THOMAS BRACKETT REED

CONGRESSIONAL LEADERS

Burdett A. Loomis

Founding Editor

THOMAS BRACKETT REED

THE GILDED AGE SPEAKER WHO MADE THE RULES FOR AMERICAN POLITICS

Robert J. Klotz

University Press of Kansas

Publication made possible, in part, by funding from The Dirksen Congressional Center.

Published by the University Press of Kansas (Lawrence, Kansas 66045), which was organized by the Kansas Board of Regents and is operated and funded by Emporia State University, Fort Hays State University, Kansas State University, Pittsburg State University, the University of Kansas, and Wichita State University.

Library of Congress Cataloging-in-Publication Data

Names: Klotz, Robert J., 1969– author.
Title: Thomas Brackett Reed : the Gilded Age speaker who made the rules for American politics / Robert J. Klotz.
Description: Lawrence, Kansas : University Press of Kansas, 2022. | Series: Congressional leaders | Includes bibliographical references and index.
Identifiers: LCCN 2021050541
ISBN 9780700633326 (cloth)
ISBN 9780700633333 (ebook)
Subjects: LCSH: Reed, Thomas B. (Thomas Brackett), 1839–1902. | United States. Congress. House—Speakers—Biography. | Reed, Thomas B. (Thomas Brackett), 1839–1902. Reed's rules. | Parliamentary practice—United States—History—19th century. | United States. Congress. House—Rules and practice—History—19th century. | Legislators—United States—Biography. | Statesmen—Maine—Biography. | United States—Politics and government—1889–1893. | United States—Politics and government—1893–1897.
Classification: LCC E664.R3 K56 2022 | DDC 328.73092 [B]—dc23/eng/20211020
LC record available at https://lccn.loc.gov/2021050541.

British Library Cataloguing-in-Publication Data is available.

Printed in the United States of America

10 9 8 7 6 5 4 3 2 1

The paper used in this publication is acid free and meets the minimum requirements of the American National Standard for Permanence of Paper for Printed Library Materials Z39.48–1992.

CONTENTS

BURDETT "BIRD" LOOMIS (1945–2021) CONGRESSIONAL LEADERS, FOUNDING EDITOR

Burdett "Bird" Loomis was a great colleague, scholar, mentor, teacher, community activist, and patron of the arts. He was often interviewed in national and regional newspapers, and on television and the radio for his insights into national and state politics. He will be missed by his family, colleagues, students, and everyone who knew and admired him for his work in the University of Kansas (KU) and Lawrence communities, in Kansas state government, and in the political science discipline.

A few years after completing his PhD in political science at the University of Wisconsin–Madison, Loomis was lured to the University of Kansas in 1979. His work on congresspersons focused more on individual orientations and behaviors than did earlier scholars, whose research tended to emphasize institutions and structures. Long before today's political dysfunction, Loomis began warning about the declining civility in Congress and the drive toward partisan advantage instead of good policy.

Loomis's legacy includes an extensive list of books and articles, including a coauthored book on interest group politics with Allan Cigler and Anthony J. Nownes that is still considered one of the standard texts in the field. Loomis also took on several administrative roles at KU, including chair of the Political Science Department. He spent a good deal of time in both Washington, DC, and in the state capitol in Topeka. As internship director, he placed dozens of students from KU and other Kansas universities in congressional and state legislative internships. Loomis was one of the first recipients of the Kemper Foundation Teaching Award in 1996 for his work in establishing that program. He also served in the administration of Kansas governor Kathleen Sebelius.

Loomis cofounded the Robert J. Dole Institute for Politics at the University of Kansas after befriending Dole while doing research on Congress. He served as the institute's interim director from 1997 to 2001. The institute has a rich collection and a program of guest speakers, media events, teaching, and discussion sessions, many of which featured him as a speaker or contributor.

Loomis was also highly active in the community, including by authoring regular newspaper columns as part of a group called "Insight Kansas." He was considered one of the leading experts on Kansas politics, particularly from the 1960s to today. He and his wife lived in a gorgeous three-story house in Lawrence filled with original art. They often hosted dinners for people at KU and in the community. In his 1994 book for the University Press of Kansas, *Time, Politics, and Policies,* Loomis used extensive interviews and participant observation to document the impact of the Kansas legislature's short, rushed sessions on the policymaking process. His final coauthored book, tracing the changes in Kansas politics from 1960 onward, is forthcoming from Kansas.

Bird Loomis had a love of life. He enjoyed his family and the arts as well as public service, teaching, research, and international travel. He is survived by his wife Michel Loomis, son Dakota, daughter in-law Krystal, granddaughter Georgia, and their newest granddaughter, Merribelle.

Michael Smith, Emporia State University
John Kennedy, University of Kansas

PROLOGUE

Inspired by self-importance, Democratic Congressman William Springer looked to finish his argument with flair. It was February 1, 1883, and Springer was delivering a routine speech in favor of reducing the tariff on chloroform, which he described as useful for tooth extractions. When Republicans suggested that tariff reduction was not popular, Springer had a ready response. He was going to adopt the famous claim of three-time Speaker and five-time presidential candidate Henry Clay. Never mind that Clay had expressed the sentiment about slavery while Springer was arguing for a fifty-cent per pound reduction on chloroform. Springer declared, "I would rather be right than president."[1]

"The gentleman need not worry for he will never be either," interrupted Thomas Brackett Reed.[2]

Agreeing on little else, competing partisan newspapers reported that the House laughed at the insult. The Republican *Evening Journal* proclaimed, "The House roared."[3] The Democratic *Argus* added an independent clause to its headline: "The House Roared and the Ass Brayed." The *Argus* elaborated, "Our Reed, our original Thomas, who like the clown at the circus turns the ring master's wise-saws into jokes to tickle the school boys. Don't Tommy, give us a little statesmanship . . . [instead of] notoriety for such puerile wit as the Springer specimen!"[4]

While the disagreement of partisan newspapers was predictable, what was less predictable was that Thomas Brackett Reed would become one of the most consequential figures in the history of American politics. Reed's significance occurred despite the fact that he, like William Springer, would never be president. As Speaker of the House, Reed transformed parliamentary procedure in the United States. Although a House minority leader once lamented that the topic makes the public's "eyes glaze over,"[5] congressional procedure is not abstract. Parliamentary procedure determines how decisions are made. It sets the parameters for settling disagreements. Parliamentary procedure is about the functioning of democracy.

Reed makes an ironic contributor to the legacy of the Gilded Age. When Reed's friend and traveling companion Mark Twain coined the term "Gilded Age," it suggested that a shiny exterior was hiding interior weakness. Reed hardly presented a gilded surface, unless one counts the bright-yellow dress shoes that he occasionally wore. Rather, Reed was known for his indifference to appearance and sparked a national sensation when he brought together his nearly three-hundred-pound frame with a gauche sash. In a rough draft of his memoir, House Speaker Champ Clark described Reed's personal appearance as "wholly destitute of personal pulchritude."[6] Clark apparently decided that was a mean thing to say and omitted it from the published version.

For his part, Reed was not inclined to pull any punches. With no hint of irony, a young Theodore Roosevelt wrote, "I swear by Tom Reed . . . I am tired of flabbiness, and I am glad to see a Republican of virility, who really does something!"[7] Reed was a combatant in timeless policy fights in the Gilded Age over taxes, government spending, monetary policy, trade, gender equality, defense, wealth inequality, election fraud, and the death penalty. More importantly, he was central to a procedural battle over the meaning of majority rule. The result of this procedural fight shapes how politics is conducted in modern America.

Although part of legislative politics throughout the United States, the Reed Rules are most pronounced in the House of Representatives. In 1890, Speaker Reed established a new system of rules that was designed to curtail obstruction and allow the majority party to govern. The Reed Rules make it more likely that the majority party will win with minimal participation from the minority party. Rather than setting general rules for all legislation, the majority party can create a different rule for every bill.[8] The minority has no realistic ability to delay consideration under the conditions set by the majority, so long as the majority holds together. Although passing legislation is never guaranteed in a democracy, the Reed Rules empower majority-party leaders to shape outcomes in their favor. The incentive to compromise is reduced.

Given his contribution to parliamentary procedure, Reed represents an ideal lens for understanding congressional leadership. Reed had a vision of the decision-making process that is apparent in his words and deeds throughout an eventful career in politics. He was able to institutionalize that vision.

Congressional scholars Jeffery Jenkins and Charles Stewart summarize his success: "A post–Reed Rules institutional structure lies at the heart of all contemporary theories of party power in the House."[9] Leaders after Reed have used the institutional foundation that he built. In short, congressional leadership occurs in the context of the Reed Rules.

Reed's leadership is timeless. More than a century after his death, his leadership tactics have been written into episodes of the television program *House of Cards*. Compared to the fictional *House of Cards*, Reed's leadership is more quorum count, less body count, but it is still marked by dramatic episodes of power politics. The Reed Rules are literally guidelines for parliamentary procedure, but they also are figuratively an approach to politics. Reed's leadership is power politics for partisan ends. To understand the hyperpartisanship of modern American politics, it is necessary to understand Reed and how he transformed American politics. The rules of American politics are the Reed Rules.

CHAPTER 1

PREPARING FOR CONGRESSIONAL BATTLE

Thomas Brackett Reed was born on October 19, 1839, in several rooms of a small house. At least that was the overweight Reed's self-deprecating account years later of his own birth.[1] More hyperbole about Reed's origins comes from a respected adversary who described Reed in a biographical sketch as being "a fighter from the headwaters of Bitter Creek." Blessed with a fighter's name himself, House Speaker Champ Clark was using southern humor about people who were eager for a fight. The saying went that the folks from Bitter Creek were bad and they got even worse the higher you went up Bitter Creek. Conflict embracers would declare proudly that they were from the headwaters of Bitter Creek.[2] In Reed's case, the headwaters of Bitter Creek were found in the Gulf of Maine. Reed was born in one room of the home at 15 Hancock Street in Portland, Maine. The house was a couple of doors down from the birthplace of Henry Wadsworth Longfellow, who immortalized Portland in verse as "the beautiful town . . . seated by the sea."[3]

Reed was born into a family with deep roots in Maine. His mother Matilda Mitchell and his father Thomas Brackett Reed, a ship captain, represented a mix of Pilgrim and Puritan origins. Reed was their first child, and he would later get a sister. They were part of a family who had already produced several generations of Mainers since coming from Britain. For his part, Reed expressed little interest in his ancestors. He was determined to be his own person. Even critics conceded that he succeeded: "[Reed] was a self-made man who worshiped his Maker."[4]

When Reed became a leading presidential candidate, there was an effort to portray him as a rough-and-tumble Mainer. The reality was that Reed was probably more tumble than rough. Apparently, Reed's classmates once watched him endure a painful fall off a wall that he appeared to be on the verge of surmounting.[5] In 1840, Portland had a population over 15,000 and ranked as the twenty-fifth-largest urban area in the United States.[6] Republican newspapers, nevertheless, celebrated Reed's background in the rugged outdoors of Maine. His aunt told newspapers about the times that she watched Reed when he was a young boy. She said, "I'm pretty sure he never went gunning that he didn't have a book in his pocket to read between whiles."[7]

Ultimately, there was more reading than hunting. Reed was an awkward youngster who did not mind spending time alone. Childhood playmates remember seeing the six-year-old Reed often carrying a stack of books by himself. His bookish tendencies contributed to Reed being called "sissy" with some frequency as a youngster.[8] The diary of a teenaged classmate described Reed as having a "reticent manner and timid disposition."[9] Reed's enjoyment of reading and the encouragement of his parents helped him finish as one of the top students at Portland Boys High School. Although focused on school, Reed was also becoming interested in politics.

For a teenager becoming interested in politics, Maine provided a unique opportunity. The importance of electoral politics in Maine was magnified because Maine held elections in September while other states voted in November. The state's bellwether reputation was encapsulated in the saying "As Maine goes, so goes the nation," which remained compelling until 1936 when Republican presidential candidate Alf Landon won only one state besides Maine. A gleeful supporter of Franklin Roosevelt exclaimed, "As Maine goes, so goes Vermont."[10] Early elections drew disproportionate attention from political parties, which sent orators to Maine to build campaign momentum.

An opportunity to hear a prominent politician arose on August 14, 1855, when Nathaniel Banks spoke in Portland at a Republican gathering. Banks was a leading candidate for Speaker of the House. As the nation grew increasingly divided, any Speakership candidate had the difficult task of showing a commitment to preserving the union while still appealing to members who were antislavery. During his speech that morning, Nathaniel Banks surprised his listeners. The person who expected to be Speaker of the House for the entire nation said that he supported union but would be "willing in a certain set of circumstances to let it slide"—those circumstances being if its "chief object" became the perpetuation of slavery.[11] Opponents attacked him as willing to sacrifice the union. Banks tried to assure the House that he was committed to union.

The Speakership race had become a sectional contest. Banks united antislavery members into a slim plurality but fell short of the required majority. A voting standstill exceeded two months. The importance of having a Speaker was not lost on the House. The answer would be a rule change that allowed election by a plurality instead of a majority. Free from the majority requirement, Nathaniel Banks was elected Speaker on the 133rd ballot. Years later, Reed recalled hearing the future Speaker give the "Union Slide" speech in which "his well-chosen language, his graceful figure and gesture, and his aggressive way carried with him the whole audience."[12]

Reed maintained his interest in politics throughout the 1856 presidential campaign between Republican John Fremont and Democrat James Buchanan. The election prompted Reed's first documented exercise in vote counting when he tabulated the presidential preferences of his classmates. It was not much of a test of his vote counting ability since Fremont won the class in a landslide. Reed counted himself a Republican.[13]

Battle-Ready College Student

In fall 1856, Reed continued his education about twenty-five miles from Portland at Bowdoin College. In the mid-1820s, among Bowdoin's approximately 150 students were four who became household names. They were poet Henry Wadsworth Longfellow, novelist Nathaniel Hawthorne, and politicians William Pitt Fessenden and Franklin Pierce. Reed gained a similar education as these distinguished alumni since the curriculum had barely changed in the intervening years. Bowdoin remained an institution devoted to teaching the classics, where an all-male student body took mostly the same courses. Faculty turnover was also low, prompting one historian to write that "some of the faculty seemed less pedagogues than landmarks on the local landscape."[14]

Reed got off to a slow start at Bowdoin. His unexceptional class rank probably had something to do with his lack of attention to the curriculum. Instead, Reed spent much of his early time at Bowdoin engaged in pleasure reading, especially novels. Years later, in an interview with legendary journalist Theodore Dreiser, Reed was matter-of-fact about his early college diversions: "I spent a little too much time on light literature, and it nearly cost me my sheepskin."[15] His progress was also impeded by financial challenges in paying for college, which prompted a brief hiatus to earn money by teaching.

Reed's participation in Bowdoin traditions merged with his dietary preferences during one delicious sophomore prank. Incoming freshmen were given a royal send-off by loving mothers who furnished them with pies and other treats to make their challenging first days at Bowdoin more pleasurable. This tradition inspired another tradition. Sophomores would ambush the freshman residence hall at night and steal the baked goodies of the hapless freshmen. Years later, mince-pie-deprived freshman Frank Dingley recalled his first encounter with Reed: "The leader of the sophomore bandits was an ogre I had heard of before. He seemed to me to be ten feet tall, four feet wide and heavier than a long ton of coal."[16]

Another Bowdoin tradition that drew Reed's attention was Military Training Day, which was a legacy of a Maine law that required college students to train one day a year with the encompassing town's militia. After the law lapsed, Bowdoin students preserved the day for dressing up in outlandish battle gear. Writing for the *University Quarterly*, Reed published his first piece of extended sarcasm as he described the day's events. Reed depicted "motly groups" of battle-ready students in "comical costume" marching through the "verdant streets of Brunswick." As described by Reed, banter extended beyond formal events: "At dinner, instead of peaceful request to pass the potatoes, rang the warlike command to march down that detachment of beefsteak, or order out that platoon of potatoes, or squadron of pie."[17]

Reed's wit extended from writing to debating. He became the informal president of a group of class humorists who went by the name "the Pentagon."[18] Humor was also central to his formal debate style. At one campus event, Reed was ostensibly less prepared than his opponent, who brought a stack of books to his desk. Reed teased his opponent that he "did not think it would be necessary for him to bring in the whole college library in order for him to maintain his proposition."[19] Reed was hitting his stride.

Reed's debating spirit extended to religion. His religious background as a youth included attending church with his mother, independently joining the State Street Congregational Church at fourteen, but leaving the church a few years later. Reed, therefore, would have been familiar with the daily prayer sessions and Sunday church services that were required by Bowdoin as part of its mission of fostering "piety and virtue." Students were also asked to read theological works. In Reed's words, "During the time I was in College I had the habit of discussing theological questions at every opportunity with anybody and everybody. I always took the opposite side, with rigid and pleasing impartiality. If my opponent was an Unbeliever I tried to convince him of the truth of Christianity; if a Christian, I asked him to answer the objections which seemed to me worthy of consideration."[20]

Reed ran short on money late in his Bowdoin career. His roommate Samuel Fessenden, who was the son of US Senator William Fessenden, was undoubtedly aware of the problem. Samuel appears to have encouraged his father to make a loan to Reed. To complete his studies, Reed borrowed $200 from Fessenden. A note was prepared, and Reed promised to pay Senator Fessenden back with interest. Just four years after graduation, Reed made his third and final payment. Apparently, the two had not calculated the exact amount of interest, which led to the odd situation of a young college graduate calculating interest owed as he personally remitted $63.25 to the Secretary of the Treasury[21]—a position to which Fessenden had recently been appointed by President Lincoln.

While in college, Reed was developing the style of argumentation that he would use in the future. In a college essay, Reed wrote, "The secret of eloquence was then, as it is now, brevity."[22] He also valued taking firm positions and not backing down from a fight. "We must have a firm earnest abiding purpose which time can not change and opposition only makes firmer," Reed maintained in another essay. Reed contemplated how he might make a mark during his life. His description foreshadows a willingness to challenge existing practices: "For better far be the forked and jagged lightning crashing through the air rousing and startling the souls of men and purifying the earth and then go out than if to be a simple star traveling through forever amid a host a myriad of others just like it. Man was made to be ambitious."[23]

By his senior year, Reed's ability and ambition had led him to great accomplishment. Decades later, Reed would describe his senior year as the hardest he ever worked.[24] He ranked first in the class for the year, which pushed his overall class rank up to fifth of nearly sixty students.[25] Earning a speaking role at commencement on August 1, 1860, Reed addressed the topic of death. His speech foreshadowed the loss of several classmates in the Civil War. Reed's friend Samuel Fessenden died just two years later on a Virginia battlefield. When Reed heard the news, he broke down in tears. Years later, he gave a tribute to his fallen friend at a speech in Portland: "He can only live in my memory, but he lives there, sublimated in the crucible of death, from all imperfections, clothed upon with all his virtues, and radiant with all the possibilities of a generous youth."[26]

After college graduation, Reed explored careers that would allow him to pursue his love of reading and intellectual stimulation. He returned to his hometown and vacillated between opportunities in teaching and the law. Reed taught for a year at Boys High School in Portland. As a teacher, Reed struggled to discipline the barely younger boys. His efforts to whip an unruly pupil once resulted in what Theodore Dreiser described as "a close victory, which a single pound more of avoirdupois added to the youth might have decided against the teacher."[27] Reed tired of teaching and resigned his position. He began studying law at the Portland firm of Howard and Strout.

Reed had given up thoughts of a life in the ministry, but he was still thinking about religion. On February 7, 1863, Reed wrote a letter to a former minister recounting the path of his religious thinking. He said that by the end of college he had decided that "the creed of the Church was untenable." While rejecting specific church doctrines and Biblical literalism, Reed reaffirmed his belief in God and the importance of doing good work on earth. In reaching this conclusion, Reed mocked the Garden of Eden as "the apotheosis of lounging" that "would have been merely a Paradise of fools." Reed wrote, "It is only by fighting the devil, that we ever get to be anything."[28]

Reed seemed like a young man ready to leave his hometown. The Union Army was certainly looking for young men hoping to become something by fighting in the Civil War. But Reed took a different path. In spring 1863, he was in the steerage section of a ship headed for adventure in California. It would not have occurred to Reed at the time that someday he would play a role in establishing a shorter path for ships through Central America.

When he arrived in San Francisco, Reed resumed his vacillation between careers in law and teaching. He taught for a few months in a small schoolhouse in Stockton, where a former student recalled Reed as a poor disciplinarian whose pupils made him "the butt of many jokes."[29] In evaluating his performance, the school committee found some promise but lamented Reed's "indiscreet remarks (which caused several scholars to leave)."[30] His evaluations were better for his legal pursuits. He passed the California bar exam after apparently impressing the exam committee with his spontaneous affirmative answer to whether recent currency legislation was constitutional. As Reed told the story years later, the examining judge explained, "What the bar of California needs is more young men who can decide great constitutional questions at the drop of a hat!"[31] Despite his legal success, he did not like California. Reed blasted the state's lawlessness in an unpublished essay: "[If a man] did not enjoy being shot at from six to eighteen times every twelve hours . . . he was called by his more robust cultivated and appreciative companions, a sick monkey." Reed confessed to being "a very sick monkey indeed."[32]

If Reed wanted to encounter less gunfire, he would have struggled to find a better role in the Civil War than the one he began in April 1864. With some assistance from Senator Fessenden, he secured an appointment as assistant paymaster in the navy.[33] He served on the ship *Sybil*, which was based in Mound City, Illinois, and provided supplies to other ships in a Union-controlled part of the Mississippi River. Reed helped pay the crew and manage supplies. He would later describe his work as having "kept a grocery store for the government" and "no getting shot at by the enemy." He elaborated, "It was a delightful life—$1300 a year and one ration, and nothing to do."[34] The money helped him to be free of his college debt when he paid the final installment to Fessenden. Reed was ready for a fresh start.

Not surprisingly, Reed chose law over teaching and Maine over California as he returned to civilian life. Reed passed the bar exam administered by a committee that included county attorney Nathan Webb in October 1865. Reed got to work building his legal practice in Portland. He handled the usual array of minor civil and criminal cases that came to a new lawyer, working hard and steadily building a favorable reputation in the legal community.

One typical way for lawyers to gain prominence was through political service. The schedule and skills of a lawyer were also a good fit for politics. Given Reed's early attraction to politics, it is not surprising that he would consider this path. His bar examiner Nathan Webb believed that Reed was well suited for politics. A former state legislator, Webb was a prominent delegate at the Portland Republican convention on September 5, 1867. Webb's support and Reed's reputation among lawyers earned him one of the party's four nominations for the Maine House of Representatives.[35]

Party identification determined the outcome of elections for the state legislature. The general election was just four days later, and there was no time for any individual campaign. Reed and the three other Republican nominees for the Maine House were running against four Democratic nominees in a multimember city district in which the top four vote getters would win election. Reed finished second as the Republicans took advantage of a substantial party identification advantage to sweep Portland's seats in the Maine House. Indeed, Republicans dominated the election to win both chambers of the state legislature and the governorship.

Confronting Stranglers in the State Legislature

On January 2, 1868, Reed joined other lawmakers at the opening of the Maine State Legislature in Augusta. Since many of the high-profile issues of the legislative session were legal in nature, Reed was fortunate to be appointed to the Judiciary committee. His greatest contribution during the session was judicial reform. Reed advocated for adding a new superior court between the city court and Maine Supreme Judicial Court to reduce the backlog of cases in the Portland courts. The bill prompted Reed's first significant newspaper coverage. The Republican *Press* praised his "very able speech,"[36] while the Democratic *Argus* credited his "know how to engineer" as instrumental in the bill's passage.[37] Although Reed's bill only added a middle-court level in one county, it foreshadowed a broader move to a three-level court system in Maine and the nation.

When the 1869 legislative session convened, the easily reelected Reed was poised to take a major role. There was even talk of him becoming Speaker. As reported in the *Portland Daily Press*, "Mr. Reed has been urged by his friends and by many members of the Legislature to allow his name to be used, but he has from the first firmly refused to accede to their wishes."[38] Although not Speaker, Reed would play a leading role in the session's two major issues. These issues were not partisan issues. In fact, at the end of the 1869 session, newspapers of all party affiliations praised the legislature for its absence of party animosity. Of course, it would have taken some doing for the 2 Democrats in the 31-member Senate and the 28 Democrats in the 151–member House to generate much party animosity. Nevertheless, Republicans would create plenty of their own dissension.

The first issue was a contest for the US Senate, which had been attracting superlatives since it had started informally years earlier. Hannibal Hamlin, who had given up one of Maine's US Senate seats in 1860 to serve as vice president to Abraham Lincoln, was determined to return to the Senate after being dropped as vice president for Lincoln's second term and subsequently losing to William Pitt Fessenden in a bid for Maine's other Senate seat in 1865. This time, his opponent was the incumbent US senator, Lot Morrill. The contest had little to do with policy, as the candidates were in general agreement, but was based on personality and who would control patronage jobs. An industrious newspaper reporter captured the extent to which Augusta was being dominated by the Senate race: "Nothing else is talked of or even thought of."[39]

Since US senators were chosen by the state legislature, these elections in practice were decided by a caucus of the members of the majority party in the legislature, in this case Republicans. Once the Republican caucus had voted, there would be a vote to make it unanimous; with all Republicans committed to vote for the same candidate, the official vote on January 20 in the full state legislature would be a mere formality ratifying the caucus vote. Prior to the vote, both sides claimed that they were ahead by a similar amount. About thirty members were being claimed by both sides. For his part, Reed was a solid supporter of Morrill.

The 150 Republican legislators were in place for the final vote at 7:30 p.m. on January 7. There was no secret ballot. To vote for Hamlin, a member walked to the front of the room and deposited a blue paper with Hamlin's name printed on it. Morrill's name was printed on a red ballot. As described by the *Lewiston Evening Journal*, "This was a hard ordeal for those who wanted to be on both sides."[40] Ultimately, 150 men deposited ballots in the box. The vote was Hamlin 75, Morrill 74, with one blank ballot. One of the red ballots had the name of Morrill removed, which was treated as a blank ballot. Hamlin was announced the winner. Under normal circumstances, Speaker Josiah Drummond's motion to make the vote unanimous would have passed. This election, however, had never been ordinary.

Demonstrating his enthusiasm for parliamentary technicalities, Reed was the first to gain the floor to object to Hamlin's victory. Reed asked for a new vote. He said that 150 votes had been cast and that a majority required 76 votes. Hamlin had only received 75 of the 150 votes. Reed maintained that state law treating blank ballots as nonexistent was not applicable to caucuses and there should be a clear majority in caucus. Since some Hamlin supporters had left after the vote, Hamlin supporters were never going to accept a revote that night. The two sides argued until after 10:00 p.m. and then adjourned.

In the days that followed, the two sides clashed. On January 13, Reed wrote his friend George Gifford describing how "Hamlin is back and with him some other birds of evil omen." His letter suggested that supporting Morrill against the desires of Speaker Drummond had cost him. Reed wrote, "Drummond puts me *fifth* on the Judiciary and explains to me that he didn't do it 'on account of this contest' which shows that he did. So you see we have to bleed as well as fight."[41] Republican bleeding ended on January 17, when Morrill withdrew after five supporters from his own county conceded that Hamlin had been elected fairly.

The second major issue facing the 1869 legislature was capital punishment. The legislature's discussion was set against the backdrop of the scheduled execution on February 5, 1869, of convicted double murderer Clifton Harris. If carried out, the execution would mark a significant change in Maine policy. An 1837 law had virtually eliminated capital punishment by requiring that prisoners sentenced to death be kept on death row for at least a year and be executed only if the governor initiated an execution warrant. Governors had objected to this judicial function, and the only execution since 1837 had been an extreme case in which a prisoner had compounded his crimes by killing the prison warden. After Joshua Chamberlain became governor, he set a date to begin clearing the backlog in order to encourage the legislature to clarify the law.

The strong disagreement in the legislature was reflected in the different labels used by the two sides. Advocates of the death penalty described the execution process as "hanging," while opponents denigrated it as "strangulation." Debate was expected to be vigorous. Reed's assessment of whether this debate would change the minds of other legislators appears mixed. On January 27, 1869, Reed lamented, "You can't make much use of personal influence because of the nature of the question." Reed described the perspective of one of his legislative opponents: "Mr. Messer considers any one who desires to abolish strangulation as 'trying to be wiser than God,' which remark he regards as closing the whole question. Against such inner light it [is] no use to burn the farthing candles of mere human reasons."[42] Four days later, he envisioned a small opening for persuasion. He wrote, "If we only had some favorable statistics to show we might perhaps make a few converts."[43]

Death penalty legislation was referred to the Judiciary committee on which Reed sat. After hearings and debate, the committee voted to change the death penalty law. The change, however, was not in the direction preferred by Reed. By an eight-to-two margin, the committee voted to make the death penalty mandatory within a year for first-degree murder. Reed contemplated the perspective of "the Stranglers" in a letter to Gifford: "The profound reasoning which led three or four of the eight to their result I will not recapitulate because I am unequal to it."[44] Reed offered a competing measure that banned capital punishment. The House would debate the two competing proposals for several days.

On February 19, 1869, Reed took the floor for his major opportunity to address the issue. He planned to speak about fifteen minutes. Reed argued that the irreversible character of the death penalty prevented correction of the inevitable government errors and led to uncertain trial outcomes since juries, judges, and witnesses "shrink" from participating in capital trials. Reed questioned the deterrence of the death penalty and observed that forgery and horse stealing in England had not increased after those crimes ceased to be capital offenses in 1829. He confronted the prevalent argument that capital punishment was God's will by saying that it was typical for a "hoary wrong . . . [to be] propped up during its last years by texts of scripture." After forty-five minutes, Reed finished by imploring undecided members to have any "doubts lead them to the side of mercy."[45] His pleas went unheeded as the House voted ninety-five to forty-five against substituting Reed's bill to abolish capital punishment for the committee bill making it mandatory.

Although Reed was on the losing side of the session's major battles, his conduct during them had increased his prestige. The Democratic *Argus*, which supported capital punishment, described Reed's speech as "candid and well considered."[46] A summary of the legislative session by the *Portland Daily Press* praised Reed's "readiness and skill in debate, his solid legal acquirements and general culture."[47]

Reed's performance in the House made him a natural candidate when an opening emerged in the Maine State Senate. Reed's competition for the Republican nomination, Charles Morris, was also a lawyer and state legislator. Despite being an intraparty contest, the two candidates were associated with different positions on a key issue. Morris was a temperance supporter while Reed had mitigated Maine's prohibition law. Reed secured the nomination in August 1869 in the closest race decided at the convention and won the general election in the heavily Republican district.

Despite his electoral success, his ability to read the political landscape still needed sharpening. In a letter to a friend, Reed admitted that he had been overconfident in assessing the low popularity of George Shepley in another contest: "I have been supposing that I was announcing not only the Lord's truth but also the Lord's transparent truth when I said that Shepley didn't have any strength here. But I was mistaken and my mouth is in the dust and my face is turned to the wall." Reed's problem was that he had not sufficiently weighed the local nature of politics. Reed joked, "When Saint Paul was elected Apostle to the Gentiles, I wonder if prominent Christians, men eminent in religious circles, came up from Garsus and laid down on Apostles and brethren from that vicinity and urged the necessity of having an Apostle from that 'locality.'"[48]

As Reed began work in the Maine State Senate in 1870, he faced an early test of his reputation among other legislators. Reed had decided to run for attorney general—an office elected by the state legislature. Since Republicans controlled both chambers, the election would effectively occur in a caucus of all Republicans serving in the state legislature. Reed secured the caucus majority on January 6 but would not begin his one-year term as attorney general until the session ended.

In his personal life, Reed made a longer-term commitment when he married Mrs. Susan Jones in Portland on Saturday, February 5, 1870. A widow, Susan Jones, born in 1840, was the daughter of Congregationalist minister Samuel H. Merrill. She lived on Bramhall just a half mile from his parent's home on Brackett Street. Somewhere on their strolls together on the Portland peninsula, they had fallen in love. It is, of course, difficult to understand a relationship from the outside. The presence of a treasure trove of love letters can make the task easier. In this case, the Reed family was more interested in privacy than in creating a historical record, and only a few brief letters have survived. One has the newlywed writing a "Dear Sue" letter. Symbolic of the dearth of surviving correspondence, Reed wrote, "I've so much to say to you that can't be written. . . . I love you, Tom."[49]

During his state senate term, Reed balanced industrial interests with other Maine interests, especially fishing. When the legislature heard a proposal in March 1870 to exempt a company from the requirement to create a fishway when building a dam, Reed objected, "The fish interest of Maine is a matter of great importance, rivaling the manufacturing interests, and one should not strangle the other."[50] Reed, however, was less concerned with stopping the progress of fish when it came to the fountain in the capitol, which was home to a small population of trout and other fish. Reed was known to reach into the fountain basin and playfully pick up the fish with his hands.[51] Like the trout, Reed was a big fish in a small pond.

Reed was starting to demonstrate a command of parliamentary procedure. He was ready with points of order and frequently offered amendments. He demonstrated the ability to offer a killer amendment to split a supporting coalition. His most consequential parliamentary maneuver during the session eliminated municipal aid to a railroad. Even though the measure had passed the committee unanimously, Reed successfully offered a surprise motion to postpone it indefinitely before many legislators were even at their desks on March 15.[52] The session ended a week later, and Reed became Maine's attorney general.

Able Attorney

As attorney general, Reed was set for a dramatic increase in his statewide profile. The position required him to travel to courthouses across the state to prosecute major crimes. Reed's previous opposition to the death penalty would not deter him from prosecuting capital cases. Since crime stories met news standards,[53] the trials guaranteed Reed substantial press coverage.

His first high-profile case presented a major challenge. The defendant had killed a man who he alleged was having an affair with his wife. There had been several recent cases outside Maine where jurors had refused to convict similar defendants, including the 1868 New York jury that acquitted General Cole for having killed a man two days after his wife confessed to a wartime affair. During the case, Reed's opposing counsel, E. F. Pillsbury, regularly quoted Bible verses about adultery and argued that Maine cherished the sanctity of marriage as much as these other jurisdictions. In his closing argument on December 6, 1870, Reed implied that the defense attorney could have made his point with fewer Bible verses: "Now, while all this scripture was being read to you, I make no doubt that it may have occurred to you that brother Pillsbury was a man more given to searching the scriptures than you had supposed before." Reed conceded that adulterers did not fare well in the Bible. He said, however, that it was important to recognize who punished adulterers in the Bible: "They were to be doomed to death after they had been brought before the proper tribunal, not sent without warning out of the world, upon a mere suspicion of an enraged and infuriated husband."[54] The case went to the jury, which initially split eleven-to-one in favor of murder. A unanimous verdict was required so deliberation continued. Finally, nine hours after taking the case, the jury returned a verdict. The jury found the defendant guilty of manslaughter. Unable to convince the holdout juror, the others had agreed to a verdict of manslaughter rather than force a new trial.[55] Although Reed received credit in the press for avoiding an acquittal,[56] a simple majority had not given him the outcome he wanted. It would in the future.

After being reelected to a second term in 1871, Reed took time out from prosecuting murderers to recover state money. This time the challenges were political. Legally, the case was straightforward: Reed was trying to collect money from sureties on a bond for which approximately $60,000 including interest was owed. Politically, nothing was straightforward. More than a decade earlier, the Maine treasurer, Benjamin Peck, a Republican, had stolen state money, leading to a deficit that became the legal responsibility of his bondsmen. Death and financial calamity had struck most bondsmen, leaving only two solvent bondsmen unexpectedly responsible for the entire amount. One of these was nationally famous Neal Dow who had been instrumental in passing Maine's temperance law and still had a significant constituency among Maine Republicans.

Although the political influence of Dow had deterred previous Republican prosecutors, Reed pursued the matter. It probably did not hurt that Reed was no fan of Neal Dow and his temperance movement. Prosecuting Dow would not help the relationship. Defeating Dow would help even less after the judge sustained Reed's argument that the defendants' role as sureties and the debt amount were unquestioned. Politics would, however, have the final say when the Republican state legislature considered whether to grant relief to Dow and the other remaining surety, who were each on the hook for over $30,000 for someone else's theft. Although Dow supporters could not get the votes to fully discharge the debt, the legislature reduced Dow's amount to $5,000 by eliminating interest and reverting to his original one-seventh share. The Dow family's resentment of Reed did not drop proportionally.

Reelected attorney general in January 1872, Reed traveled to the northeast corner of Maine to prosecute Edward Kirby for murder. In a letter to his wife, Susan, on October 18, 1872, Reed confessed to being "a little anxious about the result" since the case had been sent to the jury. As described in his letter, Reed's anxiety was based partly on his assessment of the jury: "The jury are now out and being thoroughly stupid may stay out twelve hours longer or may not agree at all." Reed suspected that the judge's instructions had favored a second-degree murder conviction, but acquittal was still possible. Ultimately, the jury would end up in the middle with a manslaughter conviction. Reed assured Susan, "I want to get home as soon as convenient to see my family—Of course I have thought of nothing but you all this week."[57]

Reed contemplated whether to seek reelection to another term as attorney general. During the fall, Reed wrote his friend George Gifford, "I did not imagine that I was to have any contest but do not purpose to retire hit or miss until considerable further effort." It is not clear how much further effort Reed exerted. In the same letter he told Gifford, "I hope to have Kennebec [County] solid but hate to call on my friends again in this matter." In any case, Reed was justifiably concerned that many legislators felt that exceeding three terms undermined "rotation in office."[58] By the time the legislature met, Reed had given up the fight. The legislature elected Harris Plaisted as attorney general. Decades later, Reed was still resentful, mocked him as "Plaisted the Conqueror,"[59] and told friends that he "was beaten for the Attorney Generalship of my state by a man conspicuously unfit."[60] It would not be the last time he would harbor a grudge against fellow Republicans.

Although Reed was no longer the state's top prosecutor, he was not giving up public service. He enjoyed government work and was open to other opportunities in politics. He served briefly on the Portland School Board alongside his friend Stanley Pullen, the editor of the *Portland Daily Press*. On March 9, 1874, he was appointed city solicitor of Portland. It was a step down from being Maine's top lawyer, but the relatively small caseload would allow ample time to continue his Republican Party activity and private legal practice.

On December 11, 1874, Reed combined these pursuits by representing Rodney Fogg, a Republican campaign operative accused of bribery. Democratic newspapers celebrated the charges as evidence of Republican corruption, and the case drew much attention. The district attorney presented two men who testified that Fogg approached them on election day with an offer of ten dollars to vote Republican and paid them later after they voted as instructed. In defending his client, Reed produced twenty-five witnesses to testify that the two men were habitual liars. After the jury found him not guilty, Fogg reportedly offered the first prediction that Reed would one day become president.[61]

It is unlikely that the title of president would have given Reed more joy than the title of father. Sadly, Reed and his wife's first child had been a son who lived only a few days. The news was happier on January 23, 1875, when Susan gave birth to a healthy girl. She was given the name Katherine, but they called her Kitty. Reed doted on her constantly. Even as she got older, she would remain "la petite," the little one, to Reed.

In his private legal practice, one important client was the Republican *Portland Daily Press*. After successfully defending the newspaper from a libel suit in May 1875, Reed was retained for a personal-injury case. Dwight Parker was suing the newspaper for negligently leaving open the gate to its elevator shaft, which he fell down during a midnight advertisement delivery, resulting in him suffering a concussion, being bedridden for eighty days, and permanently losing feeling in his legs. Parker was being represented by A. A. Strout, whose habit of personally greeting every juror had annoyed Reed in their previous cases.[62] Reed's closing argument that the plaintiff had not exercised sufficient caution in entering a dark area was praised by the *Press* as a "very able effort."[63] The disheveled appearance of the court reporter symbolized the weariness of participants after a difficult trial in which the jury reached its verdict at 1:45 a.m. The jury found for the plaintiff and awarded him $4,000 in damages. Victoriously leaving the courtroom, plaintiff's attorney Strout greeted the court reporter. Placing his hands on the court reporter's head, Strout moved the reporter's out of place hair back into place. After watching this display of triumph, Reed walked over to the court reporter and messed it back up to undo Strout's grooming.[64] It would take a few more months to undo the jury award. On appeal, the court overturned the award on the grounds that the hallway was dark enough that a reasonably prudent person unfamiliar with the surroundings "ought not to have proceeded without a light."[65]

"*Damnum absque injuria*,"[66] Reed told the court on October 14, 1875. This was probably the most common legal concept employed in his role as city solicitor. The term meant injury but no legal violation. In practice, Reed was conceding that plaintiffs were injured but arguing that the city was not legally responsible. Typically, Reed would try to show that the plaintiff was at least partly at fault for the injury. An example is the case involving sixty-year-old Mary Richardson, who sued the city for $10,000 after falling and breaking her arm on an icy sidewalk maintained by the city. Reed defended the sidewalk slope as necessary for drainage and insisted that the fall had occurred beyond the ice-covered hollow in the sidewalk. The court found the city responsible but only for a small fraction of what was sought. Reed later wrote, "The jury rendered a verdict for the plaintiff in the sum of $366.66, a sum which would seem to indicate that if there was a defect it was a very small one."[67] Overall, Reed had a successful three-year tenure as city solicitor and furthered his reputation for service to the public and the Republican Party.

Running for Congress

Defending Portland against lawsuits brought by its accident-prone citizenry occasionally stirred Reed's competitive juices, but he was eager to move to Congress. Given his previous electoral success, Reed was a quality challenger who wanted to be strategic about choosing to run under favorable circumstances.[68] Thus, his interest was sparked when he heard complaints about his district's Republican congressman, John Burleigh, who had exposed corruption and waste at the Kittery Naval Shipyard. It is tempting to view the exposure of corruption as a good thing that might strengthen one's reputation. Burleigh's actions, however, were not appreciated by establishment Republican leaders who were eager to turn military contracts into political advantage. Thus, Reed was encouraged to challenge Burleigh. The fact that Burleigh had alienated party leaders qualified as an opportunity, even if Reed had no intention of running as a pro-corruption candidate. Opportunities did not arise often, and three years had passed since being attorney general. Reed decided to run.

The contest would be resolved at the Republican district convention. With the press reporting that the two candidates had an equal number of committed delegates,[69] the Burleigh and Reed forces mobilized. Burleigh supporters emphasized a county equity argument. Maine's First District encompassed two counties—Cumberland and York. The Republican representative before Burleigh came from Cumberland County and served four terms, while Burleigh came from York County and had served only two terms before Reed's challenge. Advocates for York County offered a resolution that the Republican nominee alternate evenly between York and Cumberland County. Although removed from specific names, this resolution about geography was a test vote for the nomination since Reed was from Cumberland County. The resolution to guarantee York representation failed. Reed had the votes. On the nomination vote, Reed defeated Burleigh 134–113.[70] A motion to make the vote unanimous, which would give the party a united front for the general election, prompted shouts of "no." In his speech accepting the nomination, Reed appealed to party unity: "We all here believe in the Republican Party one and indivisible. We believe it to be the only hope of this country for progress, intelligence and increase of honorable national greatness."[71]

Since the Democratic district convention was over a month away, Republicans had ample time to continue infighting. In late July, disgruntled York County Republicans released a manifesto asserting that Reed's nomination was a setback for York County and civil service reform. The Portland *Advertiser,* which had supported Burleigh, ran a letter from an anonymous author who claimed to be friends of both Reed and Burleigh asking for Reed to withdraw.[72] Later in the campaign, however, the *Advertiser* supported Reed. Burleigh's congressional career was over, and he died within a year.

On August 3, the Democrats held their district meeting. They passed a resolution praising Representative Burleigh for his exemplary service in fighting corruption. In accepting the nomination, John Goodwin advocated for honest government and civil-service reform. This was an appeal that Democrats took around the country as they charged the Grant administration with corruption and made administrative reform a campaign centerpiece.[73] The day after accepting the nomination, Goodwin—who, like Reed, was a Bowdoin alum, lawyer, and state legislator—said that he respected his opponent and pledged to reject negative campaigning.

Goodwin's principal newspaper supporter, the *Eastern Argus,* took no such pledge and waged an almost entirely negative campaign against Reed. The *Argus* gave disgruntled York County Republicans space to air their grievances. The *Argus* also attacked Reed personally by describing him as a "known infidel [to Christianity]" and "a man whose belief is unbelief."[74] Reed's principal newspaper supporter, the *Press* downplayed the Republican defections and defended Reed against the *Argus* claims. The *Press* declared, "The statement that Thomas B. Reed is an atheist is an utter, baseless and wicked falsehood."[75]

Reed campaigned vigorously throughout the district. He spent much time in York County addressing Republican meetings. By the end, he had assuaged all but a few Republican defectors. He spoke to audiences both large and small, sometimes at the same time if judged by the crowd estimates in newspapers. Reed's address at Pepperell Square in York County, for example, was heard by 450 unenthusiastic listeners according to the Democratic *Argus,*[76] but 5,000 eager listeners according to the Republican *Press.*[77] Regardless of how many attended Reed's events, they heard a speech that lasted about ninety minutes and emphasized the South, civil service reform, and monetary policy.

On September 11, 1876, Maine voters went to the polls. Reed earned just over 51 percent of the vote and defeated Goodwin 16,232 votes to 15,212 votes, with 140 votes to Burleigh and others.[78] Speaking at a Republican victory party, Reed proclaimed, "[The outcome] shows that the people of Maine are still true to the principles for which they have been fighting for twenty years. . . . But as long as we live in a state of probation we must live in a state of warfare with wrong."[79] Reed was in good spirits. He had run behind Burleigh's margin in 1874, but he was going to Washington.

Elected to Congress at thirty-six years of age, Reed was bringing a personality and leadership style shaped by his early career experiences. Scholars have long understood that formative experiences are critical in shaping leadership.[80] Although state legislatures can provide important schooling in cross-party compromise,[81] Reed had limited experience working with Democrats in a Republican-dominated state. Based on an international survey of legislators, Payne and Woshinsky present a typology of six principal motivations for legislators, including adulation (popularity), obligation (sense of duty), status (ladder climbing), program (policy solutions), mission (transcendental life meaning), and game (political competition).[82] Reed had shown some program motivation in his eagerness to find policy solutions. Above all, however,

Reed appeared to be exhibiting a game motivation in which the "participant seeks the satisfaction of applying and demonstrating his intellectual prowess in a highly structured, challenging, and competitive situation."[83] Reed's relish of political competition was showing hints of being accompanied by a struggle to accept losing gracefully. He savored parliamentary triumphs in the state legislature and victories in the courtroom. It is striking to hear the future Speaker celebrate a partial victory when his municipal client had to pay only modest damages to an elderly woman who fell on an inadequately maintained sidewalk. Reed would not be as satisfied with partial victories in the future.

CHAPTER 2

THE BUMPTIOUSNESS OF A YOUNG CONGRESSMAN

"Every new member, like a young lawyer or merchant newly come to town, has to show what there is in him and win his own way,"[1] Reed advised a young audience about starting out in Congress. In 1877, Reed traveled to Washington to join the all-male Congress and settled into a boarding house. Temporary housing was common for members who knew that two regular sessions would only amount to about one year in Washington for a two-year term. Once members settled into town, they met with their respective party caucuses to select leadership. The minority Republicans selected Ohio Civil War veteran James Garfield as leader. House Democrats selected Samuel Randall as their leader and the Speaker of the House.

Samuel Randall was a respected figure in the House. He had represented an industrial district in Pennsylvania since 1863. Even though his support for relatively high tariffs to support manufacturing put him in the minority of his own party, he rose steadily in the ranks of the House Democratic caucus in part because of his proficiency in parliamentary procedure. When Democratic Speaker Michael Kerr died near the end of the Forty-Fourth Congress, the Democrats chose Randall to replace him. There would be no chance to ease into the position. Both parties were convinced that they had won the 1876 presidential election. As inauguration day approached without an official winner, chaos loomed as the Democratic House and the Republican Senate weighed how to resolve the competing claims of Democratic and Republican presidential electors. Ultimately, Randall helped to craft a compromise that ended the stalemate by allowing Rutherford Hayes to assume the presidency with the understanding that Republicans would scale back Reconstruction in the South. Tension from the disputed election, however, was still high.

Thus, Reed was entering Congress during a time of intense party conflict that reflected broader Gilded Age politics. Although historians disagree about the exact years of the Gilded Age, there is wide agreement that it begins sometime in the 1870s and ends around 1900.[2] During the last quarter of the twentieth century, politics was marked by vigorous party competition. The national political balance was close even as the regional strength of the parties varied. Party organizations were strong and emphasized voter mobilization.[3] Voter turnout in the era was historically high, with average turnout in presidential elections at 78 percent of eligible voters.[4] In Congress the competition was undertaken by constantly changing members who served on average only 2.4 terms in a body that averaged 42 percent new members.[5] The press was often part of the competition since partisan newspapers retained a slight majority in the industry despite growing competition from independent newspapers.[6] The era's strong party enthusiasm is partly because the winning party could fill government jobs with its supporters. The patronage system has made it tempting to suggest that elections were about jobs, not policy. Modern scholars, however, have demonstrated that there were significant ideological differences between the parties.[7] Some of these emerged from different approaches to the economic growth generated by the Gilded Age's transformation to an industrial economy. As the name Gilded Age suggests, surface wealth covered up core weaknesses. Modern scholarship has emphasized that the hidden flaws extend beyond an arguably overstated amount of corruption[8] to include such characteristics as widespread suffering from persistent deflation,[9] industrial labor strife,[10] denial of opportunities to minority groups,[11] increasing wealth inequality,[12] and reduced life expectancy.[13]

When the Forty-Fifth Congress started on October 15, 1877, it had been over eleven months since the election. A long layoff was not unusual and, in fact, the gap was two months shorter than normal because President Hayes called Congress into session early. According to the congressional calendar, the first regular session was scheduled to begin on the first Monday in December the year after the November general election, and it typically lasted until sometime in the summer. Congress would then be off from late summer until the first Monday in December, when members would return for a lame-duck session until March 4, when the terms of a new Congress would officially begin. It was not until 1935 that this calendar was changed by the Twentieth Amendment, which moved up to January the start date for both the newly elected president and the Congress.

Like most new House members, Reed got off to a quiet start. Freshmen were generally not expected to play a large role in a House that valued seniority. There was a norm against excessive floor participation, and it often took a while for a congressman to make his first extended remarks. Freshmen were generally assigned to the less prestigious committees. Reed was no exception. He was appointed to the low-prestige Committee on Territories despite his later assertion that at the time he would not have known a territory had he run into one on the avenue.[14]

Reed's first role on a substantial matter occurred on January 10, 1878. Democrats proposed a broad investigation into wrongdoing by executive departments in the Grant administration, which had left office the previous year. Reed mocked the idea that the House was designed to "investigate all the wickedness of the land," questioned the willingness of Democrats to investigate their own "special pet wickedness," doubted whether the process would remain secret as intended, and suggested that the investigation process in Congress accomplished little more than to "provide material for party purposes."[15] The *Boston Herald* correspondent described his first speech: "[Reed] looks like Dickens' fat boy . . . and has a good voice and a fluent manner of speaking . . . [and] knew how to stop when he got through."[16]

Reed gained national attention on April 12, 1878. That day the bill titled "To reimburse the College of William and Mary, in Virginia, for property destroyed during the late war" reached the floor.[17] The principal speaker for the legislation was Massachusetts Congressman George Loring who, like Reed, was a first-term Republican. In his hour-long maiden floor speech, Loring spoke about the distinguished history of William and Mary and the opportunity to heal the "sorest wounds" by a charitable measure "appealing to that tender regard for all man's endeavors to improve his moral and intellectual and religious nature, by which alone can we mitigate the horrors of war."[18]

As described by the *New York Times,* things were going along "swimmingly"[19] for supporters of the legislation until Reed took the floor. Reed suggested that Congress should ignore the emotional rhetoric and consider the bill's principle of compensating war damages. "Now, if you establish this principle you establish a principle that no other nation ever had the inconceivable folly and imbecility to establish since the beginning of time," Reed explained. He urged members to consider that 10 percent of pending bills were war claims and that this was part of a broader pattern that must be stopped: "You gentlemen opposite come forward and insist that the victorious country shall pay for the damages inflicted by it upon its enemies."[20] The debate ended without a vote on the bill.

Reed's home-state newspapers disagreed about his performance. The Democratic *Argus* mocked Reed as "screaming himself hoarse about rebel claims" on a nonpolitical bill and suggested that "Thomas fired his little gun into the wrong cover." The *Argus* said that the speech did not bode well for the future. It wrote, "It is a critical time just now for Mr. Reed. He is deciding whether he will become a statesman or a politician." Its early conclusion: "His opening effort . . . showed its author to be far more of a politician than a statesman."[21] The Republican *Whig and Courier* saw things differently: "As this grab was intended for an entering wedge for the long array of Southern war claims, it would be difficult to overestimate the service rendered the country by Mr. Reed thus early in his term of service."[22]

Deciphering Democratic Plots on the Potter Committee

On May 13, 1878, House Democrats pushed to create a special committee to investigate the irregularities of the 1876 presidential election. Minority Leader Garfield and Reed were among nine Republicans who authored unanimously approved caucus resolutions urging resistance to a Democratic proposal that was "revolutionary and destructive of the good order, business prosperity, and peace of the country."[23] The Democratic *Argus* mocked the revolutionary language of Republicans: "Republicans cry that to investigate their party's record will bring about revolution. Sorry they have such a bad record."[24] Some Democrats sensed that the committee would be the last opportunity to challenge second-year incumbent Hayes and talked openly of impeachment or resignation in the face of overwhelming evidence of fraud. Other Democrats, including Speaker Randall, maintained that the goal was not to remove the president.

Once the bill passed over Republican objections, interest shifted to whom Speaker Randall would assign to the committee. The chair would be the original resolution's sponsor, Clarkson Potter, and it would be known as the Potter committee. The committee would have seven Democrats and four Republicans. The imbalance was even greater since Speaker Randall insisted that one of the Republicans would be Ben Butler, who had been moving away from the Republican Party and later became a Democrat. That left three Republican spots. Prominent House Republicans were not pushing to serve on the committee, which would enmesh them in party conflict and lead to writing a minority report. Speaker Randall appointed Jacob Cox (OH) as senior Republican along with two first-term Republicans, Frank Hiscock of New York and Reed. Reportedly, these three Republicans were recommended by House Republican leaders and were agreeable to Randall. The Republican *Cincinnati Commercial Tribune* lamented that the Democrats deliberately excluded from the committee "any of the strong aggressive Republicans of the House . . . who would meet force with force."[25]

Republicans might have been even more concerned if they had known that Reed had no particular affinity for Hayes. In private correspondence before his appointment, Reed had criticized Hayes: "The President is a man of limited ideas and a dodger . . . [who] is moved by petty things."[26] The day after the committee was announced, Reed contrasted Hayes with his predecessor in another letter, writing, "When I think of this contest, I cannot help thinking of what Logan says about Grant 'wherever we were we knew he was thinking of us and would look out for us.'" Reed modified the sentiment to fit Hayes: "Wherever we find ourselves we know that R.B.H. is thinking of us and will look out for himself."[27] As he entered his important committee work, Reed had personal and political problems with his own party's president.

The Potter committee began its work to great fanfare on Saturday, June 1, 1878, with the star witness for the Democrats. James Anderson, the Republican registrar for East Feliciana parish, was now admitting that he had been pressured by Republicans to claim Democratic intimidation, which led to thousands of Democratic votes being discarded in Louisiana. Anderson testified that he and West Feliciana registrar D. A. Weber had quietly made a notarized joint statement saying that although the elections in their area were fair, they signed protests under Republican pressure and promises to take care of them after the election. The statement, he said, had been held back in case they needed protection in the future. Despite this union of the Felicianas, the outcome for them was anything but felicitous. Weber was taken care of, but not in his preferred manner; he was the victim of an unsolved murder, believed to be political in nature.[28] Anderson was alone telling the story, and Washington was paying attention. President Hayes wrote in his diary: "The election investigation began yesterday with calling as a witness the scamp Anderson."[29]

From the Democratic perspective, Anderson did well in his first day's testimony under the awkward circumstances of admitting to falsifying reports under pressure. Since little new evidence was expected from the Potter committee, a witness telling a revised story was notable. Anderson's role was central to the disputed election. The Democratic case for election fraud in 1876 centered on the states of Florida and Louisiana, where election returns initially showed a Democratic victory but Republican election boards responsible for the official results reversed the outcome by eliminating votes cast in Democratic strongholds under the difficult-to-quantify justification of intimidation. Democrats had long questioned the integrity of these election boards, which conducted their work in secret. Since Hayes had won the electoral vote 185–184, these states were essential to the Republican victory.

The best strategy for committee Republicans was unclear. Republicans could let the Democrats recycle evidence and produce their partisan report; later, they could dismiss the outcome as a biased committee reaching a foregone conclusion. Alternatively, Republicans could fight hard and risk extending a process designed to highlight Republican fraud. Reed would play a major role in setting Republican strategy. The committee had already divided into subcommittees, and Reed was left in Washington with Benjamin Butler the favorite Republican of Democrats. Recalling the scene in Washington after Anderson's first day of testimony, Congressman William Claflin reportedly said that he had never seen Republicans so dispirited. Talking with Claflin, Reed hinted at his upcoming strategy, saying, "I am going to cross examine that witness, and I'll tear him all to pieces."[30]

When testimony resumed after the weekend, Reed took center stage as the Republican assigned to question Anderson. Under Democratic questioning, Anderson was presented as someone who wanted to come clean by admitting to filing a false protest despite knowing that Democrats had won his parish fairly. Reed would try to show that Anderson was not coming clean but was an individual of poor character who had been open to playing both sides from the start. In so doing, Reed evoked the difficulty of calculating the effects of voter intimidation. Referencing the agreement between Anderson and Weber, Reed asked, "You say that intimidation was not legitimate means; and you also say there was some intimidation. Now, how do you make it out that the Democratic gains were by legitimate means?"

Anderson responded, "There was intimidation to some extent in both those parishes, but to a very slight extent . . . not intimidation on the day of election, not really fears of intimidation, but a fear that something might occur."

"That is, a kind of intimidation which you could swear to on one side or swear against on the other," Reed suggested. He was ready to make his case that this intention to have it both ways had reached fruition as Anderson was now taking the Democratic position on the effect of voter intimidation. Reed asked, "You gave testimony on one side [Republican] of the question before the [1877] Senate committee, did you not?"

"Yes."

"And you carefully suppressed all the evidence which had a tendency to help the other side, did you not?"

"I did." Anderson proceeded to defend his testimony as having tried to "suppress as much of the truth as possible without swearing to a lie."

Reed clarified: "So that before that committee you meant one thing in your own mind and you conveyed another meaning to the committee?"

"Exactly," Anderson replied.

After a recess, Reed resumed questioning, "When you say that some of your statements were made with one understanding on your part and another on the part of the committee, I presume you mean by that that you deceived them?"

"I mean by that, that while I was telling the truth they could put a different construction upon it."

"And you intended that they should put a different construction upon it?"

"Yes, sir."

"What in your judgment is the difference between that and perjury?"

"I think there is a vast difference."

"Will you state the difference?"

"I think the difference is this. Perjury means where you willfully deceive by telling falsehood. I confined myself to the truth."

"You did not willfully deceive the Senate committee?"

"No sir, but while I told the truth I did not state all the truth."

"You gave them an entirely wrong idea, didn't you?"

"They may have taken a wrong idea."

Reed persisted, "So that when you gave the answers that you did give, you intended to deceive them?"

"I intended to leave them under a false impression."

Reed reframed, "And you intended to deceive the committee when you conveyed that impression?"

"That is the construction that might be put upon it in the backwoods of Maine."

"Never mind what they do in the backwoods of Maine. The backwoods is not my country. Will you answer the question?"

"I have answered you."

"That you intended to deceive the committee?"

"Yes, sir."

"Under oath?"

"Yes, sir, under oath."[31]

The cross-examination of Anderson finished the next day. Having spent the first day impeaching Anderson's character, Reed focused the second day on questioning the authenticity of documents that supported Anderson's story. In the critical exchange of the second day, Reed asked Anderson about the details of Weber signing the statement asserting that they were acting under Republican pressure. Reed asked one question after another about the smallest detail of signing the two copies of the statement and was able to generate contradictions about Anderson's recollection of signing the document. A reporter for an independent newspaper said that while observers of the proceedings were perplexed at the minutiae and subtly different questions about a signing that occurred over a year ago, Reed was effectively cornering the witness into a choice between risking a forgery charge or denying the document.[32] At an opportune moment, Reed picked up the alleged Anderson-Weber document. He handed the paper to Anderson, telling him, "Look at that and say whether it is the original paper." Anderson carefully looked over the paper for some time. Reed asked, "You have some difficulty in recognizing it?"

Anderson replied, "I never saw that paper before. That is a very good counterfeit."[33] Anderson had just testified that an important piece of evidence for the Democrats was not real. Reed smiled. Anderson snapped at Reed, "Reserve your smiles until after the investigation is over and perhaps you will smile on the other side of your face."[34]

After his cross-examination, Reed became a national partisan lighting rod. The Potter committee's proceedings, especially its first key witness, were the subject of intense public interest. Reed played the major role for the Republicans in this critical period. Drawing on his prosecutorial expertise, Reed magnified the character flaws and undermined the evidence of an opposition witness. Typical of Republican papers, the *Cincinnati Daily Gazette* credited Reed with a "very forcible and effective" cross-examination.[35] On the other hand, Democratic papers like the *Boston Herald* had found a new target:

"Reed has a considerable tendency to bumptiousness, and . . . police court blackguardism."[36]

Following Anderson's eventful testimony, Democrats on the Potter committee settled into a more predictable pattern of revisiting Republican campaign misdeeds. The lack of new evidence in the months following Anderson's testimony lessened public interest. As the work dragged on, it became apparent that there was no bombshell for overturning the election results. In fact, in the early stages of the Potter committee's work, the House passed a resolution not to challenge the title of Hayes. The Potter committee, however, was reminding people of the ethical shortcomings of Republicans during the 1876 campaign. Democrats were eager to take the ethics issue to voters in 1878 and 1880.

In the summer of 1878, Reed took a leave from the Potter committee to campaign in his district. He arrived home to find that he was in electoral trouble. Economic struggles in Maine had benefited the Greenback Party, which supported inflationist policies that appealed to debt-burdened farmers. Reed asked the party for more help distributing campaign documents, especially his William and Mary speech. Privately, Reed expressed the belief that his Potter committee service had earned him party support during the campaign: "As for the District I don't believe the Republicans will let me be slaughtered while I am at the front."[37] On August 1, Reed was unanimously nominated by First District Republicans.

Two days later he was raising party campaign funds. At the time, political parties relied heavily on what were called "assessments" placed on government workers who obtained their jobs through political patronage, even though they did nonpolitical work in government agencies like delivering the mail. Thus, Reed visited the office of C. W. Goddard to collect the expected contribution. Reed probably did not realize how difficult his task would be. Hours earlier, Goddard had criticized Reed in a letter to President Hayes: "Mr. Reed, having been renominated by acclamation, made a speech in which your administration indeed your personal existence was ignored as absolutely as that of the emperor Constantine."[38] When Goddard declined to pay the contribution, Reed highlighted his role on the Potter committee to preserve the title of the Republican president. Goddard still refused and wrote another letter to Hayes saying that he refused to contribute to a candidate whose victory might be seen as a rebuke of his administration. In reply, Hayes gave Goddard partial satisfaction by writing that his administration rejected compulsory campaign assessments but that he supported Reed's reelection "strongly and without qualification or misgiving."[39] While Goddard qualified as a minor nuisance, a bigger danger lurked on the horizon.

Constituting a majority in the district, the combined support of Democrats and Greenbacks would be fatal to the first-term incumbent. Democrats hoped that the Greenbacks would also nominate the Democratic nominee Samuel J. Anderson, a successful attorney and son of a former congressman in the district. The Greenbacks, however, did not find Anderson sufficiently supportive of monetary expansion and instead nominated E. H. Gove. In accepting the Greenback nomination, the florist Gove said that the working people of Maine were suffering while the two major parties were busy investigating each other. Although the ideal of having the Greenbacks nominate the Democratic candidate was not realized, Democrats considered Gove's nomination a second-best alternative since Gove was a former Republican who might draw support from Republicans.

Reed gave stump speeches of approximately ninety minutes throughout the district. His campaign emphasized the importance of a sound financial policy. He was supported by the Republican *Press*, which praised his legislative record: "A vote for Reed is a vote against the payment of Southern claims."[40] On the other hand, the Democratic *Argus* downplayed Reed's opposition to Southern war claims, "While Mr. Reed's friends are claiming credit for him that he opposed the William and Mary College bill, we have not noticed any mention by them of the fact that the bill was a republican measure."[41] Four days before the election, the *New York Times* described the outcome of the contest as very much in doubt.[42]

Ultimately, Democrats and Republicans both saw the outcome as hinging on who could prevent their supporters from defecting to the Greenback Party. The Republican *Press* feared that Reed's fate would mirror a recent congressional race in Oregon where a Republican Greenback had taken enough votes from the Republican candidate to provide a Democratic victory.[43] The Democratic *Argus* accused Reed supporters of distributing Greenback literature in Democratic neighborhoods.[44] Newspapers discouraged defections to the Greenback candidate with dubious math. The election-day *Press* told readers, "And if you vote for Gove you vote against Reed and for Anderson."[45] Similarly, the election-day *Argus* instructed, "Every Democrat that does not vote for Anderson today gives half a vote for Reed."[46]

Of course, on election day, September 9, 1878, the math entailed counting one vote for the candidate for whom the ballot was actually cast. When district voters went to the polls, no candidate received a majority. Reed secured 13,738 votes, or 46 percent of the three-way vote, with Anderson receiving 9,473 and Gove 6,504 votes.[47] Reed had been reelected. Two of his five House Republican colleagues were less fortunate as they lost to Greenback opponents. Thus, it was with mixed emotions that Reed took the podium on election night, lamenting, "The large vote given for the wrong cause reminds us that our labors must not close here."[48]

Although focused on his Potter committee work, Reed participated occasionally in floor debate during the short session. On January 10, 1879, the William and Mary bill on which Reed had first obtained national prominence reached the floor again. Reed's attention became focused on another Republican, James Monroe from Ohio, who was supporting the measure to provide $65,000 to repair damages incurred during the Civil War. Saying that he had not heard this bill offered as anything other than a charitable measure for an educational institution, Representative Monroe insisted, "I would not vote for it or say a word for it as a war claim."

Reed interjected, "The gentleman from Ohio has said that he has not read the arguments in favor of this as a war claim. Has he taken the pains to read the title of the bill, which is "a bill to reimburse the College of William and Mary for damages?"

Monroe explained, "I understand that the friends of the bill propose to change the title."

"In other words, my friend is like the deacon who was a member of a temperance society, who said he could not drink cider, but if they would call it apple juice he would drink it."

Monroe responded, "I know the mettle of my friend from Maine; that he is not in the habit of being put down by a joke, and I tell him in all kindness that I do not mean to be put down in that way myself."

"I had not the slightest idea of putting the gentleman down. I was only meeting an argument which both he and the gentleman from Massachusetts [Mr. Loring] presented. He says that hereafter he is going to be foremost in opposition to the payment of war claims. I tell him that the time to fight is when the battle is going on, and not after it is over."

"That is true; but it is not worth while to begin the battle beforehand; it is not worth while to get up in the middle of the night and begin sounding the trumpet and beating the drum and making the fife scream when every honest man is quietly sleeping in his bed."[49] Shortly after the exchange, the House defeated the bill 127–87.

When the Potter committee was wrapping up its work in February 1879, attention was diverted by the discovery of telegrams between Democratic operatives during the disputed 1876 presidential election. These telegrams had two characteristics that generated public interest: 1) they were in secret code that had just been decoded; and 2) the messages showed Democrats discussing how to pay off the electoral boards of southern states in order to secure the electoral vote for the Democratic candidate Bill Tilden. The telegrams already had a popular moniker, the "cipher telegrams." The Potter committee would be the first high-profile opportunity for Democrats to explain the telegrams. Key operatives involved in the cipher telegrams were called to appear before a Potter subcommittee.

William Pelton, the central figure in the cipher telegrams, was the first to testify. He entered the hearing room at the Fifth Third Hotel in New York City on February 6. Pelton was the assistant secretary of the Democratic National Committee and the nephew of the Democratic presidential candidate Bill Tilden. Under Democratic questioning, Pelton presented himself as someone confronted by an electoral environment in which corrupt canvassing boards were going to steal Tilden's victory unless bribes were paid. Pelton's efforts to buy the one elector that Tilden needed to win the presidency came up a dollar short and a day late. The plot's failure confirmed for Democrats that Pelton was acting alone since the multimillionaire Tilden could afford the discussed amounts. Ultimately, all canvassing boards and electors associated with the twenty disputed electoral votes sided with the Republicans.

The crucial fiftieth telegram in the set had been sent to Pelton by Manton Marble, a Democratic operative in Florida. At the time, Pelton was living in Tilden's mansion, which is where the message was sent. As translated by the *Tribune*, Marble wrote: "Have just received a proposition to hand over at any hour required Tilden decision of board and certificate of governor for 200,000." The decoded response of Pelton was brief: "Proposition too high."[50]

When Reed cross-examined Pelton, he was methodical. Reed used his familiar strategy of asking about ostensibly harmless minutiae to get a witness to commit to details with problematic implications. Even if Reed could not get Pelton to make the desired admission (that Tilden was somehow involved), Reed wanted Pelton to evoke remembered and not-remembered details that would strain belief about how human nature operated. In cross-examination, Reed pressed Pelton on whether Tilden was aware of his activities. Reed referenced another telegram that translated as "If Returning Board can be procured absolutely, will you deposit 30,000 dollars?" Reed asked, "Did you receive a dispatch of the character indicated by that translation?"

"Yes, sir, I received a dispatch of that character."

"Did you show that to your uncle?"

"No, sir."

"Where did you receive it?"

"I have no means of fixing it; but either at the Everett House or at Liberty Street."

"Was not this quite a little event, this statement that a state could be bought for $30,000, when you were rather anxious about that time to get a state?"

"Well, I can't fix definitely at which office I received that dispatch."

"Can't you recollect where you got a startling telegram like that?"

"No, sir."

"You had not been in the business of buying states before?"

"No, and I had not been buying any then."

"Apparently not; but this was the first offer you had ever received of a state, was it not?"

"I suppose it was."

"Did not an event like that make any impression upon your mind so that you could remember where you received the astounding news?"

"It made an impression on my mind, but I do not remember where I received it."[51]

As it got late in the questioning, the number of potential offers and areas that had been discussed had become so numerous that the questioner and answerer were struggling to juggle all of them. Reed thought that he had caught Pelton for giving previous false testimony at a prior Senate hearing when Pelton denied knowledge of a telegram about buying an elector. Pelton, however, noted that the telegram in question referred to the price of a canvassing board. "There were no electors," he said.

Reed was starting to understand. He asked, "Then you make a broad distinction between the purchase of a Canvassing Board at wholesale and the purchase of an Elector at retail?"

"Well, yes, if you choose to consider it in that light."[52]

After Pelton's testimony, Republicans claimed victory and Reed received some credit for it. Pelton had admitted to making efforts, albeit unsuccessful ones, to purchase the support of several electors and boards. Although Pelton had not implicated Tilden, the corruption was getting close to the Democratic presidential candidate. The *New York Times* praised Reed's approach to eliciting additional details: "Mr. Reed had conducted it in a style of sarcasm, the humor of which gave Col. Pelton some relief, for he could laugh away his embarrassment at odd moments when the committee and the spectators were convulsed."[53]

Excitement was high the next day as the other half of the telegram to buy Florida, Manton Marble, appeared before the Potter committee. During his testimony, Marble insisted that the monetary offers were not his and that he had merely passed them on as "a matter of news." In his cross-examination, Reed asked, "Now when you sent this dispatch, 'Have just received a proposition to hand over at any hour,' and so on, you did not suppose that anybody would understand that you were engaged as the medium of bribery?"

"Precisely not."

Reed countered, "When you transmitted a dispatch which, persons not understanding your character, would have a suspicion was a proposition to assist in bribery, you call it a 'danger-signal.' That is something which I do not understand, and which must arise from your relations with Colonel Pelton. Now, explain how you supposed that Pelton, instead of mistaking it, as he naturally did, for a proposition to assist in bribery, was to understand it as a 'danger-signal'?"

"I wished him to make the Democratic committee aware that the Canvassing Board was thought to be venal."[54]

Reed proclaimed, "In the presence of these masters of the art, we Republicans ought to be ashamed of our cipher."[55] He pressed Marble on whether he had considered the consequences of his actions. "Were you not afraid that this dispatch which you sent to Pelton, saying 'Have just received proposition to hand over at any hour required Tilden's decision for $200,000,' might be communicated to Governor Tilden?"

"I had no idea about any one communicating the dispatch to him. . . . He was not in my thought at all in that connection."

"Notwithstanding the fact that you directed your telegrams to No. 15 Gramercy Park, where he lives?"

"Notwithstanding that fact."[56]

Tilden, who was struggling with health issues, testified the next morning. His voice was so soft that committee members struggled to hear. Tilden testified that he was unaware of Pelton's activities during most of the period. When Tilden found out that Pelton was pursuing a dubious endeavor, he rebuked Pelton and insisted that any activity be stopped. Overall, Tilden accepted an embarrassing lack of awareness of the actions around him ("under his own roof" in the familiar Republican refrain), but no evidence tied him to the scheme. He found a mostly receptive audience for his assertions that the presidency had been stolen from him. As Tilden was finishing, the acting chair, Democrat Eppa Hunton, made a familiar Democratic inference about the failed plots discussed over the last three days. He framed it as a softball question, "You state your belief that the Returning Boards in one or more states were purchased. You had information that led you to believe, and that, if true, would convince you that at least one of those boards offered itself for sale to the Democratic side. Now, it was not sold to the Democratic side, and is not the conclusion legitimate and proper that if not purchased by one side it was by the other?"

Reed jumped in before Tilden could answer, "I object to that question, and ask for the ruling of the chairman on it."

Ignoring Reed, Tilden answered, "That is a question of logic."

Acting Chair Hunton, unable to keep a straight face, said to Reed, "Do you expect the Chair to rule out a question he has himself asked?"

"Yes, sir, that one, with confidence," Reed replied.

"Well, the witness says it is a question of logic, and as that is not a matter of investigation, I will rule out both question and answer. That is all, Governor Tilden."[57]

After the hearings ended, evaluations of Reed proliferated. Democrats attacked him personally. The *Chicago Times* characterized Reed as a "cheerful idiot" who demeaned the proceedings: "Reed is a great, fat stupid creature, who has the most decided down-east twang."[58] The Democratic *World* editorialized, "The bearing, tone and manner of Committeeman Reed were more studiously offensive even than his language and at times more vulgarly insolent."[59] The *Argus* merged the perspectives by suggesting that Reed's style represented the incongruity of a portly, jolly Shakespearean character playing a ruthless Dickens character: "It was something like Sir John Falstaff playing the part of Bill Sykes."[60]

Republicans offered a simple explanation for Democratic attacks on Reed. He exposed the "most nauseating spectacle of battled and exposed rascality, squirming and twisting mendacity, and absolutely transparent hypocrisy, ever presented to the American public."[61] Republicans saw nothing incongruous about his style. It was a good approach to getting information. The *Graphic* suggested Reed's humor reflected a calm sincerity: "Mr. Reed, whose wit is fully a match for all the rest of the committee, must have a sort of latent honesty hidden about him, for he never goes through the farce of getting angry, as do his fellow-members, and keeps his temper under the most exasperating circumstances."[62]

The Potter committee presented its findings on March 3. The majority report ignored the cipher telegrams and emphasized the questionable behavior of the returning committees. It declared that the evidence supported Tilden's claims to the presidency. The Republican minority report highlighted voter intimidation and mocked the Democratic dismissal of the cipher telegrams as Shakespearean incongruity: "A report upon frauds connected with the electoral count in Florida, with the cipher dispatches omitted, is so patent an example of the trite performance of Hamlet with Hamlet omitted, that we can hardly credit our eyes in seeing the majority thus turn the tragedy into a farce."[63] And what would Butler do? Butler wrote his own report saying that the Louisiana violations were so egregious that the state's vote should have been discarded, which would have resulted in the election of Tilden.

Ultimately, the Potter committee reports were buried in the mounds of congressional paperwork and had little impact on the perception of who had rightfully won the 1876 election. By the time the committee did its work, people were starting to accept that a definitive outcome was unlikely. The committee left unresolved the question of whether Republican actions overcompensated for the indeterminate effect of voter intimidation. Above all, the committee had revisited misbehavior on both sides. The passage of time has done little to put the conduct of the election in a better light, and modern historians view the 1876 election as a "disgraceful chapter" in American history.[64]

The Potter committee, however, had a profound impact on Reed's career. His prominence and legislative experience were now integrally tied to partisanship. The bitter dispute over the 1876 presidential election was not only the backdrop for the start of his career, but he was also on the front lines of the struggle. Indeed, in the critical days when Anderson testified at the hearings, Reed was the only bona fide Republican on the subcommittee. Reed excelled in the struggle. He drew effectively on his legal background including his penetrating cross-examination ability. Further, his sarcasm guaranteed quotes in newspapers seeking to enliven their coverage of government proceedings. In short, Reed's persona fit well into the contentious partisan era in which his career began. The Potter committee had solidified his path to partisan leadership. He was not one to back down from a fight. Reed would always remember the dramatic start to the Potter committee when he stood alone in party combat questioning Anderson. Lest he forget, Reed need only look at the framed *Harper's* drawing of his cross-examination of Anderson that remained prominently placed in his home decades later.[65]

Exquisite Raillery

Party animosity was the signature characteristic of the Forty-Sixth Congress. It was Reed's second term and began with a special session on March 18, 1879. The parties still had not let go of the disputed presidential election of 1876. The 1878 off-year election had returned a Democratic House majority led by Speaker Randall that was not eager to work with the Republican president Hayes. Both parties were seeking any advantage for the upcoming 1880 election. Business was booming and the government was running a surplus. In short, the only urgency was to get the better of opponents. Having served on the partisan Potter committee, Reed was not well positioned to avoid these party battles. That was fine with him.

Reed dedicated most of his floor energy to criticism of adding unrelated subjects, or riders, to spending bills. Under House rules, a rider could be attached so long as it reduced spending. The Democrats, who generally supported a low revenue tariff and low spending, were adding riders to must-pass appropriations bills in order to force spending cuts. Reed repeatedly made points of order against these riders. He defended germaneness and expressed concern that the Appropriations committee was getting too much power since any subject could end up on its bills. With a solid Democratic majority, Reed invariably lost.

On April 25, frustrated by Reed's repeated objections, Democrat Ezekiel Ellis of Louisiana sought solace in a Bible verse. He proclaimed, "Mr. Chairman, it would seem, as we gather from Holy Writ, that people were sometimes attracted by the sight of a 'reed shaken by the wind,' but it is too common a spectacle in this House to excite much attention."

Reed replied, "The expression quoted by the gentleman is rather too common to be repeated by an educated man. A friend near me suggests that there is wind enough, but the reed is not shaken."

"Well, be that as it may, it requires usually but very little to shake it."[66]

Unshaken, Reed shifted his focus in fall 1879 from the breeze in Congress to the storm that was brewing in Maine. Mainers had gone to the polls in September, and the initial vote tally showed that Republicans had won both chambers of the state legislature. Since no candidate had received the required majority for governor, the new Republican state legislature would have the responsibility for electing the next governor. Three months after the presumed Republican victory, however, the Democratic-controlled council responsible for certifying the outcome released the official results, which disqualified Republican votes in enough legislative districts to relegate the Republicans to a minority in both chambers.

Reed was not about to miss this fight. He was frequently in Maine strategizing with other top Republicans. In what he later characterized as having "administered the truth in doses so large and so free from impurities,"[67] Reed condemned Democrats for their "unblushing steal." On December 18, the *New Hampshire Patriot* editorialized about his conduct: "Congressman Reed . . . is fairly blubbering with vexation and anger, and makes all sorts of wild statements, and talks incoherently about 'stealing of a state and overthrow of a state government,' as though such things were an awful crime of which republicans were entirely innocent."[68] Reed was not about to back down and spoke in Portland on December 23. The count-out, Reed argued, was not about partisanship but about a violation of fundamental democratic principles: "The sole basis on which our government rests is the control of all by majorities . . . [and] if it be, then, in the power of any set of men to permanently put aside the declared will of the people, our form of government has perished from the earth."[69]

Maine was in the midst of a constitutional crisis. The incumbent Democratic governor, Alonzo Garcelon, ignored the Maine Supreme Court's opinion that Republicans had been legitimately elected. The official state seal was seized. Democrats and Greenbacks began meeting as the official state legislature; Republicans met as a rump legislature. As talk of mob action proliferated, hundreds of state militia members were activated and arms were requisitioned. Governor Garcelon summoned Maine's Civil War hero Joshua Chamberlain to oversee capitol security. Chamberlain managed to secure the peace. Democrats and Greenbackers relented after a follow-up ruling by the Supreme Court. The crisis ended without bloodshed.

Reed was relieved by the outcome. Maine was looking like it was incapable of running a democracy, a charge that Reed would rather have leveled at southern states. Only a two-term congressman, Reed had now played a significant role in two ugly disputes about electoral integrity—one state and one federal. Reed and the Republicans were victorious in both cases. In the aftermath, Reed told a journalist, "I believe in an overruling Providence more strongly than ever before. I had doubted it sometimes, but this Maine matter has convinced me." When the journalist relayed Reed's comment, a Democratic official commented, "The man who sees a special Providence in affairs is always the man whose side has whipped the other side."[70]

Back in Washington, Reed joined party battles during the session. The minority Republicans typically took the role of trying to stop Democrats from advancing legislation. It was not that difficult. First, Democrats lacked unity; second, there was no shortage of techniques available to obstruct legislation. The first line of defense for the minority was to deny the presence of a quorum for doing any business at all. This perennial strategy was called the disappearing quorum.

It was not easy for Thomas B. Reed to disappear. He was a large man whose seat in the House was in clear view of the Speaker. Yet despite sitting at his seat, Reed was frequently not counted as part of the quorum. Neither were his Republican colleagues. They refused to vote when their names were called. Recorded as not voting, they were not counted as part of the quorum required for doing business. At first glance, the full House suggested the presence of a quorum, but it disappeared as members refused to respond to their names.

Pioneered by John Quincy Adams in 1832,[71] the disappearing quorum technique effectively stopped the legislative process from getting started. Article I, Section 5 of the Constitution specifies that a majority of the House "shall constitute a quorum to do business." By withholding its members from the quorum, the minority can force the majority party to bear the entire burden of constituting a quorum. This was especially daunting when the majority party had a narrow majority. Inevitably, some members were away for reasons such as illness or attending to business in their district. This was the case in Reed's second term as the Democrats had a 149–130 majority.

On January 28, 1880, some Democrats supported a proposal to close the loophole that enabled the disappearing quorum. The Constitution authorizes the House to "compel the attendance of absent members," but it is silent about whether they can be compelled to vote. Under House rules, members not voting were not counted as part of the quorum. Thus, the Democratic proposal provided that members present but not voting could be considered part of the quorum through "ocular demonstration."[72] In short, the Speaker could see that members were there and could count them as part of the quorum. The proposal immediately drew sharp criticism from Republicans, including leader James Garfield.

Supporting the Republican position, Reed's speech on the House floor was a strong defense of the disappearing quorum. He explained, "The constitutional idea of a quorum is not the presence of a majority of the members of the House, but a majority of the members present and participating in the business of the House." The practice of allowing members to refuse to be counted as part of the quorum was "a privilege which every minority has availed itself of since the founding of this government." This practice, Reed argued, was enshrined in political theory: "It is a valuable privilege for the country that the minority shall have the right by this extraordinary mode of proceeding to call the attention of the country to measures which a party in a moment of madness and of party feeling is endeavoring to enforce upon the citizens of this land."[73] Reed finished his speech, no doubt unaware that this would not be the last time he would hear these words. As for the fate of the proposal, no vote was taken. Even if Democrats had mustered the necessary quorum, they were too divided to pass the measure.

Later in the session, tensions flared on a spending bill to fund basic services. The bill had already passed the House, but the Senate added a rider that shifted responsibility for appointing deputy marshals from the executive branch to the courts. The House Democrats wanted to approve the Senate version without debate, but Republicans objected. This disagreement prompted days of time-wasting quorum calls and roll-call votes generated by dilatory motions about how much time should be allotted to discuss the issue. A time-consuming roll-call vote on whether to allow ninety minutes of debate, for example, was followed by a roll-call vote on whether to allow seventy minutes of debate. It was inevitable that a member would note that far more time had already been wasted than the hour or two requested for debate. This observation immediately provoked what might have been the height of petulance during the conflict. Pennsylvania Democrat Robert Klotz proclaimed, "I would rather remain here all night than agree to the demand of the other side."[74] The squabbling continued. Finally, on April 21, 1880, an exasperated member suggested that the dispute could be referred to a committee outside normal operating procedure. His proposal was to refer the matter "to a committee on common sense with instructions to report immediately."

Reed exclaimed, "That would be a partisan committee—all from this side."[75] Of course, Democrats were not willing to let a Republican committee resolve the issue. The stalemate continued. Taking aim at Reed, the *Washington Post* suggested that Congress was not the only place that was low in common sense. It editorialized, "Mr. Reed's constituents should apply for some of this commodity before the next Congressional election."[76]

On April 22, the impasse ended when Democrats agreed to give Republicans an hour for debate on the rider requiring the courts to appoint an equal number of deputy marshals for each party in each region. Democrats would soon wish they had not done so. Rather than dividing their time, Republicans gave the full hour to Reed.

Reed incorporated his criticism of the bill into a sweeping consideration of majority rule and minority rights. He first rejected the bill's aspiration to nonpartisanship, explaining, "There is no such thing as a non-partisan republic, and the moment you get a non-partisan republic that republic is tottering to its fall." Reed continued, "Parties are created for some decent and respectable purpose; they grow out of the necessities and needs of mankind; and our system of government is founded on the idea of ascertaining which party should be uppermost." The evaluation of parties is best accomplished when the parties are not "twins" and the uppermost party can be held "responsible" for its actions. Applying these philosophical principles, Reed offered his summary of how government should work: "The best system is to have one party govern and the other party watch; and on general principles I think it would be better for us to govern and for the Democrats to watch."[77]

Reed pursued a similar pattern of applied political philosophy in contemplating the impact of public opinion in democracies. Given the central role of parties in Reed's view of government, it is not surprising that public opinion acts through parties. He explained, "The people express their average intelligence every time they come to the polls, and every party expresses its average intelligence." By emphasizing averages, Reed's argument downplayed leadership: "The reason we have been right and they have been wrong has not been that they had not brilliant leaders; it is because the average of intelligence with us has been higher than the average of intelligence with them."[78]

Democrats were enraged. John McMahon began, "I have listened patiently for an hour, with my limited intelligence, to hear some important point, and when I remember that our friends on that side sat for two whole days in the persistent obstruction of the public business for this—for this and nothing more, I am lost in amazement."[79] He then attacked Reed and Republicans as hypocritical for saying they wanted fair elections when they wanted partisan oversight. Apparently, Reed had not changed any minds, and Democrats prevailed on the vote.

Reed, however, had strengthened the conviction of Republicans. The *Portland Daily Press* praised Reed: "His raillery is exquisite." Not only the style, but also the substance of Reed's speech was praised by Republican papers. They expressed a range of skepticism about Democrats being able to answer Reed. The *Portland Daily Press* editorialized that "Democrats will find the rest of the session and the campaign that follows insufficient time in which to answer it."[80] The *Philadelphia Press* thought it would take even longer: "Mr. Reed of Maine said more than the opposition will be able to answer in twenty years."[81]

In the summer of 1880, Reed returned home to campaign. Democrats and Greenbacks had become more closely aligned since 1878, but it remained uncertain whether they would unite to oppose Reed. Democrats and Greenbacks met separately on the morning of July 29, 1880. Democrats voted 175–7 for Samuel Anderson, setting up a rematch of 1878. The question was whether it would be a three-way rematch. E. H. Gove tried hard to make it one, but he lost a hard-fought contest to Anderson, who claimed both the Democratic and Greenback nominations. With a united opposition, Reed would be hard pressed to hold his seat.

His chances were helped by Republican unity. As Reed accepted the unanimous Republican nomination on August 11, he remarked that it was a more pleasant occasion than the contested nomination four years earlier. Reed claimed that national issues in the race were insignificant compared to the issue of electoral integrity in the state of Maine as manifested by the 1879 count-out of Republicans. He said that a huge victory was important to ensure that a similar electoral "crime may never again be a temptation to any scoundrel of either party so long as the world lives." Searching for a metaphor to capture the size of the Republican victory needed to send this message, Reed invoked biblical imagery that would resonate with his coastal district: "We are going to bury these worse than Egyptian foes of ours in a Red Sea of popular wrath."[82]

Reed campaigned at Republican meetings with speeches ranging from a few minutes when he was one of many speakers to two hours when he was the featured speaker. During a speech in Hallowell that the Republican *Kennebec Journal* characterized as "his usual happy-go-lucky style," Reed asked rhetorically, "Why don't God kill the Democratic Party?" He answered, "Every struggle with evil that we have gives us renewed moral power and courage."[83]

On September 13, Maine voters went to the polls. Given the infamous count-out a year earlier, both parties were suspicious about the vote counting.

When Reed went to bed, the count showed a small lead for Anderson. The next morning the *Argus* reported that it was "almost a certainty" that Anderson had won.[84] After all the votes were counted, however, Reed had defeated Anderson by 16,915 to 16,822.[85] Reflecting on another narrow win, Reed wrote, "I am getting to like the business but it is as insecure as living in a Powder mill and very often as startling."[86]

Despite the final tabulation, the Democratic *Argus* claimed that there was proof that Anderson had a majority of over three hundred votes.[87] The Republican *Press* told its supporters that the *Argus* and Democrats were trying to "steal Congressman Reed's seat."[88] The dispute would be resolved in the US House, which has the constitutional duty to judge the election returns of its members. A Democratic House would likely uphold Anderson's challenge. In the national elections in November 1880, however, the Republicans narrowly won control of the House. Anderson's challenge would not prevent Reed's reelection.

The question, however, was whether Reed wanted to stay. Maine Senator Hannibal Hamlin had announced his retirement earlier in the year, and the Republican Maine State Legislature would elect a new senator at the start of 1881. Reed's name was widely mentioned as a candidate. He had a lot of thinking to do about whether to seek the position. On November 23, 1880, Reed announced his decision in a letter to the Republican *Press*, saying he was not a candidate for the open Senate seat. Reed referenced the competitiveness of his district and said that one seat could jeopardize Republican control of the House.[89] He would be returning to the House for a third term.

First, however, he went to Washington for the lame-duck session of his second term. Reed picked up where he had left off before the campaign. He was immersed in areas of high partisan conflict, especially on questions about the conduct of elections. On the Potter committee, Reed had spent months fact finding about electoral integrity. This meant that he was the Republican most likely to be called upon to respond to Democratic allegations about the 1876 election. Even after the 1880 election, Democrats regularly condemned the 1876 outcome.

Such was the case on December 13, 1880, when Democrat Joseph Davis revisited the findings of the Potter committee about Republican transgressions in the 1876 election. Even if Davis did not have a famously grating voice, Reed would not have liked the sound of renewed charges of Republican fraud. Reed explained that he was "pained to hear this matter opened again," even if Representative Davis had spoken "so eloquently and so melodiously."

Reed reached for a metaphor to capture the "chronic" condition of Democratic election complaints. He explained, "The attitude which they have assumed for the last four years reminds me very much of a dog that I once owned. After going out into the street and getting a complete and thorough thrashing from a bigger and worthier dog he used to come into the house and lay down upon the hearth, and then with one paw rub one damaged ear and growl, and with the other paw rub the other ear and growl, and then he would rub his scarred and unhappy nose and growl, and feel bad generally." Reed ended his metaphor optimistically, "Now I am in hopes that time, after a sufficient lapse of it, may cure them as it has cured him."

A representative inquired, "The dog is cured now?"

"He is dead," Reed responded. He then ascribed significance to the Democrats not renominating Tilden in 1880: "If the Democratic Party in its inmost heart ever believed in the charge of fraud in connection with the election of 1876, they ought to have . . . presented to the people for vindication [in 1880] Samuel J. Tilden, the ablest and the keenest man that belongs to their party; and I say that after having had some experience thereof." Reed proceeded to revisit accounts of violence in the South on election day.

During his remarks, Reed was interrupted by Ohio Democrat Ebenezer Finley, who insisted on a question. He opted for a traditional congressional question format. Finley asked, "Is it not a fact . . . that in 1874 the election in Louisiana was free and fair?"

Drawing on his Potter committee experience, Reed responded that Republicans had actually won the parish in question by "two to one" in 1874. Having capitalized on his knowledge and eager to change subjects, Reed said, "I think it very possible that that may have been a fair election. Now, having embalmed that fly in the liquid amber of my discourse, I wish to proceed." With that soon famous transition, Reed renewed his documentation of Democratic transgressions.

Reentering the fray, Davis responded, "I do not desire to enter into a debate upon the general iniquity that attended the elections in Louisiana and Florida. In that I am sure the gentleman from Maine would have a decided advantage of me, as he certainly has in point of melodious voice."[90]

After the jab at Reed's voice ended the verbal sparring, the responsibility for scoring fell to newspapers. They had the most trouble finding a winner for the most "melodious voice." The *Springfield Republican* framed the dilemma: "Though a keen thinker and clear writer, he [Reed] has about the most disagreeable voice of any member of Congress. One of his few rivals is a North Carolina member named Davis." It then described the specific incident as Davis speaking "for some time in his ear-splitting fashion" with Reed then "sawing the air in his usual discordant tones with a reference to the fraud lamentation." The Springfield paper, however, was reluctant to declare a draw since Reed had made the first reference to voice aesthetics. It criticized Reed by alluding to Ben Butler, the Civil War general with an eye abnormality and a penchant for rankling his superiors: "The sheer impudence of it was Butlerian, and more than Butlerian, for even Butler would hardly reproach another man with being cockeyed."[91]

Republican newspapers celebrated how Reed had "embalmed the fly in the liquid amber" of his rhetoric. The *Bangor Whig & Courier* said that the "House roared" after Reed said these words in a "comically serious tone."[92] The Democratic *Argus* did not find it even half-comical. It editorialized, "This is our Thomas's modest characterization of the high order of his own eloquence. It is precious as amber." By the end of the editorial, subtlety was gone as it found a lesson in the event: "What an egregious ass a conceited man can make of himself."[93]

Although Reed's most visible floor activity was partisan fights, his second term also included policy advocacy. Reed regularly suggested that spending for defense was inadequate. He claimed that Democrats would rather "build a ship around an old hawse-hole" than build a new ship.[94] Given the technical impossibility, this characterization of Democratic commitment to obsolete technology exceeds for sheer exaggeration even the mock congratulation of Democratic progress that Reed would later offer: "The last declaration made by the gentleman from Tennessee was that the proper navy for the United States was a couple of logs with the American flag fastened to them. And the gentleman from Connecticut has today advanced as far as a canoe."[95]

On December 15, Democrats were again praising old military facilities. Speaker Randall explained, "Fort Sumter, after being battered, and battered, and battered, was in a better condition of defense at the end of that assault than it was when the first gun was fired."

Reed responded, "My friend says, too, that Fort Sumter was in a better condition after it was battered down than it was before. I do not know what military men may say about that, but I should be sorry to trust our defenses to forts which had to be battered down before they became of any use." Reed noted that economy was virtuous, but in excess it became the vice of "parsimony and penuriousness."

Randall defended himself, "In my action here on the subject of expenditure of public money, I have always been guided by one thought; that I had no right to be either liberal or extravagant with other people's money."[96]

Less than a month later, Reed tussled again with Randall. Reed said that a Democratic bond proposal would not be effective unless the interest rate was more attractive to buyers. He explained, "I believe that the arguments and facts and figures presented by the Speaker of this House and by other gentlemen are as fallacious as any that have ever been presented." Reed lamented, "I am sorry that the Speaker of this House has endeavored to make this matter a party question."

Speaker Randall replied, "It is rather amusing to me to listen to the gentleman from Maine, and I will try to bear his lecture with all the composure that my nervous system is capable of . . . but I really think that this lecture would have come more appropriately from some other gentleman than the gentleman from Maine; for during my long service with him in this House I have never seen him go very far beyond the lines of the narrowest partisanship."

Reed countered, "Allusion to my partisan feeling has no bearing upon the subject. I am glad to say that wherever I have taken ground there my party has been with me; and I believe that the wisdom of a good party like the Republican Party is better than all the non-partisanship that ever fooled a House or deceived a people. . . . Is my time out?"[97]

The chair confirmed that Reed's time had expired. In the bigger picture, however, thanks to the votes of fewer than one hundred Mainers in the First District, Reed's fifteen minutes were far from up.

CHAPTER 3

ELEPHANT AVOIDING MOUSETRAPS

Reed had a plan to become Speaker of the House in his third term, when the Republicans would have a majority for the first time in his congressional career. The selection of the Speaker after 1865 had become institutionalized as a prerogative of the majority party caucus acting as what modern scholars characterize as an "organizational cartel," in which majority-party members settle intraparty differences over leadership with a caucus vote and then secure organizational control by voting as a unified block in the official House vote for Speaker.[1] In practice, this meant that the Speakership was decided by building support among other majority-party members, which was a process that prospective candidates often began during the waning days of the lame-duck session of the previous Congress. The field for Speaker was open since the House Republican leader in the Forty-Sixth Congress, James Garfield, had been elected president.

When the Forty-Sixth Congress was finishing in early 1881, the *New York Times* identified five leading candidates for Speaker in the Forty-Seventh Congress. Three candidates came from west of the Ohio River (Julius Burrows of Michigan, John Kasson of Iowa, and J. Warren Keifer of Ohio) while two were eastern candidates (Frank Hiscock of New York and Reed). All candidates except Kasson were entering their third term; Kasson was returning to Congress for a fifth term after a four-year absence. The *Times* estimated that Reed was in third place.[2]

The race was shaping up as a geographic struggle between the almost evenly matched eastern and western contingents of the House Republican caucus. Reed privately doubted that a geographic combination would determine the outcome: "A majority can't safely be organised in that higgledy piggledy way."[3] The most prominent geographic argument early in the contest was made by Frank Hiscock, who downgraded the Keifer campaign by asserting that one state should not have both the president and the Speaker of the House. A lot would change, however, between the end of the Forty-Sixth Congress on March 4, 1881, and the beginning of the Forty-Seventh Congress on December 3, 1881.

The Speakership contest and American politics were altered by the death of President Garfield on September 19, 1881. Garfield had been shot in early July by a disgruntled job seeker whose bullet did less damage than the grubby hands and instruments of doctors. For his part, Reed lost a friend. He had expressed his sadness to a friend as Garfield's condition worsened: "It is hard to keep from tears when I think that at this very time the man who could not from his very characteristics have a personal enemy in the world is dying such a painful death!"[4] Nevertheless, Reed fulfilled a commitment to speak at a Boston event just two days after Garfield died.

Reed's speech put him in an unenviable position. He was giving a Massachusetts Republican convention speech, which typically would rally the troops for a tough election fight. At the same time, the nation had just emerged from a painful three-month period of wondering whether President Garfield would die. During this period the country had largely put partisanship on hold and was now mourning the loss of a president. The convention lacked its usual energy. Convention organizers struggled to find a balance between somber reminiscing and energizing Republicans for the campaign.

While eulogizing Garfield, Reed decided to give a partisan speech. He lamented that "with all their wealth, with all their knowledge, with all their treasure of love, fifty millions of people stood powerless" as their president lay dying. Reed explained that an "exalted feeling" had been necessary to deal with the crisis, but "like all things earthly" it would pass and partisanship would reemerge. Reed told his audience that there was a problem with ignoring the flawed character of Democrats: "It would be polite to do so but it would not be accurate." Reed said, "It is the fashion to say in times of political lull like this, there are no issues between parties, why not try the other one now. Would it be wise policy to put a doubtful crew on board ship simply because she sails on a fair day?"[5] Reed's choice to deliver a partisan speech opened him up to criticism from the *Boston Daily Globe*, which editorialized that Reed expressed his "ultra Republican and partisan views without regard to the feelings of anybody."[6]

The contest for Speaker was heating up in fall 1881. The early front-runner, Frank Hiscock of New York, was no doubt having second thoughts about whether one state should be able to hold both the presidency and the Speakership. Garfield's death had brought New Yorker Chester Arthur to the presidency. With Ohio less dominant in the federal government, Keifer's candidacy strengthened. By November, Hiscock and Keifer appeared to be the leaders, but both were well short of the required majority. This gave Reed an opportunity.

Reed's chances for Speaker depended on being the second choice of members committed to other candidates. On November 27, the *New York Times* laid out just such a scenario, writing, "Reed is popular with Western members, and it is probable that the Representatives from that section who desire to see Mr. Hiscock defeated would gladly join a movement to elect Mr. Reed if a man from their own section cannot be nominated."[7] Reed himself considered this outcome unlikely. He wrote his friend George Gifford in November: "You are good to hope for the Speakership for me but I have no such expectations." Reed told Gifford that he was "badly situated" because of the prominence of fellow Mainer and Secretary of State James Blaine: "Maine is hardly big enough for Blaine alone and his fortunes will be better subserved by somebody else." Reed also lamented the "trick and dicker" of the selection process.[8]

Republicans met at noon on December 3 to elect the Speaker. Since there were 146 members present, 74 votes would be needed for the required majority. On the first ballot, the vote totals were Keifer 52, Hiscock 44, Kasson 15, Reed 13, Burrows 10, Orth 8, and Dunnell 4. Balloting continued. By the sixth ballot, Reed had moved into a tie for third as the results were Keifer 54, Hiscock 34, Reed 18, Kasson 18, and Burrows 10. Would a stalemate open up the Reed scenario for victory? Substantial movement did not occur until the sixteenth ballot. Ultimately, Reed received 11 votes, which placed him third behind Keifer with 93 and Hiscock with 18 votes. While Hiscock's support was vulnerable, it shifted to Keifer and not to Reed. In defeat, Reed was most discouraged by having Hiscock cut into his support in New England. Years later, the defeat remained a source of resentment to Reed, who was convinced that he had lost to inferior opponents.[9]

Although Reed did not take losing well, he had not come away empty-handed. Consistent with the practice of keeping the party unified by rewarding rivals for the Speakership,[10] Keifer named Reed chair of the Judiciary committee. Reed fared better than another candidate Godlove Orth, who finished sixth on the first Speakership ballot but was passed over for Foreign Relations committee chair despite his seniority and diplomatic experience. The question of how Orth would respond to being snubbed by Speaker Keifer for that chair was important because the two served together on the close-knit House Committee on Rules (Rules committee), which was chaired by the Speaker and constructed to give a three-to-two advantage to the majority party. The answer came quickly. On January 5, 1881, Orth took the floor and accused Keifer of appointing committee chairs based on political reasons instead of qualifications. Concluding a blistering personal attack on Keifer, Orth announced that he was resigning from the Rules committee.

Reed's appointment to the Rules committee on January 9, 1882, was a monumental moment in his career. Reed had been well positioned to fill the vacancy left by Orth's abrupt departure from the committee. He had demonstrated expertise in parliamentary procedure and was a logical choice for Keifer. It was a classic case of a leader connecting motivation with a political opportunity.[11] The appointment put him on a committee closely tied to party leadership. Even though the committee had minimal visibility during the session, it was often immersed in partisan fights by offering rules at the beginning of the session. Reed would use his Rules committee service as a springboard to greater leadership opportunities.

Reed's policy focus during the session was on distributing the Geneva Award, which was the $25 million that Great Britain paid to the United States for damages caused by allowing Confederate ships to use British ports during the Civil War. The settlement was reached after much negotiation between the two countries. The US government quickly paid claims to American merchants who had ships damaged in the war that had not been fully covered by their shipping insurance. These uncontested claims amounted to about $15 million, which left $10 million in Geneva Award funds awaiting distribution. Congress had tried over the last decade to pass legislation to distribute the money. Both chambers and the president, however, could not agree on the same bill, and the money remained set aside. In an 1880 letter, Reed lamented that the process would probably come to nothing.[12]

Yet on May 10, 1882, Reed's majority report on the Geneva Award was on the floor. Reed argued that keeping the money in the Treasury contributed to a perception that the United States had been overpaid and had stolen money from Britain. He defended his committee's provision to pay the money to shippers who had been unable to pass on higher costs in the competitive international shipping market rather than to insurers who had profited at the time through charging higher premiums. Countering suggestions to let the Supreme Court decide, Reed said that Congress had the lawmaking power and the courts "cannot interpret laws that do not exist."[13]

After Reed closed the debate, the vote was taken. The bill had come far since its early perception as a long-shot measure. The Geneva Award passed the House in a 133–67 vote, was approved by the Senate, and signed by the president. The law was especially popular in Maine. One of the US Senators from Maine estimated that $3 million of the $10 million would go to Maine interests.[14] The *Rockland Courier* editorialized that "too much cannot be said in praise" of Reed's work on the measure.[15]

Rule Change with Jumbo Implications

After his work on the Geneva Award, Reed turned his attention to the rules but with a new sense of purpose. He began pursuing a goal to change the House rules in order to allow a majority to govern. Reed previously had been in the minority and focused mostly on the small picture of calling Democrats on parliamentary violations. After his appointment as a majority member of the Rules committee, Reed focused on the big picture of how parliamentary procedure related to the capacity of the House for legislative achievement. Reed was convinced that the House rules facilitated filibustering and prevented the majority from action.

There were numerous ways to filibuster legislation. Although its modern use typically occurs in the context of the right to extended debate in the Senate, the term "filibuster" at the time referred broadly to any time-consuming procedural device preventing a vote on final passage. As seen in the previous chapter, the disappearing quorum was often the first choice for obstruction. When the majority could produce a quorum on its own, other options were available. The most effective was to offer dilatory motions, which take various forms but have delay as the underlying objective. One example of a dilatory motion would be to move to adjourn until Wednesday at one o'clock in the afternoon, and then force a thirty-minute roll-call vote to defeat the motion. After the motion was defeated, someone could offer a slightly different motion, such as moving to adjourn until Wednesday at two o'clock in the afternoon, in order to force another time-consuming roll-call vote. Under the House rules, these motions were allowed; indeed, the motion to adjourn was a privileged motion that took precedence over other business.

Their appealing properties as a dilatory strategy had caused adjournment motions to constitute 23 percent of all floor votes in the prior Congress.[16]

Reed's history-making first foray into facilitating majority action through rule change occurred in late May 1882. Democratic filibustering was preventing Republicans from awarding a seat to a southern Republican in a contested election case. Although election dispute resolution places Congress in a judicial function of weighing evidence from election returns, the reality was that these were mostly decided on a partisan basis.[17] With Republicans keeping a quorum, Democratic filibustering centered on offering dilatory motions. The delay started on May 20. Day after day, the House sat reading names for roll-call votes on dilatory motions. Frustrated Republicans called a caucus to discuss how to stop this. At the May 26 caucus, Reed insisted on a vote after a specified number of hours, telling caucus members, "If the minority refute such a proposition . . . we must invoke the power of the Constitution and ride over their factions and partisan obstructions."[18]

Facing imminent loss of their quorum to the out-of-town obligations of several caucus members, Republicans set May 29 as the day of reckoning. Reed started the day by presenting a Rules committee resolution to change the rules to prohibit dilatory motions on election cases. Democrats began to delay. A roll-call motion to confirm a quorum consumed thirty minutes. Motions to adjourn were offered. Reed made a point of order that no dilatory motions were allowed on reports from the Rules committee. Debate ensued.

Reed was the principal speaker for the Republicans. In approaching the metaphysical question of whether rule changes had to be made under the existing rules, Reed resolved the chicken-and-egg dilemma in organic terms: "[By] the organic law of the House, the House has a right to change its rules at any time. No members or set of members have any right to use the rules which are to be changed to prevent the change which the House desires to make." Reed offered metaphorically, "There is no such thing as suicide in any provision of the Constitution of the United States."[19] In response, Democrats blasted Reed for changing the rules during the game. They mocked the idea that even though a two-thirds vote was required to suspend the rules, Republicans were claiming that a simple majority could ignore them.

The deadlock ended when Speaker Keifer sustained Reed's point of order that dilatory motions were not in order on rule changes. When appealed, Republicans sustained the Speaker's ruling on the point of order. With barely a quorum, Republicans then outvoted Democrats to establish the rule change.

Republicans moved forward on the contested election cases that had been pending for almost six months.

In the aftermath, Reed became a lightning rod for those analyzing the dramatic ten-day confrontation. The *Washington Post* reported, "When the House adjourned for the day a revolutionary precedent had been established and the minority had been temporarily deprived of an inalienable right."[20] In contrast, the *Portland Daily Press* explained, "By Democratic filibustering the work of Congress has been delayed a full fortnight, and but for the masterly leadership of Mr. Reed the Bourbon threat that the contest should be prolonged four months might have been carried into execution."[21] Perhaps the faintest defense received by Reed was in the *Philadelphia Times*: "It [Reed's rule change] is not justifiable on any rational ground, and it is measurably excusable only because it was the employment of lawlessness to defeat [Democratic] lawlessness and legislative anarchy."[22]

Reed's parliamentary maneuvers have an important legacy. First, when his point of order against dilatory motions on rule changes was upheld, it established the important precedent that Rules committee measures would be protected from dilatory motions. Being protected from dilatory motions to have reports "promptly adopted"[23] was a vital privilege that the committee would draw on in the future to become the agenda setter for the majority party. Second, Reed had changed the rules to prohibit dilatory motions on a specific type of legislative action, the contested election case. In presenting his proposal, Reed framed it narrowly as enabling the House to carry out its constitutional obligation to judge elections. Changing the rules with a simple majority vote during the session to prohibit filibustering on a certain class of activities was innovative.[24] On its own, the impact of the rule was modest. Republicans stood a better chance of seating members in a handful of election cases. It was, however, an important first step in testing House willingness for more majority governance. It would take many more battles before the House was governed by something approaching majority rule. Reed was in it for the long haul.

The inevitably partisan nature of procedural issues cemented the perception of Reed as a partisan. He increasingly found himself in partisan skirmishes with Democrats. Reed's favorite target was William Springer of Illinois. Before being elected to Congress in 1874, Springer had refused to pay the federal income tax imposed to fund the Civil War, which resulted in having his home taken by the government and which sparked more than a decade of litigation that ended with Springer himself arguing unsuccessfully in front of the US Supreme Court that the income tax was an unconstitutional direct tax.[25] Reed probably first came to dislike Springer when they served together on the Potter committee. Reed did not miss chances to put down Springer. On July 5, 1882, William Springer claimed that Reed "had made light" of his accusations of impropriety. Reed rebutted, "I will say to the gentleman that if I 'made light' of his remarks it is more than he ever made of them himself."[26]

Later in the month, Reed jumped to the defense of a House clerk who had made a tabulation error that benefited the Republicans in obtaining a quorum. Reed chastised Kentucky Democrat Joseph Blackburn for being cynical about a tabulation error in carrying a figure to the next column: "This is so plain and so palpable that if the vision of the gentleman from Kentucky were not obscured by party passion I believe he would be the very first man to acknowledge the injustice of what he has said."

Blackburn's response targeted Reed: "He is peculiar in another respect; and that is in frequently treating this House to lectures on non-partisan demeanor on the part of representatives, and painting the beauties of that supremely balanced state of mind where a man can act without the slightest bias growing out of his party affiliations. That is a peculiarly interesting spectacle that the gentleman presents; and I know of nothing in this world it reminds me of, and of but one thing in the other world, and that would be the devil undertaking to prate upon the beauties of the scheme of universal redemption."

Reed responded, "I thought that was the part of the other world with which the gentleman would naturally be familiar."

"I trust if I shall suffer such a doom as that I may at least be spared that supremest of tortures the company of the gentleman from Maine."

"You will be," Reed assured him.[27] Subsequently, Democrats chose not to pursue an investigation of the clerk. A partisan skirmish had ended. It would not be the last. Partisan skirmishes, including name-calling, accelerated in anticipation of the 1882 campaign.

The potential stable for name-calling of physically large Republicans increased with the arrival of the African elephant Jumbo in the United States. The London Zoo, fearing a rampage and frustrated with his trainer, quietly sold Jumbo to the American Barnum and Bailey circus. Jumbo was reluctant to leave the London Zoo and his weeks-long resistance to being placed in a shipping box generated free publicity for his American debut in spring 1882 at Madison Square Garden. Marketers quickly adopted the name "jumbo" for anything large.[28] The elephant had already been popularized as a symbol for the Republican Party by cartoonist Thomas Nast in the 1870s. The increasingly prominent House Republican Rules committee member and the elephant Jumbo were both large even though their exact size was unknown: Reed had said that a gentleman does not weigh more than two hundred pounds and P. T. Barnum had refused to allow Jumbo to be measured to encourage the media to exaggerate. It was not hard to link Reed to the elephant celebrity.

Reed made it even easier. On July 13, Reed set himself up by employing a metaphor in which he was a Republican elephant. He accused Democrats of taking insincere political positions for political gain. Reed offered a metaphor for what the Democrats were doing: "Gentlemen, do not go on setting mouse-traps for elephants; that is the trouble with you. You cannot rise to the dignity of any occasion."

William Springer interrupted, "You are the Jumbo!"

Reed retorted, "Oh, yes, that gentleman always rises to the dignity of an occasion suitable to himself."

When the Chair announced that Reed's time had expired and George Robeson was preparing to speak, Springer proclaimed, "Let Jumbo now retire to the rear and let the real genuine white elephant come forward."[29] Springer had managed to insult two Republicans with a metaphor that Reed had initiated. Democratic papers celebrated how Springer "suddenly retired him [Reed] from the scene, accompanied by a suitable amount of laughter."[30] Democrats had a new nickname for Reed. Sadly, the real Jumbo died just three years later in a railcar accident.

Would the voters retire Reed from the scene? Two months later, Maine voters would be going to the polls for the 1882 congressional election. Reed returned to Maine upon the close of Congress. His district, however, was gone. As a result of the 1880 apportionment, Maine had lost one seat in Congress. The task of drawing the new lines fell to the state government. On the last day of the legislative session, the Democratic governor vetoed the redistricting plan of the Republican legislature. This left Maine without any new lines for reducing its congressional seats from five to four.

As a consequence, House seats would have an unusual statewide constituency. Reed was one of four at-large Republican candidates. The Democrats and the Greenbacks returned to a combined ticket and offered four candidates that included the two sitting Greenback representatives. They emphasized Republican extravagance, especially in expanding the number of government workers who then were expected to contribute to the Republican campaign fund. The statewide constituency offered a chance to remove Reed without actually beating him in a district that he had carried three times. Looking ahead to the campaign, Reed complained to a friend: "This year will be a battle summer for me. We shall have to fight Maine all over and I grow weary at the very thought. I hate to address my fellow citizens; but I shall never let them know it this side of political extinction."[31]

Despite any misgivings, Reed worked hard during the campaign. His campaign theme was that the country had settled the major questions from the last two decades. He praised Democrats for accepting some Republican ideas but said differences remain: "If they can't say our whole creed let them roll under their tongues as sweet morsels some of our good words."[32] Reed leveraged incumbency advantage during the campaign by claiming credit for Maine's benefits from the Geneva Award.[33]

Maine voters went to the polls on September 11. The four Republican House candidates won seats as Dingley led with 73,214; Reed 72,917; Boutelle 72,680; and Milliken 72,483 votes. The closest Democrat, Daniel Thing, had 63,585 votes. As a result of the unusual statewide district, Reed had received five times his previous vote. He would be returning for a fourth term in Congress. But the election-day wish of the Republican *Press*—to "elect Thomas B. Reed to Congress and our State will have the next speaker of the House of Representatives"[34]—would not be fulfilled. Democrats regained control of the House in November 1882.

The tone of the lame-duck session that began in December 1882 was set by the election results. The Republicans had a sense of urgency knowing that Democrats had a majority in the next Congress. The Democrats wanted to run out the clock until they took over. These positions became clear in an early session disagreement about a holiday recess. Republicans suggested that there was so much to do that Congress should shorten the recess and return to work on December 26. Joining the debate, Reed noted, "We have had recreation enough during the last vacation—as much as I think most of us want." After Democrat Samuel "Sunset" Cox of New York pointed out that Reed had previously supported a longer holiday recess, Reed responded, "That was a Democratic Congress, and the country needed a rest."

"It needs a rest now," Cox rebutted. "I will say to my friend from Maine the country has already said that they do not want your services. After the fourth of March we will be busy and you will have a long, long rest."[35]

Once again, Reed had used humor to his advantage. Ironically, his foil,

Sunset Cox, had written a treatise on the nature of humor. Under Cox's taxonomy of humor functions, Reed had just used humor for "adroitly avoiding the point," which was his inconsistency on congressional vacations. Reed's broader use of humor as a leadership tool also fit Cox's theory that humor can be one of the most valuable skills for gaining public attention and "influencing" others. Cox, who had a penchant for sunlight metaphors, saw humor as especially important in legislatures because the seriousness of policymaking creates an "urgency for those gifts which cheer, brighten, and bless . . . [with] soft radiance" and soften "dark edges with sunshine."[36] In a modern study of congressional humor, Dean Yarwood finds that humor has an overall positive effect on a congressional career and gives a humorous person power over those who fear they may be ridiculed.[37]

Ultimately, the House would break between Christmas and New Year's Day, leaving Reed with some time to reflect. He composed a letter to his longtime friend George Gifford. In it, Reed expressed frustration with the national election result: "I have been of late much disgusted. We have been beaten hammered and pounded by our own people. . . . If anyone were to come along now and offer me what I am fairly worth in some other business this country would run great risk of losing a statesman."[38]

Democrats Unstrung by Special Rule

When the House returned on January 2, 1883, Republicans came eager to work on the tariff bill. At the least, they wanted to fix some problems and preempt a less preferred bill when Democrats took over in the next Congress. Tariff policy was important because of its broad economic impact on consumers and producers. It also shaped the size of the government since tariffs were by far the largest source of federal revenue. In general, Republicans favored higher tariffs than Democrats, but both parties experienced some internal disagreement based on the tariff's diverse impact on constituency economic interests. On February 3, Democrat Sunset Cox complained about a 110 percent tariff on glass, which he mocked as a tax on light. When a Michigan Republican questioned Cox about whether it was relevant for Cox to have told a story about a chandelier manufacturer lobbying for constructing a roof over Paris to increase profits, Cox said, "I go anywhere for any light; if I could get my friend from Michigan in some sort of a condition where I could put a wick into him I would illuminate this great country from Maine to the Gulf!"

Reed took the floor: "If the gentleman from New York illuminates anything it will have to be by the aid of the gentleman from Michigan, as he seems incapable of doing it alone." Easing into his policy argument, Reed rejected the idea that tariffs were leading to excessive profits, suggesting that the businessman was forced "to confine himself to a reasonable profit" or else draw many competitors. Similarly, tariffs were not placing too great a burden on consumers as evident from the fact that "there never was a time in the history of the country when the poor man's wants were so thoroughly supplied." In short, tariffs did not act as taxes that added to the cost of the product.[39]

Democrats mocked this assertion. William Springer was eager to reengage Reed just days after being immortalized as one who would never be right or president. On February 8, Springer countered, "I ask him [Reed] to state his candid opinion and expose his ignorance or wisdom before the country in answering . . . whether it [the tariff] is a tax or not."

Reed conceded, "I cannot teach the gentleman from Illinois any wisdom." Springer agreed, but undoubtedly for a different reason than Reed was about to articulate. Reed continued, "It is necessary for the plant to grow, not only that there should be seeds sown, but also that there shall be soil in which to imbed them. . . . The great difficulty is not that I cannot tell him what is the right way, if he would be instructed, but the difficulty is in making connection at the other end of the road."[40]

With a week to go in the session, tariff reform seemed unlikely. Since the House failed to pass its own tariff bill, the only realistic option for legislation was for the House to take up the Senate tariff bill and either concur or send it to a conference committee by nonconcurrence. Using the US Tariff Commission recommendation as a starting point, the Senate bill proposed significant, if uneven, tariff reduction.[41] When taking up a Senate bill, House rules provided first for a vote to concur followed by nonconcurrence options. Reed and other Republican leaders, however, did not like the Senate bill, which had higher tariffs than they were willing to accept. As the situation stood, Reed believed that under the existing rules "death awaited" tariff reform.[42]

To salvage tariff reform, Reed and Republican leaders found a solution that was destined to change forever majority rule and partisanship in the House of Representatives. Republicans held a caucus on February 22 that did not produce any consensus, except to pass the problem to the Rules committee, which Reed referred to as the "arbiters of destiny" for the bill.[43] Committee Republicans worked together on a quick response.[44] On February 24, Reed presented the first of what is now known as a "special rule" in the history of the US House of Representatives.[45] By definition, special rules bring a measure to the floor outside the normal order and set the parameters for debate and amendment. Reed's historic special rule provided the following: "It shall be in order at any time . . . by a majority vote, to take from the Speaker's table House bill No. 5,538 . . . and to declare a disagreement with the Senate amendments . . . and to ask for a committee of conference. . . . If such motion shall fail, the bill shall remain on the Speaker's table unaffected by the decision of the House on said motion."[46]

Politically, the rule represented a solution to a political problem that Reed described privately as "very peculiar."[47] Time was running out. The obvious solution, which was to concur and pass the Senate version, was not acceptable to House Republican leaders who preferred higher tariffs. The Senate bill, however, was likely acceptable to enough Republicans to combine with Democrats to pass the House. The rule was politically effective because it allowed the tariff bill to come up only on terms favorable to Republican leaders, whose ability to appoint conferees would lead to a conference report with less tariff reduction than the Senate bill. The *New York Times* noted that a compromise supported by a cross-party majority was being prevented: "If there should be a majority desiring to vote to concur, they will have no opportunity to do so under this rule."[48] After removing the preferred option for many, the rule made members choose between a conference committee or nothing. Reed and other Republican leaders outmaneuvered Democrats and some of their own members. The number of Republicans who supported the Senate bill, which has been estimated at nearly forty based on caucus behavior,[49] can never be known for sure because that vote was never taken, which after all was the point of the special rule.

Procedurally, the special rule marked a sharp departure from the way rules had worked before. Rules were general in nature and affected all the business of the House. This, in contrast, was a rule for only one bill, which was specifically named. The rule did two very important things. First, it got the bill to the floor. This is essential given that most bills die on lengthy legislative calendars without ever receiving a final vote. Second, it constrained how it would be treated when on the floor. In this case, the rule brought the tariff bill to the floor but took away the concurrence option and allowed only nonconcurrence by requesting a conference. All this was accomplished by majority vote instead of the two-thirds majority required to formally suspend the rules. In short, as described by modern political scientists, this "remarkable" proposal amounted to a simple majority "customizing" bill treatment.[50]

The marked departure from parliamentary practice is apparent not only in hindsight, but it was also recognized at the time. When Reed made his first push for majority rule in 1882, he cited precedents from parliamentary history suggesting that dilatory motions need not be recognized for rule changes on contested elections. On February 26, when Reed advocated for the special rule, he conceded that the provisions were "unusual in their nature and very forcible in their character." Democratic Congressman Joseph Blackburn placed its unusual nature in a different light: "It is an absurdity upon its face. A rule is not a provision or a declaration that reaches to a separate, distinct, specific measure."[51] The unique operation of the bill was captured well by the *New York Herald*: "It not merely changes the general rules of the House for the specific purpose of securing action on one special bill and none other, but it strictly limits the action of the House on this special bill to a special conclusion." The *Herald*'s metaphor for the rule gave it credit for ingenuity: "It realizes the Irishman's dream of a gun which should fire so as to hit the object if it was a deer, but miss it if it was a cow."[52]

On February 27, 1883, history was made as the House passed the rule by a 129–22 margin with most Democrats refusing to vote but failing to prevent a quorum. In its first incarnation, the special rule foreshadowed a unique ability to elevate partisan rancor. Applying sports language, the legislative season (session) was taking place under a set of rules. The minority party was cruising toward a rare victory in one game (bill). Rather than accepting defeat, majority party leaders changed the rules during the game. The new rules restructured the strategic choices available to the players in a way that favored the majority-party leaders. The cross-party compromise that was likely to win under the old rules was prohibited under the new rules. The game changed suddenly and majority-party leaders snatched victory from the jaws of defeat. When the season continued with the next game, the old rules were back in place. A member of the first team on the losing end of a special rule, Sunset Cox, offered his perspective on the operation of the special rule: "It is a fraud on . . . all that is just and fair in our politics."[53]

The first special rule also showed its usefulness as a tool for agenda setting. As used by social scientists, agenda setting refers broadly to determining what subjects are covered. In the context of Congress, the agenda typically refers to bills that receive a final passage vote.[54] A special rule takes a bill out of the normal order and brings it to a floor vote under conditions set by the Rules committee and approved by the House. This is agenda control at its most basic. Bills that get a special rule will be on the agenda for a final vote. Bills that do not get a special rule are less likely to be on the agenda. They will most likely never come up in the normal order.

Special rules, however, offer the potential for more than basic agenda control by regulating how bills are considered. The magnitude of agenda control varies depending on the restrictiveness of a special rule. Political scientists often characterize special rules on a continuum from open rules, which do not restrict the content of amendments, to closed rules, which restrict the content of amendments.[55] As special rules become more restrictive, agenda control increases. Amendments that are allowed by a special rule become part of the agenda. Amendments that are prohibited by a special rule are not on the agenda. In 1883, Reed not only offered the first special rule but also a highly restrictive rule. Only one option that was to go to conference was on the agenda. The first option available under the regular order, which was to approve the Senate bill, was removed from the agenda. Privately, Reed offered a metaphor for what motivated the rule: "We had to have a string tied to the Bill and somebody standing with a little hatchet to cut it to pieces if it did not turn out a good little Bill."[56] In limiting options, the Rules committee exercised sophisticated agenda control.

The Rules committee is likely to gain House approval for special rules. First, the Rules committee is structured to support majority-party leadership. When Reed presented his special rule, the Rules committee was composed of the Speaker and two handpicked majority-party members and two minority-party members. Second, the likelihood of keeping the majority party's numerical advantage is increased because of the longstanding norm that members of Congress support their party on procedural votes. A procedural vote that affects how Congress conducts its business can be distinguished from a substantive vote on public policy. The pressure on members to support their party is greater on procedural votes than substantive votes. There are many reasons for this gap, including the way that procedural votes implicate the majority party as a governing body and are less visible to constituents.[57] Historians have shown that a skilled leader can obtain policy goals by winning indirectly on a procedural vote when losing is likely on a direct substantive vote.[58] Political scientists estimate that the level of partisanship on procedural votes is 75 percent greater than on substantive votes.[59] The strength of the norm is shown in systematic findings that majority-party members offer greater support for procedural votes than for the corresponding substantive vote, and the gap increases as special rules become more restrictive.[60] Such was the case on the first special rule when Republicans approved the rule

128–4 in an outcome that political scientists statistically analyzing the vote have characterized as party trumping constituency interests.[61]

While presenting the first special rule represents a landmark event, it does not appear to have been initially part of a grand plan by Reed for majority governance. In fact, Reed seems to have placed policy concerns at the forefront. In his closing speech on the rule, Reed claimed that the legislation was necessary because "the business interests of this country are in danger from the gentlemen on the other side." Reed's subsequent assertion that a conference committee would be the best forum for promoting these interests drew derisive looks from Democrats. Reed countered, "Even gentlemen who smile out loud know what I say is the truth, and it is the truth that they raise their clamor upon." Thus, Reed's closing speech did not claim the rule as important for majority governance. Reed conceded, "I admit that unless there was a great emergency I should not be in favor of the passage of this rule."[62]

Although the rule was discussed, it is clear that the attention given to it was not commensurate with its significance. There was a very good reason for that. The session was ending in a few days. Consistent with scholarly findings about the importance of timing for legislative leaders, Reed had been able to "use deadlines strategically"[63] to obtain change that would not have occurred in normal time. There were important policy proposals at stake, and time was running out. Once the rule passed, attention immediately turned to policy questions.

Before the session ended, the Republicans passed tariff revision as a direct consequence of the rule. As expected, the conference committee produced tariff legislation that reflected the preferences of House Republican leaders for higher tariffs. The final vote showed the party cleavages inherent in tariff legislation. Republican support carried the bill to a 152–115 victory, but twenty Democrats voted for the bill while sixteen Republicans voted against the bill. The bill was signed by the president. Republicans had salvaged something from the session. Although it would not meet for another nine months, the new Forty-Eighth Congress was in place fewer than ten days after Reed presented his special rule. Reed was back in the minority.

Suffragist in the Minority

The consistent dynamic during Reed's fourth term was a fight over appropriations. Republicans supported an increase in the size of the federal government while Democrats tried to limit its growth. These positions not only fit a general ideology about federal-state relations, but they were also a practical consequence of Republicans holding the presidency since the Civil War and being able to appoint Republicans to government positions. The impetus for House Democrats under new Speaker John Carlisle to play defense was even stronger since the Republican president was joined by a Republican Senate.

To strengthen their defensive posture, the majority House Democrats adopted rules that made it difficult for the majority to act. Essentially, the Democrats returned to the rules of the Democratic-controlled Forty-Sixth Congress rather than accept the modest enhancements for majority action incorporated by Republicans in the Forty-Seventh Congress. Reed, who opted against challenging Keifer for party leadership, remained on the Rules committee. Early in the session, he proposed a new rule to extend the so-called morning hour during which nonprivileged committees could bring up and pass their preferred bills by a simple majority vote. Otherwise, a two-thirds supermajority would be necessary to take a bill out of order (through suspending the rules) and save it from certain death at the bottom of a legislative calendar that was determined by date submitted and not by importance or support. On February 4, 1884, having failed to get a quorum for his proposal during the previous Congress, Reed tried again to get his "morning hour" extension passed: "I now offer these propositions to a Democratic House in the same good faith in which I offered them to a Republican House." Reed recognized that elections had consequences and that it would be dangerous if they did not. Reed explained, "If the people do foolish things and suffer the consequences of them, they will not be likely to repeat their foolishness."[64] Apparently, the Democrats were unmoved by Reed's promise of being able to implement their foolish mandate and defeated the rule.

Although Reed was arguing for a more active Congress, on a personal level he was comfortable with not working too hard. At this time, Reed was making his way through the works of Alexandre Dumas. On February 17, 1884, he wrote to his friend, "I do so enjoy the word mongering[,] the exquisite play of expression. . . . So much has this thing grown on me that I find myself neglecting laborious days and enjoying delights." It recalled Reed's Bowdoin days when fiction took him from his schoolwork. In his letter, Reed contemplated the implications of being so easily distracted, asking rhetorically, "Do you know why I shall never be a 'statesman'?" Reed's answer: "It is because inter alias the whole world is such a chronicle of small beer compared with the bright histories of things which never happened that I can keep up no consecutive pursuit of those duties which well and sedulously performed enable the Rabbi to become the Pasha of Three yea of innumerable tails."[65]

Theater was on Reed's mind on March 5. The famed British actor Henry Irving was the talk of Washington as he was performing to packed houses including President Arthur at the National Theatre. Reed was part of a small dinner in Irving's honor at the Metropolitan Club. Bringing an outsider's perspective to the group of distinguished guests, Irving turned to Senator Thomas Bayard and commented that he looked like George Washington. Always ready to join the fun, Reed needled Bayard that he would now have to live up to Washington's character. Irving added, "And you, Mr. Reed, might have sat as a model for the Stratford bust of Shakespeare."[66]

Having the famous Shakespearean actor say that he looked like Shakespeare was a surefire way to increase Reed's fame. One supportive newspaper explained, "Mr. Reed is a very able man, whose greatness has been somewhat eclipsed by the fact that he is supposed to resemble Shakespeare."[67] At the least, it gave opponents an excuse to make fun of his appearance. Maine's Democratic *Argus* editorialized, "As to his looks, we could see no Shakespeare in his face—say rather a big apple dumpling."[68] In any case, Irving appears to have been the first to link Reed to Shakespeare. The connection with Shakespeare would follow Reed for the rest of his career. The *Troy Telegram* observed, "As nobody knows anything about the appearance of Shakespeare the compliment to Mr. Reed is not apparent."[69]

Reed resumed his criticism of the rules on April 17. He aimed his slings and arrows at Samuel Randall, who as Appropriations committee chair was able to use his committee's privileged access to the floor to monopolize House debate at the expense of other legislation. Reed joined a debate about an amendment to an appropriations bill that would change pension rules in a way that would increase spending. The amendment had drawn a point of order from Randall for violating the rule that insulated appropriations bills from new legislative provisions that would increase spending. Reed criticized Randall: "[He is] perpetuating a state of the rules which renders legislation impossible except on an appropriation bill; and then he will not let it go upon such a bill!"

Randall responded, "The theory in this House, and it should be the theory in every legislative body, is that rules are made to protect the minority. The majority can always take care of themselves."

"Not in this House," Reed answered.

Randall answered, "The gentleman from Maine, who, as a member of the Committee on Rules, took part in making these rules, should remember the magnanimity which the majority in framing the rules were willing to extend to the minority. . . . The rules provide for saving the money of the people." Randall concluded, "The country today is being legislated to death. Instead of having too little, we have entirely too much legislation."

Reed responded, "The gentleman from Pennsylvania says that there is too much legislation. I do not say whether that is true or not, but I do say that Congress sits here for the purpose of hearing the people . . . [who] are entitled to have their grievances heard, and not put where they cannot be heard."[70]

Reed's focus on rules and spending was interrupted by the issue of women's suffrage. Legislation had been introduced for a constitutional amendment that would grant women the right to vote. It was considered by the Judiciary committee on which Reed served. It became clear that the majority opposed the amendment. Reed accepted the responsibility of writing the minority report. On April 22, Reed hastily assembled his thoughts into a minority report for women's suffrage.

Reed read the draft report that night to his wife, Susan, who lay on the sofa expressing disagreement with the report. The next morning, when his wife questioned Reed's political views on the upcoming presidential race, Reed reminded her that her opposition to women's suffrage suggested that her gender made her views necessarily inferior to his. Susan soon conceded that some women were able to decide political questions. Reed relayed her shift to his friend George Gifford: "Such progress cheers one on the long road which will finally lead to emancipation."[71] Reed would have to be content with his partial victory at home. His minority report received only four of the committee's fifteen votes.

Reed's minority report made a forceful argument for granting women the right to vote. He opened by mocking how opponents of racial and gender equality claimed to be acting out of concern for the well-being of those allowed fewer rights. His sarcasm thickened as he extended the argument to children: "When it was the fashion to beat children, to regard them as little animals who had no rights, it was always for their good that they were treated with severity, and never on account of the bad temper of their parents." Rejecting the idea that opponents were motivated by a "tender consideration" for the good of women, Reed suggested the explanation of prejudice. He wrote, "Prejudices are none the less prejudices because we vaguely call them 'nature' and prate about what nature has forbidden when we only mean that the thing we are opposing has not been hitherto done." Moving beyond prejudice led Reed to a clear conclusion: "No reason on earth can be given by those who claim suffrage as a right of manhood which does not make it a right of womanhood also." The evidence, Reed argued, shows that women's suffrage would improve both women and politics. "Every citizen in the United States is made more intelligent, more learned, and better educated by his participation in politics and political campaigns," he wrote.[72]

Ultimately, history would be kinder to Reed's report than his House colleagues. While pleased enough with Reed's report to distribute five hundred copies, Susan B. Anthony captured the overall feeling of women's suffrage advocates about the 1884 session in a letter to a friend: "I keep thinking of those men at the Capitol not doing what I want them to."[73] Failing to advance as the Sixteenth Amendment in 1884, women's suffrage would ultimately become the Nineteenth Amendment on August 18, 1920. In recounting the history of women's suffrage, some historians have noted Reed's early contribution to women's suffrage. Ruth Gallaher, for example, argues that Reed's 1884 report is evidence that women's suffrage had early support even in the mainstream because, in her words, "No one can accuse Thomas B. Reed . . . of being ultra-radical, sentimental, or visionary."[74] Less qualified praise of Reed's four-page report can be found in *The History of Woman Suffrage* by Susan B. Anthony and Ida Harper: "The question of woman suffrage never has been and never can be more concisely and logically stated."[75]

First District men would determine Reed's fate the next month. Democrats and Greenbacks united to nominate Nathan Cleaves, who like Reed was a Bowdoin alum and an attorney with service as a state legislator and city solicitor of Portland. One campaign challenge for Reed was lingering resentment in Brunswick where Republicans voted 152–114 to appoint anti-Reed delegates to the district convention to protest one of his postmaster recommendations. Because of the statewide race two years earlier, Reed's district had not rendered a judgment on him since his narrow victory in 1880. Looking at the upcoming election, Reed wrote his friend George Gifford, who was in Europe, "Indeed I shall be lucky if they don't get me under this time." Reed continued, "If in your sweet seclusion you learn of my disaster mourn mildly for I am not sure that I shall at all. This business has many elements of boredom in it."[76]

During the campaign, Reed was the target of negative campaigning by the Democratic *Argus*, which accused him of having received a large consulting fee in the summer of 1883 for helping to secure Texas state lands for a

British syndicate. Was there any truth to the allegation? Archival evidence offers insight into why the accusation aggravated Reed, who privately complained about taking "column after column of abuse."[77] In fact, Reed had become involved in a Texas land deal. He had agreed to compensation that paid him only expenses if he was not successful but a "liberal fee" if he was successful. Reed could certainly be criticized for trying to become wealthy, but the evidence suggests he had failed. Among the papers of Reed's clerk is a terse letter from a Texas businessman telling Reed, "It is hardly necessary to add that you accomplished nothing."[78] Indeed, Reed was struggling months later to recoup his expenses on the deal.[79]

Reed's campaign focused on Republican prosperity and Democratic failure. His speech at a flag raising on August 20 was typical. Reed began by noting that twenty-four years of Republican rule had brought unparalleled economic growth: "In all the broad history of the world since the sun first shone on it there is no such splendid achievement." This record of Republican success contrasted with the failed record of the Democratic House. It would not, Reed said, take long to count all of the Democratic achievements in the last Congress: "You can count every achievement upon one hand if you only have one finger and a stump."[80] He proceeded to identify the two achievements as Republican measures that attracted enough Democratic support to pass.

A challenging campaign ended with election day on September 8. When the votes were tabulated, Reed's total in Brunswick had declined about seventy-five votes from his previous district election. Reed, however, did slightly better elsewhere and captured 53 percent of the district vote. His margin was lower than all of the other Republican congressional candidates in a Republican landslide in Maine. Taking the stage at a victory party on election night, Reed proclaimed that it seemed like the Democratic Party "try whatever means it may, can never beat us in this district." It was a great day, he said, "for there can be no greater blessing to a state than to be under a Republican government."[81]

CHAPTER 4

MINORITY LEADER SCOLDS DEMOCRATS

During the nine-month recess before his fifth term, Reed began a diary. The purpose was not to document a rising career but to learn a foreign language. Thus, his diary, which he kept for about four years, was written exclusively in French. Overall, his French writing lacks the nuance of his English writing; on the other hand, its simplicity may reflect unfiltered honesty. The diary was part of an overall strategy for learning French. During this period, for example, Reed regularly met with a French tutor for two-hour evening sessions. He wrote some letters in French, and he also read French novels.

One subject that Reed did not discuss publicly but that is described extensively in his diary is his health. In particular, his diary provides rare insight into what he thought about being overweight and reveals a diet that may have contributed to it. On October 4, 1885, for example, his breakfast prominently featured fish balls. He attributes his dietary preferences to a fishing ancestry while recognizing that this is not an ideal breakfast: "I love fish balls dearly. But as they make me fat I ought to give them up."[1] He also believed that his diet contributed to his most persistent health problem, which was insomnia.[2] In one diary entry, he is thankful for his political achievement but wishes, "If only God would give me sleep."[3]

Reed's French diary also offers insight into his social interactions and intellectual interests. While in Maine, he often walked from his home at 32 Deering Street to Portland's Cumberland Club, where he enjoyed reading newspapers, playing cards, and socializing. When Congress was meeting, Reed typically spent mornings with administrative tasks, such as processing the mail, and afternoons in session. He would then go to dinner with friends or with special guests, including the inventor of the telephone, Alexander Graham Bell.[4] After dinner he would often practice French. Above all, the diary reveals that he spent a lot of time with his wife and daughter, making for a close-knit trio. The family enjoyed playing games, with backgammon and the card game Tric-Trac among their favorites.

When not socializing, Reed was most likely reading. His diary documents a prodigious amount of reading. His tastes had changed little since his time at Bowdoin. Reed enjoyed reading fiction. His diary, for example, describes finishing *Le Barbier de Paris* one night and beginning *La Latiere* the next morning[5]—two works from the 1820s by French author Paul de Koch, whose depictions of Paris life found a popular audience abroad. On a recommendation, he even read erotica. His opinion is apparent without translation: "Un livre terrible plein de grossierété."[6]

Starting his fifth term in 1885, Reed had a good chance of winning the Republican nomination for Speaker. He confided to his diary that it would be an "empty honor" since Democrats had a 183–140 majority.[7] Reed was probably selling the position short. The *Boston Morning Journal*, for example, proclaimed that it was "not an altogether empty honor" because the winner would be seen as the leader of the minority party and would be consulted about Republican committee assignments.[8] The previous leader, Warren Keifer, had become immersed in a nepotism scandal and was out of Congress after losing his district's Republican nomination. To win the honor, Reed would have to defeat New York Representative Frank Hiscock.

Reed's nominating speech was given by William McKinley, who was a good person to have in his corner. McKinley had an amiable nature that attracted people to him. Born in 1843, McKinley lacked Reed's extensive formal education since he had joined the Union Army when he turned eighteen. After the war, McKinley became a lawyer and a prosecutor. He was a congressional classmate of Reed, having first won election in 1876 from the manufacturing city of Canton, Ohio. The two became friendly and enjoyed dining together. They were both rising Republican stars who served together on the powerful Ways and Means committee, where they advocated for high tariffs. Although rumored to be a candidate in his own right, McKinley had opted against challenging his friend for the position.

When the votes for House Republican leader were counted, Reed had won the secret-ballot election over Hiscock sixty-three to forty-two. In a letter to his friend George Gifford on December 14, 1885, Reed admitted that he took "plaisir" both in the margin of his victory and how he had done it. Reed insisted that he had not approached anybody to win the honor. He was able to win in what he considered the right way, which made victory even more satisfying. Reed told Gifford that he had been surprised but unshaken by the discovery that Hiscock had pursued support though "solicitations."[9]

Although Reed won the nomination, that itself offered no guarantees about future party leadership. The norm of not making assumptions about the future was broken in the Republican meeting by William Walter Phelps in his nomination speech for Hiscock. Phelps reportedly "astonished" his party colleagues by suggesting that they should vote for Hiscock to set him up to be Speaker in a future Republican Congress. The *New York Times* explained that this argument backfired for Hiscock by alienating members who considered themselves to be future candidates for Speaker and those who planned to retire. Speaking for Reed, McKinley argued that the race was only about the session's nomination.[10]

As minority leader,[11] Reed faced a challenging task. Republicans tended to favor more government action, but as the minority party they were best positioned to resist action. In a letter to a friend shortly after being chosen, Reed explained, "We are forced to help them . . . our position will be very difficult." Reed summarized his predicament: "I am like a young bear, all my difficulties are in front of me."[12]

While eschewing bear cub similes, modern political scientists offer insight into the difficulties that a minority leader faces. Matthew Green characterizes minority leaders as facing a tension between their first priority of gaining majority status and a secondary desire to pass good policy. One factor that may increase the emphasis on passing good policy is leadership of an entrenched minority party that has low expectations for gaining control.[13] In a compelling scene in the biography *Robert H. Michel*, the longtime Republican minority leader looks in a mirror and says, "Today you're going to be a loser," which captures a degree of acceptance that furthered a distinguished career of seeking compromise to pass good policy.[14] Even if Reed were the type of person who took losing gracefully, he was taking over in a different context. Party control in the House had changed three times in the last six elections, and Reed could easily envision a path to achieving the first priority of gaining majority status. Reed saw this path as facilitating Democratic failure. While modern minority leaders lack viable techniques to stop the majority party, Reed had many more tools available to stop majority action. In the future, Reed would do more than anyone to empty the toolbox for minority leaders, but for the time being he was content to exploit the available tools.

Reed found no shortage of opportunities to criticize Democrats during the session. He chastised Democrats for rejecting his invitation to establish rules that made it easier for the majority to act. Another frequent criticism was how Democrats handled appropriations bills. Democrats took pride in the historical role of appropriations chair Samuel Randall to "close the treasury vault against the lobby as an alligator does its huge jaws."[15] Reed resented that Democrats had successfully used the spending restraint argument against Republicans in the last election. He countered their argument in two ways. First, he argued that Democrats were not providing enough money to carry out essential government functions. Second, Reed suggested that House Democrats offered artificially low appropriations bills only to raise spending afterward by accepting Republican Senate increases in conference committees and using deficiency bills to make up for shortfalls. On February 25, 1886, Reed denigrated the Democratic practice as a campaign ploy so that Randall could make "his annual procession across the country with his budget of figures, explaining how economical he had been and consequently what a saving he was to the country."[16] His diary entry for the event showed his enjoyment of this part of the job. He wrote, "I encountered Mr. Randall in debate and I had some fun with him."[17]

The following day, Reed extended his criticism of Democrats to the appearance of corruption emanating from the administration of Grover Cleveland, who had narrowly defeated Mainer James Blaine in 1884 to become the first Democratic president since the Civil War. The House was launching an investigation into whether ownership of Pan-Electric Telephone stock by the attorney general and other Democrats had influenced the administration's handling of a telephone patent dispute. Reed said that he could "appreciate the natural feeling of solemnity" that was affecting Democrats: "To be stopped in the midst of a career which had for its motto the turning out of 'rascals,' to be obliged to stop and consider the question whether by some accident instead of turning them out they had not got in—is of course painful."[18] Writing in his diary, Reed referenced his failure to convince Democrats that he felt their pain: "The Democrats seemed so solemn that I could not restrain myself and I made a consolatory speech which did not console."[19]

Reed returned to one of his favorite pastimes on March 19. William Springer listened as Reed accused Congress of usurping the authority of the president by legislating the promotion of a military officer. Springer challenged Reed to explain the difference between the current bill and previous Republican action. Reed replied, "I am not giving instruction in legal distinctions to the gentleman from Illinois. It would be absolutely impossible for me; I should have to start from the ground."[20] Springer suggested that Reed's real reason for refusing to answer was that there was no difference. Later that night, Reed reflected on the event. His diary provides an admission, albeit a qualified one, that he had been less than courteous to Springer's legitimate question: "I replied brutally to Mr. Springer. I cannot restrain myself when I see that man."[21]

On April 5, Reed was more cooperative as he worked with Democrats to pass legislation authorizing construction of a new building for the Library of Congress. The existing library served members of Congress and had insufficient space for its growing collection. A new building could expand its public functions into a real national repository. In his diary that night, Reed said that the bill's passage was a victory that pleased him greatly.[22] After walking by the new library a few years later, Reed wrote in his diary, "I went to the Library of Congress building, for which the world should give me the credit, though I scarcely expect to get it."[23] His prediction proved incorrect. In her 1966 book *The Proud Tower*, the Pulitzer Prize–winning historian Barbara Tuchman wrote, "The existence of a national library is owed to Reed, whose persistent and eloquent insistence finally wore out the natural parsimony of the House to secure adequate funds for the Library of Congress."[24]

As leader of the minority Republicans, Reed provided the critical votes to pass the bill. At the time, it seemed likely that the library bill would die without a vote on the long legislative calendar. The bill reached the floor under suspension of the rules procedures that required a two-thirds supermajority. Bipartisan support was essential to obtain this margin. Democrats were divided on the 159–63 House vote, but every Republican voted to fund what became the Jefferson Building. The minority leader had been willing to cooperate with Democrats who supported the measure.

Besides legislative work, members of Congress are expected to provide constituency service. As described by political scientists, casework involves "myriad favors" for constituents.[25] Reed was no exception. On the day of his library victory, Reed spent the morning acting as a tour guide for a constituent who was visiting Washington. A desire to help an individual constituent was also behind Reed's visit to the White House on April 27. Reed was trying to secure a pardon for a Maine sea captain, William Goodell, who had been found guilty of cruelty to his crew and was serving four months in San Quentin. The meeting went well and Reed was pleased that Goodell would be pardoned. Reed confided to his diary that he would like to become better acquainted with President Cleveland but doubted whether this was possible since the president "doesn't have the time to get to know anybody."[26]

As the long session drew to a close, Reed relished reminding Democrats of their difficulty in getting things accomplished. One reason for the limited achievement had been the rules that empowered Republican filibustering and made any action difficult. The lack of unity among Democrats on key issues, especially the tariff, also hindered achievement. Reed took pleasure in Democratic divisions on a late-session appropriations bill: "When they are divided as they are it is impossible for both of them to be wrong; it gives a chance for justice and righteousness to be done in this world."[27] Reed noted that "lower organizations" are prone to splitting up but Republicans were not.[28] As Congress prepared to adjourn, Reed assessed Democratic performance during the session. He said that their large majority had created a situation of "charming Arcadian simplicity . . . for the display of their varied talents." Yet, Reed suggested, they had largely failed, and "if we should stay here any longer it seems to me that we should probably have about the same result with more expenditure of time."[29] Shortly after, the session ended and Reed returned to Maine for his reelection campaign.

Reed's campaign took full advantage of the Democratic struggles in governing. He accepted a unanimous nomination at the Republican convention with a speech in which he confessed to being unable to describe Democratic achievements in the last Congress: "Some voice better equipped than mine must take up the wondrous tale." Reed then contemplated who was to blame for the lack of achievement: "Yet I am not partisan enough to blame the Democratic Party for this outcome. I blame the people who put them in power." This blame is due, he said, because the nature of Democratic politicians was well known: "After they had been bedridden for twenty-four years it was folly to expect from them anything athletic."[30] Reed's campaign developed the theme that Democratic intransigence was threatening necessary government functions. In particular, Reed attacked Democrats for not supporting the navy. He contemplated how the Democrats planned to defend the country when they provided money for only two of the most advanced naval guns: "One, I suppose, for the Atlantic, and the other for the Pacific coast."[31]

For their part, Democrats were growing weary of losing to Reed and were gravitating toward William Clifford, a successful lawyer and the son of Supreme Court Justice Nathan Clifford. Getting a sense of his growing support, Clifford released two statements before the district convention saying that he refused to be a candidate. Nonetheless, the convention nominated him on July 28. Clifford sent a telegram declining the nomination, but the convention hall had emptied before it arrived. Ultimately, Clifford agreed to challenge Reed. On the campaign trail, Clifford criticized Reed frequently for his support for railroads. Reed was tempted to go negative and went so far as to write up an attack on Clifford, but he threw it away before even his wife could discover it.[32]

On September 13, 1886, Reed won the closest congressional race in Maine. Reed received 50.5 percent, Clifford received 46.2 percent, and the two minor-party candidates earned 3.3 percent. Reed had earned a sixth term to Congress. Having held his seat, he traveled extensively in support of other Republican candidates for the remainder of the 1886 campaign. Afterward he returned to Washington for the lame-duck session.

Reed summarized his political activity during the session in his diary: "It seems to me that I have not lost the opportunities to diminish the prestige of the Democratic Party." He continued, "It has failed in all its endeavors."[33] On February 26, 1887, he took aim at his favorite target, William Springer, for opposing naval spending: "The gentleman never got within a decade of the present in his life, and his party surrounds him where he stands."[34] On February 28, Reed again railed against Democrats for inadequate navy funding.

Reed's sustained criticism drew an immediate response from Democrat William Holman, who retorted, "I wish to say to the gentleman from Maine he scolds very well, but I could find fish-women in this town that could beat him at that game."

Reed replied, "The gentleman from Indiana—and I take his word for it—says he knows fish-women in this town who could make a better scold than I am. I admit the fact, and also congratulate him on the congeniality of his associations."[35]

After the short session ended, Reed returned to Maine and in June 1887 went on a two-month trip to Alaska that became the basis for his first major national publication. Since regular tourism to Alaska had only begun in 1881 with the packaging of rail and steam service, Reed represented the early wave of visitors, and readers of the prominent monthly *North American Review* would be interested in his experience. Reed described how a native woman and baby wearing only light shirts went about their day as "we effeminate grown men and women looked on clad in rain coats, winter ulsters, and the thickest woolens money could buy." The steamship company would have been pleased by another Reed description: "On board a comfortable steamer, without the worry of change, with no chances of bad hotels, in serene pleasure, the traveler voyages two thousand miles as if in a narrow inland sea, forever changing, and always wild, startling, and unexpected." While absorbing tourist pleasures, Reed could not take off his political hat entirely. Perhaps only a member of Congress could observe the marvels of an Alaskan waterway and find it "a pleasing anticipation to think of its figuring some day in the River and Harbor Bill."[36]

By late fall, Reed returned to politics even though he was down on the subject. He confided to his diary: "Politics is very empty at this hour. The majority of things that I desire to say is about the other side." His heightened desire to talk about the Democrats was the product of frustration with the Republican Party's likely nomination of his Maine rival James Blaine. Reed thought a Blaine presidency would be detrimental to his own career: "He has always been my enemy, having opposed me as attorney general, and always toyed with me." His October 8 diary entry proceeded into a laundry list of criticisms of Blaine, including his multiple marriages and suspicious personal finances. Reed then reminded himself why he was writing: "I don't desire to make a catalogue of Mr. Blaine's affairs. I only seek to write French for practice."[37]

A week later, Reed was also down about the potential for helping the poor. He wrote in his diary that the novelist Leo Tolstoy, author of *Anna Karenina*, captured well the difficulties associated with helping the poor: "He gives today the truth about the impossibility to do something for them."[38] Even as Reed was privately acknowledging the gap between the rich and poor, he was publicly minimizing its relevance. For Reed, what was important was that the overall standard of living in the country was improving. He told a Portland audience, "The rich have grown richer, but so have also the poor . . . richer in comforts and in happiness." Thus, Reed's private recognition about the gap between the rich and the poor in the Gilded Age would not lead to policy proposals. Speaking in Portland, Reed insisted, "I hold him to be a heathen and a publican who doubts that under the law of nature, the embodiment of which is God, the progress of the poor keeps more than equal pace with the progress of the rich."[39]

Ponderous Spear Jabs Democrats in Fiftieth Congress

The Fiftieth Congress, which began on December 5, 1887, was destined to be one of the least productive in history. The Democratic majority was reduced in the 1886 election to 169–152. It would be difficult for Democrats to make the required quorum of 165 on their own. Further, the Democrats remained split with a significant faction of protectionists. If the two wings of the Democratic Party managed to, in the words of Sam Randall, "flap together,"[40] Reed would be waiting to block measures that the Republicans disliked. If somehow that failed, the Republican Senate could thwart the Democratic House and president. Previewing the Fiftieth Congress, the *Washington Post* described Reed: "When he is at his best, he is as officious as a second trombone, as inflammatory as a pack of fire-crackers under a barrel and as busy as a bumblebee in a boy's trousers." With this backhanded compliment, the *Post* editorialized that it was "glad" Reed was in Congress since "without him we should suffer greatly from ennui."[41]

Ennui could be useful for Reed—and not just because he used the word in his French diary to describe his workdays. More significant for the future of American politics, the predictable ennui and inaction of the Fiftieth Congress would help Reed build his case for a change in the House rules. Indeed, the stage was set for a master class in how congressional rules prevented even modest legislation. Reed could make his point without having his party looking like the only obstructionists; he could count on Democratic factions to do some of the obstruction for him. On the other hand, Republicans generally wanted the national government to do more and stood ready to work with Democrats who had special reasons to support legislation. Thus, Reed could also promote legislation that might encounter Democratic obstruction.

As Congress started, President Cleveland and House Democrats were eager to reduce the surplus produced by ever-increasing tariff revenue. There was universal concern that the country was risking an economic slowdown by withdrawing so much money from the economy. Although agreeing on the problem, the two parties had very different solutions. Republicans supported high protective tariffs so they wanted to increase outflows by paying off debt and increasing spending. Most Democrats preferred to reduce tariffs, which they saw as raising the price of goods that everybody consumed. President Cleveland broke with the tradition of multisubject annual messages and limited his congressional message to tariff reduction.

An early sign of the limited desire to get things done came in the second week of the session when members debated taking an unusually long holiday recess. While Reed opposed tariff reduction, he was interested in legislating and wanted the House to work longer. When Democrats proposed to adjourn for three weeks on December 16, 1887, Reed mused that House Democrats needed time to "range themselves alongside" the president since the president's message "requires that they should traverse a very great distance before they can get alongside of their pioneer brother at the other end of the avenue."[42] Ultimately, the parties compromised on a two-week recess.

On January 11, 1888, Reed showed that he would retain his knack for irritating Democrats in the new Congress. He lamented that Democrats were refusing to support soldiers even when everyone agreed that the surplus needed reduction. Reed took aim at Missouri Congressman James Burnes: "The candor of the gentleman from Missouri . . . has not permitted him to state what was the actual condition of affairs." Reed blamed a previous Democratic House for adding a requirement that Congress act affirmatively to make pension payments.

Burnes countered, "Now, I simply place my assertion against his, and I say that, with all his prophetic vision, with all his wondrous judgment, with all his immense power, he has not divined aright the motives which actuated me or those who served with me on the Appropriations Committee." Burnes showed that the legal change had actually occurred under an earlier Republican, not Democratic, Congress as Reed had maintained. Burnes contemplated the cause of Reed's factual error: "Even this I do not impute to the gentleman from Maine as indicating a want of candor, because the House knows that he is the soul of candor, especially on political propositions. I attribute it to him rather as a mere act of forgetfulness."

Reed answered, "Mr. Chairman, it is of very little consequence, of course, whether I have made an error upon a given subject or not, but it is of some consequence whether I have stated to the House what is not so, having the means of information." Reed explained that even though the Republicans had changed the law, the next Democratic Congress could still have chosen to spend properly even if not directed by the law. "If that be so," Reed argued, "the situation remains precisely where I said it was, and the argument which I addressed to the House loses none of its force."[43]

On February 29, Reed criticized Democrats for failing to address the surplus. He chastised them for not buying back bonds to reduce the surplus. His deputy William McKinley argued that President Cleveland already had the authority to do that without congressional approval. In his diary, Reed celebrated this one-two Republican punch: "At the House today Mr. McKinley and I made a reconnaissance of force."[44] To Reed, the Democratic failure to consider other available means of reducing the surplus demonstrated that what Democrats really wanted to do was to reduce tariffs. Reed mocked the idea that people were demanding tariff reduction: "Is it that anybody is troubled about his taxation? Why, everybody seems to be earnest and agreed to keep on all the taxes we have got!"

Democrat William Breckinridge of Kentucky entered the debate to defend President Cleveland. He said that the president's message had taken tariff reduction "out of the mere dull sequence of official documents and caused a discussion from one end of America to the other that neither the wit of the gentleman from Maine [Reed] nor the eloquence of the gentleman from Ohio [McKinley] will cause to cease until the iniquitous protection of the present tariff has been reformed." Breckinridge appealed to Congress to clarify the question of presidential authority by acting to "remove the President's doubts."

Reed responded, "We are going to remove them."

Breckinridge replied, "I have no doubt in the world, Mr. Chairman, that whenever the gentleman from Maine speaks he does remove somebody's doubt, generally on this side of the House; because we have found it to be a good rule to listen to him, when he speaks, with profound gratification, and always take the other side from his utterances."[45]

On April 4, the stage was set for the session's first major exhibition demonstrating how the rules of the House undermined governing. A bill proposed to refund revenue collected from a Civil-War property tax to the states that had paid it. It was a perfect measure to split Democrats with protectionist Democrats (who liked spending the surplus) and non-South Democrats (who resented Southern states not paying the tax) inclined to support the measure. Opponents of the bill, who were about eighty Democrats, knew that they would lose any vote and committed themselves to preventing one. Opponents used the time-honored delay techniques of adjournment motions and quorum calls. The House settled into a routine of roll calls, failed adjournment votes, recesses, attempts to find missing members, and judging excuses of missing members brought to the House by the sergeant at arms. The dead time gave members ample time to write letters. One of Reed's letters on April 7 described the situation to his Maine friend Andrew Hawes. Reed wrote, "The Brigadiers are now filibustering like pirates and the other half of Dem. Party is opposing them but with bated breath. . . . This filibuster ought to help us much."[46] Technically, days into the standoff, the House was still on the same legislative day, as it never adjourned but just took recesses. The House literally was reliving the same uneventful day.

Inactivity would soon end, although not before entering the record books. On Tuesday, April 10, the House dispensed with the recesses and remained in session for twenty-six consecutive hours. The legislative day, which was still April 4, was said to be the second longest ever.[47] Of course, members were not actually conducting any business, but merely responding to their names being called. Mostly, members were trying to get some sleep in the extraordinary all-night session. Lucky members claimed parts of couches and put newspapers over their heads. The *Washington Post* described the situation as the sun rose on a new (calendar) day: "The few tramps who had taken advantage of the all-night session to take shelter in the galleries, were sleeping and scattered around in those picturesque forms in which tramps excel even Congressmen."[48]

The homeless, however, were among the few Americans impressed by this Congress, and pressure grew on Democrats to end the fiasco. Newspapers adopted a strike metaphor and calculated the cost to the taxpayer of the inactivity. The embarrassing all-nighter prompted the Democrats to caucus. The next day, the two wings of the Democratic Party entered the House united. When the key vote came on April 12, it would be a party line vote. The standoff had ended, appropriately, with a postponement. Democrats decided to support delaying consideration of the direct tax bill until December. With the direct tax bill out of the way, the House took up the tariff bill.

After a month of general debate on the tariff bill, Reed and Speaker Carlisle closed for their respective sides on May 19. Crowds filled the House galleries early in the morning, and special accommodations were made to allow additional seating on the House floor. Reed began to address the House at noon. The magnitude of the occasion was matched by his commanding presence. The *Daily Globe* observed, "Now and then the thinly coated Shakespearian head would be thrown back and the big, fat, upturned face would shine in the sunlight from above."[49] Speaking with minimal reference to his notes, he occasionally elevated an arm to amplify a point.

Reed used a hungry-dog metaphor to capture his main theme that it would be foolish to throw out a system of protection that was working. He adapted one of Aesop's fables to capture the temptation of unproven foreign markets: "Once there was a dog. He was a nice little dog. Nothing the matter with him except a few foolish free-trade ideas in his head. He was trotting along happy as the day, for he had in his mouth a nice shoulder of succulent mutton." Things were about to change for the dog. Reed continued, "By and by he came to a stream bridged by a plank. He trotted along, and, looking over the side of the plank, he saw the markets of the world and dived for them. A minute after he was crawling up the bank the wettest, the sickest, the nastiest, the most muttonless dog that ever swam ashore!"

Reed also countered the argument that protection was empowering monopolists: "Let my poor scared friend who covers his head with the bedclothes at night lest he should be devoured by monopolies take courage." Reed mocked the idea that lowering the tariff and having British companies challenge monopolists was an answer, saying, "Call in the British! When the day comes that this Republic cannot save itself from a dozen of its own citizens without aid from over the sea, I hope to be buried a thousand leagues under some respectable and permanent mountain range. What unreasonable talk this is. A dozen men fix the prices for sixty million freemen! They can never do it." Reed explained why: "There is no power on earth that can raise the price of any necessity of life above a just price and keep it there. More than that, if the price is raised and maintained even for a short while, it means ruin for the combination and still lower prices for consumers. That is one of the laws of God working for His children."[50] His speech ended at 1:55 p.m. to rousing applause from Republicans. Subsequently, making a rare floor appearance, Speaker Carlisle advocated for tariff reduction in a ninety-minute speech that was well received by Democrats.

In characterizing the style of Reed's speech, there was agreement. Reed described his own technique: "Thus far I have employed a familiar method of argumentation which is called in Latin *reductio ad absurdum*, or, in plain English, confronting the principles a man lays down with the facts of the universe and showing him the dreadful absurdity of which he has been guilty."[51] Apparently, Reed's style was transparent. The next morning's *New York Times* presented a similar assessment with enough modification to produce a negative spin: "He [Reed] can present an opponent's case as well as his own, with all the inconvenient points left out of each, and preserve the appearance of symmetrical completeness better than any other speaker on either side in either house."[52]

While agreeing on style, observers disagreed on substance. Critics suggested that his light style impeded substance. The Democratic *Argus* described it as a two-hour speech in which the "Goliath of the House, with ponderous spear, jabbing" at Democrats failed to "rise to the dignity of argument."[53] The *Portland Daily Press*, in contrast, characterized Reed's speech as convincing: "Its foundation is laid strong and deep, but the structure reared upon it has been made attractive as well as substantial."[54] Indeed, Reed's speech proved extremely popular in Republican circles. He expressed pleasure in his diary that over a half-million copies of his speech were printed. He believed that the speech had dispelled a common criticism: "There are many people who used to think that I didn't have the capacity to make a long speech, a well substantiated speech, [rather] than my small observations from time to time."[55] Reed wrote in his diary, "In truth I have arrived at the summit of the climb."[56]

Extending his critique beyond the House floor, Reed wrote an article for the July 1888 issue of *North American Review*. The magazine wanted an article summarizing the recently completed national Democratic convention. Who would be better than Reed to provide the analysis? Reed drew from his French study to explain the growing Democratic support for free trade: "The French historian, Lanfrey, seems to have been right when he said that a little charlatanism is needful to move masses of men. Mr. Cleveland's administration does not seem to lack the needful motive power." He worked his convention observations into a broader discussion of the importance of political party, explaining, "Party feeling and party fealty I have no quarrel with. They both bind men together and help make the world governable. No man ought to leave the party his judgment upholds except for grave cause; and he will not if he is wise, for it means disruption of friendship and the sundering of ties, the strength of which no man knows until they are broken." Reed suggested that the tariff issue should qualify as a grave cause for protectionist Democrats.[57]

While criticizing Democrats, Reed faced a leadership challenge in his own party related to the potential tension between a minority leader's goals to make good policy and enhance electoral prospects. Should Republicans offer a substitute tariff bill or just object to the Democratic bill? The question was discussed at a contentious meeting of the Republican caucus. Reed's position was clear: "If we should undertake to propose a bill which could pass this House it would have to be with such an abatement of Republican principle as would secure Democratic votes."[58] Ultimately, despite disagreement even in the upper ranks of the caucus, Reed prevailed and the Republicans chose not to offer a substitute. During a walk after the meeting, McKinley informed Reed that he had rejected the encouragement of other Republicans to make a claim for party leadership by offering a Republican substitute to the tariff bill.[59] Without a substitute, the key vote was on final passage of the Democratic tariff bill. The bill passed 162–149 with fewer than five defections within each party.

With the fate of the House Democratic tariff bill in the hands of the Senate, Reed penned an article for the *Independent*. Framing the article as a call to the electorate to support protection in the upcoming election, he argued that experience had shown the value of high tariffs. This success would be undermined by Democratic tariff reduction that was just a step to free trade. Reed explained that tariff reduction would increase imports with a predictable result: "More importations mean more revenue." He saw this as leading to another surplus: "When we have disposed of this surplus another will await us in less than five years and probably in less than two." Thus, Reed said, the Democrats will demand a new reduction bill with "each recurring surplus . . . until we reach the goal of Mr. Calhoun's ambition embodied in the Confederate constitution which prohibited Protection."[60] In reviewing Reed's article, the *Picayune* singled out this mechanism. It said that Reed's argument of lower taxes leading to more government revenue embodied "a contradiction so apparent that we are surprised to find that he himself did not detect it." The *Times Picayune* asked, "Mr. Reed contends that to lower the rates will be first to reduce the surplus and then to increase it. How can that be? How can the cause which does away with a surplus create a surplus?"[61]

In August 1888, rumors swirled about Reed's future. He denied interest in Maine's open Senate seat: "The papers have been sending me to the Senate for some years, but I have never been consulted about it."[62] It was also reported that Reed would retire and make money in New York.[63] This rumor would arise periodically until it actually happened. Perhaps Reed was thinking about future riches in New York, but for the time he was thinking about smaller riches. He petitioned publisher Whitelaw Reid for additional compensation because of the special burden that he had incurred in researching his *Independent* article. Reed wrote, "I had to read most all the Democratic speeches. . . . I suppose however I ought to be grateful to have escaped alive."[64]

As House Republican leader, Reed was a target for Democrats in the 1888 election. After William Clifford declined a rematch, Democrats nominated businessman and former county attorney William Emery. The major theme of Emery's campaign was that Republicans had created an unfair system in which the tariffs on luxury items purchased by the rich were low while the tariffs on common items purchased by ordinary Americans were high. Emery declared that he was "not a believer in free trade" but favored reducing the tariff on the "necessaries of life."[65] It was likely to be another close contest. Reed explained, "The enemy in my district are going to try to beat me. I cannot say how their efforts will pan out, as I understand they intend to fight very hard."[66]

Reed's campaign defended high tariffs. He argued that the living standards of ordinary Americans had never been higher than under the Republican protective tariff. Reed conceded that high tariffs resulted in some wealthy Americans. Describing himself as an ordinary man who wore a fourteen-dollar overcoat rather than a forty-dollar luxury coat, Reed said, "I do not feel any great satisfaction in seeing somebody else ride in a carriage while I do not." Yet, there was a positive economic side effect from how a wealthy man invested his money: "He must either make something with it, build something with it, or what comes to the same thing lend it to some man who will make something or build something with it."[67]

Reed continued his pattern of winning the closest congressional race in Maine. He defeated Emery by 18,288 to 15,855 votes. The Republican *Press* described the prelude to a celebratory Reed serenade: "Red and green lights were burned, and Roman candles and rockets were discharged. To this was added the booming of cannon."[68]

After securing his victory, Reed campaigned for Republican candidates across the country. Speaking in Los Angeles on November 2, Reed identified a "strawberry mark" that showed Democrats supported free trade even though they denied it. Reed suggested, "You can always tell what a man is going to build by the tools that you find in his hands. And the first tool that you find in the hands of a Democrat—and I use the word 'tool' in no disrespectful sense, because I have as much respect for Mr. Mills as a gentleman as I have lack of respect for him as a statesman—the first tool that you find in the hands of the Democracy is Mr. Mills, chairman of the Committee of Ways and Means." Having taken Mills to the woodshed, Reed sought an analogy for the choice between protectionist Republicans and free-trade Democrats. He explained, "Let me tell you here, and I tell it under solemn responsibility, that at the close of the election on November 6th, you will find that in some things besides religion, if you have not been on the Lord's side you have been on the other side."[69]

Spending election day in California, Reed celebrated as Republicans won the presidency, the House, and the Senate. For the first time since the 1872 landslide led by Ulysses Grant, Republicans had won clear control of all branches of government. There would be tremendous pressure to take advantage of this rare opportunity. There was also the potential danger of overstepping the electoral mandate. Republicans controlled all branches of government without having obtained a majority of the votes cast for any of them. Republican Benjamin Harrison lost the popular vote for president to Grover Cleveland but used narrow wins in Indiana and New York to eke out an Electoral College victory. An advantageous vote distribution also enabled Republicans to win more House seats than Democrats, even though more votes were cast overall for Democratic House candidates. Finally, Republicans retained a two-seat margin in the Senate by winning half the Senate seats that were up for election in the state legislatures.

Anything to Protect the Rights of the Minority

The lame-duck session produced another major exhibition demonstrating how the rules of the House prevented legislation. Bills to fund the Union Pacific Railroad and organize the territory of Oklahoma had substantial support, but they also had determined opponents willing to filibuster. The tactic of choice for stopping these bills was for one member to insist on a bill reading at the start of legislative days set aside for passing measures under suspension of the rules. Under the rules, the call of states and territories that served as a vehicle for time-consuming demands to read legislation happened before legislating, and thus the House never got to the business part of the day. Many Democrats were willing to tolerate wasted days because their commitment to short-term policy goals did not outweigh the risk of weakening a filibuster power that might come in handy when Republicans took over the House next session. This dynamic gave Reed the opportunity to present himself as constructive. Reed would spend much of the short session aligned with groups of Democrats who wanted to get things done. He was there to help.

Reed's first opportunity to help arose on January 4, 1889, when he presented a rule to eliminate the call of states and territories that had been abused to compel the reading of long bills. To get the rule heard, Reed had worked with Democratic Speaker Carlisle and Republican Joe Cannon to get a three-to-two majority on the Rules committee. Reed described his measure to the House in philosophical terms: "If the House finds that its rules are so employed as to be made means of obstruction to prevent the majority from controlling, then the House has the right to take into its own hands the change of its rules." Reed continued, "The very fundamental principle of our government is control by a majority; and, however wise any individual man may be, the principle of our government is that when 101 men are on one side and 100 men are on the other side, the 100 go to the wall, even if they are as wise as the [101] gentlemen."[70]

Since Speaker Carlisle supported the proposal, Charles Crisp led Democrats who did not want to see government action. Inaction was a longtime calling for someone who had entered politics to resist Reconstruction in the South. Crisp, however, was not a lifelong southerner. Born in 1845 in Sheffield, England, Crisp was the child of traveling Shakespearean actors who eventually settled in Georgia. At sixteen, Crisp enlisted in the Confederate Army and spent the last year of the Civil War as a prisoner of war. After his release he became a lawyer. In an unusual career path, he had already served several years as a judge before being elected to Congress in 1882.[71] Judge Crisp was not intimidated by Reed. Crisp countered, "My idea, sir, is that the rules of this House are made not only, as suggested by the gentleman from Maine, for the orderly conduct of the public business, but there is a greater and higher object, and that is to protect the rights of the minority, to restrain, in the language of the old law-writers, the unbridled license of the majority, to give them time for reflection, so that when passion is allayed they may return to a sense of justice if they find they have departed from it."[72]

Reed's proposal naturally led to a standstill in legislative activity. Most of the five-day impasse was spent reading names in a futile effort to overcome the disappearing quorum. The standstill prompted Democrats to schedule a caucus for January 7. Reed took credit for this in his diary: "It is always necessary for them to have a caucus each time that I have business with them."[73] In caucus, Democrats gave lukewarm support to allowing a vote on the rule change.

On January 8, Reed stood side by side with longtime nemesis William Springer on the final vote. Reed lobbied Republicans while Springer took the lead in getting Democrats to support the rule change. The *Weekly Courier-Journal* characterized the pairing: "Singular as it may seem, Springer acted as Tom Reed's lieutenant in the fight over the change of rules. His love of Oklahoma overcame his underappreciation of Reed." Democratic Congressman Amos Cummings said that as he watched them work together, he was thinking about Reed's comeback to Springer's proclamation that he would rather be right than president.[74] Springer need not worry since he will never be either.

Worry, however, was justified for Reed and Springer as they were facing a close vote. The roll call ended with a slight majority for the rule change. Keeping the vote open, Democratic leaders pressured members to vote against the rule change. After a few switches and new arrivals, Reed's victory turned into a 120–117 defeat. The *Boston Daily Globe* described the outcome: "Nothing else in the present temper of the House is half so unpopular as a motion to do any business."[75]

Reed found some vindication the next day. The failure to pass a rule limiting filibustering was followed by more filibustering. Reed injected himself into a day of legislative inactivity. He posed a rhetorical question to Charles Crisp: "I would like to inquire of the gentleman from Georgia whether there is anything else that can be done to protect the rights of the minority?"[76] That Reed felt pleased by his measured response is apparent from his diary entry on January 9. He wrote, "I made an assault on Mr. Crisp, which made everybody laugh. . . . I asked him sweetly if there was anything more that could be done to sustain the rights of the minority as he himself was at that moment at the head of the majority."[77]

Less sweetly, a disgruntled Democrat who had voted with Reed, James Weaver intensified his pursuit for something approaching poetic justice. A supporter of Oklahoma, Weaver decided that the best way to get action was to filibuster and refuse to allow the House to do anything, even routine acts, until the Oklahoma bill was taken up. Weaver's mind-numbing filibuster occupied the better part of a week, and whatever its relation to justice, it was far from poetic, unless one finds poetry in the repeated reading of 325 names. He forced these roll-call votes through quorum calls and dilatory motions, especially the motion to adjourn, which was always in order under the rules. Ranking episodes of legislative impotence is challenging, but scholar Hubert Fuller described Weaver's filibuster as the "climax" of obstruction in the Fiftieth Congress.[78] Newspapers intensified their criticism of House proceedings. It is difficult to sort out all the irony, but by giving filibustering a bad name, Weaver somehow convinced filibuster-supporting Democrats to allow a vote on Oklahoma to stop his filibuster.

While Reed accumulated exhibits for a rule change, his efforts to advance Democratic proposals were not without awkward moments. On January 14, backed by the Rules Committee, Reed supported a rule to suspend the five-o'clock adjournment to allow the House to work later into the night as a way to wear down filibusterers. This meant later nights, which probably would be spent doing nothing. Reed described in his diary what happened when he made his proposal for a longer day: "Immediately all the Republicans began to excuse themselves."[79] His use of "all" was hyperbolic, but the measure was not popular in his own caucus. When Republican Lewis Payson offered the routine procedural motion to recommit and effectively kill the rules proposal, an unusual scene transpired. The entire Republican caucus except for Joseph Cannon voted against its own leader. Despite the internal Republican drama, there was little drama about the outcome as Democrats easily outnumbered Republicans and defeated Payson's motion.

Republican drama continued when the House voted on the original motion to rescind the five-o'clock adjournment. Reed had not stopped attacking Democrats even as he supported their proposal as furthering the cause of majority rule: "I do not purpose to stop the business of the House simply because . . . they have taken an unrighteous method of getting out of this difficulty instead of a righteous one."[80] Anticipation grew to see if Reed's supporters in the party would interpret the dispute as a challenge to his leadership and support him on the actual motion. Some did, but Reed was outvoted in his own party eighty to thirty-five.[81]

Newspapers framed the rule change proposal as the first battle in the looming contest for Speaker of the House. By virtue of their November victory, Republicans would control the next House and contestants for Speaker were emerging. The first sentence of the *Boston Globe* story about the rule proposal summarized the outcome: "The fat candidate for speaker, Thomas B. Reed of Portland, met with his first severe repulse today." The second sentence elaborated, "His discomfiture was witnessed with suppressed emotion by the thin candidate, Joseph G. Cannon of Danville; the swarthy candidate, William McKinley, Jr., of Canton, and by the candidate with the boss lungs, Julius C. Burrows of Kalamazoo." [82] For his part, Reed was proud that he had stood firm. He wrote in his diary on January 14, "I made a very lively speech—If one expects a man trembling before the face of a crowd because of his desire to be Speaker, one does not find that in me."[83] The *New York Times* saw a different outcome: "Mr. Reed has lost the control of his side."[84]

In the waning days of the session, Reed remained frustrated with the legislative inactivity of the House. In addition to the usual delays, the House regularly set aside time to pay tribute to members who had died. Reed had long believed that too many days were lost to sparsely attended memorials. Thus, he was annoyed on February 23, when the House took off the afternoon to eulogize Missouri Representative James Burnes. Although Reed felt that congressional time was unnecessary for the task, he devoted a diary entry to remember Burnes. Reed wrote, "During the time he was in the flesh, he was a man without fear, without scruples, a liar who never hesitated a moment to hide the truth, to violate all the obligations of good faith."[85] Burnes had been right not to question Reed's candor earlier in this Congress.

Although Reed technically lost many of the procedural battles during the Fiftieth Congress, he made progress in his longer war against House procedures and was ready for a victory lap. It took the form of an article titled "Rules of the House of Representatives" in the March 1889 issue of *Century* magazine. Reed's diary describes how he finished the article even though the editor only gave him a day to write it: "I am sick today, but nevertheless I finished the article . . . [having written] 3,000 words in 18 hours, eight of which were spent in bed."[86] The article places the Fiftieth Congress in a historical context of reduced opportunities for action under House rules. "If the majority do not govern," Reed wrote, "the minority will; and if the tyranny of the majority is hard, the tyranny of the minority is simply unendurable."[87]

CHAPTER 5

NEW SPEAKER ESTABLISHES MAJORITY RULE

The start of the Fifty-First Congress in late 1889 brought to an end the yearlong contest for Speaker of the House. There were five major candidates: Julius Burrows, Joseph Cannon, David Henderson, William McKinley, and Reed. From early on, newspapers framed it as a two-horse race between Reed and McKinley. More than ten months before the caucus vote, the *Washington Post* observed, "The most conspicuous rivalry in the pending contest is between Reed and McKinley."[1]

The contest was typically described as friendly. Both Reed and McKinley expressed pride in refusing to solicit votes by offering promises of committee appointments. The campaigns reportedly agreed not to punish their opponent's supporters in committee appointments. Newspapers reported that the candidates remained on good terms and interacted socially. When asked to endorse criticism of Reed's war record during the campaign, McKinley refused and left the room in disgust.[2]

While newspapers conveyed friendly relations between competitors, Reed was not pleased with having to compete for a position that he felt was rightfully his. From Reed's perspective, he had been chosen as leader before and the higher stakes should not change anything. Privately, in a letter to a friend, he wrote, "The speakership—or indeed any other place—never seemed much worth longing for but having twice been selected when the party was out of power it would seem rather a rebuff not to have it."[3] More privately, Reed singled out McKinley for criticism in his diary, writing that McKinley "was wrong in presenting himself as a candidate for the Speakership."[4] Reed softened the "shivers of disgust" he felt about the competition by philosophizing about the motivation of his competitors: "But then men are men."[5]

McKinley, however, rejected Reed's notion that it would be inconsistent for the party to change leaders now that it was in the majority. McKinley supporters recalled the debate during the 1885 election of Reed over Hiscock as minority leader in which McKinley's nominating speech insisted that the choice was for the moment and not for establishing future preferences.[6] McKinley advocates were not being unrealistic in hoping that caucus members would judge a leadership candidate's likelihood of goal achievement differently depending on whether the party was in the minority or majority.[7] Describing Reed as having the qualities of not just a bulldog, but a "thoroughbred bulldog," the *Boston Globe* wrote that these qualities fit Reed "for leading an opposition party and yet totally unfit him for leading his party when it is in the majority."[8]

To manage his campaign, Reed chose Henry Cabot Lodge. Born in 1850, Lodge came from a wealthy family and earned a PhD in history from Harvard under the guidance of Henry Adams. His luxurious home in coastal Massachusetts and stylish dress earned him the nickname "the Dude of Nahant." In navigating Boston politics, he showed that he would not back down from a fight. Winning a congressional seat in 1886, Lodge was impressed by Reed, his party's leader in the House. Lodge wrote letters to his mother that told stories about Reed and expressed admiration for his "remarkable" friend.[9]

Lodge was a good choice to run a strong but subtle campaign. He seems to have kept the balance that Reed was seeking in a low-key race. Lodge would be constrained by Reed's refusal to make the customary promises to gain support.[10] The campaign had not been aggressive, but by mid-November Lodge was working hard and meeting with caucus members to solidify support for Reed.

During the Speakership campaign, Reed also received support from non-House members, most notably Theodore Roosevelt. Born in 1858, Roosevelt also combined a tough but cultured personality. Roosevelt already had written a well-respected history of the navy and shown his resilience by standing up to powerful entrenched bureaucracies in Washington and New York in his pursuit of civil-service reform. Although Reed was generally not a fan of civil-service reform, he reportedly said, "I don't like it straight, but mixed with a little Theodore Roosevelt, I like it well."[11] For his part, Roosevelt was encouraged by the possibility that Reed could improve the functioning of Congress. Reed and Roosevelt also got along well personally. Roosevelt captured his views of Reed in a letter to his friend Henry Cabot Lodge in the summer of 1889: "He is a loyal friend and as true as steel."[12]

Roosevelt's civil-service reform constituency and geographic appeal made him valuable. Roosevelt was popular in his native New York, where Reed sought a unified delegation, and respected in western states, where Reed hoped to chip into McKinley's support. A full year before the vote, Theodore Roosevelt championed Reed for Speaker at the Federal Club in New York City, saying, "I hope Tom Reed . . . will be Speaker. . . . He is an excellent parliamentarian and presiding officer, a clean, strong man of very unusual ability, with courage, tact, and decision peculiarly suited to control a House as narrowly divided as the next is likely to be."[13] Roosevelt found other opportunities to lobby for Reed. As an example, after learning that a railroad executive was likely to be influential with two Minnesota House Republicans, Roosevelt contacted the executive and then wrote a letter to Reed assuring him that things went well.[14]

Reed also benefited from the context of a narrow majority and the expectation that rule changes might be necessary to implement the Republican platform. Reed had years of expertise in parliamentary procedure while McKinley was perceived as weak in the area. In the run-up to the vote, Reed was asked about the prospects for procedural change. His answer made clear that it was an issue in the race: "We will have rules under which the business of the House can be transacted when the majority gets ready to transact it."[15] On the other hand, if Republican members wanted to minimize the likelihood of a contentious session, Reed's disposition might give them pause. They could be drawn to McKinley who, in the words of the *Boston Globe*, was "essentially diplomatic" and the "antithesis of Reed."[16] In short, personality mattered since leaders with different strengths and weaknesses were competing for a strategically placed position in an environment open to change.[17]

McKinley's ability to avoid alienating people positioned him well for a second ballot if the first ballot failed to produce the required majority. McKinley's public persona was consistent with private encounters showing that he did not make things personal. This is apparent in an incident relayed by Theodore Roosevelt to Henry Cabot Lodge in the summer of 1889: "I saw McKinley the other day; and explained to him that I was supporting Reed; he was as pleasant as possible."[18] McKinley's charms, which had once worked well on Reed, were quickly wearing off. Reed's diary at the time was presenting a different take on McKinley's congeniality: "He [McKinley] always has his wand and his mysterious airs, which stun journalists but he is a man of little scope, believe me." Continuing, Reed predicted that McKinley would soon be "exposed to critics, and the result will be that one will find that he is at present above his own level."[19]

McKinley's diplomatic nature was also seen as reflecting his desire to be president. A Reed deputy tried what the *Boston Journal* called an "ingenious" approach to persuading McKinley to withdraw from the race. Harry Bingham referenced the widely held expectation that if McKinley did not become Speaker, he would be named chair of the Ways and Means committee responsible for tariff legislation. Bingham speculated, "Now if a McKinley tariff bill should go through the next House and be a success, then hardly anything would prevent Major McKinley from coming forward as a promising presidential candidate."[20]

McKinley nonetheless believed that winning would be better for his career than losing, and his supporters continued to work hard. Building on strength in his large home state of Ohio, McKinley made western outreaches and enjoyed substantial support in the South. His tariff support positioned him well to win votes in the industrial states of New York and Pennsylvania. McKinley supporters were confident that they had a path to victory. The *New York Times* observed, "McKinley's workers are doing more boasting than all the other candidates combined."[21]

The conventional wisdom was that Reed's biggest problem was the potential for western representatives to unite behind a single candidate. Reed was criticized during the campaign for his indifference to western interests, especially his opposition to silver coinage. McKinley spoke of incorporating western interests into a tariff and played up the idea of a western candidate: "I am of the opinion that the Speaker will be a western man, but whether it will go further west than Ohio I don't know."[22] This, of course, was a dig at Reed who was the only candidate from east of Ohio. Rumors of a western combination intensified after the four other candidates ate dinner together the night before the vote. Reed had been invited, but he said that prior commitments prevented his attendance. No western combination was emerging. Reed's competitors reportedly had a problem in uniting against him: "Each insists upon being the beneficiary of any combination that may be formed."[23]

Decision day arrived on November 30, 1889. One newspaper that morning offered a playing card metaphor for the common prediction that Reed was in the lead but short of the required majority: "He [Reed] has the best hand in the game, but must draw to fill."[24] With 165 Republican members present, 83 votes were needed to win. The first ballot matched newspaper projections, with Reed polling the most votes but falling short of a majority. Reed received 78 votes, including all 23 New England votes, 33 votes from Pennsylvania and New York, and 22 votes scattered around the country. McKinley received 39 votes, including all 16 votes from Ohio, the most southern votes of any candidate (9), 6 votes from Pennsylvania, and 8 votes from elsewhere. Of the 48 votes for the other three candidates, 31 came from their home states. McKinley's hopes for a second ballot were realized, but he would not have wanted Reed to be so close to a majority.

The caucus prepared for a second ballot. A late arrival meant that a majority was now 84 of 166 votes cast. Reed would need to keep his seventy-eight votes, add the recently arrived Reed supporter, and have five switch to him to reach a majority. As the roll call got underway, there was little change. A western combination was not emerging. Early in the alphabetical reading, Bergen changed from Henderson to Reed. After all the names had been read, six members had switched to Reed from other candidates. Reed had just become the Republican leader and presumptive Speaker. McKinley made a motion to make the nomination unanimous, which was approved. Reed made a brief statement to bring the party together after a tough race. He addressed the caucus, "While I am grateful to the warm friends who have supported me, there has been no opposition of which I have a right to complain."[25]

Since Reed had won with only one vote to spare, the victory could be credited to almost anything. Theodore Roosevelt, for example, received credit for helping Reed win the second ballot support of western Republicans.[26] The resonance of any explanation varies with the interpretation of how close McKinley came to winning. On the final 166-vote ballot, Reed tallied 85 votes, McKinley 38, and the other three candidates combined for 43. How close did McKinley come to winning? A century after the contest, best-selling author Kevin Phillips enumerated the result as McKinley "came within one vote of being chosen by his party as Speaker of the House."[27] If McKinley can be credited with being one vote short, then surely the other three candidates could make the same claim. The dubious math depends on the one vote representing a western combination that did not materialize.

Two days later, the Fifty-First Congress opened. Reed was voted Speaker by a vote of 166–154 over Democrat John Carlisle. Reed then received an escort from Carlisle and William McKinley. The *Bangor Whig & Courier* described the procession to the Speaker's chair: "He [Reed] crooked both elbows, and then the little fellows, for little they are compared with that giant, caught on and he sailed down the aisle about half a foot in advance of his conductors."[28]

As he took over the Speakership, fifty-one-year-old Tom Reed cut an imposing figure that was tailor-made for editorial cartoonists. He stood six feet, two inches tall and weighed almost three hundred pounds. Although he had risen to the second highest place in American politics, Reed did not care much for appearances. He allowed a straggly mustache to grow. He was not interested in fashion. He was, however, living in style. He had recently moved a few blocks closer to the White House from his longtime Washington residence at the Hamilton House (Fourteenth and K Streets) to the newer and more comfortable Shoreham Hotel (Fifteenth and I Streets).

Quorum Challenge

Speaker Reed faced the profound challenge of leading a party whose majority was so narrow that it would struggle even to obtain a quorum. Under Article I of the Constitution, it takes a majority of the House to constitute a quorum that can legally do business. After the death of one Republican at the outset of the Congress, the US House consisted of 329 members; 165 members constituted the quorum needed to conduct business. Since Republicans had 168 members, they could afford the absence of only three members if they wanted a quorum on their own. Typically, member illness and being called away (whether on business or pleasure) would mean a significant number of members would be absent. Getting a quorum on their own would be almost impossible for Republicans. They, therefore, would be vulnerable to the disappearing quorum. If Democrats refused to vote when their names were called, the apparent quorum would disappear. It was a strategy that Reed knew well, since he had used it when he was in the opposition.

The stage was set for a battle between Democrats and Republicans, who were enjoying their first unified government in years with a Republican president and Congress. If House Republicans hoped to win the fight, they would need more advantageous rules than historically had been used in Congress. This is exactly the course that Republicans were hinting at in the months leading up to the start of the December 1889 session.

The most prominent of the efforts was by Reed himself. Reed intensified his pursuit of new rules with a speech at a July 4, 1889, celebration at Woodstock, Connecticut. His speech began, "It was no less a person, I believe, than the Duke of Wellington who remarked [that] 'there is only one thing more demoralizing than defeat, and that is victory.'" Reed argued that the Republican election win in November 1888 would be demoralizing if Republicans were unable to act in the Congress that was set to begin in December 1889. The reason that Republicans might be unable to act, Reed said, was that Congress operated under "the worst set of rules that ever afflicted a decent community." He singled out the disappearing quorum as "the most effective" filibustering technique. Reed lamented that the public seemed indifferent to this: "A minority—simply because it is a minority—stops legislation, and the country looks on as if it were a trivial matter."[29]

To change this perception, Reed wrote an article in the October 1889 issue of *North American Review.* Reed argued that the rights of the minority were overstated: "The rights they [minorities] have, and ought to have, are simply those which will serve to guide the whole House acting by its majority to safe and correct conclusions." He maintained that less delay would improve debate and legislation. Avoiding specifics, Reed suggested that the rules would change: "There will be an effort to establish rules which will facilitate the public business—rules unlike those of the present House, which only delay and frustrate action."[30]

Democrat Roger Mills joined the battle over rules with a follow-up piece in the December 1889 *North American Review*. Mills insisted that there was no emergency demanding a revolutionary overhaul of House rules and predicted, "The great difficulty in the way [to Republican action] is the quorum which the Constitution requires to do business." Mills foreshadowed the primary Democratic argument: "The responsibility is on the majority party to make the quorum, and instead of scolding the members of the minority for refusing to share in the responsibility of bad legislation, they should call their own delinquents to account for abandoning the post of duty."[31]

Although producing a quorum was an immediate problem for Republicans, it was likely to get easier later in the session after contested election cases had been resolved. Under the Constitution, the House is the judge of its members. In practice, this meant that the House was charged with resolving the handful of cases in which the election of a member had been contested, typically on the grounds of fraud. Despite the ideal of Congress acting judicially, the House typically resolved these on a partisan basis with Republicans seeing facts one way and Democrats the other way.[32] Consequently, the majority-party view of the facts could be expected to prevail, and the majority party would expand its majority as cases were resolved by unseating some minority-party members and replacing them with majority-party members.

The Fifty-First Congress had seventeen cases to resolve. Some Republican cases were stronger than others. Where Republicans had evidence of fraud in southern elections, they could expect to be unified to unseat the challenged southern Democrat. Like everything else in the session, the rules fight loomed over disposal of contested election cases.

For the first month the major point of contention was that Reed had chosen to lead without adopting formal rules. Typically, the Rules committee would have reported standing rules and the House would be operating under them. Reed's leadership of the committee showed that consensus building among the five members—two Republicans, two Democrats, and the Speaker—was not a high priority. Reed did not call any meetings of the committee in the first month. One of the two Democrats whom Reed appointed to the committee was Samuel Randall, the former Speaker. Based on experience, Randall was well qualified to serve on the committee, but he was gravely ill and could not attend any meetings. Reed did not have to worry about replaying his previous confrontations with Randall but rather sent a letter to Randall on January 15, 1890, in which he wrote, "I respectfully invite any [rules] criticism on your part or any suggestions which will be read to the committee."[33] The other Democrat on the committee, former Speaker John Carlisle, received incomplete information about the committee's work. The two Republicans on the committee, William McKinley and Joseph Cannon, reportedly were less supportive of strong majority rules than Reed.[34] In the absence of meetings, Reed worked with his clerk to prepare a set of rules.

In the meantime, Reed was operating the House under what he called general parliamentary law, which he defined as the accepted practices in public bodies across the United States. Where ambiguity existed, it would be up to Reed to determine what general parliamentary law demanded. Democrats did not like this situation from the outset. Ridiculing the idea of widely recognized general parliamentary law, Democrats promised obstruction if rules were not presented to the House. Despite all the talk about obstruction, the session began with little actual obstruction. Between waiting for committees and the holiday recess, Republican leaders had done little except routine actions.

As the session picked up, Reed had a choice. He could allow Democrats to obstruct for a while, which would provide further evidence in his case for procedural changes against obstruction. Alternatively, he could rest his case on past practice and resist even the earliest signs of obstruction by Democrats during the session. The bud-nipping strategy of Reed became apparent on January 20, 1890. After Reed recognized a majority for Republicans on a standing vote, Democrats offered the routine motion to confirm the standing vote with a teller vote, which entailed appointing tellers from each party to count the votes. Judging it a dilatory motion, Reed refused to order the teller vote. The next day, Democrats protested when the journal omitted Reed's denial of the teller vote. Charles Crisp accused Reed of hypocrisy for having maintained earlier "the House is entitled to tellers if they are demanded." Reed countered that although he had previously chosen to have a teller vote, it did not constitute a right.[35]

The dispute sparked press interest in Congress. In fact, Reed had just complained about the lack of congressional coverage to a reporter. He said, "If we could manage to sprinkle half a column of baseball news into the Congressional report the newspapers would print it fast enough."[36] The Louisville *Courier-Journal* extended the sports metaphor by alluding to Reed's teller vote denial: "It is well, however, for Brother Reed that the House is not a baseball aggregation, for if he performed his duties as umpire with the same degree of fairness as he performs those of the Speakership, the distinguished gentleman's head would soon be as bare of scalp as it already is of hair."[37]

The dispute also prompted the two parties to hold caucuses to set strategy. On January 24, Charles Crisp told his Democratic colleagues that Republicans planned to bring up the contested election case from West Virginia. Democrats talked about the need to resist. Three nights later Republican members caucused. Some House Republicans were nervous about what would happen if it became easier to move bills that they opposed this session and especially next Congress if the Republicans were returned to the minority. The caucus passed a modest resolution saying that it was imperative for all Republicans to show up when the West Virginia election case was brought forward on January 29. The *Washington Post* reported that the outcome was "an indication that the Speaker hardly contemplates adopting the radical course of counting as present members not voting in order to secure a quorum."[38]

Parliamentary Upheaval

On the morning of Wednesday, January 29, 1890, anticipation built in the House that there would be some early shots in the rules fight. The morning's *New-York Daily Tribune* announced, "To all appearance the Democratic campaign of filibustering and obstruction is about to open."[39] Republicans planned to bring up their strongest contested election case, *Smith v. Jackson* from West Virginia, despite the fact that no rules had yet been presented to the House. They would be bringing it up in a chamber marked by the absence of at least half a dozen Republicans, which left the Republicans just short of a quorum on their own. As the gallery waited for the first shot in the battle, Reed sat in the Speaker's chair. He was about to surprise nearly everybody. He had not even told his top two deputies of his intentions.[40] Reed was steeling himself not only to fire the first shot but also to deploy massive artillery. He was about to count a quorum that included unwilling Democrats.

On schedule at noon, the Republican chair of the Elections Committee brought up the West Virginia election case for consideration by the House. The vote was on whether to bring the case to the floor. The vote was predictable. Republicans voted in the affirmative while Democrats implemented the disappearing quorum strategy and refused to vote when their names were called. The clerk announced the final vote in which only 163 votes were cast. The vote had fallen short of the 165 votes required for a quorum. Democrat Charles Crisp proclaimed, "No quorum."

Reed responded, "The Chair directs the clerk to record the following names of members present and refusing to vote." A loud cheer arose from the Republican side. Democrats went ballistic.

Crisp announced, "I appeal. I appeal from the decision of the Chair."

Reed began reading the names of non-voting Democrats, "Mr. Blount, Mr. Breckinridge of Arkansas, Mr. Breckinridge of Kentucky."

Kentucky Representative William Breckinridge interrupted, "I deny the power of the Speaker and denounce it as revolutionary." Democrats burst into applause. Reed continued reading the names. He got up to McCreary.

James McCreary challenged Reed, "I deny your right, Mr. Speaker, to count me as present, and I desire to read from the parliamentary law on that subject."

Reed countered, "The Chair is making a statement of the fact that the gentleman from Kentucky is present. Does he deny it?" By now, Democrats were out of their seats and yelling at the Speaker. Reed announced, "The gentleman must not be disorderly."

Democrat Joseph Wheeler challenged, "Must the representatives of the people remain silent in their seats and see the Speaker of this House inaugurate revolution?"

Charles Crisp managed to be heard over the chaos, "I trust that I will be recognized for the purpose of taking an appeal."

Reed explained, "The Chair will state the question. The question of quorum was raised, and the Chair treats this subject in orderly fashion, and will submit his opinion to the House, which, if not acquiesced in by the House, can be overruled on an appeal taken from the decision."

"By brute force," Crisp interrupted.

"The Chair proposes to give a statement accompanied by a ruling," Reed explained, "from which an appeal can be taken if any gentleman is dissatisfied therewith."

"In advance I enter an appeal," Crisp said.

Reed began with a brief defense of his actions. His primary argument was constitutional: "There is a provision in the Constitution which declares that the House may establish rules for compelling the attendance of members. If members can be present and refuse to exercise their function, to wit, not be counted as a quorum, that provision would seem to be entirely nugatory." For precedent, he cited examples of leaders in New York and Tennessee who had made similar rulings in state legislatures. Reed pronounced, "The Chair thereupon rules that there is a quorum present within the meaning of the Constitution." After Crisp renewed his appeal, Reed stated, "The gentleman from Georgia appeals from that decision, and the question before the House now is, shall the decision of the Chair stand as the judgment of the House?"

Crisp insisted, "I desire to be heard on that."

As the bedlam continued, Reed recognized Illinois Republican Lewis Payson for the purpose of preempting debate on Crisp's appeal. Reed said, "The gentleman from Illinois moves to lay the appeal on the table." The parliamentary steps were in motion to hold the vote without debate.

Crisp insisted, "I claim the right to be heard."

Reed countered, "The motion of the gentleman from Illinois is one which he had a right to make." After Crisp pleaded that he had the floor, Reed insisted that the House was going to move on.

Crisp responded, "I submit to the Chair that it is unfair, unjust, and unmanly to refuse to us an opportunity of presenting our case to our fellow members. . . . Mr. Speaker, I appeal to your fairness as a man. Gentlemen [turning to the Republicans], I appeal to your fairness as men, to give us simply an opportunity to reply to the argument which the Speaker has seen proper to make."

Republican Benjamin Butterworth asked Payson to withdraw the motion to lay the appeal on the table. Butterworth said, "This is an important question and gentlemen have a right to be heard." Democrats applauded. Payson agreed to withdraw his motion, and Crisp maintained the floor.

Crisp attacked the decision: "When you vote to sustain the ruling of the Chair you will not only overturn the uninterrupted practice of one hundred years in this House, but you will vote directly in opposition to the views of many of your most distinguished leaders." Crisp then moved on to name prominent Republicans who had supported the right of members to refuse to vote. He said, "I say to you, gentlemen, on the authority of Mr. Blaine, that the decision just made by Mr. Speaker Reed, if sustained by your votes, will lay the foundation for the greatest legislative frauds ever committed in this country." He also cited President Garfield. He was ready for the grand finale. Crisp continued, "I now present you the argument of the distinguished gentleman from Maine, now the Speaker of the House." He quoted Reed's 1880 speech on the disappearing quorum: "The constitutional idea of a quorum is not the presence of a majority of all members of the House, but a majority of the members present and participating in the business of the House." Crisp pleaded, "I appeal, Mr. Speaker, from Philip drunk to Philip sober." Democrats loved it.

Reed announced, "The House will have the kindness to be in order."

Crisp would return to the inconsistency argument: "I have not read all of the remarks of the distinguished gentleman from Maine, but I think I have read enough to show it is a conclusive reply to the argument of the Speaker from Maine today." [41]

After a final plea by Crisp, Reed deputy and fellow Rules committee member Joseph Cannon took up the mantle for Republicans. Evidence that Cannon had not been informed of Reed's plan is that his speech was mediocre. Cannon conceded that just three months ago he would have said that Reed's actions were a violation of precedent. This seems to confirm reports that Cannon had been advocating for rules that retained more minority rights. No matter, he proceeded to defend the ruling of Reed. The House would subsequently adjourn.

The next morning's newspapers had different perspectives on the excitement, which was described by one newspaper as "Pandemonium Reigned Supreme!"[42] Republican newspapers defended Reed. The *Lewiston Evening Journal* suggested that Reed made a common-sense ruling that had prompted a "rebel yell" from Democrats.[43] On the other hand, Democratic papers attacked Reed and praised Charles Crisp. The *Atlanta Constitution* described how Crisp had condemned "Reed's various arbitrary decisions, and completely took the hide off him, so to speak."[44] With Reed's hide removed, so to speak, the Democratic *Boston Globe* laid bare Reed's true intent. The *Globe* editorialized, "At the present rate of Mr. Reed's autocratic development it will not take him more than a year or two to buckle on spurs, abolish Congress, invade the White House, tip out the misfit President and get himself crowned king, emperor, sultan, czar, or something of that sort."[45]

Nobody expected calm the following day when the House reconvened. William Springer began the day with a motion to adjourn. It lost. On the motion to bring up the previous day's journal, the Democrats refused to vote. Reed directed the clerk to record the names of those present but not voting. Democrats protested. On the subsequent motion to approve the previous day's journal, the Democrats refused to vote. The Republicans could provide only 162 affirmative votes, which was short of the 165 needed for a quorum. Again, Reed directed the clerk to record the names of those present but not voting. Democrats continued to condemn Reed as a revolutionary tyrant. Progress was minimal even as Reed counted a quorum a third time against unwilling Democrats.

William McKinley then got the chance to defend Republican actions. Like his fellow Rules committee member Joseph Cannon, his defense would be awkward. McKinley responded to Democratic jeers about previous Republican use of the disappearing quorum. McKinley addressed the inconsistency with a confession: "I have sat here and filibustered day after day in silence, refusing to vote, but I cannot now recall that I ever did it for a high or a noble or a worthy purpose." This drew cheers and applause from Democrats. McKinley finished the mea culpa: "There was never a time I did it that I now remember when I did not feel ashamed of myself."[46]

On January 31, the House galleries were packed in anticipation of the third day of the parliamentary crisis. After the House defeated Springer's motion to adjourn just after it convened, it turned to the previous day's journal. The motion to bring up journal approval prompted a lengthy roll-call vote in which Republicans mustered 160 votes to proceed while Democrats refused to vote. Reed counted a quorum to the protest of Democrats. This was followed by a lengthy roll-call vote on actual approval of the journal. Republicans managed 161 votes to approve the journal, but Democrats did not vote. Reed counted a quorum to the protest of Democrats. Reed refused to recognize another motion to adjourn. Springer declared, "Well, this is tyranny, simple and undiluted."

Democratic protests against being counted and not having motions recognized grew more personal, most notably by William Bynum who was able to prompt a rare response from Speaker Reed. Bynum challenged Reed's action, "I am standing here as their representative to sustain their rights against the arbitrary, the outrageous and damnable rulings of the Chair. . . . You have the power, backed up by a mob."

"Gentlemen will refrain from expressions of opinion," Reed announced.

Subsequently, Bynum initiated a broader critique of Republicans. He said that Reed's actions were "in keeping with the practices of your party when you stole the presidency and counted in a man who was not elected." Bynum had not been impressed by Reed's explanation of the decision to count the quorum: "You went forward day and night to vamp up some feeble show to sustain your rulings. No tyrant ever ascended the throne but who attempted to vamp up some feeble show of title to amuse the people while he gained possession of the kingdom." Bynum closed with a promise. He explained, "Now, Mr. Speaker, proceed in this manner; but, in the language of the immortal Emmet, we propose to dispute every inch of ground, burn every blade of grass, and the last intrenchment of liberty shall be our graves." As Democrats applauded, Springer moved to adjourn. Reed ruled the motion out of order. Democrats appealed.

Reed said, "Gentlemen will please take their seats. . . . The Chair rules that motion to be not in order." He was about to take aim at the second key strategy of obstruction—dilatory motions. After most of the first two days focused on the quorum, the repeated motions to adjourn had opened the door for Reed to address the issue of dilatory motions. Reed explained, "The object of a parliamentary body is action, and not stoppage of action. Hence, if any member or set of members undertakes to oppose the orderly progress of business, even by the use of the ordinarily recognized parliamentary motions, it is the right of the majority to refuse to have those motions entertained, and to cause the public business to proceed." He alluded to Bynum: "When a gentleman steps down to the front, amid the applause of his associates on the floor, and announces that it is his intention to make opposition in every direction . . . it is then the duty of the occupant of the Speaker's chair to take, under parliamentary law, the proper course with regard to such matters." Reed pronounced, "The question of the appeal from the refusal of the Chair to entertain the motion will be put to the House for its judgment."

Springer interjected, "Upon that I desire to be heard." Republican floor leader McKinley struggled to be heard. McKinley made a motion to set aside Springer's appeal. Springer protested as McKinley's motion was recognized.

Reed ruled, "The gentleman from Illinois is not in order."

"Yes, I am, but the Chair is out of order, and I desire to be heard upon the motion to lay on the table." The vote continued over Springer's objection. Republicans set aside Springer's appeal with 163 in favor and Democrats not voting. Reed counted a quorum of unwilling Democrats. Springer moved to adjourn again. Reed refused to recognize the motion. Springer maintained that since some business had been conducted, it was in order to make another motion to adjourn.

Reed disagreed: "There has also been a decision by the Chair as to that class of motions, and the decision has been sustained by the House, and it now becomes the duty of the Chair to execute the will of the House as expressed by its vote."

Springer asked, "Then when will it be in order for someone to move to adjourn?"

"It will be in order at the proper time," Reed declared.[47]

After resisting adjournment motions, the House actually got around to debating the contested election case that had started the upheaval two days earlier. Republicans chose the case because they felt it was their strongest case, and many Democrats recognized it as one of their weakest. For Republicans, the signature element of the case was how West Virginia's Democratic governor had counted a three-character, written-out number beginning with *tw* and ending with a sloppily written letter that appeared to be an *e*. The governor read the "twe" as an abbreviation for twelve and not the number two, thereby adding ten votes to the Democratic candidate and turning a three-vote deficit for the Democrat into a seven-vote advantage for the governor's fellow Democrat. In discussing the case, Republican Dalzell highlighted this detail of the contested election. He explained, "Twe is not now, never was, and, as is said in the report, probably never will be among sane men an abbreviation of either twelve, or twenty, or any other word known to an American. The governor knew, furthermore, that this word represented a number, and there is no number in the English language written with three letters, the first of which is 't' and the second 'w,' except the single number 'two.'"[48]

Democrat Charles O'Ferrall countered that counting "twe" as twelve was actually the conservative estimate of the vote received by the Democratic candidate. O'Ferrall explained, "The governor, being called upon to construe the returns, in construing and ascertaining what was meant by the three letters 'twe,' held that it was an unfinished word, and as t-w-e were the first three letters of only two numbers, twelve and twenty, he gave the benefit of the doubt against his political friend and in favor of his political opponent, and counted it twelve."[49]

At "twe"-o'clock noon on February 1, the House reconvened for the fourth day of the parliamentary upheaval. The disorder was becoming routine, and newspapers noted that spectators had declined from the third day. That did not mean, however, that the day would not begin without Springer's motions to adjourn. In refusing Springer's motion, Reed gave a rare opening to his opponents. Reed explained, "It would be an act of simple justice [to allow a vote on Springer's motion] if there were time, but inasmuch as very many sick men are being kept here by the procedure being indulged in, it would be unfair to them."

Springer responded, "I move to adjourn in order to let these sick people go home."

Reed ignored Springer and proceeded to count a quorum of unwilling Democrats to approve the journal. "If the gentleman will be in order the business of the country may proceed," Reed said.[50] Contentious debate continued on the contested election case. Springer offered futile motions to adjourn. The crisis was over.

The four-day parliamentary upheaval produced much analysis, including some from Reed himself. As Speaker, he had been limited to a few brief explanations and many pleas for order. In an interview with the Associated Press on February 2, Reed expressed resentment that he was pressuring ill Republicans to attend while "140 lusty Democrats sit silent in their seats, doing no public duty except to draw their pay." Reed asked, "Is it possible that the United States is paying those gentlemen $13 a day without even the poor privilege of counting their silent forms?"[51] He reiterated his argument that the constitutional provision to compel attendance presumed that members would vote when they got there. Reed suggested that alternative expectations were absurd. Later in the month, Reed wrote a *North American Review* article linking this to the intent of the Framers: "Our [founding] fathers knew nothing of this modern system of metaphysics whereby a man could be present and absent at the same moment; could be visible to demand his yeas and nays, and invisible when they were called." Reed recalled when the presiding officer of a state legislature implemented the disappearing quorum. Reed characterized the result: "Thereupon the friends of tyranny of that period, in the person of Mr. Cooper, made the point that the Chair was present, and the Chair decided that he was not!"[52]

Democrats reiterated that previous history and democratic theory demanded that majorities actually produce a majority to do business. They suggested that Reed's alternative was the one that was absurd. Democrats argued that Reed had made Democrats complicit in Republican policies that they opposed. Former Speaker Carlisle told the *Globe*, "We simply contend that these revolutionary schemes shall not be consummated by the aid of our votes."[53] The Republicans, they argued, had not ruled by majority rule, but, in fact, were a minority faction seeking to control the government. The Democratic *Argus* editorialized, "Majority rule, therefore, as Republican leaders attempt to act it out, means the passage of measures by less than the constitutional majority of the House, and the compelling of Democrats to share in the wrong doing."[54]

Democrats hammered the argument that Reed's actions contradicted his own previously stated views. Reed's 1880 speech in favor of the disappearing quorum became the most quoted speech in America. Every hour or two, Democratic floor speeches presented the highlights. Democratic newspapers piled on. The Democratic *Argus* summarized: "Consistency is evidently not one of the jewels that shine in the crown of Czar Reed."[55] The Republican *New York Daily Tribune* countered, "It is to his [Reed's] credit that he has been able to do so without caring for the fact that in the past he has worked as a member under the rules and customs as they stood."[56]

The two sides also disagreed about whether Reed had undermined freedom. Articulating Democratic concerns, the *Boston Globe* editorialized that "the precedent which Speaker Reed seeks to establish is full of peril to the liberties of the people."[57] Republicans, however, mocked the idea that fundamental liberties were at stake. The *Portland Daily Press* wrote, "The inalienable right of a Congressman to move an adjournment every fifteen minutes, and to demand a roll call has also been assailed. . . . The Cradle of Liberty should immediately be set to rocking, the descendants of the minute men of Concord and Lexington should be ordered under arms."[58]

On both sides the parliamentary crisis was personalized to Speaker Reed. Democratic newspapers demonized Reed. One Democratic legislator adapted the doxology: "Curse Reed from whom all evils flow; Curse him all creatures here below; Damn him above ye heavenly host; Damn Reed with his infernal boast."[59] The Democratic *Chicago Herald* envisioned some old-fashioned justice. On February 2, it editorialized, "Speaker Reed deserves to have been dragged out of the House by the hair of his head and hanged to the first tree in the capitol grounds, until he was dead."[60] The *Herald* seems to have forgotten that Reed was bald.

In contrast, Republican papers celebrated Reed. Republican poets matched Democrats stanza for stanza: "Count, Mr. Speaker, count with care. Count every Democrat in his chair. Brains or no brains, count him there. Whether he howl or whether he swear."[61] Republicans also invoked religion: "In the New Testament we may read, Something about a shaking reed, But 'tis not so at Washington, At the present House session, No shaking Reed is planted there."[62] Even some House Democrats articulated a grudging respect for how Reed had handled the crisis. The *Boston Globe* quoted an anonymous House Democrat: "I should feel perfectly justified in being one of a half dozen men to depose the Speaker by physical force, and yet thoroughly as I detest Reed I admire him for his nerve and magnificent sang froid."[63]

These characteristics naturally prompted talk of Reed as a presidential candidate in the 1892 election. The *Boston Globe* reported, "Republicans are already talking about him [Reed] as the next nominee for the presidency . . . [who] will go before the convention on his reputation for courage and back bone."[64] For his part, Reed brushed off the talk. A reporter asked whether Reed was thinking about the presidency. Reed responded, "No, not much, it seems to be someone else who is thinking of it." Reed considered how he might go over with Republicans at the convention: "In my judgment they might do worse, and they probably will."[65]

One lingering question was why Democrats had not simply left the chamber before the roll-call vote began in order to deny a quorum once Reed had counted a quorum for the first time. Democratic papers had been hinting at this strategy throughout the crisis. The *New York Times* predicted, "Should the Speaker force his decision upon the House by attempting to employ the silent but visible Democrats to constitute a majority, it is expected the Democrats will then withdraw from the House."[66]

Democrats, however, did not adopt the strategy. Why? A lot of credit goes to former Speaker Randall, who although too ill to be in the chamber, sent a message to caucus members urging them to stay in the chamber and fight. Indeed, some Democratic papers promoted the idea that Randall himself might lead the charge. A *Boston Globe* headline announced, "Randall May Enter House on Cot and Attack Speaker."[67] Even if some Democrats were reluctant to fight, they also recognized that running away might look bad. Many Democrats also preferred to put Republicans on the record for what they did, which required being in the chamber. Democrats routinely described how the public would vindicate them. Finally, Democrats expressed confidence that the Supreme Court would thwart Reed. On the first day of the crisis, the *New York Times* speculated, "The first bill passed by less than a majority vote will be tested as to its legality in the Supreme Court."[68]

While conceding defeat, Democratic representatives and newspapers articulated the consistent theme that Reed's victory would come at a heavy cost. In a newspaper interview, Springer predicted, "The party that enjoys the latitude furnished by those rules will be like Actaeon in the fable—doomed by his own dogs."[69] Perhaps the most creative application of this argument was undertaken by Representative Henry Turner. He joined other Democrats in using Reed's own words against him. Unlike most Democrats who made the obligatory reference to Reed's now-famous 1880 determination that a quorum included only members choosing to participate, Turner focused on Reed's July 4, 1889, speech at Woodstock in which Reed foreshadowed his rules reform. Reed opened his Woodstock speech, "It was no less a person, I believe, than the Duke of Wellington who remarked [that] 'there is only one thing more demoralizing than defeat, and that is victory.'" Unfortunately, the second line of Reed's speech was the following: "I have not taken the trouble to verify the citation, because the truth is so solid and sound that it needs no buttress or support from even the most illustrious name."[70] That is usually not a good sign. Turner reminded the House that the duke was actually a victory man. Turner explained, "The gentleman [Reed] inverted the saying of the duke, but he stated a truth inadvertently with more pith than did the famous warrior." Reed's inversion of victory and defeat opened him up to irony. Turner concluded, "In his decision . . . [Reed] has been again unmindful of the truths of history, and that victory to his party today may be more demoralizing than defeat!"[71]

Analysis of Reed's leadership over the four-day parliamentary crisis has never really ended. One unresolved question is the level of support that Reed had within the caucus for his decisive action. His caucus had previously voted to encourage Republican members to show up for work. There is a huge gap between this and Reed's decision to break longstanding precedent about how to count a quorum. Was Reed acting on behalf of his caucus? There is a rich debate by modern scholars about the extent to which congressional leaders are constrained by their caucus. One perspective is that leaders act as agents implementing the preferences of caucus members who function as the principal in a principal-agent relationship.[72] An alternative perspective suggests that leaders act more autonomously to take actions beyond their caucus preferences.[73] In this case, the evidence supports autonomous action in the midst of known disagreement within the caucus. Reed's genuine uncertainty about whether he had caucus support is reflected in how he made plans to retire from Congress if he were not upheld.[74] Aware of caucus disagreement, Reed acted without telling his top two deputies[75] whose lack of warning was reflected in their clumsy speeches defending Reed's actions. Weeks earlier, a bare majority of his caucus had voted for him on a second ballot when his primary competitor was reluctant to overhaul House rules.

Of course, the true preferences of members cannot be determined since their votes occurred in the context of how events played out over the four days. In shaping this context, Reed made strategic choices that increased the likelihood of success. His choices affected the reactions of Democrats and Republicans. One of Reed's strategic choices that has been singled out by political scientists is his decision to count the quorum on a contested election case, which was likely to inspire partisan loyalty and make a rebuke of the Speaker less likely.[76] Whatever Reed's level of support at the start, his bold and sudden action prompted his caucus to rally around him.

Reed Rules

After the previous week's turmoil, there was relative calm on Monday, February 3, when the House met for a final vote in the West Virginia contested-election case. The galleries were less crowded. What was more crowded, however, were Republican seats in Congress after leaders exerted strong pressure on members to be present for the final vote. Democrats extended the debate as long as possible.

The final Democratic speech was given by West Virginia Democrat William Wilson, who mocked Republican inconsistency on the disappearing quorum. Wilson began, "There is no more inspiring sight in the eyes of all virtuous and right-minded men, none more full of encouragement for youth, than when hoary and notorious sinners, who have long persisted in wicked ways, publicly acknowledge their sins, and transgressions and promise in the sight of all men to be virtuous, honest, and righteous." Wilson analogized, "I can not but liken them to a story I read, long years ago, of an Alpine village which the devil had so thoroughly debauched and corrupted that it was a terror to all the region round. But as a punishment for his misdeeds the devil was forced to assume the garb of a priest and go among them and preach so eloquently that he converted every one of them into the fold of the true church." He summarized: "I fear it would be not allowable, under general parliamentary law, for me to say in this instance who the devil he is, but I think, Mr. Speaker, I have him in my mind's eye." To Democratic applause, Wilson concluded with a mock Republican mantra under the new procedures: "We will legislate with no rules to protect the Treasury. . . . We will appropriate; we will educate; we will irrigate, and whatever we do, we will never hesitate. . . . And we will go home, every one of us, with a public building. . . . We will take home rivers and harbors to our constituents."[77]

The end of the debate brought about a final vote on the contested-election case. The vote was to unseat the Democrat Jackson. The roll call showed 166 Republicans in favor and 163 Democrats not voting. The motion carried. For the first time all year, Republicans produced a quorum on their own. Reed was not required to count a quorum. Democrats had no recourse as a Democrat was unseated and replaced by Republican Charles Smith, who was immediately sworn into office. It was 8:30 p.m. Democrat William Springer assumed the floor. He asked, "Is this a proper time to move to adjourn?" Reed permitted the adjournment motion, which carried.[78] It had shaken the foundations of government, but Republicans had another member.

When Congress met the next day, Reed was pleased to have the election case behind him. The *New York Times* described his appearance: "Fresh as a rose, and as cheerful as a cricket, Speaker Reed this morning resumed his chair in the House, prepared to repeat his arbitrary and harsh treatment of the minority, to which he still refuses the privilege of knowing by what law its utterances and actions are to be governed."[79] Other Democrats renewed the criticism of being governed by an ambiguous general parliamentary law interpreted by Reed. Democratic Representative Amos Cummings prepared to offer a resolution to make copies of a recognized book on parliamentary law so that members could see by what they were being governed. William Springer told Cummings, "Never mind, just get 329 photographs of Reed, and put one of them on each member's desk."[80] The order for the photos and book reprint would be unnecessary. Reed was ready to replace general parliamentary law with formal rules.

In their final form, the rules proposed to establish majority rule in the US House of Representatives. The two hallmarks of obstruction—disappearing quorum and delaying motions—were emasculated. The rules allowed the Speaker to include members who were present but not voting as part of the quorum. The rules formally gave the Speaker the ability to refuse to entertain motions offered for the purpose of delay. While Reed had assumed both powers under general parliamentary law, the new rules formally recognized them. The rules also enhanced the discretion of the House in taking pending legislation off legislative calendars. The emerging role of the Rules committee in guiding legislation was facilitated.

In short, the new set of rules paved the way for the majority party to legislate. In the language of modern political science, the Reed Rules sought to "explicitly empower a partisan majority to order the agenda of the House."[81] Although analysts at the time did not have modern political science's theoretical and empirical understanding of agenda control,[82] they were already articulating how the Reed Rules would fundamentally change politics. The *Washington Post* summarized the proposed rules: "In short the whole effect of the rules is to permit the majority to take up or proceed with any measures it desires, consider it as long as it wants to, cut off debate when it wants to, and secure a vote on final passage."[83]

On Monday, February 10, the rules were presented to the House. While the House regularly took weeks to debate rules, Joseph Cannon proposed to end debate on the new rules on Wednesday. Democrats were furious. They argued that it was unfair to fundamentally change the rules of the House with so little debate. Reed pushed forward with the motion by Cannon to end debate. Cannon's motion failed by a vote of 58–149. Many Republicans had sided with the Democrats. After Cannon's motion failed, Springer offered a successful motion to spend the entire week on the rules.

During the debate, Democrats took on the two major innovations of ignoring dilatory motions and counting nonvoting members as part of the quorum. Springer attacked the new rule about not allowing dilatory motions: "I have looked in vain in the textbooks, and there is nowhere, in Cushing, or in Jefferson, or in any other writer upon parliamentary law, a place where a dilatory motion is defined." In the absence of a clearly defined dilatory motion, Springer argued, the Speaker was given the power "to determine the motive of every man upon this side of the House." This had profound implications: "Gentlemen, you are introducing here a most dangerous precedent; and I warn you that before this year is out you will repent in sackcloth and ashes if you can, as your consciences are so seared, of the time when you clothed your Speaker with this unconstitutional, autocratic, and despotic power over the proceedings of the House."[84]

The last hours of debate and the final vote on rules took place on Friday, February 14. Democrats ended much as they began by highlighting the inconsistency of Reed. Charles Crisp proclaimed, "I now quote from another gentleman." Members were no longer surprised that the anonymous authority for the disappearing quorum would be Reed. Crisp quoted Reed's prior assertion that there was minimal risk in allowing the disappearing quorum since it only meant that the minority could "upon great occasions demand that every bill which is passed shall receive the absolute vote of a majority of the members elected." Crisp continued, "That language was used by the honorable gentleman from Maine, now the Speaker of this House."

"The Chair recognizes it," Reed said.

Crisp continued, "Now gentlemen, I have no idea that you intend to strike out this proposed rule; but I do believe that you yourselves, in view of the statements of these distinguished men, are doubtful as to its constitutionality." Crisp offered as additional evidence of Republican doubts about the quorum counting method a letter that Republican leaders had recently circulated to their members urging attendance for the rules debate because "we must be able to show a quorum of our own members."[85]

Ultimately, the rules passed despite the failure of Republicans to produce a quorum. The final vote was 161 yes, 144 no, and 23 not voting. Democrats chose to go on record in opposition to the rules. Given that for months they had asked Republicans to present rules, it would have been difficult to refuse to vote on the rules. The House adjourned.

The House met for the first time under its new rules the following day. Many members had taken the opportunity to leave town overnight since the rules fight had ended. The vote to approve the journal was 128 yes, 1 no, and 190 not voting. Reed applied the new rules to count a quorum: "The clerk will read the names of members noted by direction of the Speaker under clause 3 of Rule XV."[86]

The adoption of the Reed Rules was a monumental event in the history of the US House of Representatives. The majority party was empowered to legislate. Before the Reed Rules, the majority party had struggled to enact its policies. The Reed Rules were designed to improve that record and allow the majority to govern. Textbook political science recognizes the adoption of the Reed Rules as a "watershed moment" in the history of Congress.[87]

While there is scholarly consensus that adopting the Reed Rules was a watershed moment, there is a rich debate about why the transformation to majority rule happened in February 1890. Modern political science has shown that there was a favorable institutional context for strengthening majority-party governance during the Fifty-First Congress. Reed's actions did not occur in a vacuum but built on the inherited rules of the House, such as the 1811 establishment of a previous question motion and Reed's parliamentary moves in his third term "allowing a simple majority to modify a two-thirds rule."[88] Reed's predecessors, especially James Blaine, Samuel Randall, and John Carlisle, had provided some targeted institutional tools that could be helpful to majority rule, especially strengthening the power of recognition and converting the Rules committee to a standing committee, even if their unwillingness to challenge the disappearing quorum had made them vulnerable to obstruction.[89] The willingness of majority-party members to empower stronger House leaders was also made more likely by the majority party securing organizational control over the House after 1865 instead of the ad hoc and regional coalitions that had previously often elected the Speaker and organized the chamber.[90] Increasing membership size favored restrictive procedures.[91] The explosion in the number of bills by the 1870s made floor time scarce and strained previous practices for floor consideration.[92] The recent history of obstruction, which can be measured as a percentage of obstruction motions in the previous Congress, favored a reduction of minority rights.[93] Stronger party governance was also more likely given the high level of policy agreement within the political parties and disagreement between parties.[94] Republican control of other parts of the government and the small numerical House majority also seemed to favor efforts to strengthen the procedural imperatives of majority-party leaders.[95]

Although institutional factors are important, leadership also matters. It is hard to account for the magnitude of the change represented by the Reed Rules without reference to Reed's strong leadership. Even if ideological polarization was comparatively high in a long-term perspective, the level was similar to the previous four Congresses, which had experienced a "golden age of gridlock and obstructionism."[96] One compelling scholarly perspective is offered by Randall Strahan, who argues that even if a favorable institutional context may have been necessary, it is insufficient to explain such dramatic change. A satisfactory explanation, he argues, must recognize that Reed was an innovative leader who had the skill and vision to take advantage of a critical moment when Congress was out of equilibrium.[97] Douglas Dion also captures well the limitations of institutional factors for explaining the adoption of the Reed Rules: "A final factor, though one shudders to bring it up, is the personality of Thomas Brackett Reed . . . [who] represented a level of political leadership and responsibility that is difficult to theorize about."[98] As described by Aldrich and Shepsle, Reed's "instrumental behavior" to "grease the skids for the majority party" occurred in an institutional context, "but the imaginativeness of the ploys remains a puzzle."[99]

While some enhancements to majority-party governance were likely under any leader given the institutional context, the evidence suggests that Reed's "more sweeping rules reform" was unlikely to emerge from alternative Republican leaders.[100] William McKinley, for example, was a well-known conciliator who had just finished second to Reed for the Speakership taking a less aggressive posture to minority obstruction. Properly classified as exercising personal leadership,[101] Reed literally wrote the text of the rules with the assistance of one clerk. They are properly called the Reed Rules.

The vote on February 14, 1890, marked only the initial adoption of the Reed Rules. Whether or not they would take hold was a question for the future. Ultimately, Reed's leadership would also play a large role in their institutionalization. In February 1890, however, there was genuine uncertainty about what would happen to the Reed Rules. There was also uncertainty about their policy impact, which was probably the greatest concern for Reed's contemporaries. The *New York Times* contemplated, "The majority is now in full and untrammeled possession of all the powers of the House, and it will be interesting to see what it will do with them."[102]

CHAPTER 6

THE MAJORITY PARTY LEGISLATES

"You seem to be the brains of the G.O.P.—Reed on the other hand appears to be the balls (No offense to you)," wrote W. S. Bigelow to his friend Henry Cabot Lodge in 1890.[1] In private correspondence and public life, Reed was the talk of the nation. His bold actions were either glorified or reviled. Reed was inundated with requests to give speeches throughout the country. Some invitations were easy to turn down. On March 1, 1890, Reed declined an invitation to speak in Kentucky because the inviting organization's president, Jay Durham, had previously threatened him. Reed wrote, "Now Jay F. Durham assured me during the late 'disturbances' that if they had me in Kentucky they would kill me. Knowing the said Durham to be a journalist, his declarations to me import absolute verity."[2] Outside Kentucky, speeches had significant appeal to Reed. They were especially important since he had lost one potential forum for articulating his views. As Speaker, Reed followed the tradition that Speakers did not vote or talk about policy on the House floor. Embracing the role of a public Speakership making external policy appeals,[3] Reed prepared speeches after the rules fight when committees were preparing bills and the floor was quiet.

The relative calm was broken on March 4, 1890, when Speaker Reed disciplined Democratic leader Charles Crisp. Republicans were using their newfound power to unseat another Democrat and seat a Republican in a contested-election dispute. Pushing forward on a roll call, Reed demanded order in the chamber. Charles Crisp was talking in the aisle when Reed insisted, "Gentlemen will take their seats and cease conversation." Crisp took offense at being singled out to sit down. Reed maintained, "The Chair did not point out the gentleman from Georgia," but then undermined his claim with the defense that "the gentleman's back was turned, turned so the Chair did not look particularly at the gentleman from Georgia" even though he was "looking in that direction." Crisp rejected the no-eye-contact defense and said that the Speaker had gone "too far."[4] Symbolically, it was powerful as Reed exercised the most basic schoolhouse discipline by ordering the Democratic leader to sit down and be quiet.

By May 1890, bills were ready and Republicans were prepared to legislate under the new rules of the House. Legislating in a closely divided chamber, Reed would utilize all the resources that he had developed over his congressional career. With filibustering crushed by rule changes on the quorum and dilatory motions, final votes would not be delayed. For bills presenting special political challenges, floor action would begin when the Rules committee issued a special rule, which Reed had pioneered back in 1883 but which had not been used since then. Once approved by the majority caucus, a special rule would constrain the options available to the House and set a time for a final vote. The importance of the House floor and committees declined relative to political party.

The first major bill moved by House Republicans under the new rules was tariff reform, which was their highest legislative priority. William McKinley and his Ways and Means committee crafted the bill in regular consultation with Speaker Reed. The final product, usually called the McKinley Bill, provided unexpectedly large tariff increases. Under the new majoritarian procedures, Republicans set a definitive time for a vote on final passage of the bill. The Rules committee presented a special rule that allowed twelve days of debate with a final vote set for noon on May 21. Republicans were aligned against amendments that originated outside the Ways and Means committee. The twelve days were significantly less than some earlier tariff debates, but Republicans saw the time period as sufficient. After debate ended at the prescribed time, the House passed tariff reform 164–142.

In the aftermath, a provocative and enduring statement was attributed to Reed. It apparently emerged from a discussion in which Reed criticized the Senate for providing too much deliberation. The contrast with the House was stark. As reported by the *New York Star*, Reed said, "Thank Heaven, the House is not a deliberative body."[5] Given the published variations, there is some doubt about whether Reed uttered exactly these words. When Reed wrote a follow-up article about legislative debate, he left enough ambiguity to preserve the quote for posterity. On the surface, Reed's article rejected the nondeliberative characterization by saying that "in order to make laws wisely the [legislative] body must be a deliberative body." Yet, in taking a shot at his critics, Reed conceded, "Deliberation implies thought, and not necessarily words, except as they are food for thought."[6] Democrats were not eager to be nourished by Reed's food for thought. Reed's quote in the *Star* became shorthand for Democratic arraignments of Reed.

The session's second major piece of legislation, which involved the currency, required Reed to be even more creative in using the new rules to press forward with Republican legislation. A majority of the House appeared to favor the free coinage of silver, which was anathema to Reed as undermining the gold standard and fostering inflation. If given the chance, a handful of western Republicans, who represented silver-mining constituencies, were likely to work with Democrats in supporting a free-silver bill. The key was not to give them a chance. This was done through the Rules committee issuing a special rule preventing a vote on a free-silver amendment. Further, the special rule limited debate to a few days and set a definitive time for a final vote on June 7. Rather than let floor managers allocate debate time, Reed personally oversaw the process. On June 5, members gathered around Reed's desk to request speaking time. He was trying hard to ignore the clamoring of William Springer. Feeling ignored, Springer insisted, "Mr. Speaker, I want to know if you have put me down yet."

Reed responded, "I have put you down more than once, Mr. Springer, but the trouble is I can't keep you down."[7] Reed had less trouble keeping down free-silver advocates, and the currency bill passed the House without a vote on a free-silver amendment.

Later, when a free-silver bill passed by the Senate was sent to the House, Reed faced a fight in keeping it away from free-silver supporters who wanted to vote on it immediately. Reed referred the Senate-passed bill to the Coinage committee, which opposed free silver. Democrats were furious the next day when they learned of Reed's action in the House journal. Democrats decided on the strategy of trying to delete from the journal the statement that Reed had referred the bill to committee. In defending the Democratic position, Representative Springer attacked Reed for denying a vote on something the people wanted: "You may ignore it, and put down the representatives of the people on this floor, but the people will put you down, sir, at the polls in November."[8] Republicans defended Reed with one of them going so far as to remark that Reed had always been correct even if the results were not always pleasing. Democratic Representative Crisp retorted, "Yes, during this whole session the gentleman and his party, if I may be permitted to borrow a simile, have seemed to bow before the Speaker of the House with much the same feeling with which the Hindoo bows before the hideous image of his god. He knows that he is ugly, but he feels that he is great."[9] Crisp's insult notwithstanding, silver Republicans were not in the mood to bow to Speaker Reed.

After two days of fighting, Democrats enjoyed a rare victory over Speaker Reed. On the vote to "correct" the journal by eliminating the statement that Reed had referred the bill to committee, Democrats benefited from seven Republican defections to win 121–117. They backed up that win with other procedural vote victories. Democratic papers rejoiced. The *New York Times* celebrated what it called "the first rebuke to the autocrat of the House."[10] Democrats expected that the journal correction would bring the bill to the House floor.

Reed rebounded the next morning. He told the House, "The refusal to record a fact did not obliterate the fact itself, any more than the destruction of a deed would prevent the transfer of property which had already taken place, or the scuttling of a boat, which had carried a man across a lake, would re-land him on the other side."[11] It was time for a final vote on appealing Reed's action. As described in the *Washington Post*, "Everybody in the well-filled gallery had come to see a Democratic victory. They saw a Democratic Waterloo."[12] The Francophile Reed probably appreciated the historical analogy and was pleased not to be playing the role of Napoleon. His decision to refer the bill was upheld 144–117. Ultimately, drawing out the process allowed time for anti-silver Republicans to get to Washington and to raise doubts among a few Democrats. Days later, a compromise version that rejected unlimited silver coinage but authorized $4.5 million of silver coinage passed the House. By mid-July, the Sherman Silver Purchase Act was law.

House disposal of the silver bill marked an important event in the operation of the new rules. Although Republicans were mostly united on tariff reform, they had significant differences on silver coinage. The new rules for the first time would be used against a significant block of Republicans. Majority rule did not mean that majorities would emerge in a free-flowing way on the House floor. Above all, the rules meant that the views of the majority of the majority party would prevail. Some modern political scientists have described this as the difference between majoritarian government in which the median person in the entire chamber is decisive and party government in which the median person in the majority party is decisive.[13] Reed's preference is captured in his famous assessment that the best system would entail Republicans governing and Democrats watching.[14] While Democrats watched, Republican party leaders were governing using the Rules committee to limit the choices that would be available to the House. Although many members failed to appreciate the new governing model, it was possible to grasp the effects of the new rules. Charles Crisp, for example, during the debate on considering the Senate silver bill, challenged the nature of majority rule implemented by Reed. He explained, "A mixed majority here now desire to do business. I believe the chief advantage claimed for our rules is that they enable a majority to do business, and yet when we seek, under the rules you have established, to do business, you . . . deprive us of the right to do so."[15]

After passing currency legislation, Reed and House Republicans began the final push for the session's third major piece of legislation—to establish federal supervision of elections. The measure was a response to southern states preventing the votes of blacks from being counted by such techniques as discarding ballot boxes, intimidation, literacy tests, poll taxes, purging registration rolls, and violence. By empowering federal election supervisors, the bill represented a renewed effort by Republicans to guarantee the Fifteenth Amendment right of blacks to vote after the Civil War. The original effort had evaporated with the contested election of 1876 in which Hayes was awarded the presidency, but there was an implicit concession that a more hands-off approach would be taken in the South. The issue of black disenfranchisement had remained on the back burner for years until Republicans secured unified control of the government in the November 1888 election.

In support of the elections bill, Speaker Reed published an article in the June 1890 issue of *North American Review*. Reed had become frustrated with southern allusions to electoral inconsistencies in the North, especially in his own district. He explained, "This kind of answer is so common, and so reminds one of the beam and the mote of Scripture. . . . Is robbery by violence to be tolerated and approved until we have utterly abolished petty larceny?" Reed maintained, "No really valid objection can be urged against Federal supervision, for an honest count can hurt no one." Reed framed the issue as justice not only for blacks, but also for Republicans: "To put this whole matter in a nutshell, the Republican party alleges that it is deprived by all manner of devices—differing in different States, but having one common purpose—of votes which under the Constitution of the land that party is entitled to." Reed even had a specific number in mind. He said that Democrats wrongfully held twenty seats by suppressing black voters who disproportionately voted

Republican. He summarized, "All we ask is that in national matters the majority of the voters in this country may rule."[16]

Democrats attacked the bill in many ways. A political-philosophy critique was leveled at the bill as a violation of federalism through federal intrusion on a state government's constitutional right to control its own elections. A political-impact critique condemned the bill as a plot by Republicans to take control of the government. William Springer argued that the bill was "intended to perpetuate the ill-gotten power of the Republican Party in this House and in the country."[17] Some opposition was also racist. In floor debate, for example, Allen Candler said that it was necessary to protect the integrity of elections from the African-American man who does not take voting seriously: "He goes to the polls as he goes to the circus or to a public execution—for a frolic. . . . The negro is admitted by all, I believe, to be an inferior race intellectually."[18] The combination of philosophy, politics, and prejudice made the elections bill the type of proposal that would have been defeated under the old House rules, which enabled a determined minority to stop legislation. During the rules debate, Republicans directly connected procedural reform with passage of this party-building bill.[19]

Under the new rules, the House could end filibustering on the elections bill. On June 25, the Rules committee brought forward a rule that limited the opportunity for amendments and set a final vote for July 2. After the end of scheduled debate, Reed recognized Democrats for routine motions to recommit and adjourn. Trying to put off the vote until the next day, William Springer insisted on a reading of the engrossed bill with all amendments incorporated. To great surprise, Reed produced the engrossed bill, which he had asked clerks to prepare in advance. The *Washington Post* described what happened next: "The Clerk glanced at the immense pile of manuscript, looked imploringly at the Speaker and then began at a 200-words-a-minute rate."[20] After only two hours, the seventy-six-page bill had been read. Democrats had run out of options. The bill passed 155–149.

With major legislation out of the way by spring, the House was set for a long, hot summer of minimal activity. The House kept busy with routine matters, including working through a large number of pension bills. As far as major legislation, however, the House was mostly waiting for Senate action on measures that the House had already passed. The lack of high-profile business diverted attention to the trivial.

The most trivial matter that became a national obsession was surely Speaker Reed's attire in the Washington summer heat. Specifically, Reed was wearing a sash. Although sashes were making inroads into the broader population, they were still unusual and not long removed from their origin in the so-called "dude" culture of young, flamboyant men. Thus, Reed's choice to don a sash in the summer of 1890 was an endless source of amusement for the press. A Texas representative proclaimed, "Look at Tom Reed wearing a dude belly-band!"[21] Above all, by drawing attention to Reed's waist, the sash offered newspapers an irresistible opportunity to remind readers that Reed was overweight. The New York *Sun* described Reed's sash as "the glowing equator that circumscribes the outsides of the capacious insides of the Man Who Looks Like Shakespeare and has quorums in his eyes."[22]

His sash also became a bridge to policy and leadership attacks. The quantity of textiles in the sash led to faux analysis that its construction had implications for international trade. Newspaper writers speculated whether the high-tariff-supporting Reed lived up to his convictions by using only domestic materials. Other critics tied the sash to Reed's broader leadership. The *Saint Paul Daily Globe* editorialized, "That bright sash worn by Speaker Reed will prove to be the frippery of the clown rather than the belt of the ringmaster."[23] Of course, some lamented that newspaper coverage of the sash could have gone to policy issues. Columnist Robert Graves said that Reed's "broad blue belt has been more talked and written about throughout the length and breadth of the land than any other feature of the congressional session," which he said was an illustration of "the fondness of the American people for the practical things of life, for the commonplace and the comic."[24]

Democrats wanted to dethrone the Speaker in Maine's September 1890 election. The Democratic campaign, however, got off to an inauspicious start at the First District Democratic convention. Democratic speakers seemed unsure of the name of their nominee, whom they nominated as both Melville P. Frank and Melvin P. Frank. In a brief acceptance speech, M. P. Frank supported lower tariffs, trust regulation, and the secret ballot. Ultimately, Frank gave few speeches and allowed party supporters to speak for him. Throughout the campaign, the Democratic *Argus* combined the usual criticism of Reed's appearance with references to autocratic leadership: "The imperial head of the Kaiser and the elephantine figure that supports it."[25]

Reed was treated as a conquering hero by Republicans when he returned to Portland for a brief campaign. The last stages of his journey home included traveling on a special train carrying a railcar with likenesses of Reed on both sides. Reed stopped briefly in several cities along the way to address crowds. His speeches emphasized how congressional Republicans had implemented all their campaign promises. At Portland City Hall on September 4, Reed pronounced, "Party responsibility has begun, and with it also the responsibility of the people. . . . Responsibility will wait on power, and wherein the people, with full knowledge that their servants can act, will choose those who will worthily carry out their will." The *Press* described the scene as Reed ended the speech: "[The] audience, in its eagerness to catch every word, calmed down to the stillness of a vast forest and then like the rushing of a hurricane into the trees came the burst of applause which suddenly broke forth as it was seen that he had finished."[26] The Democratic *Argus* reported the same moment less picturesquely as the audience "made a rapid bolt for the door."[27]

In confronting the Democratic opposition, Reed benefited from his friend William McKinley's willingness to travel to Maine to speak on his behalf. During the 1890 campaign, McKinley praised Reed in a number of speeches in Maine. At Old Orchard Beach, for example, McKinley said that the tariff reform could never have passed "had it not been for the famous ruling of the Speaker."[28] As recognition of their special friendship, Reed broke with tradition and shared his last campaign appearance with McKinley on September 8 in Portland's City Hall. Reed said that he was cutting his speech short in order to highlight McKinley, whom he introduced as "a friend to me, faithful to his party and an honor to his country." McKinley discussed the tariff and alliteratively acknowledged Reed's achievement: "I wish I had the words to paint to every citizen of this district the scenes through which that brave, bold, brainy man has passed in the last nine months."[29]

Republicans rolled to a huge victory in Maine's election. Reed earned his largest margin ever by defeating Frank with over 57 percent of the vote. He addressed happy Republicans at an election night gathering at city hall. Reed proclaimed, "I suppose we never shall know what it is to possess the earth entirely, but I think that we have got rather an adequate notion of it after all."[30]

When Reed returned to Washington, he was greeted with gifts and congratulations from his Republican colleagues. Democratic newspapers contemplated a newly empowered Reed: "It is to be feared Speaker Reed will be obliged to wear his sash band around his head, which is much swollen over his late success."[31] Reed, however, had little time to ponder new fashion statements. He decided to press forward with another contested-election case. This time, the plan was to unseat Democrat Edward Venable and seat Republican John Langston because of vote suppression in a Virginia district.

When Republicans called up the contested-election case, the session's second parliamentary upheaval was underway. This time, Reed did not confront Democrats hurling abuse and waving fists; there was often only one Democrat in the chamber. Democrats had adopted the long-hinted strategy of absenting themselves from House business. Technically, they would show up for the quorum call to avoid arrest but slip out the side door before the roll-call vote. When Democrats left, Republicans were woefully short of a quorum. Republican leaders exhorted their members to attend. The futile process wasted a week. One Republican, Joseph Cheadle of Indiana, even admitted that the evidence appeared to favor the Democrat. There was discussion about whether to back off the contested-election case since the session was ending in a few weeks. Would Reed press forward? Yes, he would. To be successful, he needed more Republicans in town or a way to keep Democrats in the chamber.

On September 18, 1890, Reed ordered the exit doors locked, including the major thoroughfare between the chamber floor and the members' lobby. Maine Republican Nelson Dingley was caught in the members' lobby when the door was locked and was forced to listen to the proceedings from the other side of the door. He would have heard Democrats in an uproar. Among the angry Democrats was Representative Kilgore, who approached the doorkeeper at the members' lobby exit and asked to leave. The doorkeeper refused. Kilgore then planted one leg and kicked the door with the other leg. The wicker door broke off the hinges and flew into Dingley who suffered a bloody nose. Democrats approached a second exit. The doorkeeper backed away and Democrats exited the chamber. No quorum was present. In the words of the *Sun*, Democrats had drawn "first blood" in the second parliamentary upheaval.[32]

The escape became a national sensation. Constantine Buckley Kilgore lived up to his longstanding nickname "Buck" and left a strong footprint on news reports of the incident: "With characteristic energy he planted a No. 11 boot, made by a cobbler in Van Zandt county, Tex., squarely in the middle of the doors."[33] Shoe companies shipped numerous shoes to Kilgore and hoped for an endorsement. Democratic newspapers celebrated the iconic boot. The *Daily Gazette* proclaimed, "Col. Kilgore's kick is likely to go down to posterity as a vigorous protest against autocracy."[34] Republican newspapers condemned Democratic lawlessness. The *Baltimore Herald* editorialized, "The unfortunate circumstance of Mr. Dingley, of Maine, having his proboscis shivered into sundry fragments, added to the stampede of a small gang of lawmakers from the legislative hall, constituted a spectacle that was neither creditable nor edifying."[35]

After repeated failures, Republicans hoped for a quorum on September 23. Even though some members had returned to Washington, they were short when voting began. Republicans stalled to give members more time to arrive. When Representative Sweney entered, he was greeted with hugs. Democrats had to keep one person in the chamber to call no quorum. Counting the lone Democrat, the minimal quorum of 166 members was met. Republican papers delighted in the irony: "He remained in the hall to make the point of no quorum [but] was caught and counted by the Speaker as the 166th member present."[36] After unseating Venable, Republicans voted to seat the Republican Langston and immediately gave him the oath of office.

What happened next came as a surprise to most members, including absent Democrats. Republicans brought forward another election case from South Carolina. In a matter of seconds and with no debate, Republicans voted to unseat Democrat William Elliott and seat Republican Thomas Miller. Given the unexpected turn of events, it is not surprising that Miller was not on hand to be sworn in. Whatever swearing was done was by Democrats after they discovered what had happened. In about five minutes, the Republican majority had increased from 173–153 to 175–151.

With the session ending in a week, attention turned to finishing major legislation. Most importantly, the tariff bill was emerging from conference. The conference committee had done little to mute the high tariffs in the original House bill. It was passed by both houses and signed by the president. It became the final major law in the historic first session of the Fifty-First Congress, which had both transformed parliamentary procedure and made major substantive shifts in public policy.

Reed Rebuffed

Afflicted with smallpox, President Lincoln reportedly said, "Tell all the office-seekers to come at once, for now I have something I can give to all of them."[37] He was expressing the widespread frustration with the seemingly endless number of job seekers who occupied so much time of elected officials. In an era before civil-service protection, federal government positions were filled on a largely partisan basis. Members of the president's party in Congress, in particular, had the prerogative to make recommendations for filling various federal positions in their constituency. People who wanted federal jobs applied to their member of Congress in hopes of being recommended. For the individual job applicant, the stakes were high as the process was used to fill many of the best jobs in the federal government, including postmasters and customs house officers. From the perspective of members of Congress, the process was a mixed blessing since they could distribute scarce and valuable jobs to electoral supporters but ran the risk of alienating people who did not get the job. After finishing the time consuming and politically risky process of making a recommendation, members of Congress expected to have their recommendation accepted. Even though Congress established a civil service through the Pendleton Act of 1883 in the aftermath of President Garfield's assassination by a disgruntled job seeker, it started as a small "hodgepodge,"[38] and pressure on members lessened only slightly.

During the final days of the session, Reed pressured not only Democrats on policy matters but also Republican President Benjamin Harrison on appointing Portland's port collector—a position that had been vacant for almost half a year. The collector was widely considered the most important federal position in the state because of its high pay and its usefulness as a political-machine power base. Symbolic of the power of collectors at major ports was that Chester Arthur took the presidential oath just three years after serving as collector of the port of New York.

The appointment for collector reflected a power struggle in Maine. On one side, Fred Dow was being championed by both US senators from Maine and Secretary of State James Blaine. Dow had previously held the position but was removed by Democrat Grover Cleveland for political reasons. On the other side, Reed supported Wes Milliken for the position. Further, Reed hated Fred Dow. While Reed and Dow allegedly did not get along as schoolmates in Portland, their professional animosity probably began when Attorney General Reed insisted on suing Fred's father, Neal Dow, on a decades-old debt that other Republican politicians in Maine had chosen not to pursue. Soon after, the two emerged as Republican rivals whose relationship was marked by intermittent political slights and animosity. The rift exploded when Fred Dow was appointed collector in 1883 by President Arthur on the advice of Maine senators without consulting Reed.[39]

On September 29, 1890, President Harrison appointed Fred Dow as collector for Portland. In an unusual step, the Senate did not refer his appointment to committee but immediately confirmed him. Reed supporters were outraged. Reed had repeatedly backed administration policies and used his power to allow Harrison to avoid tough vetoes, most notably on the silver bill. The *Whig and Courier* editorialized, "We fear that it will look to the country as ungracious as would be disciplining and humiliation of a successful commander in the very presence of the troops he had just led to a brilliant victory."[40] For his part, Reed "fulminated against Harrison in profane language" and never again had cordial relations with him.[41] Democrats, on the other hand, mocked Republican infighting: "Two insignificant citizens of Maine wanted the proud position of collector of taxes on cabbage-heads, potatoes, cheeses, beans, peas . . . etc. and this glorious land of the free and home of the brave, has been shaken."[42]

Despite his anger over the Dow appointment, Speaker Reed was eager to take the Republican record of achievement to the people in the national campaign. Since he had already won reelection in Maine's early elections, Reed traveled to districts where he determined that his visit could "do the most good" for other congressional Republicans.[43] On a typical day, Reed appeared at one or two major events, where he spoke in front of audiences ranging from three thousand to fifteen thousand. His hour-long major speeches were often supplemented with five-or-ten minute speeches at train depots. Parliamentary procedure was a key topic. Reed blasted Democrats for the quorum fight: "I don't deny that empty benches may very often properly represent the Democratic Party. . . . Nevertheless, a sensible people do not pay men $5,000 a year in order to procure their absence. There are a lot of men here who would stay away from almost anything at a less price than that."[44]

Reed's campaign speeches described the Republicans as the party of action while Democrats were the party of criticism. He suggested that "the Republican Party must take positive ground on some known spot of earth" while Democrats "are free then to skirmish through the rest of creation."[45] Although he saw party identification as mostly fixed, Reed considered the Republican commitment to majority rule as the type of issue that could draw in other voters: "There are times, I say, when men have an opportunity to free themselves from partisan bias, to express their faith in the fundamental principles which underlie the free government of this country."[46] Naturally, Reed saw the party changers as Democrats being won over to Republican ideas. He, however, did leave open the possibility for a Republican to switch to the Democratic Party. He told his audiences about a Republican who "tired of progress" and, consequently, "became tired of the Republican Party, and had to be pitched out at the tail end of the Republican cart, when he found himself at the head of the Democratic Party."[47]

Reed's campaign tour gave the highest priority to his friend William McKinley. He spent three days in Ohio where McKinley was in electoral trouble because his district had been gerrymandered. Reed's appearances in

McKinley's district drew wide attention from the press. Democratic papers relished the chance to hit two Republican leaders at once, such as the *Daily Critic* evoking the famous nicknames of each: "The Czar and Napoleon are now friends and allies, and the former will respond to the latter's cry for help and go over into the latter's district and endeavor to bamboozle the Buckeyes into returning the High Priest of Protection to Congress."[48]

After stumping for McKinley, Reed moved farther west to an area of the country where the residents did not know him very well. They were eager to be acquainted. On October 21, Reed went to Champaign, Illinois. He spoke to an audience of ten thousand, boosted by the university giving a half-day holiday to students. He then traveled to Peoria, where he was well received by a large Republican evening audience. Democratic newspapers were less sanguine about how Reed played in Peoria. Reviewing his Illinois speeches, the *Herald* highlighted Reed's regional idiosyncrasies: "Mr. Speaker has an apparently congenital detestation of one letter in His Majesty's alphabet; there is no *r* in the lexicon of the Yankee who talks about the democratic pa'ty and who introduces 'wuh' as the equivalent of an old word called in these regions 'were.'"[49]

While Republicans greeted Reed as a conquering hero, Democrats intensified their attacks. He was regularly criticized for supporting monopolies and the tariff. The Democratic Party distributed a campaign document in all districts in mid-October featuring the Reed quote, "Thank God the House of Representatives is no longer a deliberative body." Reed's first visit to cities also seemed to open the door for Democratic editors to mock his physical appearance. Calling him "Baby Elephant Reed,"[50] the *Chicago Herald* dispensed with the subtext: "He presents the spectacle of a large, fat man in hard times." When Reed was joined by a band on stage, the *Herald* reported, "Sometimes his hands were uplifted and sometimes his back was bent so that his paunch rested on the head of the tuba player."[51]

Ultimately, Reed's campaign trip failed to produce the desired results. It was not for lack of effort. Reed traveled for an entire month and, when he left New York on November 1, he was exhausted and suffering from a cold. Republicans lost the seat in almost every district that Reed had visited. The losing candidates who hosted Reed in their district were not low-hanging fruit. They included such distinguished Republicans as two future Speakers of the House (Henderson, Cannon), a future vice president (Sherman), and a future president (McKinley). In assessing the success of Reed's tour, the *Springfield Republican* looked to history: "In all American history it is doubtful if such another political stumping tour, attended by equal noise and so humiliating results, can be found."[52] Overall, Democrats picked up nearly eighty House seats to turn their minority into a nearly 150-seat majority in the next Congress. The *Morning World-Herald* offered an infelicitous interpretation of the results: "Speaker Reed will now have an opportunity to go out and hang himself with his own sash."[53]

The electoral defeat left Reed dejected and looking for answers. In a letter to friend and fellow sash wearer Henry Cabot Lodge, Reed wrote, "Well I find it a trifle difficult to put the thing into words! Don't you? It looks just for the moment as if this was a world made mostly for cowards and laggards and sneaks."[54] He also blamed President Harrison: "A party which was yelling for its Chief Betrayer hardly deserved a better fate."[55] Publicly, he tried to blame the defeat on unrealistic expectations about the tariff bill since prices rose quickly but benefits took longer. Asked by a reporter why his party had lost, Reed reportedly said, "The women did it,"[56] even though the only women who had cast congressional ballots were in the Republican state of Wyoming. Writing in the *North American Review,* Reed explained, "Every woman who went to a store and tried to buy went home to complain."[57] Whatever the cause of the defeat, Reed started looking ahead. In his November 5, 1890, letter to Lodge, he advised: "However there is but one thing to do and that is close the ranks for the next fight."[58]

Lame Duck Sprinting

Having absorbed an electoral drubbing, House Republicans faced the question of whether they would press forward with their policies in the lame-duck session. Republicans would control the House until the Fifty-First Congress adjourned on March 4, 1891. They still had rare unified control of the major branches of government. Yet, the electorate had repudiated their policies and procedures. What would Reed do? There is no evidence to suggest that this was a difficult decision for him. Reed pressed forward.

Opposing Democrats had the calendar on their side. House Republicans had two months to complete legislation, which could still be held up in the Senate. Above all, Democrats wanted to run out the clock on the bill establishing federal oversight of southern elections. In resisting legislation, Democrats reminded Republicans about the 1890 election. On January 19, William Springer said, "The American people spoke at that election in opposition to the conduct of this House and of the Senate not only upon the rules, but also upon the McKinley bill, and especially upon what is known as the force bill or the elections bill." Springer concluded that Reed and the Republicans were "defying the voice of the people and endeavoring to force that bill upon us in the closing hours of a Congress which has been repudiated most emphatically by the people of this country."[59]

Any obstruction in the House was short lived. On February 20, Democrats offered a dilatory motion to recapitulate a vote, which would verify the outcome. Reed replied, "The Chair is of the opinion that there is no possibility of any error existing which can affect the result in the record of a vote of 150 to 8."[60] Yet such tallies could still run into quorum troubles, and in Reed's eagerness to count a quorum, he counted some members who were not in the chamber during the roll call.

This drew a stern rebuke from Charles Crisp, who said that he had been out of the building when the roll call began. Crisp explained, "I merely desire to say this, so that the House and the country may understand the method in which the presiding officer of this House makes up and falsifies this record."[61]

This counting error became the centerpiece of an impeachment resolution on February 23. Whereas Reed had improperly counted a quorum to advance legislation that would provide jobs to Republicans, a Democratic resolution proposed a constitutional amendment establishing an impeachment procedure for House Speakers. Under the proposal, falsifying a quorum count was "a high crime or misdemeanor with such penalties by fine and imprisonment, removal from office, and disqualification for holding office."[62] Predictably, the proposal went nowhere.

While Reed thwarted Democratic delay in the House, he could not do anything about delay in the Senate. Most disappointing to him would have been the failure of the Senate to pass the bill providing federal oversight of national elections to guarantee voting rights for blacks. Early on, it was recognized that the intensity of the opposition meant that the bill would not pass the Senate without a rules change. On one key occasion, Vice President Morton, who frequently presided over the Senate, refused to follow Reed's example and count a quorum by including those present and not voting.[63] The Senate Republican caucus had reportedly agreed to press forward with the bill, even if it took a rules change. The support of the caucus declined as time passed. The ostensible majority for a "Reed-like solution" had evaporated by the second session.[64] A group of Republicans made a deal with Democrats to set aside electoral reform to move forward with other legislation.

This had profound consequences, according to historian Thomas Upchurch: "The defeat of the Federal Elections Bill marked a turning point in American history. . . . Not until the advent of the civil rights movement more than a half-century later would African Americans be able to count on the federal government to protect their rights."[65]

On the last night of the session, William McKinley visited the Democratic side of the House to find someone to offer the customary resolution of thanks to the Speaker. By tradition the resolution was given by a member of the opposing party. In the previous Congress, for example, Reed himself had presented the resolution thanking Democratic Speaker Carlisle, which was approved unanimously. McKinley inquired about which Democrat would be willing to offer the resolution. It was a final task for deputy leader McKinley in a successful collaboration that historian Edward Heald characterized as the affable McKinley having "smoothed over rough spots left by Reed's harshness."[66] On this occasion, however, the social skills of McKinley were no match for Democratic resentment of Reed's leadership. He returned to the Republican side without a volunteer. McKinley would have to take the unusual step of presenting the resolution himself.

Before the resolution was offered, the House met all night, wrapping up the business of the legislative session. Time was dwindling before the session ended at noon on March 4. Some Democrats were counting every minute. Springer proclaimed, "The country is to be congratulated that the era of Treasury-looting is now at a close. Only 55 minutes more of opportunity to put your hands in the people's Treasury and squander the people's money."[67] Beyond the usual anticipation of the end of the session, there was interest in the gratitude resolution. Newspapers had been reporting that the Democrats would give a lengthy speech against the resolution. Reed left the chair and allowed a deputy to preside. McKinley's resolution stated, "Resolved, That the thanks of this House are presented to the Hon. Thomas B. Reed for the able, impartial, and dignified manner in which he has presided over its deliberations and performed the arduous and important duties of the Chair."[68] Opting against a speech, Democrats simply asked for the yeas and nays.

The vote on the resolution to thank the Speaker would be no ordinary roll call. Members voted definitively over the crowd, which was so large that family members of representatives were allowed on the floor. Democrat William Cowles proclaimed, "Not, no, put me down twice if you can." Another technique for voting no twice was when Democrat Thomas Skinner was called and his young daughter mimicked her father with another loud "no," to the delight of Democrats.[69] Republicans also gave demonstrative votes. When the roll call ended, the vote stood 151–116. On the resolution thanking Speaker Reed for his impartiality, every Republican had voted yes and every Democrat had voted no. A loud roar arose from the Republican side when it was announced that the resolution carried.

Taking the chair, Reed said, "Political action can never be justly viewed from a near standpoint; Time and distance are needed for a ripe judgment, and the verdict of history is the only verdict worth recording." He offered an early verdict "that the highest commendation will be given us in the future." Reed ended on a personal note: "To members on my left, with whom I am politically associated, I beg to tender my most sincere and heartfelt acknowledgements. No man ever received more ungrudging and unflinching support from a band of men more unselfish and more patriotic. . . . The honors of the Fifty-First Congress belong to you alone."[70]

The refusal by Democrats to support the resolution to thank Speaker Reed drew much attention. Democratic newspapers piled on by saying that Reed had received more "no" votes on the resolution of thanks than any other Speaker ever—a record that he would keep for more than a century. The *Argus* explained, "Mr. Reed was the first Speaker who had to get a party friend to introduce such a resolution, and the first Speaker to have every vote of his opponents recorded against him."[71] Republican newspapers asked readers to consider the source. The *New-York Tribune* editorialized, "It is a great compliment to him that the lawless and revolutionary members refused their assent to the vote of thanks."[72]

Following the close of the Fifty-First Congress, Republicans celebrated their legislative achievements. The *Philadelphia Inquirer* editorialized that more had never been "accomplished . . . by any party in time of peace."[73] At a gathering of prominent Republicans on March 6, Reed summarized the achievement of the Fifty-First Congress: "We have shown to the people of the United States that there is in this country a possibility of responsible government."[74] This set him up for an easy criticism by the Democratic *Sun* later in the week: "It must be sad, however, for Mr. Reed to reflect that the people of the United States declared with so much vehemence last fall that they didn't want responsible government in which Mr. Reed was responsible for the government."[75]

Another speaker at the dinner was Republican rising star Theodore Roosevelt who mocked the idea of Reed as a polarizing figure. Roosevelt explained, "To hold the Speaker in any wise responsible for the inevitable friction and disorder produced by the suppression of filibustering is a good deal like holding a sheriff to account because in capturing a dangerous and brutal criminal it is sometimes impossible to avoid a fight." Roosevelt looked to the future: "Beyond question the historian who in the future shall write a history of representative government through a legislative assembly will have to credit Speaker Reed" who is owed "a great debt [from] all those all over the world who believe in responsible popular government."[76]

While Republicans congratulated themselves, Democrats took a different perspective on the legislative output. Privately, Democrats condemned "the most disagreeable Congress"[77] and celebrated "the good news that the 51st Congress was dead."[78] Publicly, on March 9, the Democratic New York *Sun* used historical appropriations committee data to conclude that federal spending had increased from never more than $820 million in previous Congresses to $1,009,270,471 in the Fifty-First Congress. The Fifty-First Congress had just got a nickname. The New York *Sun* christened it the "Billion Dollar Congress." It placed the Fifty-First Congress in a historical context: "It has been no ordinary season of extravagance and prodigality. It has been a rake-hell orgy of expenditure."[79] The Republican shattering of previous spending records became the overriding theme in Democratic papers that lampooned the "Billion Dollar Congress."

The Democratic christening of the "Billion Dollar Congress" prompted one of Speaker Reed's most famous quotes that he did not originate. The Republican defense of federal government expansion was framed mostly as the size of government catching up to the rapidly growing population. Reed himself used this argument in a March 6 speech: "This country, with 60,000,000 of people, cannot be governed as this country could be governed when it had but 3,000,000."[80] The argument caught on that the United States had become a "billion dollar country." Many publications at the time and through the present give Reed credit for originating the aphorism "billion-dollar country." The phrase, however, did not originate with Reed. In a *North American Review* article, Reed praised the "Billion-Dollar Country" argument for increased government spending but implied that he had not come up with the phrase.[81]

Posterity has also given Reed and the Fifty-First Congress credit for things that actually happened. It is not the two big priorities of tariff reform and currency policy that have the most enduring legacy. It is the other legislation that got cleared from a long backlog of measures awaiting action. The Fifty-First Congress, for example, passed the Sherman Antitrust Act, the first major regulation of business consolidation and the foundation of monopoly regulation into the twenty-first century. By establishing a role for the federal government in certifying food quality, the Meat Inspection Act of 1891 was a forerunner of broader federal regulation of economic activity.[82] The Fifty-First Congress laid the foundation for a strong navy by authorizing three new battleships in the Navy Act of 1890. After two decades of failed forestry bills, the Fifty-First Congress passed the Forest Reserve Act, which authorized the president to set aside land as a national forest; it has been called "the most important legislation in the history of Forestry in America" by Gifford Pinchot.[83] French spoliation claims languishing for over a century were cleared, and a direct tax from the Civil War was refunded. The expansion of pensions for veterans whose disabilities were unrelated to the Civil War in the Dependent Pension Act of 1890 established a broader entitlement that is seen by modern scholars as a "milestone in the development of American welfare policy."[84] Two new states were admitted to the union during the Fifty-First Congress. Addressing a backlog of cases for an overworked Supreme Court, the Fifty-First Congress established the modern judiciary by adding an intermediate level, the Circuit Court of Appeals, between the district courts and the Supreme Court. Congress also passed a copyright law, which Theodore Roosevelt credited to rule changes that helped erase the "lasting shame to us that this [copyright] law was not enacted fifty years ago."[85]

More than policy, however, posterity has credited the Fifty-First Congress with fundamentally transforming congressional procedure. At the outset of the Fifty-First Congress, the House was overdue for a pendulum shift away from extreme obstruction in the direction of greater efficiency. An obvious target would have been a reduction in the prerogative of a single person to tie up the House for days. This was a predictable pendulum shift that would have been likely under competent leadership. This is not what happened in the Fifty-First Congress. Reed was not content to ride a pendulum shift to marginal change in the direction of more efficiency. Against fierce resistance, Reed and the Republicans fundamentally changed how the House legislates. By stopping filibustering, Republicans obtained final votes on bills. They also shifted the operation of the Rules committee to strengthen agenda control. Even though Speaker Carlisle had on rare occasions used the Rules committee to bring a bill to the floor out of order on a simple majority vote, Congress had not adopted another special rule that changed standing rules for an individual bill since Reed's 1883 special rule. Reed and Republicans institutionalized the special rule that had been a one-off in 1883 by approving ten special rules, including six that can be characterized as restrictive.[86] Significantly more than before, the House majority party determined which proposals would obtain final votes. In an official House document, Library of Congress historian George Galloway summarized the change: "By empowering the Speaker to prevent obstruction, the reforms of 1890 went far to regularize House procedure, to expedite the conduct of its business, to enhance its dignity, and to fix legislative responsibility upon the majority."[87]

The extraordinary leadership skills required to transform the intransigent House was recognized by those who participated in the process. Besides Reed, the closest to the situation would have been the two Republican members who joined him on the five-person Rules committee that was responsible for parliamentary procedure in the chamber. These were Joseph Cannon and William McKinley, who would go on to become a powerful House Speaker and a president, respectively. In reflecting on the events of the Fifty-First Congress, Joseph Cannon said that only Reed could have accomplished what was done. Cannon acknowledged that despite his leadership skills and those of McKinley, the two of them were not up to the task of transformation.[88] After challenging Reed for the Speakership as a more conciliatory alternative, McKinley told audiences after the Fifty-First Congress that he would "undo" his challenge with hindsight about "what this great leader has done."[89]

The passage of time and the application of modern methodological techniques have reaffirmed the importance of Reed's leadership skills in guiding the Fifty-First Congress to revolutionary change. Modern political scientists have created impressive data sets that try to explain procedural changes across all Congresses with an array of institutional variables such as ideological cohesion of members. It remains difficult to understand the dramatic change of the Fifty-First Congress without acknowledging Reed's leadership ability. Douglas Dion, for example, found that explanations of historical procedural changes necessitated including Reed in his model. In mathematical terms, Reed was operationalized as a dummy variable (0=absent; 1=present) that was statistically significant in a positive direction at the high .001 level of statistical significance.[90]

Accounting for the quality of Reed's leadership presents a challenge not only for modern math but also for vocabulary. Scholar William Riker decided to make up a word for the type of leadership that Reed represents, explaining, "Thomas B. Reed, a bold, creative parliamentarian . . . carried off one of the greatest heresthetical maneuvers."[91] Reed's actions no doubt were heretical to established practices in the House, but the middle "esth" takes them to an entirely different strategic level. Riker coined the term "heresthetics" to represent leadership that structures choices to make victory more likely, such as how Reed made it difficult for his caucus to oppose him. Riker, however, undersells Reed's heresthetical legacy as one maneuver. Reed created a Congress that has repeatedly empowered majority-party leaders to use the Rules committee to structure choices to make victory more likely.

Ultimately, whatever words or numbers are used, the inescapable conclusion is that Reed demonstrated tremendous leadership skills in the Fifty-First Congress. He was willing to risk his Speakership for the principle of majority rule. Reed identified the most favorable conditions under which to take the risk. A number of Republicans were skeptical of eliminating the disappearing quorum, which they had practiced recently themselves and might one day want to practice again. Reed chose to apply the principle to the facts of a contested-election case on which Republicans would agree.[92] Rather than allowing obstruction and hype to build, Reed surprised even his top deputies by counting a quorum. As a new leader, he set the tone and did not allow old practices to reemerge.

While Reed's leadership stands the test of time, the immediate verdict must also be recognized. Reed and House Republicans endured a disastrous electoral outcome. The 1890 election reduced their seat share from a majority to 26 percent, which shattered the record for lowest returning percentage for a previous majority party held by the House Whigs, which went from a majority to 32 percent in the 1842 election.[93] Thus, when the terms of dozens of defeated Republicans ended on March 4, 1891, they were heading to private life. Although Reed remained on the public payroll, the *Ohio Democrat* said that "Reed is as powerless as the smallest politician in America . . . and he will never more be allowed to boss the House."[94] The *New York Times* suggested that Reed should headline a speaker series with his defeated colleagues. It contemplated some of the lectures that Reed might be able to deliver, including "When I Was a Czar: A Narrative of Personal Experience" and "The Rights of the Minority: A Farce with Some of My Rulings for Illustrations."[95] From Reed's perspective, this would not be such a bad idea. He could use the money.

Portrait of a Leader

If any House Speaker had ever earned a vacation, it was Reed, who sailed for a three-month European vacation on March 21, 1891. Describing his time in Italy to his friend George Gifford, Reed wrote, "The paintings, churches, monuments, and countryside gave me all the pleasures of youth." Reed got a chance in Paris to try out the French that he had been practicing for so many years. In his letter to Gifford, Reed reflected on the outcome: "I am able to speak French like a native—of the U.S."[96] A reporter from the French daily *Le Figaro* who interviewed Reed describes him as speaking French reasonably well, if in the American manner of plodding to the correct words. Even when Reed misspoke, the reporter found a "cachet d'originalité"[97] that did nothing to undermine "l'erudition vaste"[98] of Reed. Regardless of Reed's proficiency, he found the French to be patient with his struggles and wrote Gifford, "We can butcher the language and nobody ever laughs."[99]

Ultimately, the legacy of Reed's time in Paris is the portrait of him by John Singer Sargent. Before the Fifty-First Congress closed, a group of Republican congressmen led by Henry Cabot Lodge, who had been painted by Sargent the previous year, each contributed fifty dollars to commission a portrait of Reed. Taking longer than planned, Sargent summarized the painting challenge in a letter to an art patron: "His [Reed's] exterior does not somehow correspond with his spirit and what is a painter to do?"[100] Sargent wrote his friend Augustus Saint-Gaudens, presumably in jest, about his problems capturing Reed: "Perhaps a full length nude would have been the thing to do."[101] Despite his musings, Sargent completed a conventional portrait of a politician, including a serious expression and head illumination to show thinking.

When the final product was displayed at the Capitol later in 1891, the immediate reaction was less than enthusiastic. The *New York Times* art critic described it as "a picture without salient qualities . . . [that] has made Mr. Reed out a decidedly commonplace large person, with a very thick neck."[102] Democratic papers had a field day with the portrait. Even the rare Democratic critic who credited Sargent with matching Reed's spirit used it against Reed: "Czar Reed's portrait, which now adorns a wall in the national capitol, is said to be atrociously bad. So is its subject." [103] Publicly, Reed played along with the notion that the portrait was not good. Standing by the portrait with others, he said, "I hope my enemies are satisfied now."[104]

Privately, Reed expressed satisfaction with the painting. After Sargent had finished, Reed wrote Lodge and said that he was pleased with the effort: "I am under the dreadful thrall under which I am told all Mr. Sargent's subjects are, and am not in the least moved by the criticism of so many, except perhaps I am willing to admit that the picture is not so good looking as the original."[105] After it was hung in a House gallery, Reed cared enough to ask Speaker Crisp to move the painting so it would receive better light. This vanity prompted a jibe from the Democratic *Brooklyn Citizen*: "If Reed could only get out of the bad light in which he placed himself as easily he would have less to fear than he has from the impartial judgement of history."[106]

The passage of time has not significantly improved the reputation of the portrait. Some scholars have incorporated the picture into a theme that Sargent was more successful depicting women and children than powerful men. One Sargent biographer dispenses with broader themes and attributes the picture's flaws to Reed: "Reed's huge bulging figure was not acutely pictorial . . . [and] seemed more an image of an overstuffed porker than a Speaker of the House."[107] Despite its modest artistic reputation, the Reed portrait is probably the most valuable painting in the House Speaker's lobby and was part of the 2007 debate about whether Congress erred in exempting the lobby from a smoking ban that applied to other public buildings in Washington.[108]

Ultimately, the painting symbolizes the difficulty of capturing the essence of Reed. If the calling card of a portrait painter is to evoke the strongest characteristic of the sitter, the paradoxes of Reed pose a challenge. Although some observers have claimed to find the essence of Reed in the Sargent portrait, they have identified different essences. Most notably, in a rare complimentary review, the art critic for *Harper's* in 1891 saw a face "where force and humor join."[109] Another art critic said that it captured his essential "truculent" attitude.[110] Reed could certainly demonstrate all these characteristics. It is easy to regard Reed as a challenging sitter for a portrait painter without resorting to the juvenile "porker"[111] name-calling by some Sargent partisans. Perhaps Sargent himself said it best: "Mr. Reed's portrait was a difficult job."[112]

Despite the challenges, Sargent was not the only prominent artist who depicted Reed. Of course, editorial cartoonists could not get enough of Reed or make him large enough. Indifferent to scale, editorial cartoonists attached Reed's head to midsections as large as the Capitol. Compared to editorial cartoonists, the sculptor Burr Miller's depiction of Reed is downright modest. Miller decided that eight feet tall would be sufficient. The sculpture, which like Sargent's portrait was made in Paris by an American, conveys how Reed towered over the House as it graces the Western Promenade in Portland. Another larger-than-life image of Reed was made by Frederic Vinton, whose full-body portrait is displayed in Maine's statehouse, where Reed once served as state legislator. Although his work on Mount Rushmore qualifies as larger-than-life, Gutzon Borglum opted for the traditional bust size in his sculpture of Reed that is housed in the Capitol.

Returning from Europe, Reed spent several days in late 1891 in Ohio campaigning for his friend William McKinley, who was running for governor. Reed stayed one night at the home of Cleveland businessman Mark Hanna, McKinley's campaign adviser and fundraiser. Hanna had managed McKinley's failed campaign to win the Speakership against Reed in December 1889. Now on the same side, Hanna and Reed enjoyed their time together. After the visit, Reed wrote McKinley to tell him that his time with the Hanna family was spent "so delightfully . . . that if you ever want to coax me to do anything you had better send Hanna."[113] The goodwill was mutual as Hanna described Reed as a "charming" guest.[114] According to a Republican paper, audiences were also charmed by the former Speaker: "They discovered him to be the jolliest and best natured czar that ever came to Ohio to rule for an hour over the judgment of the buckeyes who crowded about to hear him."[115] After the votes had been counted, Reed telegraphed McKinley: "I am much rejoiced over your victory."[116]

CHAPTER 7

GLADLY TAKES OWN MEDICINE

On December 8, 1891, House Republicans gathered to select their leadership for the upcoming Fifty-Second Congress. The caucus was now so small that the traditional congressional seating arrangement of two sides and an aisle was abandoned as Democrats spilled over into what they called "conquered territory" on the Republican side.[1] Given the magnitude of the 1890 defeat and Reed's role as a target for Democratic attacks during the campaign, would House Republicans select a new leader to give them a fresh start? For his part, Reed was running again to remain leader. In the weeks prior to the meeting, it had become apparent that no opposition was emerging. After Reed was unanimously reelected, the Democratic *World* editorialized that House Republicans had shown the "courage of their catastrophe."[2]

While the defeated Republicans were off to a smooth start, the victorious Democrats were not. After seventeen ballots at the caucus meeting, no candidate had a majority so Democrats adjourned for the night without a leader even though the start of Congress was imminent. The standstill prompted one newspaper to propose a compromise candidate: "Mills, Crisp, and Springer might settle their quarrel by uniting on ex-Speaker Reed. Each would then have ample revenge on the other and the country would not suffer."[3] With time running out, Democrats settled on Charles Crisp, not only because his less ambitious policy goals alienated fewer members but also because of the parliamentary skill that he had demonstrated in his clashes with Reed. Reflecting on the Democratic start, Reed later wrote, "When the House of Representatives of the Fifty-second Congress met, it met as a mob, and has kept up that interesting form of organization ever since."[4]

Although they were outnumbered three to one, Reed and House Republicans were well positioned in the Fifty-Second Congress. First, the broader political environment ensured that laws passed by the Fifty-First Congress would not be reversed despite the electoral landslide. The year 1890 was not a presidential election year so Republican Benjamin Harrison remained president. With only one-third of seats contested in 1890, Republicans kept a narrow majority in the Senate. Second, House Democrats were deeply divided. These divisions were especially prominent on the two major economic issues of the day. On currency reform, southern and western Democrats favoring more inflationary policies, especially free-silver coinage, were opposed by hard-money eastern Democrats. There were also divisions on tariff policy not only over the level of tariffs but also over whether to take a piecemeal or wholesale approach to revision. The combination of these factors put Reed in an enviable position. He could taunt House Democrats into pursuing policies that fostered internal conflict, knowing that they would never be enacted.

Democrats were eager to refight some of the battles from the last Congress. On January 26, 1892, Democrats proposed rules similar to the Fiftieth Congress, which had been plagued by filibustering. Most noticeably, the disappearing quorum was permitted. Alternatively, the Republican minority proposed retaining the majority-empowering rules of the Fifty-First Congress. The irony that the Republican minority proposed rules that empowered majority rule while the Democratic majority proposed rules that empowered minority obstruction was widely recognized.

The opening day of debate on the rules was marked by Reed's denial of the accusation that he had been inconsistent in supporting the disappearing quorum in 1880 as a minority member and eliminating it in 1890 as Speaker. Reed took the chamber back to his famous 1880 speech in which he defended the disappearing quorum as essential to liberty: "It seems to me that it would be a suitable and proper reply to say to him that the constitutional idea of a quorum is not the presence of a majority of the members of the House, but a majority of the members present and participating in the business of the House."[5] Reed said that he had "purposefully and intentionally" prefaced his remarks with the verb "seems" to reflect doubts that he was already entertaining about the practice. Reed suggested that he offered this qualification to allow him to revisit the issue: "I had at that far distant time my own ideas about it, from not the slightest examination, and in the hurry and rush of debate I said 'it would seem' to be a sufficient answer to speak as I did."[6]

During most of the ten-day rules debate, Reed developed a broader theme that the majority should rule. He asked, "Why am I desirous that the majority should rule? It is because it will give to the people of the United States whenever they go to an election a sense that an election really means something; that it is a decision; that it is a determination on their part, not a whim to be corrected afterwards by the House of Representatives manacling itself."[7] In a *North American Review* article published during the debate, Reed argued that the American political system had "so many safeguards" in the form of an executive and two different legislative chambers that action was already difficult without a new obstacle. He wrote, "If to all these be added the divine right of a minority to stop all business, surely this government, of which we have made rather frequent and obtrusive boasting as being a government of the people, is only an irresponsible despotism."[8]

Defending their rules, Democrats argued that voters rejected Reed's actions in November 1890. Democratic Rules committee member Benton McMillin described the election outcome: "The gentleman from Maine himself was hurled from the Chair and put back on the floor."[9] Representative Thomas Catchings alleged that Reed was refusing to hear the people's message: "The country has heard the gentleman's attempt to vindicate himself; he has discussed this question until it is threadbare; he has made speeches and written magazine articles, and the country has passed judgment upon him."[10]

The most literary approach to tying Reed's rules to the electoral outcome was an extended analogy from Benjamin Enloe. He suggested that the Republican electoral casualties from Reed's aggressive rule changes evoked a famous episode from the Crimean War: "When I remembered how the gentleman and his party had charged over the minority in this House . . . I thought how like it was to the charge of the Light Brigade." Democrats laughed at Enloe's allusion of how bad leadership had led the British cavalry into a brave, but suicidal, charge into a valley occupied by enemy Russians. Enloe then adapted Alfred Lord Tennyson's 1854 poem immortalizing the Light Brigade to Reed's House leadership: "Their leader had blundered. . . . All that was left of them, Less than one hundred."[11]

Another consistent Democratic theme was the hypocrisy of Republicans generally and Reed in particular. Indeed, much of Democratic criticism was directed at Reed personally, which was partly by default since just about every other prominent House Republican had been defeated in the 1890 bloodbath. Reed's 1880 speech defending the disappearing quorum was cited repeatedly by Democrats, who praised it as no less than "the most lucid and conclusive statement of our view of the [quorum] question . . . ever uttered by mortal man."[12] Reed was challenged directly on the hypocrisy issue on February 2, 1892. Representative Bynum asked, "Will he tell us why it was, then, that in the different Congresses in which he was in a minority he was always found among the filibusterers?"

Reed replied, "Simply because I exercised the power that was given me by the House and . . . it may be done again. Do you not see that if the House gives permission for piracy some gentleman may choose to go into that interesting and lucrative business?"

"That is," Bynum responded, "you want the rule to keep you from being bad?"

Reed replied, "I want it not only to keep me from being bad for I shall need it, but also to keep a good many other gentlemen from being bad who will need it a good deal more."[13]

Perhaps no Democrat delighted in Reed's predicament more than William Springer. During the rules debate, Reed explained why he was quoting Springer's 1880 speech opposing the disappearing quorum: "I do not, of course charge that the gentleman from Illinois . . . entertains that opinion now, [but] I read it to the House upon account of its inherent beauty and to have the continued weight of his authority." Springer's recourse was obvious. He read extended quotes from Reed's 1880 speech supporting the disappearing quorum. The scene of Reed quoting Springer and Springer quoting Reed was too much for other members to take. Representative Allen inquired, "Would it not be well, in order to stop this controversy between the gentleman from Illinois and the gentleman from Maine, that the gentleman from Illinois adopt the speech made years ago by the gentleman from Maine and the gentleman from Maine adopt the speech made by the gentleman from Illinois."[14]

Emboldened Democrats attacked the weakened Reed for even minor inconsistencies. During the rules debate, Reed criticized many of the smaller reversals that Democrats had made that would hinder majority action. He lamented that Democrats had returned to "a morning hour that is limited to sixty minutes"[15] instead of continuing the Republican practice of allowing the morning hour to be expanded to pass more legislation. He also supported an amendment that would minimize time lost to memorial services by arguing that memorial observances in the last Congress had consumed "over twenty-four days, nearly a month."[16] This gave Representative Asher Caruth a narrow opening to ridicule Reed. Caruth lampooned, "My friend from Maine . . . has such peculiar ideas upon the subject of time that he says twenty-four days make a month, and objects to sixty minutes being an hour."[17]

Finally, on February 4, the House approved the Democratic rules. The Republican substitute to retain the rules of the Fifty-First Congress was soundly defeated. Reed warned Democrats that they would come to regret their decision: "I wish I were able, by some miracle or other display of power, to transfer to this audience at the commencement of the session the wisdom and the experience which they will have at the end of it."[18]

Although Democrats generally returned to rules that allowed filibustering, they retained the power of the Rules committee to report special rules. While the Reed Rules gave the Speaker broad authority to reject dilatory motions, Democratic rules tied the power of rejecting dilatory motions and forcing cloture to a special rule from the Rules committee. In granting this power, Democrats arguably conceded the lynchpin of the Reed Rules. This prompted some opposition within the caucus, including Joseph Bailey, who chastised fellow Democrats: "If you adopt this rule, you are estopped hereafter to criticise the Fifty-First Congress and the distinguished gentleman who presided over its deliberations. It embodies the very essence of his philosophy in transacting the public business."[19] Ultimately, the Rules committee power was sold to the Democratic caucus on the basis that special rules would be offered rarely and only if a majority of Democrats agreed. Even if not intended to be used as often, Democrats were validating a central procedural tool pioneered by Reed. An important component of majority rule was being institutionalized in the House. Reed offered mock congratulations to the Democrats for preserving the committee's power: "I hail every advance of the Democratic party with very great satisfaction, because I am a sincere believer in the doctrine that in order to have an army take a new march the rear guard must be got up. I do not say this in any reproachful fashion."[20]

Reed gained another rules victory when the Supreme Court upheld his quorum counting procedure on February 29. During oral argument, the solicitor general and future president William Howard Taft defended as constitutional a law passed in the House when Reed had counted silent Democrats as part of the quorum. Writing for the unanimous Court, Justice Brewer agreed. Article I, Section 5 of the Constitution establishes that "each house may determine the rules of its proceedings" and states that "a majority of each [chamber] shall constitute a quorum to do business." The Court found that one of the rules that Congress was empowered to make was how to ascertain the "presence" of a quorum. Since the Constitution did not specify a specific method for ascertaining whether a quorum was present, Congress could adopt any "reasonable" method. The method adopted by Reed and the Republicans was reasonable and met the minimal constitutional requirement.[21]

Basking in the glow of a Supreme Court victory, Reed claimed one victory that was rightfully his and one that was not. Interviewed about the decision, Reed expressed satisfaction that his actions were upheld despite "the spectacle presented" by Democrats at the time. Reed summarized his view of the ruling for the reporter: "In every variety of expression, the court proclaims the doctrine that the presence of a majority of the members constitutes a quorum."[22] Embracing this interpretation, Reed accused House Democrats of acting in "defiance" of the Supreme Court by not counting silent members as part of the quorum.[23] But Reed was overreaching. The Court listed counting only quorum call respondents as one of several reasonable options open to Congress in ascertaining whether a quorum was present. According to Democrat Henry Turner, the 1890 election showed that the people believed that Reed chose the wrong option: "This question was tried on every stump in the United States, and it was decided by a majority unprecedented in our political annals."[24]

Tired of this attack, Reed rebutted, "The gentleman . . . has seen fit to refer to the last election. . . . [and] that great argument has already been fully exploited. How often in the history of the world have the righteous gone temporarily to the wall. Why, in the year 1653 Oliver Cromwell . . . stayed the persecution of Christians in every land: yet, in 1660 the people of Great Britain, with loud acclamations, welcomed back the monarchy with Charles II." Reed asked, "Which would you rather honor the memory of today: Charles II, admired for the moment by the English people, or Oliver Cromwell, admired by all mankind forever? It is not victories in politics or in war that are finally triumphant, but it is the Lord's truth; it is the sound principles; and in the sign of those principles, the Republican Party will be ultimately victorious."[25] Of course, the implication of Reed's analogy was that American voters had also erred by choosing a Charles II over a Cromwell. With the passage of time, Reed was increasingly blaming a misguided electorate for its repudiation of House Republicans. Reed explained, "Whenever anything is to be done the country elects Republican officers to do it, and then with that strange inconsistency in human nature they generally punish them for doing it."[26]

During the session, Reed received a piece of correspondence that would prompt arguably his most famous epigram. The correspondent asked a simple question: "What is a statesman?" Reed pondered the question and settled on a reply. He wrote, "A statesman is a successful politician who is dead." Proud of his answer, Reed showed it to his friends.[27] His epigram was soon widely circulated in newspapers. Reed's pithy definition of a statesman is now immortalized through wide distribution in print and online.

Knockdown Electoral Arguments

Given that statesmanship was out of earthly reach, Reed was free to plot against the renomination of Republican President Benjamin Harrison. On April 3, 1892, he wrote his friend Henry Cabot Lodge, "How full of peril is this sinful world—B. H. will be beaten *delenda est Carthago*."[28] Carthage must be destroyed; Reed was adapting the Roman desire for total destruction in the Punic Wars to his disagreement about internal Republican Party politics. While not adopting his historical parallels, many Republican leaders shared Reed's doubts about Harrison. Like Reed, a number of these leaders harbored patronage-related grudges. The anti-Harrison forces gravitated to James Blaine, who was endorsed by the chair of the Republican National Committee in May.

Reed followed with his own Blaine endorsement, which was anything but enthusiastic. In a May 31, 1892, letter to his clerk Asher Hinds, Reed framed his choice as the lesser of two evils: "At any rate I could not do anything but say that I preferred J. B. to B. H. by a very small majority—so small that the back towns would have to be estimated to pull through." The same letter showed that Reed preferred a different nominee: "If JGB drops out—which I think he won't do—then I shall act for myself—I shall be in Minneapolis next Monday morning."[29]

Indeed, Reed had a strategy for winning the Republican nomination. It would be a classic dark-horse strategy. The two front-runners, Blaine and Harrison, were both objectionable to significant parts of the party. As long as one of the two did not get a majority on the first ballot, the convention could become wide open. Many of the convention delegates were technically unpledged and had a vested interest in nominating a candidate who increased the likelihood of a Republican win in November. The *Boston Globe* reported, "Well informed Republicans declare that Reed is hoping to stampede the convention, and as a 'dark horse' rush to the front and be nominated for president."[30] If successful, Reed would be following in the footsteps of three of the previous four Republican nominees who had less than 10 percent on the first ballot, including Garfield who went from zero votes on the first ballot to victory on the thirty-sixth ballot in 1880.

On the opening day of the Republican convention in Minneapolis on June 6, 1892, Reed unexpectedly took the leading role. He did not have any formal role in the convention but was merely sitting in the invited guest section of the audience. The convention was occupied with routine business, including adopting the rules of the Fifty-First Congress to govern the convention. When the temporary chair mentioned Reed's role in the Fifty-First Congress, shouts of "Reed" spread through the audience. People waved handkerchiefs and called on him to speak. Reed shook his head to dissuade further encouragement. He relented and delivered what would be difficult to characterize as anything but an undistinguished speech. He described the party's past achievements: "Wealth has been poured into the lap of all our people by the great system which we believe in and which we have carried out."[31] The *Press* summarized the first day's proceedings: "There was a very evident inclination on the part of the delegates today to start out the dark horses on trial heats; but Mr. Reed was the only one who was bold enough to appear on the track and let the spectators see his shape and form."[32]

Reed's hopes for the nomination were dashed a few days later when Harrison secured 59 percent of the first-ballot votes. The implications of the perfunctory Reed effort were unclear. The Democratic *Argus* framed it as a bust for Reed: "Considering that Tommy got only four votes for President in the Minneapolis Convention, it would appear . . . his Presidential bee will buzz no more."[33] This was an unduly harsh assessment since Reed was never an announced candidate and knew his chances depended on a deadlocked convention. Theodore Roosevelt offered a rosier assessment in a letter to Reed: "Not excepting Wolcott or McKinley you made more out of the convention than any one else . . . [and] I believe you have a better chance for a career worthy of your character and capacity than ever before, no matter how disagreeable the situation may be for you at the moment."[34]

Although presidential politics had not worked out, the legislative victories kept coming for Reed. Despite their large majority, Democrats struggled with the disappearing quorum and dilatory motions. House passage of currency legislation required a cloture rule from the Rules committee. When Democrats approved the rule before reading the previous day's journal, Reed proclaimed, "They themselves [Democrats] have overridden what they call the sacred rights of the minority with a heavier horsehoof than they were ever ridden over before."[35] When currency legislation returned on July 13, the House defeated a rule to bring the Senate version to cloture. Angry that Republicans and hard-money Democrats prevented a vote on unlimited silver coinage, Populist Tom Watson spent the next two weeks ignoring House norms by accusing members of being drunk and otherwise lashing out in frustration. When Reed tired of Watson's antics, he left the floor and told a friend that observing Watson had finally enabled him to grasp the full meaning of the Biblical phrase "colt of a wild ass."[36] On August 1, there was a brief government shutdown after a continuing resolution failed to obtain unanimous consent. Four days later, the session ended.

Writing in the *North American Review*, Reed reflected on the session's legacy: "In history it will present all the dead level of a Dutch landscape with all its windmills, but without a trace of its beauty and fertility." The failing grade Reed assigned was largely a product of House rules: "Not only have they done nothing, but at the very beginning they deliberately established a system of rules which made it a foregone conclusion." Reed contrasted the Fifty-Second Congress that had "shirked its duties, and led a gelatinous life, to the scorn of all vertebrate animals" with the Fifty-First Congress that succeeded in "doing all the work put before it."[37] The article drew rave reviews from Theodore Roosevelt, who praised it in a letter to Reed: "I have just read, and reread your 'Two Congresses' in the *North American*; it is the best thing of the kind I have ever seen."[38]

Returning to his district for the 1892 campaign, Reed faced a better-organized Democratic Party and a quality challenger. The Democrats unanimously nominated Darius Ingraham, the mayor of Portland. Ingraham's principal campaign theme was that Reed's focus on national affairs had caused him to neglect his own district. Presenting his Washington work to maintain constituent trust,[39] Reed released a list of specific projects and policies that directly benefited the district, including local harbor improvements, the mackerel bill, and French spoliation claims. He noted that his recent efforts to help Maine industries had been defeated by the Democratic Party, which he reminded voters was in control of the House of Representatives. Reed elaborated on Democratic performance in front of audiences that the Republican *Press* described as eagerly waiting for "the chin-music they expected to hear from their distinguished representative."[40] Reed jabbed, "The very best thing there is about the Democratic Party is that it never does what it says."[41] Reed's lampooning prompted the Democratic *Argus* to speculate that Reed would "pine away and die" if he could not "abuse" the Democrats. The *Argus* suggested that death might only temporarily stop Reed: "Even in heaven, if so improbable an event can be imagined, he would feel lonesome unless permitted to lay down his harp and make a red hot Republican speech."[42]

While partisan blows were not new, what was new in the 1892 campaign was the method of voting. Maine had adopted the "Australian ballot," which is distinguished by having government-printed ballots cast in secret. No longer would the Maine electorate vote openly through party-printed ballots. The reform gave hope to Democrats, including Reed's opponent Darius Ingraham, who told a campaign audience that "the Australian ballot law is the first crack in the iceberg that will go through to the centre and split the Republican Party."[43] Voters, however, needed to learn how the new process worked. Thus, the two parties sponsored an unusual joint educational forum that allowed attendees to go on stage and practice casting a ballot. Some found the novelty a bit overwhelming. The *Argus* reported that "the peace and good nature of the gathering was threatened when one man fell off the stage in his excitement in making his escape from the ballot box."[44]

The tumbles continued the following night during a Reed speech in South Berwick. As reported by the *Press*, "A man who was leaning back in a chair in the very front of the house, lost his balance and fell to the floor, at the same time overturning two chairs in the immediate vicinity." The incident, however, is notable for more than the rare acknowledgement by the Republican *Press* that there were empty seats at a Reed campaign event. Even though an audience member fell and became entangled in two additional chairs, Reed managed to keep his poise. When the noise subsided, Reed quipped, "A perfect, knock-down argument you see."[45]

Democrats failed to strike any new knock-down arguments against Reed during the campaign. When First District voters went to the polls, they reelected Reed by 53 to 47 percent over Ingraham. That night the Republican victory parade came to Reed's home. Reed emerged to thank his supporters: "I call upon you now, everyone, to give three good cheers for the best thing in the United States, the Republican Party."[46]

Having secured reelection in Maine's early September elections, Reed was available to participate in the 1892 national election campaign. Despite his reservations about the Republican ticket, Reed hit the campaign stump in October. His major theme was that Democrats opposed progress and were always "going back to yesterday unless they can get back to the day before yesterday."[47] Reed, however, was less comfortable extolling the virtues of the Harrison administration. In a lengthy speech in Lynn, Massachusetts, for example, Reed referenced Democratic presidential candidate Grover Cleveland by name ten times, but he had zero mentions of Harrison. His lack of enthusiasm for the Harrison candidacy was thinly veiled. Reed explained, "From a political point of view, there are no good Democrats; it is always safer to vote for a Republican that you don't like than for a Democrat that you do like."[48] Reed's refusal to praise Harrison became a running joke in Democratic papers. The *St. Louis Republic* editorialized, "Ex-Speaker Reed has made twenty-two speeches and still persists in his refusal to disclose the name of the Republican candidate for President."[49]

Reed's spring prediction came true in November as Harrison was beaten by Democrat Grover Cleveland. Republican problems at the top of the ticket reverberated below where Democrats kept control of the House and took the Senate to secure the first unified Democratic control of government since before the Civil War. For his part, Reed was not above saying "I told you so." On November 9, Reed reflected on the election results in a letter to his friend Henry Cabot Lodge: "The result of this election is not in the least bit on my conscience for, as you very well know, I took my political life in my hands and warned everybody what the result would be."[50] In writing to Nelson Aldrich a few days later, Reed had grown more reluctant to say "I told you so": "I am not writing to say that I told you so for I didn't tell you half so much."[51]

The following week, legislating in the lame-duck session was halted by filibustering. On February 6, door-kicking Texas Democrat Buck Kilgore forced time-consuming votes for each of his varied motions to recess and adjourn. To make things worse, Kilgore did not object to the bill on the floor but to another bill that could arise later in the day. Reed defended Kilgore's right to make dilatory motions, explaining, "You know, I do not approve the system, but I would like to have it carried out, because it has, when carried out, a logical beauty."[52] In his diary, Reed compared Kilgore's ability to stop a bill supported by over two-thirds of the House to a presidential veto: "Something that not even the President can stop, can be ruined by a simple member from Texas!" According to Reed's diary, Speaker Crisp approached him right after the incident and confided that Democrats should have adopted Reed's rules and ended the folly of being bound by rules that had not bound Republicans when they controlled the House.[53]

On March 4, 1893, the Fifty-Second Congress was ready to adjourn. Although new initiatives were few, Congress maintained the regular operations of government. Speaker Crisp struggled with filibustering except on the rare occasions when the Rules committee forced cloture. Crisp managed to resist counting a quorum despite Democratic difficulties in providing a quorum on their own. Then it was time for the traditional resolution to thank the Speaker. Offering the resolution, Reed could not resist adding a qualification: "Notwithstanding we do not approve of the parliamentary law of the Speaker . . . we tender to the Speaker of this House the expression of our belief that he, like all his predecessors, has performed the trying duties of his office with upright intention and honorable purpose."[54] The resolution was approved unanimously.

Democrats Go Part of the Distance on Rules

The new Fifty-Third Congress was called into special session three months later by President Cleveland to address the economic turmoil that would become known as the Panic of 1893. Unemployment surged as manufacturers and farmers both struggled. Since the crisis began in the financial sector, many blamed the functioning of the currency and how silver was monetized in the Sherman Act of 1890. President Cleveland urged Congress to solidify the currency by repealing the law. Even though the Sherman Act was passed by the Fifty-First Congress, Reed did not object since it had been a compromise addressing time-specific conditions.[55] Summoned by a Democratic president, the pressure on Democrats in Congress to act was great.

Beyond the immediate financial crisis, the Democrats perhaps had greater incentive to act than any time since the Civil War. They had unified government controlling the presidency, House, and Senate. Having been out of power for so long, the party faced many pent-up policy demands. Most notably, many Democrats wanted to reduce tariffs. High tariffs were a constant complaint of Democratic farming constituencies in the South and West, who believed that they were being held back to pay bounties to rich eastern industrialists. Democratic desires to undo Republican policies extended beyond the major economic issues of the day. Democrats were also eager to admit new states and overturn remnants of Reconstruction in the South. There were also contested elections in which a Democrat could be seated.

The special session began on August 3, 1893, and Congress organized itself. The Democratic caucus unanimously reelected Charles Crisp as Speaker. The Republicans unanimously chose Reed as leader. The vote for Speaker was Crisp 214, Reed 122, and Populist Jerry Simpson 7. Simpson, whose signature fashion statement of not wearing socks was a protest against high tariffs and a way to distinguish himself from an opponent "whose tender feet are encased in fine silk hosiery,"[56] stopped at Reed's desk a few days later to pick up documents. To others around him, Reed reportedly said, "Every man has a niche to fill in this world and the Populist and Anarchist and Socialist probably all have their mission to perform under the direction of Providence [as] often times we learn wisdom from fools." When Simpson responded, "I presume you mean me when you refer to Populists and fools," Reed elaborated, "Not necessarily meaning you, but including you."[57]

After the Sherman Act was quickly repealed with the support of a majority of both parties, the stage was set for a month-long showdown over establishing new rules for the House. Many Democrats favored rules that would enable majority governance. The near paralysis of the Fifty-Second Congress in the face of persistent Republican filibustering was a fresh memory. The costs of inactivity would be higher under unified government. Yet some Democrats had reservations about strong majority rule since they maintained an ideological commitment to minority rights, represented districts whose constituency interests were opposed to mainstream Democratic positions on the tariff and currency, and recoiled at doing anything that would ostensibly validate the Reed Rules.

Democratic leaders proposed rules facilitating majority rule, but they were determined to make it look like they were not following Reed's example. To force a final vote without giving the Speaker unilateral power to reject dilatory motions, Democrats strengthened the Rules committee's authority to classify motions as out of order. It was a technical point. A time-wasting motion would not be heard in either case, but in the Fifty-First Congress Speaker Reed would dismiss it, while in the Fifty-Third Congress the Rules committee would prohibit it. Without a special rule, however, Democrats would remain vulnerable to a filibuster in a way that a Speaker with continuous power to prevent delay was not.

Although the strengthened Rules committee weakly approximated the Speaker's refusal to recognize dilatory motions, Democrats had no way to make it easier to obtain a quorum without following Reed's principle of counting nonrespondents. Democrats were not willing to accept Reed's principle.

As in the Fifty-Second Congress, the disappearing-quorum technique was allowed. Democrats hoped that it would not matter as they had a significant majority even if it was smaller than in the Fifty-Second Congress.

As debate began on the rules, Reed found himself in a win-win-win position. The minority Republican alternative was a return to the rules of the Fifty-First Congress. The Democratic proposal also facilitated the majority governance that Reed supported but accomplished it through enhanced use of the Rules committee. If members rejected both alternatives and insisted on strong minority rights, Reed would also win by exploiting the opportunities for delay to prevent Democratic legislation.

On August 29, Reed opened the rules debate with mock praise. He congratulated Democrats for making progress toward majority rule but expressed regret that Democrats had not seen fit to go all the way to adopt the rules of the Fifty-First Congress. He focused his criticism on Democrats giving so much power to the Rules committee, which was composed of the Speaker, two Democrats specially chosen by the Speaker for their loyalty, and two Republicans (who would be ignored as customary for the partisan Rules committee). Reed pondered, "Do you not think, gentlemen on the other side, it is a little pitiful after declaiming so much against interference with the rights of the individual member, standing upon his sole leather and his conscience to stop the business of the House that you should now depute three gentlemen to put an end to him so abruptly?"

Although the rules debate was just beginning, Speaker Crisp had already heard enough. Crisp defended the Democratic rules, "Under this system whenever it is the desire of the House that all dilatory motions shall be avoided and presented, the House has the power to reach that result through a report from the Committee on Rules." Offering a contrast, Crisp continued, "The gentleman from Maine believes that the power should be lodged in the Speaker absolutely, without any reference of the question at all to the House, to decide what is a dilatory motion." Crisp concluded by defending the unusual act of a Speaker joining the debate: "What I have said now has been provoked by the arrogant assertion that the Fifty-First Congress, in its rules and in its methods, was an example which should be followed by all Congresses which should come after."

In reply, Reed feigned having second thoughts because of the Speaker's comments: "These gentlemen are walking humbly in our footsteps. That is right. Let us give them the credit they deserve; and perhaps I am unreasonable in expecting them to go the whole distance."[58]

Throughout the debate, Democrats distinguished their rules from the Reed Rules. On September 6, 1893, William Springer insisted that Democrats were offering rules to allow the majority to govern, while Reed's quorum counting actually was empowering the minority to govern since it was conducting business when only a minority was actively participating. Based on these differences, Springer maintained, "We can not be justly accused of any desire to adopt or even to palliate what we believe to have been the objectionable features of the rules adopted by the Fifty-First Congress."

Reed could not resist taking on his old nemesis from Illinois. Relying on his expansive reading of the Supreme Court decision upholding his quorum counting, Reed said, "When I find the gentleman from Illinois and the Supreme Court of the United States in opposition, of course, it would be a very puzzling matter to me if I did not have some convictions of my own. I am sorry that the gentleman can not seem to understand the matters involved . . . and I realize the truth of the old proverb that a match for the very gods is lack of knowledge—to put it in no harsher fashion."[59] Reed struggled to resist harsher fashion. In reported off-the-floor comments during the session, Reed said that whenever Springer opened his mouth, he never fails to "subtract from the sum of human knowledge."[60]

Democrats adopted their version of rules enhancing majority rule in the House. Reed argued that the result was equivalent to the Fifty-First Congress, except that the minority Republicans had accepted majority rule without all the "choice epithets" and unruliness that Democrats had several years earlier. He summarized, "The Democratic Party on this occasion had either to resort to everything which they had previously denounced or they had to be beaten. They had their choice between humiliation and defeat, and with a vigor characteristic of their party methods, they chose humiliation."[61] Ultimately, House Democratic rules limited filibustering but did not allow the Speaker to count quorums or reject dilatory motions. Although this logistical variation gave Democrats a political argument that they had not followed Reed, they instinctively gravitated to a metaphor that undermined their argument. The *Albuquerque Morning Democrat* proclaimed, "Dr. Tom Reed is much incensed at being compelled to swallow some of his own medicine."[62]

While the Democratic House legislated, the Democratic Senate was mired in filibustering. Throughout October, as the nation suffered in economic misery, the Senate faced increasing criticism for its rules. While in Ohio stumping for the reelection of William McKinley, Reed joined the chorus, joking that the Senate was the place where all good Americans go when they die. This was a longstanding motif for Reed who had previously explained a Senate reading of Washington's Farewell Address as "each one has slowly bored each other so that all the Senators had an imperious need to hear another dead person speak."[63] Characterizing Senate membership as "most of them venerable with years, some of them venerable with wisdom," Reed mocked Senate inaction as making decisions by "physical endurance" instead of majority rule.[64] Although some Senate Democrats pressed for rules similar to the Reed Rules, they were unsuccessful. Senate delays gave Reed a cushion as he prodded Democrats to exert majority rule in the House.

When the regular session of Congress began in December 1893, Reed focused on Democratic efforts to reduce the tariff. He believed that weakening protection would further undermine the American economy. Writing in the *North American Review,* Reed argued that tariff reduction benefited foreigners at the expense of American manufacturers. He explained, "[British industrial gains] may afford satisfaction to those whose hearts have so enlarged that they have become citizens of the world; but those who have only reached that stage of development which causes them to be content with being mere citizens of the United States will still cling to the provincial and Philistine feeling that happy cities this side the Atlantic on our shores interest them more than happy cities on any other shores."[65]

During consideration of the tariff bill, an income tax provision was added that would establish a new tax on high-income earners. Reed identified a contradiction in attaching an income tax to a tariff reduction bill. Reed explained that industrialists "will, probably, by the operation of the main portion of this bill, be deprived of all power to contribute in the blessed manner alluded to" by income tax supporters.[66] Populists took a prominent role in trying to push reluctant Democrats to accept a graduated income tax with 1, 2, 3, 4, and 5 percent tax brackets. On January 30, 1894, Populist Lafe Pence summarized Reed's role in Congress: "The gentleman who heads the Republican minority here is always a mentor to his own side and a tormentor to the other."[67]

On February 1, Reed gave the major closing speech for the Republicans on the tariff bill. Speaking without notes for ninety minutes, Reed argued that the United States had enjoyed unrivaled prosperity under the protective tariff and was risking it for an untested proposition. Even if American products were superior, Reed said, in the survival of the fittest they could not compete against low-wage workers elsewhere. He offered metaphorically: "Compare the strong bull of Bashan with a salt-water smelt. Who doubts the superiority of the bull? Yet, if you drop them both into the Atlantic Ocean, I will take my chances with the smelt."[68]

Speaker Crisp countered, "The gentleman from Maine, with a facility that is unequaled, when he encounters an argument which he is unable to answer passes it by with some bright and witty saying and thereby invites and receives the applause of those who believe as he does, but the gentleman does not attempt . . . to reply to the real arguments that are made in favor of freer trade and greater liberty of commerce."[69] A restrictive rule would soon force cloture. Even though seventeen Democrats voted against the bill because of concerns about the income tax and district impact, the tariff bill passed the House 204–140.

Burglarized Crow Eaten

A quorum fight was brewing by mid-February 1894. Democrats had a significant majority in the chamber but increasingly were finding it difficult to make a quorum on their own. The chamber had 356 members so a quorum as determined by the Constitution was one-half plus one or 179. Although Democrats had about 220 members, their forty-member buffer had largely evaporated. Family or personal illness had taken a number of members from the chamber. Modest salaries meant that members often pursued work on the side and were sometimes called away to complete it. If members represented districts far from Washington, travel significantly extended their absence. The various reasons added up to Democrats regularly having only about 160 members in the chamber. For Democrats, this was their worst nightmare. They had felt compelled not to give the Speaker the ability to count unwilling participants as part of the quorum so as not to follow Reed. Even though there were regularly about 235 members active in the chamber, Democrats would not make the quorum of 179 if Republicans chose not to answer.

Reed and the Republicans used the disappearing quorum on just about everything from matters as routine as approving the journal to major legislation. The process was simple. The regular quorum call would indicate that about 235 members were present (about 160 Democrats, 70 Republicans, and 5 Populists). When it came time to vote, names would be called and opponents would not respond to their names. The quorum had disappeared. Reed delighted in the Democratic dilemma, which had been self-inflicted both because they could not get all their members there and because they had denied the Speaker the ability to count opponents who were present but remained silent.

Democratic leaders made desperate efforts to get their members in the chamber. They increased the authority of the sergeant at arms to arrest members and escort them to the chamber. This was helpful for members in the cloakroom or Washington bars, but it was not so helpful in finding members back in their constituencies. On February 22, Reed needled the Democrats for a progress report from the sergeant at arms: "I understand that some gentlemen are under arrest [and] I think we had better have the regular daily jail delivery this morning."[70] Weeks passed in failed quorums.

Taking a page from Reed's playbook, Democrats brought up a contested-election case on March 27, 1894, to close ranks. There were about 230 members present. Once a motion was made to begin considering the case, the chamber was left with only about 165 Democrats. There was no quorum, and the House adjourned. There was no quorum the following day. Democrats proposed to strengthen enforcement against absent members on March 29. Reed protested that the House could not change its rules to increase penalties against members when a quorum had not voted. Speaker Crisp determined, "No such absurd contention as that could be right or ought to be enforced; on the contrary, it has been uniformly held that the House in the absence of a quorum may do anything looking to obtaining a quorum."

Reed feigned sympathy, "I am not one of those who criticize the measures which gentlemen seem to think necessary to compel the action of their own friends [since] doubtless they know them better than I possibly could."

Stepping down from the chair to reply, Crisp revisited the proceedings of the Fifty-First Congress. He insisted that Reed had coerced members to approve quorum-counting procedures that they disliked: "When the gentleman from Maine had by his course of conduct in the chair put his party in a position where they either had to vindicate his action or denounce him, they sustained his action in counting a quorum and the gentleman knows as well as he sits in that chair that prior to that time he never could get a Republican caucus to authorize a rule to count a quorum."

"I never tried," Reed said.

"The gentleman from Maine," Crisp continued, "is known to the country as having a hobby, and gentlemen on that side blindly follow him, no matter how their own convictions may differ from his. He is the great leader on that side. You will hear them privately saying 'Reed ought not to do that' or 'This is wrong' but when Reed says 'Do it' they all step up and do it. . . . [Meanwhile] members over here follow the dictates of their own consciences." After addressing Reed, Crisp implored Democrats to attend session: "I want to say a word to this side of the House. . . . The leader that they follow without question has one great thought, one great idea in his mind, and that is to force this side to count a quorum. Every other question, no matter how great, no matter how important it may be, sinks into insignificance."[71]

The antipathy resumed the following day. The routine approval of the previous day's journal was preempted by Reed's insistence that reference to Speaker Crisp's ruling against him be amended to "the Chair overruled the point for no reason stated." When Crisp ignored him, Reed inquired, "Upon what ground?"

Crisp replied, "No member on the floor has any right, when the Chair has made a decision to rise and ask 'upon what ground' any more than a gentleman would have such right in a court or any similar body after a ruling had been made against him."

"I think," Reed replied, "that looks like tyranny."[72] As the day continued, Reed and the Republicans fought tyranny with the disappearing quorum. Reed drew attention to a prior quorum count. He moved to the front of the chamber to double-check the clerk's tabulation on the upcoming vote. Crisp told members to be in order and take their seats. Maintaining his position by the clerk's desk, Reed insisted, "I would like to be permitted to see the roll call taken."

"The gentleman will take his seat," Crisp repeated.

Reed feigned humility with a bow and cautious movement toward the aisle. "I am going to do it," Reed said.

"The Sergeant-at-Arms will ask the gentleman to take his seat," Crisp insisted as he turned and faced Reed.

The *Washington Post* described Reed's response: "He staggered and turned as if he had been shot. His face flushed and he looked scornfully at a black-haired deputy, who, in response to the Speaker's command, now stood in front of his burly form." Glaring at the Speaker, Reed sounded out each word, "That is entirely unnecessary!"

"It is not," Crisp retorted. "Instead of taking your seat you respond to the Chair every time." In his anger, Crisp had slipped into an unparliamentary use of the personal pronoun "you."

"Certainly I do, because the Chair has attacked me."

Crisp countered, “The gentleman will resume his seat, and public business will be suspended until the gentleman from Maine conforms to the order of the Chair in the execution of the rules of the House.” The *Washington Post* described Reed’s subsequent reaction: “Reed hesitated just a moment, and then, amid a deathlike silence in the House, he moved across the area from the Democratic to the Republican side . . . like a man following a corpse . . . his feet weighted with unwillingness, dragged heavily . . . [as] the eyes of the Speaker were riveted upon his every movement, watching him as a cat watches a retreating mouse.”[73]

As Reed slowly retreated, Democrat Culberson whispered, “See Jumbo go back to his stake.”[74]

Upon arriving at his desk, Reed swung his chair nervously, and glared at the Speaker. He sat down. The awkward silence was broken by the cheering of Democrats.

It was hard to deny the drama of the event that had just unfolded in the House of Representatives. A former Speaker was forced to sit by the current Speaker. Reed had been protesting at the front of the chamber. In the House that he had formerly ruled, he was forced to return humbly to his seat as the sergeant at arms enforced the Speaker’s rebuke. The drama increased because the event was almost the reverse of what had happened four years earlier when Reed forced Crisp to sit. The big difference was that Speaker Reed disciplined merely a rising Democratic leader while Speaker Crisp had disciplined a former Speaker who had transformed the House of Representatives. Champ Clark, a House Democrat who knew and liked Reed, reckoned that Reed was never able to forgive Crisp.[75]

An angry Reed was not about to let Democrats off the hook for failing to provide a quorum on their own. Republican use of the disappearing quorum intensified. Democrats strengthened their efforts to arrest missing members. On April 12, frustrated Democrats decided to supplement the arrest procedure with a new system of fines. They offered a rule to fine members ten dollars through payroll deductions for missing a vote. Reed mocked Democrats for being unable to function “without turning this House into a justice of the peace shop, with $10 jurisdiction, less than one-half of what we have in the little State of Maine.” Reed said that a new system of fines would need to be established by a quorum, which Democrats lacked.

Rebutting Reed, a frustrated Democrat offered an innovative reason why Democrats could not do the straightforward thing and count nonrespondents in the quorum. Joseph Hutcheson conceded that it was a good rule but maintained that Reed had so poisoned its use that future Congresses had to forego its benefits. In the eyes of Hutcheson, then, Reed's credit claiming was worse than blasphemy: "It [Reed's quorum counting] should be a crown of thorns upon his head instead of a crown of glory, because by his abuse he made a good rule so obnoxious to liberty-loving people that it can not again be adopted in a liberty-loving body. . . . I claim that he nailed it [quorum counting] to the cross and crucified it by an unjust use of it, and we are tired of the crucifier claiming to be the father and the originator. He should be branded as its murderer."[76]

The following day, Reed and the Republicans prevented the Democrats from approving the journal through the disappearing quorum. Only 156 members voted on the journal, twenty-three short of a quorum. The Democrats were stuck. Months of inactivity were taking its toll. Speaker Crisp insisted that he would not count a quorum. Meanwhile, William Springer was trying to sell quorum counting to the Democratic caucus. Democrats held a heated evening caucus on April 13 that lasted well over three hours. Reed cast a long shadow over the meeting. Supporters of the rule concluded that facilitating business required the rule change "even if it infringed in a slight measure upon the exaggerated patent of Mr. Reed." In opposition to the rule, Amos Cummings told the caucus that it should be called "a rule to nominate Thomas Brackett Reed for president of the United States."[77] What would they decide?

On April 17, the Rules committee introduced a rule supported by a majority of the sharply divided Democratic caucus. The outcome of Friday's Democratic caucus was summarized by the *Worcester Daily Spy*, whose reporting would test the limit of horse metaphors: "Finally, Springer of Illinois, one of the liveliest jockeys in the democratic stable, seeing that the coach would be upset and the team utterly spoiled, got up a clumsy but effective imitation of Reed's curb and applied it in spite of Crisp's objections."[78] Indeed, Democrats resigned themselves to adopting the same principle of quorum counting that they had previously condemned. Introducing the rule, Democrats emphasized that their rule was different from Reed's because it provided that two tellers be appointed to count those present and not voting instead of having the Speaker do it. Democrats knew that nobody was fooled. To reduce the discomfort of adopting Reed's principle of quorum counting, they proposed to allow only thirty minutes of debate. Reed objected and defended the right of Democratic opponents to speak.

Reed yielded to Democrats who opposed what their caucus was doing.

Democrat Benjamin Russell proclaimed, "With a Democratic majority on this side of 70 or 80 . . . we come here and present this humiliating spectacle to the American people, confessing that we can not transact the public business without invoking the exceptional and revolutionary methods of the Fifty-First Congress." Having given most of his time to the other side, Reed took a few seconds to say that "this scene here today is a more effective address than any I could make" and congratulated the House on its wise choice.[79] On the final vote, despite being in the minority, every Republican voted to enhance the majority's power by counting those present but not participating as part of the quorum. Democrats voted 126–47 for approval. Applause greeted the results of the vote. The Fifty-Third Congress had just adopted a quorum counting rule and in so doing had institutionalized another component of the majority rule established by Speaker Reed.

The timing of Reed's triumph coincided nicely with the release of his new book. *Reed's Rules* had just come out and was available for purchase. The book was a guide to parliamentary procedure and was advertised as essential reading for "all who are connected in any way with public life or corporate bodies."[80] More than a century later, the book remains an oft-cited resource for parliamentarians.

Having given Reed a victory by adapting his rules, Democrats utilized their majority-empowering rules to enact a tariff reduction bill. The 1892 Democratic platform promised tariff reduction, and the House passed a bill with significant tariff reduction. In the Senate, however, Democrats had a smaller majority, and some members were under great pressure to protect industries in their state. After months of debate and filibustering, the Senate passed tariff legislation, but its amendments to the House bill minimized tariff reduction to the dismay of President Cleveland and Democratic House sponsors. The House rejected the Senate bill and proposed a conference committee to reconcile differences. After the Senate refused to budge, House leaders caved and proposed to pass the Senate version under a restrictive rule allowing no amendments and little debate.

While House Democrats were not happy about passing a watered-down bill, Reed was pleased that Democrats largely had failed on their campaign promise for substantial tariff reduction. In the final debate on August 13, 1894, Democratic sponsor William Wilson lamented that he was "not gratified" by the bill but said that he and other reformers would "continue to march" toward more tariff reduction. Reed asked, "Has not this country suffered enough during the last twelve months that these men should come and assure it that their ravages are to continue?"[81] Speaker Crisp came down from the chair to say that even though he was disappointed with the bill, as a practical person looking beyond "theory" he had to "believe in [the] homely phrase that when people are starving, 'half a loaf is better than no bread.'"[82]

Reed countered that "even the practical, plain, homely person that the Speaker today described himself to be with tremendous accuracy" should recognize that any businessman would struggle "as long as his feet rest upon the shifting sands." Reed speculated that the reason Democrats were not in their "usually sweet temper" was that they had eaten something that "disagreed" with them: "Perhaps it is indigestion that makes them adopt such a course as we have witnessed here."[83] Reed had some ideas about what they ate. Democrats were eating crow, yes, but a special kind. Talking off the floor, Reed mocked House Democrats for passing a bill that was technically in the possession of the Senate: "I have known of crow . . . being eaten, but never before of its being burglarized."[84]

To add insult to injury, House Democrats resorted to a restrictive rule to pass the tariff bill that they did not like. Reed blasted Democrats for their willingness to "climb over every legal obstacle in order to get at the nauseous meal which has been set before them." He attacked the limited time allowed for debate: "You are going to give an hour on a side to discuss six hundred amendments, no one of which has been touched by this House, one-tenth of a second for each amendment!" Giving what little answer was left for Democrats, Henry Turner said, "I am commending to his [Reed's] own lips the medicine which he has so often devised for us."[85] Indeed, the medicine did work and Reed's criticism did little to change the outcome when later in the day the House approved the Senate version of the tariff bill and ended the major work of the session.

In pressing Democrats to eliminate the disappearing quorum and impose restrictive rules, Reed had shown outstanding leadership. The hallmarks of his Speakership had been further institutionalized by a Democratic Congress. The adoption of his key procedural innovations by Democrats were instrumental in removing them from a partisan context as they had now been adopted by both parties. While political scientists have written extensively about 1890, Reed's achievements in his return to minority leader are given far less attention. In some ways, however, Reed's actions as minority leader show the importance of congressional leadership even better than his actions in 1890.

Indeed, Reed's role in getting his procedures institutionalized by

Democrats is a great example of how leadership matters. Institutional context does not tell the whole story. Since drawing from formal powers is an important component of institutional context explanations of leadership style,[86] Reed's success in preserving caucus support and achieving his desired outcome with minimal formal powers as minority leader in 1894 may be more dependent on leadership skills than his accomplishments with extensive formal powers as Speaker in 1890. This success occurred when broader institutional factors were not aligned for Democrats to adopt strong party control. Political science frameworks predict that stronger party control is more likely when there is a narrow margin between cohesive parties.[87] This was not the case in 1894. Although reduced from the previous Congress, Democrats still had a substantial margin in the Fifty-Third Congress. Democrats were also not particularly united on any clear agenda. Yet they adopted two hallmarks of strong party control. They did it in a Congress marked by comparatively low party voting. The rate of party votes in the Fifty-Second and Fifty-Third Congresses averaged 5 percent compared to 43 percent in the Fifty-First Congress.[88]

Characterizing the institutional context as not favoring the outcome probably undersells Reed's leadership. Partisan theories of legislative organization typically assume that outcomes reflect majority-party preferences.[89] In a sense, as minority leader, Reed briefly turned upside down both major political-science models of party government. While disagreeing on the likelihood of strong party government, the two frameworks share a focus on majority-party members. Conditional party government considers both parties but emphasizes the choice of majority-party members to give power to majority-party leaders when certain conditions are met;[90] consistent party government perceives majority-party members functioning as a cartel that regularly grants agenda setting power to majority-party leaders.[91] In 1893, however, the impetus for stronger majority-party control did not come from the majority party but from the minority party. Minority Leader Reed acted as the most visible and consistent proponent of stronger majority-party control. On the vote to adopt the key party control measure of eliminating the disappearing quorum, which had a six-decade history as a potent tool of obstruction, every single member of the minority party voted yes while the majority Democrats split. Further, Republicans did not vote this way because their policy preferences were aligned with Democrats who supported the change. No Republican, for example, voted for the final Democratic tariff bill aided by the quorum rule change while only eleven Democrats voted against what

Reed characterized as burglarized crow. Even in frameworks that identify a role for minority-party members in rule changes as part of cross-party coalitions,[92] there is no systematic explanation for why a minority party would be the driving force behind rule changes to give power to the opposition against its policy preferences.

Overall, the evidence suggests that there was nothing automatic about Democrats adopting these rules. While systematic political-science models improve understanding of congressional behavior, there is still room for leadership at critical moments.[93] Given their substantial margin, Democrats should not have needed the rule change, and institutional factors did not predict it. There was also another obstacle to reform: Democrats who supported strong party control were restrained in their enthusiasm because they could be perceived as implementing the same methods that they had recently condemned. Further evidence that it was not automatic was the brutal fight in the Democratic caucus over adoption and the genuine surprise by many that Democrats made that decision.

The broader interdisciplinary literature on leadership provides a useful perspective on Reed's leadership skills. Scholars have distinguished between tactical leadership, which emphasizes technical short-term approaches, and strategic leadership, which requires a broader long-term vision.[94] Reed's tactical skills shone as he found creative ways to exploit Democratic weaknesses despite facing long odds. His short-term tactical maneuvers were aligned with long-term strategic plans. The long-term effect was to facilitate House lawmaking, which would benefit Reed's Republican Party in the future since it supported a stronger federal government. In short, Reed used his expertise in arcane parliamentary procedure to promote a vision of how democracy functions. Even in the minority, Reed's leadership made an indelible mark on national politics.

No matter how large a mark they make on national politics, members of Congress must still win election in their districts. Thus, Reed was back on the campaign trail in summer 1894. He was facing a quality challenger in former Portland mayor John Deering, who distinguished his plan to "tax the classes" from what he described as the Republican policy to "tax the masses."[95] In hour-long stump speeches, Reed defended Republican tariff policy as supporting high wages and offered his assessment of Democratic performance in the last Congress. Democrats, he said, lacked a unified plan for positive action. Their deep divisions made it impossible to tell what Democrats want, much "like a baby crying in the night."[96] If a simile was not forthcoming,

Reed had a ready metaphor. Reed said that the Democratic Party "had always been a cart, and a cart can stand still if it wants to, but a horse has to move, and when they tried to be a horse they found they were a cart just the same."[97]

While Reed campaigned for reelection to Congress, Republicans anticipated his next likely campaign. At nearly every campaign stop, he was introduced as an imminent presidential candidate. On one occasion the introductory speaker became so enthusiastic as to nominate Reed for president. The *Argus* tried to make Reed's higher ambitions an issue in the campaign, accusing him of "plainly and undeniably booming himself for the Republican nomination for President in 1896" on the congressional campaign trail.[98]

When voters went to the polls on September 10, 1894, Reed earned his largest victory ever, defeating Deering 17,086 to 8,901 votes. The victory was part of a Republican landslide in a state where economic turmoil had been associated with Democratic rule. Reed addressed supporters during an election night rally: "There does not seem to be much of any Democratic Party left, and I shall miss it."[99] The magnitude of the victory left the Democratic *Argus* grasping for a silver lining: "The trouble with the Republican victory—so far as its future effects to the party are concerned—is that it is too large."[100]

CHAPTER 8

CONSPICUOUSLY BEATEN FOR PRESIDENT

Reed's presidential campaign began in earnest following his September reelection to Congress. Most of the nation held elections in early November. This left Reed with almost two months to campaign for other Republicans. Traveling with his daughter, Reed embarked on a national tour during the 1894 congressional campaign. While the ostensible purpose was to energize the party base and support local candidates, the visits offered the side benefit of increasing his visibility for the upcoming presidential campaign. Reed spoke to hundreds, if not thousands, of Republican voters at each campaign stop. He also had the opportunity to network with Republican leaders, who would be grateful for his visit to their locality. This was the pool of future delegates to the 1896 Republican convention. There would probably be no better chance to reach these delegates. During this era, there was still a strong norm against active stump speaking in pursuit of a party's presidential nomination. An overt campaign for the nomination in late 1895 or early 1896 would violate the norm and run the risk of being perceived as too eager to obtain power. Essentially, this was the first and last opportunity to hit the campaign trail.

Reed talked mostly about the economy in his campaign speeches. With the country in economic turmoil and Democrats at the helm, Reed presented the argument that Democrats had caused the problems and a high tariff was the remedy. He offered a metaphor for how two years of Democratic rule should have alerted voters to the dangers of free trade: "The ordinary dog when he sees the shadow of a trolley car as a rule gets out of the way [but] when the car runs over his tail he is convinced that trolley cars are dangerous." Reed saw the signs of coming electoral disaster for Democrats: "It has been said that whom the gods wish to destroy they first make mad; have you ever seen such madness as the madness of the Democratic Party?"[1] There was an answer to avoiding the cycle of madness and crushed tails. Reed endorsed the protective tariff: "If I did not believe that protection was the best method to distribute to any and all of the people the great gifts God has stored up for them in the earth and in the water and in the air of this country I would not be a loyal American."[2]

Voters were receptive to the message of Reed and the Republicans in fall 1894. Early in the campaign, Reed predicted that the Democrats would be buried in trenches. After a Republican landslide, Reed confessed to a slight inaccuracy: "I should have said that we would bury them in trenches until the supply of trenches gave out."[3] Indeed, the metaphor of death dominated Reed's analysis of the election. This recurrent metaphor gave Reed sympathy for Democrats. He wrote, "The verdict of the people was so overwhelming at the last election that there is upon us all that soberness which one cannot help feeling for the dead even when they did not die in the Lord and can have no desire that their works shall follow them."[4]

Reed returned to Washington after the election for a lame-duck session of the Fifty-Third Congress, during which he made an unusual hedge on financial issues. As the Treasury faced deficits and a continuing drain on gold, Reed offered compromise legislation that used the ambiguous term "coin" rather than specifying gold redemption for new bonds. Reed regarded his action as taking "risks" to solve a problem, even if it might raise consternation among hard-line gold standard supporters.[5] Critics charged Reed with trying to have it both ways. The *Chicago Record* contemplated, "If there is any acrobat in this country who is inclined to be conceited because of his skill, let him watch Tom Reed in his great specialty of standing on both sides of the money question at the same time."[6] Reed's position was often interpreted as making a play for western silver producing states in the upcoming presidential contest. In a reply to an angry banker, Reed wrote, "Would it not be wiser for you to suspect me of patriotism than of ambition?"[7] Buried in a Republican trench in the election, William Springer failed to see patriotism and bantered that Reed's currency views might qualify him to be the Populist Party candidate for president.[8]

If Reed seemed unsure on financial issues in the lame-duck session, it was possibly related to his own financial calamity. Reed had long placed his savings with the investment firm of his friend Stanley Pullen. Thus, it came as a shock in early 1895 when Reed learned that Pullen had misused Reed's money to finance his own failed investments. On February 9, an angry Reed wrote Pullen that he had "taken from me almost all I have."[9] When Pullen begged for forgiveness to preserve a longstanding friendship,[10] Reed refused to discuss the matter. Although he saw himself as a victim of more than an "error in judgment," Reed assured Pullen that he would not harm him by telling others about the wrongdoing.[11]

Of course, keeping the incident quiet insulated Reed from public embarrassment about his financial management. As he tried to regain his financial footing, Reed expressed sensitivity about appearances in a letter to a friend: "I can see that it would have been awkward for me to have had a dispute, still the loss don't quite fall where it ought."[12] Indeed, Reed was never a particularly good investor. He had even been burned by Pullen before. In a diary entry eight years earlier, Reed described how Pullen had invested his funds with a dishonest banker and calculated losses at $4,000.[13] His communication with Pullen over the years reveals an active, if insecure, investor who had "cold chills" during market movements.[14] Perhaps he would have better success managing the American economy in Congress.

Returning his attention to national finances on February 14, 1895, Reed worked a rebuke of William Jennings Bryan into a defense of sound money. Bryan, the former preacher from Nebraska, had been taking shots at Reed throughout the debate over how to replenish the gold being drained from the Treasury. He had mocked Reed as having offered "a pretended coin position" because he lacked the "courage" to reveal his true position. Bryan, who thought that currency policy was too hard on debtors and not sufficiently supportive of silver coinage, ended his closing speech on a bond bill with a rhetorical flourish in which he proclaimed that "the oppressive demands of our eastern friends shall heal the divisions in the west and south" and restore opportunity to the people.

Reed deadpanned, "That doctrine of the union of the south and west has been preached before and by prophets whose inspiration lasted longer than that of the gentleman from Nebraska but it has been a failure [and] it always will be a failure."[15] Reed maintained that the problems were caused by the Democratic failure to raise enough revenue to pay for its spending. Ultimately, in a vote that split party lines by region, President Cleveland's proposals for new gold bonds supported by Reed and other easterners were defeated. In a letter to a friend, Reed reflected on the day's minor victory, writing, "That ass Bryan gave me an opening and I broke for it."[16]

On March 3, 1895, the final session of the Fifty-Third Congress ended, and it was time for the customary resolution to thank the Speaker. Minority Leader Reed declined to offer the resolution so the task passed to Joseph Cannon. It was a standing vote in which members rose and applauded the speaker. Reed remained seated. Would other Republicans join him? The Democratic *Plain Dealer* described the outcome: "To the honor of the Republicans be it said, only two sycophants . . . followed Reed in playing the baby act."[17] The Republican *Zanesville Courier* countered, "Tom Reed may not have been magnanimous in not voting for the resolution declaring Crisp was fair and impartial as Speaker, but he was consistent and honest."[18] Reed stayed consistent in his summary of the session in the *North American Review*: "There is a limit to the evil which any one Congress may do, and even the incompetent get tired of the exercise of their own incompetency."[19]

Reed next turned to presidential politics. He intended to run the same type of low-key campaign that had won him the Speakership in December 1889. He was going to stand on his record. This strategy afforded ample vacation time. In the spring of 1895, Reed announced, "I shall plunge into the woods early this summer and stay there as long as possible."[20] He fished in Quebec. He spent time at the beach, where he joined the nation's bicycle craze. Reportedly, a special-order bicycle was prepared in order to accommodate Reed's size. The *Sun* described Reed's successful mount: "He bestrides his wheel like a Colossus."[21] Balance issues required a little more work. Reed practiced diligently to the amusement of onlookers. Nobody seemed concerned about whether soiling a white sweater by falling off an oversized bicycle looked presidential.

While the incipient Reed campaign was spinning its wheels, the campaign of his opponent William McKinley was making steady progress. As hard as Reed worked in the 1894 off-year election, McKinley worked even harder. By one count, McKinley gave 371 campaign speeches during the fall campaign, including twenty-three speeches in Iowa in one day.[22] Commenting privately on McKinley's feverish 1894 campaign schedule, Reed wrote, "McKinley is going everywhere but I doubt if that helps much."[23] McKinley was going south in early 1895. Mark Hanna bought a large house in Georgia and invited McKinley down for occasional visits that coincided with the visits of southern Republican leaders. McKinley's congeniality appeared to be winning over southern Republicans.

The 1896 Republican presidential nomination was shaping up as a rematch of the 1889 contest between Reed and McKinley for Speaker.

Throughout the campaign, Reed saw parallels to the earlier race. He wrote Henry Cabot Lodge, "McK seems to be trying the alternating current rushing South to fill Northern newspapers with his Southern gains and North to fill Southern newspapers with his gains in New England. It really seems like 1889 back again."[24] Since he had won in 1889, the similarities gave Reed an underlying optimism. He conveyed his feelings to friend William Chandler: "New England was going to betray me in the 51st Congress. The same tactics were resorted to as to both N.E. & NY and some how I feel the same about it as I did then—that it would work out solid and all right."[25] Seeing parallels to 1889 became easier when Reed retained Henry Cabot Lodge and Theodore Roosevelt as campaign advisers.

The race offered much contrast in personality but little in policy. A McKinley biographer summarized the personality differences: "Where McKinley was soft, he [Reed] was harsh. Where the Major was kind, he was rough. Where the Ohioan was conciliatory, he was outspoken."[26] On the other hand, both Reed and McKinley held mainstream Republican policy positions. As the two candidates agreed on national financial policy, they also shared shortcomings in their own personal financial management. Both had suffered huge financial losses from a friend's betrayal. In early 1895, Reed quietly absorbed his losses, which were probably in the tens of thousands of dollars as he recalled investing about $7,000 with Pullen in just the most recent year.[27] For his part, McKinley repeatedly endorsed the bank notes of a friend apparently thinking they were renewals instead of new notes, which put him on the hook for $130,000. McKinley's $8,000 salary as Ohio governor left him no way of meeting his obligations, which became public knowledge through his friend's court proceeding in February 1893.[28] Contributions from McKinley's wealthy friends and supporters, including John Hay, who privately conceded that McKinley's "folly . . . is simply inexcusable,"[29] liquidated his debts and kept his promising political career on track.

As 1895 progressed, the active campaign of McKinley was offering a sharp contrast to the quiet campaign of Reed. As word of McKinley's activity spread, Reed and his advisers were confident that they were on the right path. Roosevelt advised, "It seems to me as yet too early to try to make any aggressive movement; it would be imitating McKinley's mistaken tactics."[30] In a letter to Lodge, Reed agreed, "To say much at any time will be troublesome also."[31] An October 1895 assessment by the *Washington Post* suggested that Reed's tactics were working: "There is no doubt about it; Reed is far and away in the lead for the Republican nomination."[32]

The Fifty-Fourth Congress was set to begin on December 2, 1895. The House Republican caucus, buoyed by nearly 150 freshmen elected in the 1894 Republican landslide, met to name its leader. Reed was chosen by acclamation. Accepting the nomination, Reed reflected, "History will accord us praise for what we did in the 51st Congress, and it may accord us its praise in this for what we do not do."[33] The expectation of minimal House activity was reinforced when a reporter asked Reed to identify the biggest problem facing the country. "How to dodge a bicycle," Reed reportedly answered, "at least I judge so from my own experience since I came to Washington."[34]

The minimal goal for legislation stood in sharp contrast to Reed's goals as Speaker in the Fifty-First Congress. The Fifty-First Congress had a Republican House, a Republican Senate, and a Republican president with a backlog of important policy goals. In contrast, as this Congress began, Republicans had solid control of only the House. The divided Senate lacked a reliable working majority. President Cleveland was a Democrat who was partly estranged from his own party. There was also little agreement on the major policy issues of the tariff and currency. The Senate leaned toward support for free-silver coinage, which stood in contrast to the sound money principles of the House and President Cleveland. Republican congressional support for strengthening protective tariffs would be opposed by President Cleveland. These disagreements made action unlikely despite the fact that the country had been suffering economically since the Panic of 1893.

During the first month of the session, Reed's attention was dominated by committee assignments. As Speaker, he made all committee assignments and named all chairs. He was inundated with requests. When one member wrote Reed that he was not asserting any claims based on his seniority and was supporting whatever Reed thought was best, Reed thanked the member and filed the member's letter with the notation "A rare curiosity to be preserved for future generations."[35] Reflecting on the committee selection process, Reed described it as the most "worried" task of his career.[36]

On December 21, 1895, Reed announced committee chairs, going against the tradition of seniority on the two most important committees. He chose Nelson Dingley of Maine as the Ways and Means chair over Sereno Payne of New York. He also chose Joseph Cannon of Illinois to be Appropriations chair over Iowa's David Henderson. Reed insisted that his selection process was guided not by politics but by the goal of legislative achievement. The best evidence for this was his selection of fellow Mainer Dingley over a large-state competitor. The *Chicago Times Herald* made fun of Reed's choice as a presidential strategy: "The list of House committees shows that Mr. Reed is holding onto his Presidential boom by Maine strength."[37]

As the committees went to work, the tariff and bond bill were likely exceptions to the inactivity that was expected for most of Congress. They also provided a potential showcase for the House to demonstrate that it could get things done. President Cleveland had just urged Congress to address the nation's pressing deficit. Republicans had little interest in Cleveland's recommended solution, but they were prepared to act quickly on the deficit. Republican action was facilitated by having adopted the rules of the Fifty-First Congress until permanent rules could be established. The Ways and Means committee met on Christmas to prepare the tariff bill. A bond bill had also been prepared. Reed and his deputies planned to pass the tariff on December 26 and run the bond bill on December 27. It was not clear that anything could stop the House from passing these two pieces of legislation after only minimal consideration.

As planned, the tariff bill reached the floor on December 26 under conditions that allowed for rapid passage. It was the first time that the House had seen the bill, which was expected to generate over $40 million in revenue. The tariff revisions affected almost every product, including adding a new tariff on wool. The Rules committee proposed a rule that allowed four hours of debate and prohibited amendments.

If Republicans saw the tariff increase as a Christmas gift to the nation, Democratic leader Charles Crisp did not. He described being summoned to the Ways and Means committee the day before, when public offices were closed for the holiday, to see the finished bill. Although he had used restrictive rules in the last Congress, Crisp said that the Republican effort stood out for the magnitude of the policy and restrictiveness of the rule. Crisp complained, "I defy any gentleman to point to any rule reported by any committee of any Congress heretofore in the history of the country whereby a general tariff bill was to be disposed of in the House of the people's representatives in about four hours, without the right to offer a single amendment." When a Republican questioned why amendments were prevented, Crisp took the opportunity to needle Republicans whose district interests might be adversely affected by the legislation. He explained, "It is designed not only to gag us, but also to gag gentlemen on the Republican side who might be disposed to rebel against the party whip which is being applied in this summary manner."[38] Quickly brushing aside the protests, House Republicans passed the tariff bill 228–83.

The bond bill was next. Some Republicans requested that three days be devoted to such an important measure instead of the one day planned. Reed rejected their offer, but he extended the debate to ten hours, including both December 27 and 28. The Republican leadership bill increased the borrowing capacity of the government and authorized a new length and interest rate for bonding authority. Democrats objected, but the sharpest attack on Reed came from disgruntled Republicans. Grove Johnson protested his lack of choice: "I am simply kneeling at the feet of the political Gamaliels who run and control the Republican Party here. I am simply swallowing the drippings of the sanctuary, not the sweets of the inner table."[39] Johnson joined fifty other Republicans in opposing the bond bill, but the measure still passed.

Combined, the rapid passage of the session's two major bills was a stark reminder of the House's capacity to act. With about fourteen hours of debate and no amendments, the House passed the session's two major bills, which constituted its principal response to the major economic crisis facing the nation. Committees had just been named earlier in the week, and the session had only begun earlier in the month. Republican papers praised House leaders for maintaining focus during a crisis. The *Philadelphia Inquirer* explained, "There was no claptrap oratory and there was no room for rhetorical outbursts with a view to making party capital."[40] The Democratic response in the Baltimore *Sun* was full of implements: "Mr. Reed has used his gavel both as a sceptre and a whip."[41] A troika of implements also characterized the critique of the *Wheeling Register*: "They did it under the lash, spur and gag of that eminent political bully Tom Reed."[42] The bills, however, had no practical impact. Reed showed that House Republicans could act, but their actions would not be acceptable to others. The Senate never passed either measure, and the deficit crisis persisted.

The first few weeks of 1896 were spent debating House rules, which were less about practical concerns than principle. Republicans needed little help from the rules to get things done in this Congress. They could easily make a quorum on their own. With a greater than two-thirds majority, Republicans hardly needed rules at all since the rules could be suspended by a two-thirds vote. Reed, however, was determined to institutionalize the parliamentary procedure that had been adopted by the Republican Fifty-First Congress and substantially upheld by the Democratic Fifty-Third Congress. The majoritarian rules passed with minimal resistance. The *New York Times* was perplexed: "Just why so much stiffening of the rules should be regarded as necessary to a Congress whose motto is to do as little as possible remains to be seen."[43]

Like political assessments at the time, modern social-science frameworks are challenged to explain the rules of the Fifty-Fourth Congress. Institutional context explanations for giving more power to majority-party leaders include factors such as narrow party balances, distinct policy agendas, and a broader political system favorable to implementation.[44] This model fits the Fifty-First Congress with its narrow margins, pent-up demands, and unified Republican government. In the Fifty-Fourth Congress, however, the margins were large and House legislation was unlikely to be enacted with a Democratic president and a Democratic-Populist-Silverite majority in the Senate. Compelling explanations of the rules outcome must include an important role for congressional leadership. In this case, Reed was committed to carrying out the principle of majority rule that he had been advocating for many years. Even when immediate policy outcomes were possible without rules enhancing majority-party control, he pressed to cement his procedural innovations.

Presidential Campaign Comes Unhinged

As the presidential campaign heated up in February 1896, the tactics adopted by the candidates aligned with their overall strategies for winning. Reed adopted a traditional strategy to win a convention brokered by party leaders after a first ballot failed to provide the required majority. An impasse was likely because state conventions often sent their delegations to the national convention ostensibly supporting not one of the major national candidates but the state's favorite son. From the delegation's perspective, this had the advantage of honoring a prominent person in the state on the first ballot and facilitating negotiation on later ballots. Other delegations obtained flexibility by sending uninstructed delegates. Reed could afford to allow favorite sons in other parts of the country to take their state's support to the national convention. The *Kansas City Star* praised Reed's restraint: "In refusing to poach upon the preserves of other Presidential candidates, Tom Reed shows good manners and good politics."[45]

Although Reed was not campaigning throughout the country, he was highly invested in the race. He was playing not to lose. Specifically, Reed was playing not to lose the support of New England. A unified New England delegation would give him a solid base of support for negotiation at a brokered convention. Symbolically, it was important that the region unite behind Reed to project strength. Thus, Reed and his campaign team spent much time shoring up support and worrying about anyone who might break the united front. Even one defecting Boston newspaper editor prompted Reed to write Lodge: "The news seems to be spreading that Mr. Stanwood is to come out for McK—It looks rather absurd."[46] Being the ostensible front-runner was taking its toll on Reed. Theodore Roosevelt wrote his sister: "I have seen a good deal of Reed; the weight of the struggle is very evident in his face and I can see how hard it is. The presidency is a great prize! And there is a bitter fight for it."[47]

William McKinley, on the other hand, lacked confidence about winning a brokered convention and formulated a strategy to win a majority on the first ballot. He and his campaign manager, Mark Hanna, implemented a national strategy to build popular support. To get instructed McKinley delegates, they often confronted party organizations that viewed the favorite-son model of nominating a leading state figure as the most effective way to negotiate for patronage and other party benefits. If McKinley fell short on the first ballot, his aggressive strategy would have built resentments that jeopardized later ballot support.

Early contests were held in the South. Since the South was solidly Democratic, this was neutral territory for Reed and McKinley that did not raise the issue of invading another's region. The Republican Party organization in these areas was often weak. The time that McKinley and Hanna had been spending in the South was garnering results. The McKinley organization's determination to win permeated its supporters. A Louisiana supporter, J. Madison Vance, characterized his successful fight in late February to win Louisiana for McKinley: "I had to go in and make my own fight against Kellogg's manipulations and money—and plenty of it—with a strong Reed sentiment to combat."[48]

Reed and McKinley campaign managers issued dueling weekly press releases assessing the progress of the race. As of March 1, McKinley's campaign manager estimated that McKinley had already won 193 delegates of the just over 900 total delegates. The Reed campaign showed a much lower total for McKinley. Reed's campaign manager, Frank Aldrich, told reporters that he doubted the McKinley figures: "The desperation of the McKinley managers to effect the nomination of their man before the convention meets is as laughable as it is farcical. The order has apparently gone out, 'Now boys, all together, one concentrated whoop for little Mac, and it will all be over.'"[49]

Although some of the difference in estimates was spin, there was also uncertainty about delegate commitment.

McKinley's strategy of challenging favorite sons faced an early test in Minnesota, where the state convention was scheduled for March 24. Minnesota had been a good state for Reed in the 1889 Speaker's race. The state had a strong favorite son in Senator Cushman Davis. While Reed and other hopefuls were content to allow Davis to retain the delegation, McKinley forces mobilized support for instructed delegates. As the Minnesota convention approached, Davis got the bad news about St. Paul from his two campaign advisers: "McKinley's friends have been working up a sentiment in his favor, and without our knowledge they had the town pretty thoroughly organized and committed in his favor."[50] On the morning of the convention, Davis telegraphed that he was withdrawing from the race. Another favorite son, Senator Pettigrew in South Dakota, met a similar fate. The *St. Louis Republic* editorialized, "McKinley's unexpected capture of these two states . . . has given an impetus to his candidacy."[51]

If knocking off favorite sons was supposed to be easy, nobody told Reed or his enthusiastic New York supporter Theodore Roosevelt. Although Reed mostly avoided fighting favorite sons, he tested the waters against New York favorite son Levi Morton. Theodore Roosevelt explored whether a Reed delegation was possible. Henry Cabot Lodge assured Roosevelt that Morton could be defeated: "I may be over sanguine about you and that fat man from Maine and you may laugh at me but I am a better politician than the pair of you rolled into one."[52] Roosevelt's experience on the ground suggested that Lodge was overly sanguine: "There is evidently at present quite a movement for Morton in New York."[53]

The Reed campaign expected an uneventful contest in Vermont. Senator Redfield Proctor had been assuring Reed that Vermont would continue its tradition of uninstructed delegates. Thus, it came as a shock to Reed when, on April 29, Vermont Republicans voted for instructed McKinley delegates and Proctor joined them. This defeat put a hole in the Reed strategy of a solid New England. In the aftermath, Proctor deflected the blame: "The feeling of Reed's friends does not trouble me. They seem to think that it was an entirely easy and proper thing for me to do to try to override the plain sentiment of the State."[54] Later in the year, when Lodge informed Reed that he was going to Vermont, Reed requested, "If Proctor should die while you are there telegraph me at Portland Farmington and Grand Beach. Be sure however that he is really dead."[55]

The campaign's big delegate prize was the following day at the state convention in Illinois, which had long been the flashpoint of the campaign. Illinois favorite son Senator Cullom expected to win the support of his home state. Rather than defer to the established Republican organization that was comfortable with the favorite-son tradition, the McKinley campaign confronted Cullom and the party organization by pursuing instructed delegates. Knowing how tough it would be, the McKinley campaign recruited Charles Dawes in early 1895 to organize the Illinois effort. Dawes told McKinley that they might have to "make the machine sick before we get through with them."[56] Cullom lamented that "McKinley forces are organized all over my State . . . [with] agents tramping around . . . to make the state solid for McKinley."[57] By convention day, Cullom chose to step aside rather than be defeated. McKinley had just won the big delegate prize of Illinois. He now had a good chance of getting a first-ballot majority.

As the convention began in mid-June, Reed's chance for the nomination was down to a long shot that McKinley's delegate support was soft. There were also 165 contested delegates. This broke the previous record and happened because supporters of Reed and other minor candidates abandoned official local conventions in the wake of McKinley control and held separate rump conventions to choose different delegates. With some McKinley defections and delegate challenges, the anti-McKinley forces might make a run at forcing a second ballot. Reed supporters put on a brave face as they left by train for St. Louis, almost all going in a southwest direction.

Reed's daughter and wife were also not giving up. In a letter to a Reed backer, Reed's twenty-one-year-old daughter, Kitty, underlined her determination: "If we fight to the end we will be more conspicuously beaten, and that at any rate is the thing next best to winning."[58] Without his knowledge Reed's wife, Susan, wrote to campaign adviser Henry Cabot Lodge. She requested, "I hope you will make a brave fight and when you make your nominating speech not allow yourself to be overshadowed by defeat."[59] Reed's own letter to Lodge echoed his wife and daughter: "I hope our people will stand up like men. . . . The joining the enemy at this time is too silly."[60]

Reed supporters were shocked when a top Reed adviser, Joseph Manley, conceded the nomination to McKinley in spontaneous remarks to reporters after the credentials committee seated McKinley delegates in contested delegations. When asked about Manley's statement, Reed told reporters that it must have been a fabrication since Manley would not have conceded. After publicly admitting that he had said that McKinley would win, Manley wrote an apology to Reed on June 12: "It was a great mistake and I shall regret it all my life."[61] In a letter to Lodge, Reed struggled to express his anger: "Manley's conduct is too disgusting to characterize."[62] A few days later, Reed managed to offer a characterization. A kitten metaphor emerged in a letter to his friend Gifford: "Of course the Hon Manley has made bad even worse. Did he sell us or was he only a weak coward. Who can say? As Tom Platt has said how can you cowhide a kitten? Even a bad one."[63]

On June 18, 1896, Republican delegates prepared to vote for a presidential nominee. In formally nominating Reed, Henry Cabot Lodge mostly lived up to Susan Reed's exhortation to make a brave fight with a thirteen-minute speech praising Reed's "courage" and "entirely fearless" nature.[64] When Lodge finished, the woman on the stage who was responsible for displaying the Reed picture to the crowd began waving it. The unfortunate outcome was described by the *Saint Paul Globe*: "Before she could faint, go into hysterics or go crazy as women who have essayed similar role before have done, the picture came off the standard and fell to the floor."[65] That Reed's campaign had literally become unhinged was confirmed by the roll-call vote of state delegations. William McKinley secured a first-ballot nomination with 661.5 votes. Reed finished a distant second with only 84.5 first-ballot votes. A western candidate and a few favorite sons shared the rest of the votes. After McKinley won on the first ballot, Reed manager Henry Cabot Lodge successfully moved that the vote be made unanimous.

The remaining question for Reed was whether he would accept the vice presidency. The convention was packed with delegates who liked both McKinley and Reed. The two complemented each other geographically, and they had worked well together in the House. The McKinley-Reed ticket, however, was not to be. Before Lodge left for St. Louis, Reed gave him a written statement that he was not willing to serve as vice president and that Lodge should make this known. Reed did nothing to show that he was having second thoughts. With the "obvious"[66] choice for vice president out of the picture, delegates settled on New Jersey's Garret Hobart. In declining to serve as vice president, whose major responsibility at the time was presiding over the Senate, Reed passed on the chance to extend his legacy of stopping filibusters. The *Daily Inter-Ocean* lamented that the public "would have enjoyed seeing Tom close up debate in the Senate in his good old way."[67]

In the aftermath, Reed blamed his defeat on unethical activity by the McKinley campaign. In a letter to his friend George Gifford on June 14, 1896, Reed wrote, "I have had the great good fortune to hold it [the Speakership] twice without mortgage or even a shadow on the title. Was it not too much to expect the Presidency on the same terms?"[68] Reed's daughter agreed with her father. Kitty wrote Republican backer Charles Marseilles after the election: "We were defeated by patent medicine tariff craze, $, promises of office, and treachery."[69]

Given that Reed supporter US Senator Jacob Gallinger privately conceded during the campaign that McKinley was "scrupulously honest,"[70] what best explains Reed's failure to win the Republican presidential nomination in 1896? And make no mistake, it was a dramatic failure. Reed went from a presumptive leader in the winter of 1896 to a distant second by the convention in June. In New Jersey, for example, a *Herald* survey of Republican legislators in January 1896 found that Reed had ten more votes than McKinley,[71] but its survey of Republican officials four months later showed McKinley ahead 135–16.[72] Reed lost to an opponent whom he had soundly beaten in their first contest and who had worked under him in the House. Reed lost in a race in which he was widely perceived to have the most gravitas. The Democratic *Argus* foreshadowed Reed's convention defeat: "As Reed is a great man and McKinley is a little man, there should be solid ground for hope—but alas! at national conventions the little chappie usually downs the big man—witness the case of Harrison, Polk, Pierce, Taylor, Scott, and R. B. Hayes."[73] It helps when the little chappie runs a better campaign.

McKinley ran an excellent campaign. He had the foresight to see that the role of public opinion was increasing and that party machines supporting favorite sons could be defeated. The strategy was crystallized in the McKinley campaign slogan "The People Against the Bosses." Starting early, the McKinley campaign recruited enthusiastic leaders to organize McKinley clubs that turned out supporters at the state and local Republican meetings where delegates were chosen. Supporters were attracted by the consistent message that McKinley's protection policy would lead to prosperity. The message was helped by the fact that the suddenly popular 1890 tariff increase was called the McKinley bill by virtue of McKinley's position as chair of the committee of origin (to which Reed had appointed him). At the end of the campaign, Reed gave credit in his own way to his opponent's public-relations acumen: "There has been an hallucination about 'McKinley and Protection' but it has not been without creators."[74]

Reed, on the other hand, ran a poor campaign. After deciding to run for president, Reed selected Frank Aldrich to be his campaign manager. There was nothing in Aldrich's record that suggested he was a good person for the position. He was serving a second term in Congress after having been Chicago's commissioner of public works. Indeed, Aldrich was shocked to be considered for the position and told Reed that he had few national Republican connections.[75] Admitting that one lacks a key qualification is an unusual job interview strategy, but it seems to have worked on Reed. As part of his passive strategy, Reed resisted fundraising. At one point in the campaign, Reed approved a meeting between Aldrich and railroad tycoon Collis Huntington, but he would not allow Aldrich to accept a contribution, even as Huntington told Aldrich that the other candidates all understood that money was necessary to mount a successful campaign.[76] By the end of the campaign, Reed had agreed to a modest $12,000 fund from friends.[77] Although Reed has been praised for "not willing to be politically expedient to raise money for a presidential campaign,"[78] the monthly *Peterson Magazine* estimated in 1895 that it would cost at least $50,000 to run a "vigorous canvass for a presidential nomination."[79] The lack of resources was a constant source of frustration for Reed supporters like Clarence Johnson, who lamented that the campaign was unable to supplement buttons with a pamphlet: "The buttons I sent you are the only indications I have seen of an active Reed campaign. . . . From the way the McKinleyites are gathering in the delegates, I am beginning to lose faith in buttons alone as a means of salvation."[80]

Further, Reed's simultaneous actions as Speaker undermined his presidential campaign. Within the Reed campaign there was great hope that Reed would benefit from taking over as Speaker in December 1895. In the words of Theodore Roosevelt, "Luckily, with your entrance into the Speakership, we shall have you where men's thoughts will all be turned towards you, just at the right time."[81] Yet, in accepting the caucus nomination, Reed promised minimal achievement. Having pioneered a brand of partisan politics that made it difficult to reach compromise, Reed seemed to throw up his hands about the prospects of meaningful reform under divided government. While inaction can be appealing, it can be a difficult sell during hard times—exactly what the nation faced following the Panic of 1893. The *Portland Daily Press* made a valiant effort to frame Reed's resistance to legislation as more admirable under the circumstances: "In the midst of this deplorable financial chaos the Speaker of the House stands like a rock, immovable and not afraid."[82] Even some supporters, however, questioned Reed's strategy. Speaking anonymously to a reporter in early 1896, a Reed supporter said, "The country is not satisfied unless we do something."[83]

The inaction campaign strategy also backfired because it was out of character for Reed, who made his reputation by doing and saying compelling things. The *Evening Press* explained, "The new men in Congress, who came there with an idea that Tom Reed was a corker, a hummer, and all that, find him as slow as a cart horse."[84] The inactivity no doubt dampened the enthusiasm of the Reed campaign. The head of the Massachusetts delegation and Reed supporter George Lyman wrote Lodge: "Ours is a campaign of solid good sense and pure Americanism, but it lacks enthusiasm—an element which their campaign possesses to a startling degree." Ultimately, the campaign failure implicated Reed's leadership. As the campaign floundered, Lyman conceded, "McKinley has out-generaled us all to pieces."[85]

In addition to an inferior campaign, Reed also was hindered by two institutional challenges. First, McKinley provided a bigger home-state electoral boost since he was from the highly populated swing state of Ohio, whereas Reed was from the less populated solid Republican state of Maine. Second, Reed's position as sitting Speaker probably worked against him. Reed was trying to become the first sitting Speaker to win the presidency and the second person to serve as both Speaker and president (James Polk was governor in between). Although many Reed supporters thought the Speakership would help him, the position had potential pitfalls. Speaker Reed would have to reject more committee chair aspirants and project requests than he could approve, thereby alienating potential supporters. Further, while Speaker Reed was occupied with congressional business during the campaign, McKinley had just finished his term as governor and was free to campaign full time. By one account, McKinley worked fourteen-hour days with an emphasis on letter writing during the peak months of the campaign.[86] It is also possible that House Speakers are perceived as having legislative instead of executive skills, especially someone like Reed who built his reputation on parliamentary procedure. To this day no sitting Speaker of the House or Maine resident has become president.

Despite some good reasons for his defeat, Reed did not take losing well. He again succumbed to his impulse to turn political differences into personal animosity. His former friend William McKinley bore the brunt of this. In a letter to his friend Gifford, Reed used creative punctuation to pack a lot of punch into one sentence: "To have endorsed paper you could not pay, to have your debts liquidated by gentlemen who are not charitable, to have exploited for your own benefit 'Industrials' dependent on your public service, to have been and to be Mr 'Facing-Both-Ways,' to have tried to betray in two conventions and made open failure; who would have thought this was the way to high honor two thousand years after the Crucifixion!" After contrasting McKinley's behavior with his own, Reed wrote, "If God sells all things at a fair price is not also the devil a good merchant? I would not dare to write this to anybody else but you, not for fear of detection but because nobody but you would understand that this is not personal but impersonal acidity."[87]

A Name That's Never Spoken

A bitter Reed seemed ready to retire from politics. The pain of rejection by the party that he had served so long was still fresh. Reed had already achieved the goals that had motivated his legislative career. Citing an unnamed Reed intimate, national columnist Walter Wellman reported that Mrs. Reed wanted to leave Washington and that Reed intended to gain financial security through legal work in New York City.[88] As summer 1896 began, the timing was right for a Reed retirement announcement. If Reed stepped aside, Maine First District Republicans could name a new Republican candidate in time for the fall 1896 election.

Would Reed step down? After reflection, Reed surprised many by running again for the seat that he had held for twenty years. He privately suggested that his motivation for seeking reelection was that the Democratic silver-coinage proposal had increased what was "at stake" in the election.[89] Given his motivation, it is not surprising that Reed's campaign appearances would take the form of discourses on the currency issue. He usually began by acknowledging that these were tough times for people. Farmers, though, didn't need Reed to tell them that they were receiving low prices for their products. Yet, on August 26, 1896, he told his audience that under the Democratic administration, "you get only 12 cents for wool." When an audience member shouted, "Only 10 cents," Reed turned the correction to his advantage: "Yes, that is the way I always understate the facts; you can always retail what I say at a profit."[90]

Despite the tough times, Reed warned his audiences, free coinage of silver was too dangerous. At the Biddeford Opera House on August 28, 1896, Reed told his audience that "of all the foolish things I have ever heard men say the most idiotic is this: 'Let's try this thing! There may be no sense in it but things can't be worse.'"[91] The Democratic proposal would, he said, make things worse by weakening confidence in money. As a result, Reed explained, lenders would not loan money if they were to be paid back in a devalued silver currency after good currency had been driven out of the market. Reed searched for an analogy that would resonate with his oceanfront constituency, explaining, "Human experience in every walk of life teaches us that those who have blundered will blunder again, and that the wisest course is not to employ a ship captain who has not yet emerged from his last ship wreck but the safe sailor who has never lost a ship, a passenger, or a letter."[92] Reed urged patience until things turned around. Reed said, "Our remedy is peace, tranquility, sound money, general confidence, and business—all will follow in regular order."[93]

Consequently, the principal strategy of Democrats against Reed was to attack his position as doing nothing as the nation struggled. Although Reed's opponent, businessman E. H. Staples, was not on the stump, Maine Democrats invited other prominent officials to make the case that Reed was indifferent to the plight of the suffering electorate. Out-of-state critics relished the chance to deride the Speaker. Picking up on Reed's "remedy" language, they exchanged familiar Czar Reed monikers for a new doctor moniker. Coloradoan H. H. Eddy told his Maine audience that Reed was offering a "faith cure." Eddy joked, "The doses are prescribed and all this over the signature of Dr. Reed."[94]

The second major strategy of Democrats against Reed was to ridicule his animosity toward Republican presidential nominee William McKinley. Although he ignored McKinley, Reed was eager to discuss the Democratic nominee, William Jennings Bryan: "If Mr. Bryan could be elected for 24 hours, I should be in favor of electing him just so that the people could find out what he represents but I don't want four years of time just to educate the rest of you."[95] In the campaign's major speech, Reed spoke for over an hour to six thousand people and declined to name McKinley even as he named Bryan five times.[96] Reed's reluctance to mention McKinley on the campaign trail prompted the Democratic *Argus* to break into verse: "There's a name that's never spoken; There's a big man's heart that's broken."[97]

On September 14, 1896, Maine voters delivered Reed and the Republicans a massive victory. Reed enjoyed his largest victory ever as he doubled his Democratic opponent, 19,329 to 8,720. A happy Reed addressed supporters on election night. His brief remarks abandoned his usual interpretation of a Republican victory. Rather, Reed said, "It was a victory which belongs to good men of both parties and cannot fail to do good to the whole country."[98]

After winning Maine's early September elections, Reed was asked to participate in the national campaign for McKinley and the Republicans. Was Reed willing to travel the country in support of his rival McKinley? If he accepted, he would have to confront two growing dislikes—McKinley and travel. Reed had recently expressed his increasing frustration with campaigning: "I object to being exhibited from the tail end of a train or on the platform like a criminal on his way to jail."[99] Ultimately, however, Reed felt the 1896 election was too important to sit out.

His 1896 schedule would send him all over the country and entail thousands of miles of travel from Maine to California. While Reed was undertaking a demanding travel schedule, McKinley was at his Canton home running a traditional front-porch campaign. In the words of the *St. Louis Post-Dispatch*, "While Mr. McKinley takes the cigar, poor Tom Reed takes the stump."[100] On October 16, the rigors of the campaign caught up with Reed when he was struck with the flu in Illinois. He was bedridden, speaking in a whisper, and under the care of two doctors. After canceling several speeches, Reed resumed campaigning, telling audiences to be extra quiet because he could not speak loudly.

Although struggling with the flu, Reed was determined not to miss the opportunity to undermine Jerry Simpson. The Kansas Populist had lost in the Republican groundswell of 1894 but was trying to reclaim his House seat. Reed hoped to generate some enthusiasm for Simpson's Republican opponent. Thus, on October 24, Reed was speaking to thousands in Wichita, Kansas. If audience members were hoping to hear the current Speaker of the House attack a third-party legislator, they would not be disappointed. Reed said that the Republican incumbent had dramatically improved representation of the Seventh District from the Simpson years when it was represented by "chaos."[101] Simpson was furious that the sitting Speaker of the House would go into a member's district and disparage his service. Simpson, however, did get a measure of revenge by defeating the Republican incumbent.

To overcome his dislike of McKinley, Reed dusted off a strategy that had worked well when he was campaigning for Benjamin Harrison. He refused to mention McKinley by name. Reed instead discussed financial policy. In Boston Music Hall, Reed reflected, "Corporate cooperation has been born into the world and unites poor and rich into one chain of destiny from which there is no separation."[102] If the reluctance to mention McKinley was noticeable in his own campaign in August, it was downright awkward in a national campaign to elect McKinley. The *Washington Post* offered a half-hearted defense of Reed's refusal to mention McKinley: "Why cannot he be permitted to treat McKinley as the Latin writers did the substantive, and leave him to the imagination of the reader?"[103]

The beleaguered Reed finished the campaign in San Francisco. California had a proposition for women's suffrage in 1896, and advocates were hopeful that Reed would endorse the measure. Earlier in the campaign, after speaking to several thousand men in a tent in Wichita, Reed affirmed his support for women's suffrage in an auditorium speech to several thousand women: "You are as deeply interested in the results of this campaign as your husbands, whom I have left across the street in the tent . . . [so] I wish you had some of the voting to do."[104] This time, however, Reed disappointed Susan Anthony and other suffragists by glancing over the issue.[105] It is likely that Reed also disappointed his daughter, who again traveled with him while his wife remained in Maine. Reed's 1896 campaign manager, Frank Aldrich, wrote privately that nobody ever managed Reed, but the closest that anyone came was his "charmingly droll" daughter, Kitty, who was Reed's "constant companion and counsellor."[106]

Ultimately, Kitty would make the fight for women's suffrage her own. In 1906, she founded a San Francisco-based magazine, the *Yellow Ribbon*, that supported women's suffrage. She later suggested that women should set up a nonpartisan educational organization. When the League of Women Voters published a book about its history, Kitty was given credit for having planted the kernel that led to the creation of the organization.[107] Returning to Maine, Kitty served as president of a state convention in 1916 for women's suffrage. She successfully lobbied the state legislature to put a suffrage amendment on the ballot. When Maine went to the polls in September 1917, the amendment lost 38,838 to 20,684. Although this effort fell short, Kitty would live to see the ratification of the Nineteenth Amendment in 1920, guaranteeing women the right to vote.

On November 3, 1896, Republicans achieved a landslide victory. They retained control of the House, which all but assured that Reed would remain Speaker. Republicans also won the Senate. Reed telegraphed McKinley, "Congratulations on the state of the Union."[108] The telegram was hardly sincere. Reed remained bitter even as many of his Republican friends had come to appreciate McKinley. Theodore Roosevelt wrote Lodge in November 1896: "I am very glad McKinley seems inclined to be so friendly; I'm really a good deal worried by Reed's seeming purpose to refuse to be on good terms with him."[109]

With a Republican president in sight, congressional Republicans had limited incentive to legislate during the lame-duck session. On March 4, 1897, the modestly productive session ended minutes before the presidential inauguration of William McKinley. A resolution was offered to thank Reed for presiding in an "able, impartial, and dignified manner." The resolution prompted loud cheering and unanimous approval. In accepting the gratitude of the chamber, Reed said, "I am sincerely grateful for the kind expression of your confidence and esteem, but I am still more grateful for the daily kindness and goodwill on the part of every member on both sides of the House."[110] Leaving the House chamber, he proceeded to the inaugural festivities for President McKinley. Reed felt that he should have been the one taking the oath of office as president.

CHAPTER 9

WAR SPEAKER

When the Fifty-Fifth Congress convened on March 15, 1897, Republicans outnumbered Democrats 206–122. The aftermath of the 1896 election had sharpened the differences between the parties, with Republicans more industrial and Democrats more rural.[1] An unusually large number of third-party members joined Congress as Populists, Fusionists, and Silverites capitalized on the transformative election of 1896 to win twenty-nine combined seats. The normal nine-month layoff between the old and new Congress was eliminated when President McKinley called a special session to begin just ten days into his administration. Reed won the Republican nomination without a significant canvass, which ensured that he would return to the Speakership. There was greater uncertainty about who would replace the deceased Charles Crisp as minority leader.

Democrats chose Joseph Bailey, who presented a sharp contrast to Reed. Born in 1863 to a father serving in the Confederate Army, Bailey was the youngest member of Congress when first elected in 1890. He projected a smooth style as he tried to rebuild Democratic fortunes after a crushing defeat in 1896. He differed with Reed on the major policy questions of the day, including support for low tariffs and free coinage of silver. Bailey's first electoral win came when he defeated his own father to become a convention delegate.[2] Reed, of course, was old enough to be Bailey's father. The stage was set for a struggle.

In moving forward on the tariff that was the purpose of the special session, Reed and the Republicans used many of the tools favoring the majority that Reed had pioneered during his career. At the beginning of the Fifty-Fifth

Congress, Republicans adopted the rules of the Fifty-Fourth Congress. While obstruction by Democrats was minimal, Speaker Reed stopped dilatory motions and counted a quorum when needed. The Rules committee prevented amendments that might lead to uncomfortable votes for Republicans. Democrat Champ Clark offered a culinary simile for Republican tactics: "Whenever any attempt is made to abolish trusts here, you Republicans squirm like skinned eels in a hot skillet, and resort to every parliamentary trick ever devised by the ingenuity of man to protect them from our assaults."[3] The Rules committee set definitive dates for voting. When the conference committee reported the tariff bill, Republicans ignored Democratic pleas for several days of debate and approved it at midnight that same day.

While Congress sat in a four-month special session charged with increasing revenue through tariff increases, Reed prevented the House from taking up other business by refusing to appoint the committees that were responsible for doing the work of Congress. Without committees there was no place for bills to go, and so they went nowhere. In closing off other legislative activity, Reed retained the support of most Republicans. Although a small group of frustrated House Republicans met to discuss how to force action and issued an anonymous press release suggesting that Reed had lost faith with the Fifty-First Congress, House Republicans were mostly quiet so as not to antagonize the powerful Speaker.[4]

As the session continued, complaints grew louder. Democrats delighted in pointing out that Reed had empowered the majority party to act but was now preventing action. On April 7, 1897, Populist Jeremiah Simpson characterized Reed's failure to name committees as "an autocratic and despotic power granted to the Speaker that deprives the people of the United States of their representation in this body." Simpson also raised an old grudge against Reed: "The Speaker came into my district last fall in the campaign and . . . took occasion to say that for four years the Seventh district of Kansas was represented by chaos." When the laughter subsided, Simpson resumed, "Chaos means lack of organization . . . and until those committees are appointed this House and its members are in a state of chaos. Not the Seventh district of Kansas alone is represented by chaos, but all the districts in the United States."

Defending his delay, Reed explained that the unusually short time between congressional sessions prevented him from assessing committee memberships. Reed reminded Simpson that the Speaker did not have the last word on committee appointment or any other procedural issue: "If the

House thinks that any occupant of the chair is not carrying out its wishes, is not acting as its representative, the remedy is in the hands of the House at any time."[5]

Simpson was emerging as the heir apparent to William Springer, the opponent who eagerly sparred with Reed despite the likelihood of coming out on the losing end. On May 3, Simpson proclaimed, "The Speaker, in withholding the appointment of committees, holds such power over the members of the Republican majority in this House that they dare not vote against any resolution which represents his wishes . . . for fear they will not get on good committees." Simpson accused Reed of having gone from stopping filibusters to stopping legislation and becoming "himself the filibusterer."[6] Again, during journal approval on May 13, Simpson condemned Reed for running the House in "violation of the rules." Taking its cue from Reed, the House ruled that Simpson was out of order and must sit down. A stunned Simpson asked, "Now, Mr. Speaker, I would like to inquire where am I at?"

Reed replied, "The Chair has never been able to find anybody who could answer that question."[7]

The press gave tremendous coverage to the altercations between Speaker Thomas Reed and Jeremiah Simpson. There was even an obvious name since the two men were better known by their nicknames. Long used as an expression for characterizing squabbling boys, "Tom and Jerry" had inevitably become a popular mixed alcoholic beverage. The *Springfield Daily Republican* lamented the "Tom and Jerry statesmanship of the House."[8] Decades later, the pairing was immortalized in cat and mouse cartoon characters. The names were properly aligned. Reed was definitely the cat.

While Reed enjoyed his tiffs with Simpson, he may have enjoyed even more the fights between Simpson and Bailey. While Populists and Democrats agreed on many issues, the two leaders had policy and personal differences that led to conflict. Early in the session, for example, after Simpson criticized Reed for not appointing committees, Bailey said he rather liked not having committees. Bailey explained, "We are not disposed to insist upon the Republican Party legislating, because we sincerely believe that the country suffers when the Republican Party legislates."[9] On another occasion during the special session, Simpson mistakenly said that Bailey had voted for a rule that he had actually voted against. Bailey admonished Simpson, "I suggest to the gentleman from Kansas that he go and inform himself, for that is not true."

Speaker Reed cautioned, "Gentlemen must not interrupt each other, and must not make unreasonable requests."[10]

Trying to Dissuade a Cuban Cyclone

Tom-and-Jerry episodes provided only a temporary distraction from congressional concern about the situation in Cuba. In the spring of 1897, despite more than a year of repression by General Weyler, the bloody conflict between Cuban rebels and Spanish colonialists was continuing unabated. Summoned to Cuba in January 1896, Weyler had tried to isolate rebels by taking away their support from peasants in the countryside. The Spanish army laid waste to the countryside and forced peasants to move into tightly controlled urban areas called reconcentrados. At the time, a presidential committee estimated that over 200,000 Cubans had died from starvation and disease.[11] "Butcher" Weyler's atrocities were widely condemned by American newspapers and religious groups. In addition to the humanitarian crisis, American politicians were also concerned about the economic implications of instability so close to American soil. Other politicians saw the crisis in Cuba as an excellent opportunity for a new foreign policy marked by a revitalized Monroe Doctrine in which America would be more assertive in removing European colonial powers from the Americas. For all these reasons, there was a strong feeling in America that something should be done about the situation in Cuba.

For many Americans the least that the United States should do was to recognize the Cuban insurgents as something more than people lashing out against a legitimate government. In legal terms, the United States should recognize the belligerency of the Cubans. Without recognizing the Cubans as belligerents, the United States was affirming that the Spanish government was the only legitimate government in Cuba. Cuban rebels were not afforded equal treatment under American law. American entities, for example, were constrained in their interactions with Cubans, including selling armaments. On the other hand, granting belligerency rights risked alienating the Spanish and complicated the diplomatic efforts of President McKinley, who opposed recognizing belligerency. Support for belligerent rights to Cuba was generally associated with stronger Cuban sympathy and support for more assertive US foreign policy. For his part, Reed opposed belligerent rights. He faced increasing pressure as instability continued in Cuba.

The pressure on Speaker Reed and the House to recognize the belligerency of Cubans increased dramatically on May 20, 1897, when the Senate passed a belligerency resolution. Not only had the resolution passed in the Senate, but also it had passed easily, forty-one to fourteen. The margin reflected popular sympathy with the Cubans and widespread disenchantment with the lack of diplomatic progress by the administration. Support for the resolution in the House was also estimated to be high. The question was whether there would be a vote on the resolution during House consideration of President McKinley's universally supported emergency request for $50,000 to help distressed Americans in Cuba. Since the House was legislating on Cuba, a belligerency resolution was germane. Consequently, Reed and the Rules committee brought the Cuban aid bill to the floor under a rule that prohibited amendments. Even though the House was legislating on Cuba, it was not allowed to vote on the belligerency resolution.

As the House debated the Cuban aid bill, Democratic leader Joe Bailey moved to amend the bill by adding the recognition of belligerency—what came to be known as the Bailey Resolution. His motion prompted the galleries in the House to burst into applause. A Republican made the point of order that the amendment was out of order since the rule did not allow amendments. The conflict would be resolved by the Speaker of the House. Before Reed issued a decision, there was debate on the point of order. It was not so much debate as allowing Democrats to vent.

In defending his resolution, Bailey emphasized that a clear majority of the House supported it. He explained, "There is not a gentleman on that side of the Chamber who does not know that, if this House were once permitted to vote upon the direct proposition to recognize the belligerency of Cuba, it would carry by an overwhelming majority." Bailey tied it to majority rule: "When we are denied the opportunity to bring that question before the House, it is not the will of the majority which you are enforcing, but it is the will of the majority which you are suppressing."[12]

As debate was ending, Bailey offered the ill-timed motion to appeal Reed's decision. Bailey insisted, "I recognize, Mr. Speaker, that no amount of argument will change the ruling of the Speaker, and I appeal from that decision, and on that I demand the yeas and nays." The only problem was that Reed had not actually ruled yet.

Reed pointed this out, "The Chair has not made any ruling, but the Chair will make a ruling in accordance with what the gentleman from Texas evidently thinks is the proper parliamentary ruling, which is that the amendment is in no wise in order." Bailey denied that he thought Reed should uphold the point of order, but that a Republican told him Reed would rule that way. Reed countered, "The Chair thinks the gentleman from Texas probably had a more inner light than that."[13] Reed upheld the point of order. The House voted aid to distressed Americans in Cuba but did not vote on the belligerency resolution. The Democratic *Fort Worth Register* accused Reed of having "muzzled" the government: "Three-fourths of the members of the house would like to vote for . . . the recognition of the belligerency of the Cubans, but they are not allowed to do so. . . . [Thereby] the farce of calling the house a legislative body goes on, like the butcheries in Cuba."[14]

Democrats tried a number of strategies over the next several months to get the resolution considered. Securing the floor under the guise of personal privilege, they would transition to the argument that the integrity of the House was being sacrificed by not being able to vote on the resolution. One tactic that held promise was tying arguments about the refusal to appoint committees with the belligerency resolution. Democrats came up with the plan to demand that Reed name a foreign affairs committee, which would then have the belligerency resolution in its jurisdiction. Throughout the intermittent attempts to consider the belligerency resolution, Reed held his ground in refusing consideration.

Anti-interventionists were happy to have Reed in the saddle. The *Biloxi Herald* wrote, "Speaker Reed does well to keep the bridle on the house and a firm hand on the rein."[15] Probably those happiest with the situation were Democrats who did not like intervention. They could have it both ways and relished it. They could be happy that their preferred policy was being carried out, while at the same time preserve the narrative of Reed as the power-grabbing czar. The *Eastern Argus* editorialized, "If the Speaker's autocratic methods blocked nothing more important than this jingo belligerency resolution the country would view the innovation with equanimity."[16]

Democrats insisted that Reed was acting against popular opinion. On July 1, for example, Representative Evan Settle digressed from a minor parliamentary issue about amending the journal into a speech declaring that the House had "acted in utter defiance of public sentiment." Settle made a prediction about "that great battle that is to be fought in 1898, and of that still greater battle that is to be fought in 1900; that battle which in my judgment will prove to the Republican Party both its Armageddon and its Waterloo."

Reed failed to follow Settle's reasoning. He offered, "Certainly the gentleman from Kentucky would not maintain that the battle of Armageddon has anything to do with the present question [to amend the journal]."[17]

Democrats were not done yet, however, and on July 7 they caught Republicans off guard by bringing up the belligerency resolution on a suspension day when a two-thirds majority could bring bills to the floor out of order. The resolution may well have been able to get two-thirds of the House on a direct vote. Thus, when Benton McMillin rose to suspend the rules and pass the resolution, it was a major event. There was a pause. Reed looked at fellow Maine Republican Nelson Dingley. Dingley knew what to do; he made a motion to adjourn. Republicans who would have supported the belligerency resolution on a direct vote would not oppose their party on a procedural vote to adjourn. The House abruptly adjourned for the day. Less than three weeks later, the special session ended. The House never voted on the belligerency resolution.

While Congress was winding down, Theodore Roosevelt was emerging as a national spokesperson for a more aggressive military posture. In spring 1897, Roosevelt began work as second-in-command to naval secretary John Long. While Roosevelt's reputation for boldness raised some concerns with Secretary Long and President McKinley, he also had friends in high places advocating for his appointment. One of these was Speaker Reed under whom John Long had served in the Fifty-First Congress. In fact, the private correspondence of Massachusetts Republican Party leader George Lyman credits Reed's support as decisive in Roosevelt ultimately getting the position.[18] Roosevelt would bring his trademark unbounded energy to the job, which would stand in contrast to the lesser energy of his much senior boss Secretary Long.

Although Secretary Long was cautious about adding battleships, Roosevelt publicly advocated for a massive naval buildup while Long was on vacation. On July 23, 1897, he told an audience of Ohio naval reserves that they might be called on to uphold American "dignity in whatever misunderstanding we may have with foreign nations."[19] Roosevelt informed his friend Henry Cabot Lodge that his Ohio speech "nearly threw the Secretary into a fit, and he gave me as heavy a wigging as his invariable courtesy and kindness would permit."[20] It would be a long, hot summer in Washington. Roosevelt wasted no opportunity to remind his boss of this. Roosevelt wrote Long, "I hope you are having a very pleasant time, and if things go on as they are now there isn't the slightest earthly reason for you to come back for six weeks more."[21]

Also enjoying summer in New England, Reed entered the public debate over the navy. He spoke at a banquet in Portland on August 19. Reed did not directly criticize Roosevelt, but he articulated the desire for a modest naval increase. Reed offered the metaphor of an insurance policy for the nation's navy. He explained, "If a man waited to pay insurance until his house was on fire, either he or the [insurance] company would be bankrupted."[22]

Learning of Reed's speech, Henry Cabot Lodge wrote Reed and inaugurated a compelling exchange about the role of the United States in the world. Lodge began his August 20, 1897, letter to Reed by complimenting him on his speech: "I read your speech and thought it very good." Lodge praised Reed's insurance metaphor. He wrote, "The point you make about the Navy and forts being the insurance covers the whole case." As a supporter of a more assertive military, Lodge used the letter to advocate for naval spending: "I hope you will not let [appropriations chair] Cannon make his economies on this insurance."[23]

Reed extended the metaphor in a reply. He explained, "Insurance is a good thing but over insurance creates what the insurance men call Moral Hazard; meaning the hazard which there always is that an over insured man will set fire to his house."[24]

Lodge responded, "I am sorry to see in you a disposition to attenuate the good things you have said, and to indulge in casuistry. We are not over insured; we practically have no insurance at all, or at best very little, and our risks are enormous." Lodge closed the subject, "I am sorry that your extreme pro-Spanish prejudices should warp your otherwise just mind."[25]

Replying on August 27, Reed protested, "'Pro-Spanish' seems a little hard but it chords with the rest of the argument." He elaborated, "I should really prefer to be 'Pro American' and prefer also not to spill any American blood for either until the advantage to America should clearly appear."[26] On September 13, Reed resumed the correspondence by defending his position in the last Congress against the belligerency resolution: "If we take that action under such circumstances it is an expression of ill will." Reed elaborated by contemplating a future scenario: "What is to be feared is that the Recognition conferring as it does power of search will by some accident and fervid persons are liable to accidents lead us into war." Reed's letter drifted into a broader consideration of US foreign policy. He wrote, "I do not think we can lay much stress on the idea that we ought to help colonies throw off the yoke for that would pledge us to Canada as well, and has not been our history." Reed concluded, "Of course all this is crude and sounds almost cynicle perhaps but to have this nation stopped in the beginning of a recovery . . . seems unwise."[27]

Lodge wrote back on September 15, defending his support of the belligerency resolution in the Senate. He explained that he had voted for belligerency but would rather have voted for independence. He explained that

Cuban independence would be followed by other South American nations. "My desire is to get Europe out of America, because the presence of Europe here is a continual source of anxiety and trouble, and when there is rebellion, as in Cuba, it hangs over business all the time, the threat of war," he philosophized. Lodge concluded with what he may have intended to be gentle teasing: "I notice with pleasure that you boldly adhere to the natural method of spelling 'cynical' by giving it the termination of 'icle.' . . . I may not be able to argue with you successfully on Cuba, but in spelling I think I have you."[28]

On September 17, Reed replied, "That was very low down in you to criticise my spelling, because it is universally admitted to be beyond criticism." Reed added some gentle teasing of his own. Reed wrote that even if he had spelled a word incorrectly, Lodge at least "could read it which is more than can be said of the most untranslatable writing I ever saw to wit yours."[29] Reed and Lodge would not have to trouble themselves with handwriting and spelling shortcomings as this letter appears to have ended the exchange, and their subsequent correspondence was minimal.

While Reed and Lodge exchanged letters, Theodore Roosevelt was keeping busy. Privately, he was increasingly critical of Reed. In late summer, Roosevelt wrote a friend, "I am rather afraid that there is a very foolish feeling growing that we now have enough of a Navy, Tom Reed, I am sorry to say, being one of the men who have given expression to this feeling."[30] He was less critical of Secretary Long in whose absence he had increased naval readiness. Roosevelt elaborated in a September 24 letter to Lodge: "[Secretary of the Navy John] Long is just a dear. . . . I have at times been a little nervous in the effort to steer the exact course between bothering him on the one hand, and going ahead with something too widely divergent from his views, on the other."[31]

The culmination of Reed's activity in summer and fall 1897 was an article against an expansionist American foreign policy titled "Empire Can Wait," which was published in the December 4, 1897, issue of *Illustrated American*. Reed began his article with the premise that empires were destined to fail: "The very extension of an empire, seems by its own power and nature to plant the seeds of that decay, which has been thus far universal through all time." He argued that overexpansion produced differences that were hard to assimilate and placed a "heavy strain on our institutions." Noting that the country may spread naturally, Reed concluded, "But those empires which hope for eternity can wait."[32]

Reed was well prepared as the regular session of the Fifty-Fifth Congress convened on December 4, 1897. He did not have to spend the first few months working on committee assignments since those had been announced on the last day of the special session. The tariff bill had already been finished in the special session. Although new gold discoveries had reduced the issue's salience, there remained some anticipation about the currency questions that had animated the 1896 presidential campaign. Reed's friend Nelson Dingley, Ways and Means chair, had demurred to give primary responsibility for legislation to the Committee on Banking and Currency chaired by Massachusetts Republican Joseph Walker, in whom Reed had little confidence. On December 25, while the House of Representatives was on holiday, Reed's sarcasm was not. In a letter to a friend, Reed wrote, "Walker has gone to New Hampshire to ride horseback, hunt and generally to get up his muscular system so that true finance may not suffer from mere physical weakness. If all the others of the committee get themselves into athletic trim all will be well."[33]

Domestic politics, however, was destined to take a back seat to foreign affairs. Members were still thinking about Cuba. The layoff had not lessened the desire to recognize the belligerency of the Cubans. It seemed a repeat of the special session when on January 19, 1898, Democrat Ferdinand Brucker offered a belligerency resolution, but Reed prevented a direct vote on the resolution.

Everything would change, however, because of the USS *Maine*. The American battleship sailed into Havana's harbor on January 25, 1898. Although expressly promoted as a friendship mission, administration officials also saw its deployment as part of a broader strategy of war preparation. On the morning of February 15, 1898, there was an explosion on board the USS *Maine*. The ship sank and 266 Americans lost their lives. Was the explosion an accident or sabotage? Many believed that Spanish sabotage was responsible. Calls for war to protect the national honor grew louder.

In the aftermath of the USS *Maine* explosion, Reed resisted pressure to act quickly. From the outset he believed that the explosion was an accident. He insisted that new defense spending follow regular procedures and meet spending targets. Thus, Reed did not grant an expedited path for a bill to fund two artillery units. His efforts slowed for three weeks the consideration of the artillery bill. In the Senate, Eugene Hale, also of Maine, was urging caution on the Naval Affairs committee. The Democratic *Argus* suggested that Reed's cautious approach to naval spending was reasonable: "Congress would be likely to hesitate before expending more millions in the construction of warships that may blow up at any time."[34]

During this period, Theodore Roosevelt and others privately and publicly blasted Reed. In a letter to Secretary Long on February 19, Roosevelt wrote, "I was informed that both Speaker Reed and Senator Hale had stated that we must cease building any more battleships, in view of the disaster to the *Maine*. I cannot believe that the statement is true, for of course such an attitude, if supported by the people, would mean that we had reached the last pitch of national cowardice and baseness."[35] Reed and Hale were also getting public criticism. The Washington *Times* editorialized, "Is Spain to get all the loose warships and we none? Probably, if Senor Tomaso Reed and Senor Dupuy de Hale can have their way."[36]

Other criticism regularly directed at Reed was even more personal. First, critics pointed to Reed's admittedly modest war record. The Omaha *World-Herald* editorialized, "Thomas B. Reed was an assistant paymaster of the Navy, and as such was in constant danger of being inoculated with the bacilli of disease that lurks in the folds of the deadly greenback. After surviving these dread dangers it is not surprising that Speaker Reed is unwilling to again expose himself to danger."[37] Second, Reed was portrayed as a stooge for financial interests. The New Mexico *Independent Democrat* suggested, "In the furtherance of the ends of justice, if it becomes necessary, let Boss Reed, or Czar Reed, be crucified. Better men than he have been crucified, and he has proven himself to be a tool of Wall Street."[38] Further, at the time, Reed was being paid well to serve as the referee for twenty-eight insurance companies. The Washington *Times* editorialized, "They [life insurance companies] realize that the coming castigation of Spain may make some death losses to the partial demoralization of their tables of expectation . . . [and in opposing the war] they have a conservative as well as an able 'referee' in the Speaker's chair."[39]

Rather than confronting Reed directly, President McKinley worked with other congressional leaders to accelerate defense spending. On March 6, McKinley called House appropriations chair Joseph Cannon to the White House. McKinley said that he did not want to jeopardize diplomacy by recommending defense spending, but he hoped that Cannon could submit a $50 million appropriation for defense preparation. Other congressional leaders met with McKinley the following day. Although Reed had been left out of the negotiations with the White House, he undoubtedly was aware of the parameters of what was being offered, and on March 8 he recognized Cannon, who proceeded to make the motion for $50 million to be spent at the discretion of the president for defense. There was no doubt about its passage. When the unanimous vote was ending, Speaker Reed made a rare request: "The Clerk will call my name." The clerk read his name, and Reed responded "yes" to the applause of the chamber.

Although Reed voted for the appropriation, he was not pleased at the circumstances surrounding the vote. According to Cannon, Reed approached him that evening as he was leaving the Capitol and asked, "Joe, why did you do it?" After Cannon replied that he could not have asked for advice in good faith because he was determined to introduce the bill with or without Reed's support, Reed replied, "Perhaps you are right" and never raised the issue with Cannon again.[40] Reed also expressed disapproval of the tone of the debate to his assistant: "Here we are standing here lashing our tail and rolling our eyes, and telling how dignified and peaceful we are."[41]

Opposition to war increasingly centered on President McKinley and Reed. Despite public pressure, President McKinley pleaded for more time to negotiate with Spain. Reed continued to stand up to a Republican caucus that was becoming restless. The two men were well placed to slow progress toward the war. Forty-five days after the USS *Maine* exploded, Theodore Roosevelt summarized the landscape for a friend: "I think it about a toss up whether we have war or peace. The trend of events is for war. Congress is for war. All it needs is a big leader; but the two biggest leaders, the President and the Speaker, both of whom have enormous power, are almost crazy in their eagerness for peace, and would make almost any sacrifice to get peace." Roosevelt concluded, "Under such circumstances it will be very hard for the majority to force action."[42]

On March 30, the pressure in the House for action on Cuba finally erupted with the presentation of a resolution to declare Cuba independent. The measure was opposed by the McKinley administration, which saw it as infringing on the Article II power of the president to recognize governments by "receiving ambassadors." Introducing the resolution, Joseph Bailey argued that the United States should stand up for freedom by allowing Cubans to fight for their independence. The proposal earned huge cheers from the large galleries; an immediate vote would put the large number of strong Republican supporters of Cuba in a difficult position. Reed was determined to avoid such a vote. He refused to recognize the Bailey proposal as a privileged motion. After intense lobbying, Republicans supported Reed on the procedural vote of whether to allow it to come up, giving him the benefit of the doubt, even though a reported fifty-six Republicans had met the night before to discuss how to force a vote.[43] Only two Republicans defected on the procedural vote.

Two days later, President McKinley consulted Reed on the situation. They made a curious pair trying to preserve peace. Reed harbored bitter resentment of McKinley's alleged duplicity in winning the 1896 election. Reed's resentment was well known, and he received some praise for backing the McKinley administration when the easiest thing would have been to lead the majority in the House that thought McKinley was dragging his feet. McKinley asked Reed how much more time he had before Congress would take the initiative and act on its own. Reed told McKinley that time was running out. Publicly, Reed compared preventing the war push to trying to "dissuade a cyclone."[44]

Finally, Reed relented on April 13, and an overwhelming majority of the House was ready to support a resolution authorizing American force to liberate Cuba from Spanish rule. The Rules committee brought the resolution to the floor with only forty minutes of debate, and it passed easily. Since the Senate had passed a different resolution, the two versions had to be reconciled before becoming law. The most significant difference was that the Senate version recognized Cuban independence, but the House version did not. Reed and his deputies lobbied to keep their caucus behind the House version.

On April 18, the House again took up the resolution authorizing the president to use force against Spain. Reed wanted to prevent the possibility that enough Republicans would defect to join Democrats in support of recognition of the insurgent government and Cuban independence. The session began at noon, and Reed supporter Nelson Dingley and Democratic leader Joseph Bailey both sought the floor. Reed recognized Dingley, who moved the previous question, which immediately ended debate and forced a vote on the House version without the Senate amendment. Bailey's protests prompted a sarcastic reply from Reed that Bailey "will gradually learn parliamentary procedure" by watching Reed's rulings.[45]

By allowing no debate and no amendments and making it the first vote of the day, Reed believed that he was giving his preferred measure the best chance of success. His strategy was vindicated by the vote on the previous question, which carried 179–156 with fewer than predicted Republican defections. The result of the early vote made defection less likely as the Senate and House shuttled their versions between chambers. The *St. Albans Daily Messenger* evaluated the vote: "Instead of a stampede from the Republican ranks, only twelve members of the House were 'faithless among the faithful found' and Thomas Brackett Reed won the greatest parliamentary victory of his life."[46] Sitting in the House gallery, famed British observer Beatrice Webb was less impressed by the House rules. In her diary, Webb described the resolution as passing the House by means of an "extraordinary procedure—which seems customary—of closing all opposition" by not allowing debate or amendments and otherwise making the House proceedings "so extravagantly absurd that one feels as if one were looking at a comic opera."[47]

By standing firm, House Republicans would be negotiating from a position of strength in conference with the Senate. With debate prevented, House members sang war songs in the lobby. Finally, the Senate relented and the chambers proceeded to vote on the same resolution just before 3:00 a.m. After passage in the Senate, the resolution authorizing force passed the House by a 310–6 vote. Consistent with practice, the Speaker did not vote.

Was Reed in line with his caucus? Three days later, he took a break from presiding and handed the gavel to Samuel McCall, who was one of six members voting against the resolution. Reed later told McCall, "I envy you the luxury of your vote; I was where I could not do it."[48]

Path of Empire is Opening

A few days after authorizing the president to use force, both chambers formally declared war against Spain. As the war began, Commodore Dewey and the American navy attacked the Spanish in the Philippines and sank all the Spanish ships in Manila Bay. Dewey had been placed in charge of the Asiatic fleet in October 1897 after some maneuvering by Assistant Navy Secretary Theodore Roosevelt when Secretary Long was on vacation. Learning of Dewey's Philippine victory, Reed reportedly said that he should leave immediately.[49] Dewey did not. The question of what to do with the Philippines, however, would wait for another day.

As the nation mobilized for war, the House of Representatives focused on a previously stalled proposal to annex Hawaii. President Benjamin Harrison submitted a Hawaii annexation treaty in February 1893 but failed to get the required two-thirds majority. Less than a week after taking office in March 1893, President Cleveland withdrew the Hawaiian annexation treaty. In opposing the treaty, Cleveland emphasized how the American role in the

Hawaiian queen's overthrow in January 1893 would make it an ill-gotten gain. When he took office in 1897, President McKinley shared the view of Harrison and supported annexation of Hawaii. Opposition in the Senate remained, however, and the annexation treaty languished. McKinley looked to the example of President Tyler's successful annexation of Texas through joint resolution, requiring a majority in both chambers instead of a supermajority in the Senate. This alternative posed its own challenges. Opponents framed annexation as a windfall for Hawaiian sugar growers and a dangerous step toward imperialism. There did not appear to be even a simple majority in the Senate, and if there was a majority in the House it was difficult to outmaneuver Speaker Reed, who was opposed to the resolution.

The annexation debate changed with the outbreak of war in April 1898. The war offered a reason to do something that expansionists had long wanted to do. The United States had been using Hawaii to refuel ships at the outset of the war, which put the technically neutral Hawaii in an awkward position. President McKinley immediately highlighted the strategic importance of Hawaii and began framing annexation as a war measure. On May 4, Nevada Representative Francis Newlands introduced the resolution to annex Hawaii. The House Foreign Affairs Committee promptly approved the annexation resolution by a ten-to-four margin, with every Republican on the committee voting in favor. Members of the committee and annexation supporters were eager to bring it to the floor. The resolution had a limited range of options to get to the floor and avoid certain death at the bottom of the legislative calendar. It would need unanimous consent or a special rule from the Rules committee. Annexation supporters pressed for a special rule. Dominated by the Speaker, the Rules committee declined to give a rule to the annexation resolution that he strongly opposed. Reed was criticized for standing in the way of a war measure that appeared to have strong support in the House. It was becoming more difficult for Reed to prevent the resolution from being heard.

Reed knew he was in the minority, but he had a plan: to hold out on Hawaii long enough that routine congressional business could be finished and adjournment was feasible. An early adjournment would be desirable to many members who would rather not spend a hot summer in Washington. Tackling the Hawaii issue would take time and perhaps waiting on the Senate. Reed rationalized that most House Republicans probably would support annexation "if obliged to vote, but many prefer not to have the question come up because it will lead to delay."[50]

As May progressed and Reed held firm, he was widely credited with sole responsibility for preventing action on Hawaii. The *Boston Globe* characterized Reed as "the single obstacle in the path of annexation."[51] The irony of using the Reed Rules to delay business was not lost on a nonpartisan newspaper, which observed, "If Mr. Reed is actually suppressing the majority, they are merely being hoisted with their own petard."[52] It was also not lost on President McKinley, who issued press releases questioning how long Reed could undermine a majority of his own party.[53] Supporters of annexation often maligned Reed as a tool of the sugar trust that feared tariff-free Hawaiian competition. For opponents of annexation, Reed became a hero. On May 18, the *St. Louis Republic* editorialized, "Every citizen whose dreams are disturbed by fear of the annexation of Hawaii should sleep peacefully now that Tom Reed has again sworn to kill that scheme."[54]

The policy conflict over Hawaii was framed as a dispute between McKinley and Reed. The *Tacoma Daily News* characterized the "McKinley-Reed fight" over Hawaii as determining whether the Republican Party would "be committed to a future policy of colonization and imperialistic development."[55] The *Evening Post* contemplated how McKinley might be able to thwart Reed: "The administration would get ahead a great deal faster if it could muster up courage enough to seize Hon. Tom Reed, instead of Hawaii, as a military necessity."[56]

Republicans restless with Speaker Reed decided to circulate a petition to show that a majority of Republicans favored annexation. A petition for a caucus on Hawaii began circulating on May 24. Over one hundred Republicans quickly signed the petition.[57] There were also a number of Democrats publicly expressing support for annexation. Reed was keeping his plan of early adjournment.

On May 29, House Republicans presented Reed with the petition showing overwhelming support for bringing up annexation. The petition had one especially important and surprising name on it. It was Nelson Dingley, Reed's friend, Maine colleague, and chair of the committee working on the session's war revenue bill. Dingley had signed the petition without talking to Reed. The magnitude of the list and the inclusion of Dingley's name was hard for Reed to comprehend. When Reed asked Dingley to remove his name, Dingley refused. Reed told his assistant Asher Hinds that he felt "abandoned."[58]

His abandonment would become even more personal and public on May 31. Speaking on the Senate floor, Reed's longtime friend Henry Cabot Lodge attacked Reed for having broken faith with his legacy as Speaker. Lodge, who had managed Reed's campaign for Speaker, described himself as part of the history-making Fifty-First Congress. Reed and House Republicans had ended the "travesty" of obstruction and acted "on the great principle that in this country the majority ought to rule." Lodge then asserted that this principle had lost and minority rule had reemerged. He explained, "The minority has been changed, but it is still the minority that rules. It is now a minority selected by a majority at the start [by choosing the Speaker and Rules committee], instead of a fortuitous group, but the principle of minority rule is unchanged." Lodge threatened, "If a helpless majority in the two Houses of Congress are unable to give him [the president] in certain directions the legislation he needs, he can employ the war powers [to obtain it]."[59] In making this suggestion, Lodge was echoing President McKinley, who had also been discussing the annexation of Hawaii by exercising his powers as commander in chief.

The end had come. Reed could not hold out any longer, and he agreed not to block the bill. Reed, however, was not going to have any part of it, and he told Dingley and other Republicans that they would be responsible for it. By June 3, newspapers were reporting that Reed was going to allow a vote on annexation. While some expected that it would come within a week, Reed proceeded with other business ahead of annexation on the calendar. For the rest of the week and into another week, other business squeezed out Hawaii. Although Reed was not blocking the House resolution, his decision not to take any role made it difficult for the Hawaii resolution to come up. Almost any controversial legislation would typically come to the floor by special rule from the Rules committee, but that was not going to happen if Reed was not taking an active role. How would the Hawaii matter get to the floor when so much regular business was ahead of it in the regular order?

The answer was an obscure motion proposing that the House move to public business on a day reserved for private business. According to the *Washington Post*, the procedural device had not been used in fifteen years.[60] The unusual nature of the motion and the priority of other bills gave Reed ample ground to rule the motion out of order. To the surprise of many, he did not rule it out of order, saying the House majority could vote to sustain the motion. The majority did want to consider the Hawaii resolution. Unanimous consent was reached to allow three days of debate.

One big question was whether Reed would participate in the debate. Although House Speakers almost never participated in debate, debate on a transcendent issue was the type of event that could justify an exception.

Reed and his assistant Asher Hinds discussed whether Reed should give a speech.[61] The *Springfield Daily Republican* editorialized that a speech from Reed would be valuable to the debate: "A speech in this crisis from Reed would be as appropriate as ever a speech from Webster on the Union or from Lincoln on slavery."[62] Reed decided not to give a speech. Debate continued without him as annexation supporters touted its military value and opponents warned against the dangers of imperialism.

The final vote occurred at 5:00 p.m. on June 15, 1898, and Reed was not presiding. He sent word of an illness. The roll call went as expected with a huge majority for annexation. The magnitude of support for annexation in Reed's own caucus was finally known with certainty. Of the 182 Republicans who voted, 179 voted for annexation and 3 voted against annexation. Democrats were more divided with 18 in favor and 77 against. As the roll call was ending, the acting chair, John Dalzell, announced that he had been instructed to say that if Reed had been present he would have voted no.

After passing the Senate, the resolution became law when President McKinley signed it on July 7. Congress adjourned its regular session the following day, and members left Washington to return to their districts. The congressional elections of 1898 were less than four months away.

Ending talk that he would retire after his Hawaii defeat, Reed announced his intention to seek reelection on August 2. For the first time he would be running against a former member of Congress. Unfortunately for his opponent, Luther McKinney, the previous victories had come from New Hampshire voters. McKinney was also hampered by reduced Democratic animosity toward Reed. In fact, the Democratic convention that nominated McKinney also unanimously passed the following resolution: "We heartily commend and approve the course of the present representative of this district in Congress in his determined and consistent opposition to the efforts of the present Republican administration's policy of imperialism as demonstrated in the annexation of the Hawaiian Islands."[63]

Citing the war, Maine Republicans decided not to campaign actively. At the end of the non-campaign, Reed attended a Republican gathering at the Portland Club. His brief remarks suggest that he was not involved in event promotion: "I was somewhat astonished when I read the circular sent out and saw that I was to deliver an address." He said that he was pleased that Republicans had chosen not to campaign and would not "break away from any rule at this late day." Reed assured his fellow Republicans that it was not a serious matter if the Republican margin of victory dropped a little this year. He, however, did qualify this by saying that he did not want it to drop too much: "Because this has not been a talking campaign is no reason why you should conclude that the Governor and I, who usually talk to you, can be dispensed with."[64]

Republicans again rolled to a landslide victory in Maine. As Reed recommended, they had not overexerted themselves to increase their margin, but the victory was large enough. Reed defeated McKinney with 60 percent of the vote. Content with his victory, Reed opted out of the national congressional campaign.

When Congress returned in December 1898 for the lame-duck session after a convincing November 1898 victory for congressional Republicans, the focus was on ratifying the treaty to end the Spanish-American War. The treaty gave the United States control of Puerto Rico and Guam as indemnity. It also included a payment of $20 million from the United States to Spain for the Philippines. As a treaty, it would need a two-thirds vote of the Senate. Thus, Reed and the House would sit this one out.

Reed took recourse in making brief, caustic critiques of American policy. He privately wrote, "What with saints who want to correct the heathen, and sinners who want to spoil the Egyptians, the path of Empire is opening wide."[65] He joked about the electoral implications of territory acquired in the war: "How can Porto Rico help going Democratic?"[66] Reed reportedly told one member that the nation had to save money because it was "buying Malays at $2 a head."[67] In early December, a Boston reporter traveling in the same smoking car of the train reportedly overheard Reed belittle American policy to bring "canned freedom" to the Philippines.[68]

Reed soon found himself at the center of the struggle over the building of a canal that would dramatically shorten the water route between America's east and west coasts. Although he had resisted outlays for the Nicaraguan Canal in the last Congress, supporters of the canal had renewed hope in the Fifty-Fifth Congress. While passageways through both Panama and Nicaragua had been considered, the Nicaragua Canal proposal had momentum and prominent supporters like Theodore Roosevelt. The Senate voted forty-eight to six to approve a Nicaragua Canal construction bill in January 1899.

The question was whether the House would have a chance to vote on Nicaragua Canal construction. It would not be easy without the support of Speaker Reed, who viewed the project as too costly and poorly planned. Reed did not allow the Rules committee to bring the bill to the floor. Although popular, the bill was not likely to get the two-thirds majority needed to bring it to the floor by suspending the rules. Pressure built on Reed, including from the McKinley administration, which supported moving ahead with a canal.

With routine procedures failing and time running out, advocates sought to hitch the Nicaragua Canal bill to must-pass legislation. An amendment was offered in the House to add the canal project to an appropriations bill. Reed ruled the amendment out of order and converted the issue into a procedural question about riders on appropriations bills on which he was able to preserve sufficient Republican support to be upheld. As the House failed to act, the Senate took the matter in its own hands by adding a Nicaragua Canal provision to the session's $30 million rivers-and-harbors bill that dispersed projects across every congressional district. Senators suggested that there would be no rivers-and-harbors bill unless the House voted directly on the Nicaragua Canal. The canal-supporting *Los Angeles Times* was delighted that the Senate had taken this extreme step: "If the Hepburn [Nicaragua] bill goes on the River and Harbor Bill, as is almost sure, no power on earth can kill it and Speaker Reed will have met the neatest parliamentary defeat he ever had the pleasure of experiencing."[69] When the Senate bill came to the House with a Nicaragua amendment, Reed referred it back to committee and instructed the committee chair not to report it to the House where members on a direct vote might very well concur with the Senate amendment. Reed resisted pressure for a Nicaragua Canal vote for the duration of the session. This time, there would be no caucus revolt as on Hawaii.

Ultimately, Reed's determination to stop the Nicaragua Canal changed history. The massive appropriation would have accumulated sunk costs for a canal through Nicaragua. Opponents of the canal recognized this and lavished praise on Reed. The *Minneapolis Times* editorialized, "Speaker Reed remained master of the situation up to the close of the last Congress and . . . is entitled to the credit of killing the proposed $115,000,000 Nicaragua canal raid on the treasury."[70] Instead of funding Nicaragua Canal construction, Congress was forced by Reed to accept only a modest expenditure for more study of two potential routes. Reed defended this outcome in a postsession article. He wrote that enthusiasm for the Nicaragua Canal had caused people to underestimate the challenges posed by that route: "The influence of the wishes of ourselves and others never will cease to affect estimates of costs, but it never affects actual expense."[71] As engineers accumulated information, Panama emerged as a better location than Nicaragua for building the canal. In 1906, President Theodore Roosevelt used the first foreign trip by a sitting

American president to visit the construction site of the Panama Canal, which opened for traffic eight years later.

On a personal level the short session was a trying time for Reed. On December 20, Lodge wrote Roosevelt about his interactions with Reed: "Reed is terribly bitter, saying all sorts of ugly things about the administration and its policy in private talks, so I keep out of his way, for I am fond of him, and I confess that his attitude is painful and disappointing to me beyond words."[72] On January 13, 1899, Reed was saddened and further isolated by the death of his longtime friend and Maine colleague Nelson Dingley. As the session ended, the *Washington Post* described Reed: "On pleasant days he lumbers along the Avenue on his way to the Capitol, silent and alone, occasionally stopping to gaze at something attractive in the store windows."[73]

On March 4, the short session was ending. The Fifty-Fifth Congress had been a momentous one. Congress declared war, which was followed by military success. By one vote, the Senate approved the treaty ending the war. Congress approved a new policy of expansionism that included annexing Hawaii and holding multiple territories after the war. When its work was done, the House began its closing ceremonies. Democratic leader Joseph Bailey offered the traditional resolution thanking the Speaker for the "able, impartial, and dignified manner in which he has presided over its deliberations and performed the arduous and important duties of the Chair." Loud applause from both sides of the chamber greeted the Speaker as he entered. Reed said, "Notwithstanding any differences of opinion or of party, you have given me your confidence in all which pertained to my duties here in a manner so full and ample that my memory of it will never pass away."[74]

After the final gavel fell on the Fifty-Fifth Congress, speculation turned to the Fifty-Sixth Congress and whether another Republican would challenge Reed before it convened in December 1899. The McKinley administration was depicted as trying to encourage a challenger who would support its priorities. The *St. Louis Globe-Democrat* editorialized, "Mr. Reed has gone too far already with his sardonic coldness for Republican policies . . . [and the McKinley] administration has cares enough without contending against a more than unsympathetic Speaker."[75]

Others were talking about Reed for an even higher office. His actions in the Fifty-Fifth Congress had made him arguably the most visible anti-imperialist. On March 9, anti-imperialist Moorfield Storey wrote his friend Senator Hoar: "If he [Reed] would come out [as leader of anti-imperialists] I think he might readily be the next president, for I assure you that the feeling everywhere is deep and growing and it only needs leadership to express itself in a way that cannot be misunderstood."[76] The conflict between Reed and McKinley was often framed as a precursor to a fight for the 1900 Republican nomination. As imperialism questions were raised during the session, one newspaper observed, "Republican congressmen must line up as partisans of McKinley or Reed, and the first gun of the next campaign for the presidential nomination will have been fired."[77] Most administration supporters, however, did not take a Reed challenge seriously. The *Seattle Post-Intelligencer* penned an editorial that must have been particularly grating to Reed by putting a new twist on the repartee that had helped to begin it all: "Speaker Reed's continued hostility to his party's policies gives rise to the suspicion that he'd rather be wrong than president."[78]

Jekyll to Hide

Reed left Washington for a vacation. He was invited to stay with his friend John Moore, a wealthy businessman, on exclusive Jekyll Island off the coast of Georgia. On March 17, 1899, noting his arrival in Brunswick, Georgia, a common departure point for trips to Jekyll Island, a newspaper reporter asked what he would be doing on the island. Reed responded, "Rest, simply rest." When asked about the prospect of a political summit on the island, Reed responded, "There is not to be a gathering of men prominent in national affairs on Jekyll Island during the time I am there as far as I know."[79] Why would a reporter ask about a summit off the coast of Georgia? President McKinley was expected to arrive on Jekyll Island shortly for his own vacation at a different millionaire's cottage about two hundred yards from where Reed was staying. McKinley's people also said there was no political purpose to the trip and that they had learned of Reed's presence on the island through the newspapers.

The press and public were not ready to believe that the two most powerful men in America would vacation on the same island on the same day by accident. The most common theory was that Reed and McKinley were coming together for a reconciliation, probably at the behest of mutual friends. Getting the actual story would be next to impossible. The remote Jekyll Island was owned by a club of wealthy members who enjoyed their privacy. Guests needed permission from a member, and there were no exceptions for the press.

The much anticipated meeting of Reed and McKinley occurred on March 21 during their respective vacations. It took place at a reception open to all islanders. Perhaps the most accurate report of the meeting was provided in the *Atlanta Constitution*: "In the course of the evening the president and Speaker Reed found time for a short talk, which may or may not have political import."[80] Regardless of what was discussed, there would have been some awkwardness between these two formerly close friends who had become bitter rivals at the pinnacle of American political power. This awkwardness would have increased because of the presence of Mark Hanna, who had managed the 1896 campaign that defeated Reed and was now accompanying McKinley on his vacation. Reporters learned that Hanna and Reed had held a longer meeting earlier in the day. The *Boston Globe* described, "At 11 am Messrs Reed and Hanna came arm in arm out of Mr. Reed's apartments . . . [and] shook hands with great cordiality."[81]

What did McKinley and Hanna say to Reed in their brief visits on Jekyll Island? It is difficult to imagine that it will ever be known. There simply were not many people there, and the principals were not talking. The most interesting possibility is whether McKinley, or more likely Hanna, suggested that the administration would support another candidate for Speaker of the next Congress. In his memoir, legendary journalist William Allen White describes Hanna as having essentially "deposed" Reed as Speaker at a "behind closed doors" meeting in which the two "had their differences out."[82] If this story is true, and there is good reason to question whether Hanna and McKinley would have thought it a good idea to confront Reed, who privately insisted that "nobody could have prevented" his reelection,[83] it is difficult to see how these two people who did not like each other would have had a better chance to talk than on Jekyll Island.

More than a century later, the mysterious summit at Jekyll Island continues to stir the imagination. In 2000, Brent Monahan wrote a historical novel that used the McKinley-Reed meeting as prologue. The novel characterizes the meeting as "bringing Reed down and pitting him against McKinley, like throwing two game cocks into a ring." The novel then diverges from historical events with a murder at the Sans Souci lodge where Reed was staying on Jekyll Island. Speaker Reed emerges as a potential suspect who has the size and opportunity to have committed the murder. Ultimately, Reed is exonerated, and the murder turns out to be pedestrian.[84] Perhaps the real events were equally pedestrian.

Whatever happened on Jekyll Island, Reed was preparing to step aside. On April 19, 1899, Reed announced that he was accepting a full-time position with a New York law firm. Why did Reed leave Congress? His farewell statement thanked his constituents but did not explain his departure. This prompted the Democratic *Argus* to "call on Mr. Reed to give the country his reasons for retiring from public life."[85] Reed had never listened to the *Argus* and was not about to start. Privately, he claimed that he had deliberately made his message unclear so that people would wonder why he did it. He explained to his friend George Gifford: "The best good of the cause would be subserved by doing what no man has yet done. Resign a great place and then people would ask why and find out not by my direct outpourings but by their inferences. When a man finds out a thing for himself he is prouder of it than if it were told him by Shakespeare."[86]

Speculation proliferated. Some focused on the disparity between Reed's policy preferences and those of President McKinley and other Republicans. A Republican version was articulated by the *San Diego Union*: "The true explanation probably is that the ex-Speaker realizes that he is not in touch with the administration as to a part of its policy, and that under the circumstances he could not throw himself into his work in Congress as he formerly did."[87] The same argument could also take a Democratic spin: "The folly of the expansion policy of the President is too patent to the Boss for him to approve it, and not having the courage, it seems, to use his great power to check his party in its visionary schemes, he prefers to retire."[88] The *Seattle Post-Intelligencer* offered a multifaceted psychological explanation: "The motives inducing Mr. Reed's retirement are . . . probably because he is tired of the constant load of care and responsibility, because he has achieved the very summit of his official career, because he does not care to continue Speaker under less authoritative conditions than heretofore, and because his talents guarantee him remuneration commensurate with their scope and quality."[89] In short, it was mission accomplished for Reed. People took greater pride in their own findings than if they had been told by the man who allegedly looked like Shakespeare.

Weighing the historical evidence, a combination of two reasons for his retirement seems most compelling. First, Reed was ready to earn money. He had thought about making money as a lawyer in New York for years. In private correspondence and in his diary, Reed had expressed the desire to become financially secure. Second, he was concerned about leading a party with which he disagreed so strongly on the major issue of the day. This was the reason that he gave to his friend George Gifford. Reed wrote, "Had I stayed I must have been as Speaker always in a false position aiding and organizing things in which I did not believe or using power against those who gave it to me."[90]

There was more than a little irony in Reed leaving the House because he was alienated from his party. He had been a lifelong champion of the Republican Party. As a rising legislator, he built his reputation on investigations and procedural matters in which partisan advantage is often transparent and members are expected to vote with their party regardless of underlying policy preferences. In his first Speakership, Reed became a partisan hero for his parliamentary mastery and his sheer determination to resist Democratic obstruction. He subsequently strengthened the majority-party's ability to govern. He formally appointed the first party whip to build support for party measures.[91] House Republicans enacted their policy goals under his leadership. Reed was more responsible than anyone for increasing the importance of political party in the House.

While his pioneering changes left an indelible mark on Congress, Reed could no longer find a place for himself in the institution that he had transformed. The new House made it difficult to reconcile intraparty differences on the major issue of the day. Even though Reed believed that fundamental American values were being undermined by how new territories were being governed, he chose to step aside. One consolation for him, as Reed described to his friend William Crane, was that he "did not do the sowing" and did "not want to reap that harvest" at a time when "having sown the wind, the whirlwind begins to peep above the weeds."[92]

CHAPTER 10

CASHING IN

A post-Congress life presented Reed with many options. He made a three-year commitment to working for the law firm of Simpson, Thacher and Barnum, which was renamed Reed, Simpson, Thacher and Barnum. Reed would be a rainmaker for the firm, but legal work would not take all his time; he would also have time to convert his political expertise into lobbying opportunities. New York was not far by train from Washington, and Reed's work for political clients ensured that he would keep one foot in the political world.

Perhaps Reed's most visible role would be a presumed candidate in waiting. He was only fifty-nine years old. He was famous and could easily return to politics. Many observers believed that he was just waiting for the right time to make another presidential run. It was widely suggested that Reed had made a strategic choice to move to a state with a bigger electoral prize. No president had ever come from Maine, but New York was another story. Of course, Reed's prospects would be brightest if enthusiasm for American expansionism should fade. He was well positioned as an early skeptic of American imperial policy to be an alternative to other Republicans who had embraced expansionism.

The aftermath of the war left Reed feeling vindicated about his position on the Philippines. He lamented, "Nobody will get credit for being right at the right time."[1] After the peace treaty did not grant independence to the Philippines, the United States went from fighting for the Filipinos to fighting against them. On November 13, 1899, Filipino rebel leader Emilio Aguinaldo advised his followers to disband and return to their homes to continue the fight as a guerilla war.[2] At the time, the American military was closing in on Aguinaldo, and he fled to the mountains. Aguinaldo escaped, but news reports suggested that other members of his family were not so lucky. When Reed showed up at his law office, he teased a law partner who was supportive of the war, saying, "What, are you working today? I should think you would be celebrating. I see by the papers that the American army has captured the infant son of Aguinaldo, and at last accounts was in hot pursuit of the mother."[3] In fact, the US military had captured both Aguinaldo's young son and elderly mother on November 14. Aguinaldo himself was not caught until March 1901.

Although still thinking about foreign policy, Reed's major focus was on making money through his legal work. His salary at the law firm was $50,000 per year, which far surpassed the $8,000 he had made as Speaker.[4] There would be opportunities to supplement that salary with lobbying, investments, and writing. Reed was ready to cash in.

The identity of Reed's client in his first New York Supreme Court appearance showed that his legal practice was off to a good start. In terms of wealthy clients, Reed could have done worse than a Rockefeller. In fact, he did better. Reed was representing not only a Rockefeller (William), but also three other industrial titans: John Moore, Henry Rogers, and Grant Schley. In essence, Reed was defending the principals in the Brooklyn gas consolidation against a lawsuit brought by William Logan, who claimed that he had not been justly compensated for stock put into the syndicate. Reed argued that Logan was an overconfident businessman who had been outmaneuvered in a routine business transaction. On December 16, 1899, Reed made his closing argument. He summarized, "It was a struggle of human selfishness on each side. . . . We were endeavoring to consolidate, and he [Logan] was trying to get as much out of us as he could." In this contest, Reed explained, "what the law requires of men is that they shall keep within the Revised Statutes. The law requires that they shall be honest in their transactions. That is all it requires."[5] Reed's argument prevailed when a referee recommended the dismissal of Logan's action. Building on this success, Reed notched a victory for Carnegie Steel in a patent case.

The start of the new century appears to have brought Reed both resolution and isolation. He resumed writing in his French diary. He may have tried to get more exercise, including walking over five miles on one occasion.[6] His January 1, 1900, diary entry shows the effect of his increasing isolation from the Republican Party on his general outlook on life: "The things that had interested me very much no longer interest me at all. The party to which I have been a member is going its way and I am going my way."[7]

Although foreign policy began the rift, Reed was also diverging from the Republican Party on the domestic issue of regulation of the increasingly large companies dominating the economy. The Industrial Commission, part of legislation signed by President McKinley, began investigating monopolies. Fresh from defending Standard Oil executives, Reed penned an article for the February 1900 *Saturday Evening Post,* arguing that monopolies should operate without government interference. He asserted that large companies were actually most vulnerable to market correction: "Those who make too much [money] are in the worst danger, for when capital starts to flow it overflows, and too much gets in, and what was already in shares the loss."[8] It was a risk that monopolists were eager to take.

The 1900 election marked the first time that Reed was not on a federal ballot in a quarter of a century. He wrote Gifford, "We are to have a nice campaign but it is a blessing to be out of it." Reed was increasingly blaming the influence of political parties for some of the nation's recent problems: "Party government so absolutely essential drills everybody into submission until such time as revolt becomes simultaneous."[9] He lamented, "It is curious to see how all political arguments turn on the amount not of gold there is in our party but of dross there is in the other."[10] Looking back on the 1900 election, he wrote, "It was certainly a hard case when one had to choose between the dishonesty of one and the plain blank foolishness of the other."[11] Applying Reed's analysis, dishonesty defeated foolishness as McKinley and his new running mate, Theodore Roosevelt, trounced William Jennings Bryan in November 1900.

In May 1901, the United States Supreme Court ruled on the constitutionality of the McKinley administration's policy on newly acquired territory. Going into the case, Reed hoped that the Supreme Court might overturn the policy. He wrote Gifford, "The Supreme Court might rectify it all but no court ever can escape the pressure of events. . . . If the court can make a difference between Porto Rico and the Philippines saddle us with the one and spare us the others it will fulfill our highest hopes."[12] In the landmark *Insular Cases,* however, the Supreme Court essentially upheld the administration's policy toward the new possessions.[13] This prompted an angry letter from Reed to Gifford on May 29. He wrote, "If the Supreme Court has failed us that may end it." Reed drew broad implications from the decision: "The whole occurrence seems to show how impossible it is to provide for the future wisdom of the world by written constitution unless the spirit of the people continues steadfast."[14]

On September 6, 1901, American politics was transformed by the shooting of President McKinley in Buffalo, New York. A week later McKinley was dead and Theodore Roosevelt was president. Any hope that Reed had harbored to win the 1904 Republican presidential nomination was now diminished by the prospect of facing an incumbent president. Future presidential politics, however, was on hold as the nation stopped to grieve for the fallen president.

Reed did not join the national mourning for McKinley. Indeed, the outpouring of affection for McKinley in death increased the resentment that Reed felt for the man who had defeated him in 1896. On the day of the funeral, the nation observed five minutes of silence, including a stop in road traffic. According to prominent journalist William Allen White, he and Reed were eating lunch when everything went silent. Recognizing that the silence was for McKinley, Reed offered his own tribute. White tried desperately after the meal to record Reed's exact words, but he was unsuccessful. White's autobiography conveyed only the general sense of what Reed had said about McKinley: "As the cabs and drays pulled up and stopped in the street below our window, Reed literally hauled off, smacked his flapperlike hands heavily on the table, stiffened up and began—not a prayer but a diatribe. . . . I have never heard such exquisitely brutal, meticulously refined malediction in all my life. . . . It was rage, chilled into sarcasm and frigid contempt."[15]

To find a happier reconciliation between Reed and McKinley, one must look to a 2011 biography of Reed. According to author James Grant, "When President McKinley passed through Portland that summer, Reed invited him to visit his home (it was Susan's idea). The two of them had a nice talk."[16] Grant's footnote for the paragraph about the presidential visit, however, suggests that he misread the date of the diary entry as September 3, 1900, when it was actually September 3, 1902.[17] By then, a McKinley visit to Reed's home would have been complicated by the fact that McKinley had been dead for a year. When Reed wrote in his diary that Susan had encouraged him to invite the "President" to visit his home,[18] it was 1902 and not 1900, and the president was Theodore Roosevelt and not William McKinley. In short, there was no reconciliation. Reed harbored a deep resentment of McKinley until McKinley's death, or more accurately, until Reed's death. Indeed, months after McKinley's death, Reed used a biblical analogy to criticize McKinley's desire to force help on the Cubans. Reed wrote Gifford, "That's like all of

McKinley's business. He was like Adam before the Fall. He doesn't know the difference between good and evil."[19]

Reed was concerned that Americans, especially Republicans, had lost faith with Abraham Lincoln. Reed argued that McKinley's policies violated the principles espoused by Lincoln: "To declare that we cannot have two systems of government one free and the other slave seems clear enough ever since Lincoln proclaimed that a House divided against itself could not stand."[20] On February 19, 1902, Reed wrote, "What a curious result . . . that we go on celebrating the memory of a man [Lincoln] whose thoughts uttered and once praised have to be avoided because they throw contempt on our practices." Reed lamented that he had recently submitted an essay about Lincoln to newspapers for Lincoln Day but could not get it published. He saw a glimmer of hope for the nation to restore Lincoln: "But the democrats now are quoting Lincoln and his thoughts are taking root in their minds. . . . It does not seem possible and yet they are now making all the Republican speeches which are made except those of [Senator] Hoar." Reed asked, "Would it be strange if the Democratic Party should become the nucleus of the reaction for liberty?"[21]

Reed was still making frequent trips to Washington, where he had the opportunity for lucrative lobbying. In early 1902, for example, he earned a $5,000 lobbying fee for supporting the domestic beet sugar industry. Reed had a ready audience in former colleagues, though he did not think of himself as capitalizing on his previous position. His diary explained, "It is necessary to understand that I told my clients before Congress that I always refused to use my influence. I will give advice to my clients and figures and facts to members. That's all!"[22]

On March 17, 1902, Reed joined Mark Twain and other friends for yachting in the Caribbean. The yacht was owned by Henry Rogers, president of Standard Oil and a friend of both Reed and Twain. Yachting with Rogers was a good indication of improved finances. It was for Mark Twain who had gone from debt to riches after Rogers began managing his business affairs. It was also true for Reed as Rogers and other New York friends began to give Reed the quality investment advice that he had lacked previously. Reed wrote a playful letter to Twain about an investment opportunity that they could share with Rogers: "You and I can live happily ever afterwards, while Mr. Rogers will start in on his third (or fourth?) hundred million, with a consciousness that he has aided the deserving poor (that's us) and promoted the progress of the world, getting due reward for virtue at the same time."[23] Reed himself had not reached the hundred-million dollar range, but his investment portfolio had certainly ballooned into the mid-hundred-thousands. For the first time in his life, Reed was a rich man.

Calm as Jove on Olympus

Reed's new wealth gave him the freedom to reduce the legal work that was increasingly boring him. He quit the law firm when his commitment ended. He had won some cases and made a lot of money. He confided to his diary, "I've had good success here but I don't have the time to become a renowned lawyer."[24]

Reed may have told his colleagues that he was quitting to spend more time with his family, and he meant it. Reed, his wife, and adult daughter formed a strong trio. Reed's longtime private secretary, Amos Allen, once described Reed's family life: "I never observed in any family an affection closer than that which existed between himself and his wife and daughter."[25] Reed's wife and daughter provided balance. Kitty shared Reed's enjoyment for politics and accompanied him on various political trips. While Susan seldom did more than tolerate politics, she shared much of his interest in culture. Reed's correspondence reveals that she occasionally read his draft publications and recommended books to him.[26] Reed's shared intellectual interests with both his wife and daughter built on his love for them as husband and father. Retirement would allow him more time at home and at their beach cottage. He did not intend, however, to give up his professional life completely.

Now free from financial worries, Reed was poised to become a writer. This was a regular theme in his diary. He wrote, "I have a great desire to write a book on the human race—a large enough subject!"[27] His preliminary thoughts were incorporated into a speech on June 25, 1902, at the centennial celebration of his alma mater, Bowdoin College. Reed offered a sweeping interpretation of the world on an overarching arc toward progress, though it may not be apparent to those living through setbacks. One commentator on the speech suggested that Reed's presence mirrored his grand themes: "T. B. Reed, the Philosopher—calm as Jove on Olympus, nay, Jove on Olympus was Small Potatoes compared with this Great Man." The writer, however, could not resist a jab at Reed: "Has he never regretted an act of renunciation which retired him from greater work for his nation, for lesser work for clients who have more than they know what to do with?"[28]

Two months later, Reed received a stark reminder that he was not in the arena anymore when President Roosevelt toured New England. Urged by his wife, Reed invited Roosevelt to visit their home. On August 26, Roosevelt arrived by train in Portland and gave a speech in which he praised Reed: "Government by the majority in Congress had practically come to a stop . . . [until] Mr. Reed, at the cost of infinite labor, at the cost of the fiercest attack, succeeded in restoring that old principle."[29] Roosevelt then joined other local dignitaries in Reed's home. Roosevelt and Reed exited side by side, walking down the steps to the street in front of a large crowd. According to Reed's diary, the gathering prompted some "rapprochement between the party here and me."[30]

On Sunday, November 30, 1902, Reed arrived in Washington. He attended the Monday opening of the second session of the Fifty-Seventh Congress, prompting newspaper reports that he was organizing opposition to President Roosevelt's proposed legislation to regulate monopolies. Reed contributed to these rumors by criticizing the ambiguity of the proposal: "An indefinable something is to be done, in a way nobody knows how, and at a time nobody knows when."[31] Reed denied that he was lobbying against monopoly regulation. In any event, he was not feeling well. Supposing it was indigestion, he returned to rest at his nearby hotel, the opulent Arlington Hotel on Vermont Avenue between H and I streets.

Reed returned to the Capitol the next morning. While visiting the Senate, he suddenly felt ill. Pain caused him to slump in his chair. During his time in the House of Representatives, Reed had famously joked that the Senate was where great Americans went to die. Would his life have one final irony?

The ailing Reed was taken to his hotel, where a local doctor diagnosed a flare-up of appendicitis. Surgeon T. L. MacDonald visited for a consult the next morning, but he did not think Reed was a good candidate for an appendectomy. MacDonald noted, "The patient was sixty-three years of age; was waxy and flabby in the extreme." The good news was that the soreness around the appendix had decreased and surgery seemed unnecessary. The bad news was that the appendicitis flare-up appeared to exacerbate kidney disease.[32] To confirm MacDonald's diagnosis, Dr. Goodno, a specialist, came in from Philadelphia. It did not take a specialist to see that Reed's condition was worsening. He drifted into a coma in the afternoon. By evening, he was conscious, but his condition remained critical.

People were becoming aware that the ex-Speaker was fighting for his life. President Roosevelt sent dispatches checking on his condition. Citizens could follow his vital signs in the newspaper. Based on updates provided by the doctor, Friday's *Portland Evening Express* reported his temperature as ninety-nine and his pulse as eighty-four. The newspaper described him as "cheerful" and showing "marked improvement."[33] Positive news was fleeting, however, and kidney failure was taking its toll.

On Saturday, his condition was grave. As Reed teetered near death, his family was there. His wife and daughter had rushed to Washington when they learned of his illness, and they remained at his bedside. Reed had his quorum of two. Coincidentally, many of his political colleagues were downstairs in the same hotel that night engaged in the revelry of the annual Gridiron dinner. Gridiron attendees included Henry Cabot Lodge, Joseph Cannon, Joseph Manley, Speaker Henderson, and Mark Hanna. They were entertained by music, roasts, and a live bear.

Unfortunately, as they dined, Reed drifted off to sleep and did not wake up. He was pronounced dead at 12:10 a.m. on December 7, 1902. By his own definition, the successful politician Tom Reed was now a statesman.

CHAPTER 11

CONCLUSION

As a statesman, Reed retains a strong presence in American politics. The Reed Rules did not die with Reed. After summarizing the part of Reed's Speakership that has not survived, this conclusion analyzes the use of the Reed Rules following Reed's death. The Reed Rules are most pronounced in the House of Representatives, where they continue to serve as the institutional foundation. The passage of time and methodological advances have deepened appreciation for the functioning of the Reed Rules and their shaping of House leadership. The Reed Rules, however, have moved beyond the House. Their impact can also be seen in the Senate and throughout American politics. The Reed Rules emerge as a lens for understanding American politics.

Pretty Authoritarian by the Way

The key aspect of Reed's House leadership that has not survived is the magnitude of unilateral powers possessed by the Speaker. When Reed retired in 1899, the Speaker singlehandedly controlled much of the legislative process. The three major ways to get bills to the floor were through Speaker recognition, a special rule issued by the Rules committee, and privileged floor access exercised by chairs of prestige committees. In addition to the recognition power, the Speaker had functional control of the Rules committee by virtue of being its chair and appointing the other four members (two from each party). The Speaker also appointed the chairs and members of all other committees. In assessing the power of the Speaker in the immediate aftermath of

Reed, the political scientist and future president Woodrow Wilson explained, "The power of appointing the committees, which the House has conferred upon its Speaker, makes him the almost autocratic master of its actions."[1]

Speaker Reed was not shy about exercising his powers. Ironically, having facilitated legislation in the Fifty-First Congress, Reed directed much of his power toward blocking it in the Fifty-Fourth and Fifty-Fifth Congresses. This is readily apparent in his refusal to name committees at the start of the Fifty-Fourth Congress. The House literally could not work since the committees that start the legislative process did not have any members. He delayed popular legislation in the Fifty-Fifth Congress. He blocked Hawaiian annexation for months with the support of only three members of his caucus. Symbolic of the difficulty of getting around the Speaker's power is that even after Reed stopped blocking the Hawaii bill, the House struggled to pass it. Without help from the Speaker-dominated Rules committee, there was no obvious way to get the bill to the floor. Ultimately, the House resorted to an obscure motion that had not been used in over a decade. The name "Czar Reed" stuck because it fit.

In the modern era it has become possible to overlook Reed's autocratic ways. He left office voluntarily. He was often transparent in his use of power, such as deciding on a special rule and then telling the Democratic members what "outrage" had been perpetrated against them. In a history of the House Speakership, Booth Mooney credits Reed with combining humor and autocracy: "Reed could laugh at himself, even at his own autocratic pretensions."[2] The Speaker of the House one century after Reed, Tom Foley, reflected on his predecessor: "My admiration and interest goes to the great Speakers of the 19th century who were pretty authoritarian Speakers by the way. My favorite is Thomas Brackett Reed who was an enormously powerful Speaker and a very witty one."[3]

Members of Congress were not laughing at the time. Whether or not he was likely to be deposed, Reed's ways were wearing thin. After he retired, Reed was replaced by David Henderson, who had served with Reed on the Rules committee. Henderson continued a partisan leadership style,[4] but employed it with weaker leadership skills.[5] Henderson was succeeded by Joseph Cannon, who had been a top Reed deputy. Cannon picked up where Reed left off and used the Speaker's individual power to prevent legislation that had wide support in the chamber. Even though a procedural majority is willing to accept a lot, there is a limit. Cannon had reached the limit in March 1910, and the House revolted. Thirty-four Republicans joined with Democrats on the key procedural vote of whether a resolution to change the rules was in order.[6]

The revolt eliminated some key exclusive powers of the Speaker. The unilateral power of the Speaker to appoint all committee chairs and members was removed. The Speaker was thrown off the Rules committee. The era of the all-powerful Speaker drawing on formidable formal powers was over. In defining eras of Speaker power, political scientists characterize the period from Reed until the revolt against Cannon (1890–1910) as the "czar era."[7]

Reed Rules in the House

Although power is now less concentrated in the Speaker, the ability of the majority party to govern continues. When the Speaker's exclusive powers were removed in 1910, they did not disappear but became shared more broadly among majority-party members, including with the Speaker, the Rules committee, substantive committee chairs, and the full majority-party caucus.[8] In the modern House, for example, substantive committee members are nominated by each party's committee on committees and approved by the party caucus. Despite fluctuations in the location of power over time, the majority party has had at least a baseline ability to control the House agenda since the Reed Rules.[9] Quite simply, there has been no return to the extensive filibustering and limited discretion in bringing measures to the floor that existed prior to the Reed Rules. Reed's innovations are the twin pillars of the majority-party's agenda control in the House.

The first pillar is the ability to stop filibusters. Before Reed, filibustering was rampant; after Reed, majorities can end a filibuster. The Reed Rules allow the Speaker to reject dilatory motions. Reed put an end to the disappearing quorum. Of course, the technical process of counting a quorum is not as important now as it was earlier since attendance is much higher and members can use modern transportation to get to Washington. Stopping the disappearing quorum, however, is symbolic of the broader ability of the Reed Rules to end any type of ostensibly permitted filibustering. This is captured well in Reed's parliamentary manual provision that rule "changes can be made by a majority . . . even if the rules already adopted provide that two-thirds or any larger number alone shall make changes."[10]

The second pillar is the use of special rules to shape which proposals receive final votes. Before Reed, the majority party struggled to secure votes on preferred measures and to prevent votes on disliked measures; after Reed, the majority party has substantial control over which proposals receive final votes. The Reed Rules give congressional leaders flexibility in taking bills off calendars. They also allow leaders the ability to tailor how a bill is treated on the floor.

The importance of the Reed Rules in altering the institutional foundation of the House has been long appreciated. Scholars writing in the aftermath observed the difference. In her 1896 study of the Speakership, M. P. Follett summarized the effect of the Reed Rules as having "fixed the responsibility for legislation, to a much greater degree than ever before, upon the majority."[11] Woodrow Wilson wrote his dissertation on congressional government based on observations in 1883 before the Reed Rules, and he wrote a follow-up book based on lectures given in 1907 after the Reed Rules. While his dissertation described legislation impeded by filibustering,[12] Wilson later characterized the House as an "efficient instrument" that "looks to the Committee on Rules to sweep aside the ordinary routine of procedure whenever necessary."[13] It became clear over time that filibustering had stopped and the majority party had greater agenda control. Thus, Reed has been given something close to official credit for landmark institutional reform. As the head of the Office of the House Historian, Robert Remini wrote a House history that credits Reed with having "inaugurated the era of the modern Speaker."[14] The Committee on House Administration supervised a chamber history that recognizes the critical contribution of Reed: "The 'Reed Rules' that he devised and advocated not only changed the way in which the House did business a century ago, they continue to shape the House today."[15]

The application of modern social-science and historical methodologies has deepened appreciation of Reed's contribution to establishing the institutional foundation of the House. The enduring impact is perhaps best captured in the innovative work by Cox and McCubbins on agenda setting in the House. They created a dataset of non-unanimous legislation brought to the House floor since 1877. Building on the pioneering work of Poole and Rosenthal establishing historically consistent assessments of member ideology,[16] Cox and McCubbins analyze over a century of bill outcomes under the same framework. Since it is a work of quantitative political science, Reed himself is measured: "Our main independent variable is $Reed_t$, which takes the value one for Congresses operating under Reed's rules and zero otherwise." As coded, the Reed Rules have been in effect since 1890 with the exception of the Fifty-Second Congress. Even though Reed was minority leader, the Democratic Fifty-Third Congress is coded as a Reed Rules Congress because it adopted Reed's quorum rule for stopping filibusters and used special rules to set the agenda. Their conclusion is striking: "We find that the proportion of proposed policy moves that favored the majority party . . . increases abruptly, substantially, and permanently with the adoption and later readoption of Reed's rules."[17] Specifically, they find that the probability that a bill getting a final vote constitutes a policy shift toward the majority party increased from 57 percent to 81 percent under the Reed Rules.[18] The importance of the Reed Rules is also captured by rate changes in party rolls (when over half of party members are on the losing side of a final passage vote): The roll rates for minority parties go up significantly and the roll rates for majority parties go down significantly after the Reed Rules.[19] Cox and McCubbins summarize that the "modern (i.e., post-Reed) House of Representatives" gives the "majority the ability to control the agenda."[20]

While providing a valuable tool for party leaders, the Reed Rules do not guarantee success. Cox and McCubbins emphasize that the Reed Rules are most effective in giving majority parties a substantial baseline of negative agenda control—or the ability to prevent votes when it will get rolled. While negative agenda control has been largely consistent since Reed's time, there has been more variation in positive agenda control or the ability to obtain final votes on preferred policies.[21] Winning final votes is also necessary for the ultimate goal of policy change. In short, the Reed Rules provide a significant, but limited, advantage to the majority party. Writing for a Dirksen Center project on congressional leadership, Barbara Sinclair captures this well: "Since the institution of the Reed Rules, which deprived minorities of the ability to obstruct, House rules have provided the potential for strong majority party leadership."[22]

Whether the potential for strong party leadership is realized depends on a variety of factors. A synthesis of a rich scholarly literature would recognize that institutional context and leadership both affect the magnitude of party government in the House. Above all, political scientists have found that stronger party government is more likely when the congressional parties are polarized with greater homogeneity within parties and greater differences between parties.[23] The institutional context sets the basic parameters for leadership power and style.[24] Provided that party leaders want to exercise power,[25] their skills will affect the likelihood of achieving desired outcomes in the party context that they are facing.

Thus, the House has experienced variation in the strength of party government on top of the raised baseline from the Reed Rules. The 1910 revolt against Speaker Cannon had a negative effect on the majority party's agenda control but far smaller than the positive effect of the Reed Rules.[26] The 1970s constitute a dividing line between an era of weaker party government and an era of stronger party government. Democrats controlled the House from 1937–1960 for all but four years, but they were vulnerable to a conservative coalition of southern Democrats and Republicans. This included the Rules committee, which gave Democrats an eight-to-four margin, but two of the eight Democrats, including Howard Smith, who took over as committee chair in 1955, often sided with Democrats on conservative coalition issues to impede progressive legislation favored by the broader Democratic caucus. Although majority-party leadership largely reclaimed the Rules committee after a 217–212 vote added three seats to the committee in 1961, Democrats continued to struggle with the conservative coalition. A Democratic member of the Rules committee in the 1960s, Richard Bolling, did not view the Democratic challenges in the midst of the conservative coalition as a flaw in Reed's "brilliantly reformed" House rules but as a manifestation of a "deformed" House Democratic Party.[27] By the mid-1970s, the Democratic House majority had made reforms that strengthened party government, including giving the Speaker the ability to nominate the majority party's Rules committee members at the start of each Congress. The independent power of committee chairs was weakened by creating a more centralized budget process, strengthening subcommittees, facilitating Speaker referral of bills to multiple committees, and having the party caucus elect committee chairs by secret ballot. Combined with the decline of the conservative coalition as conservative southern Democrats were replaced by Republicans, these reforms ushered in a period of stronger party government that has continued to the present. A lynchpin of this is the Rules committee, which was structured to give a greater than two-to-one advantage to the majority party in 1975 and has provided a nine-to-four advantage for the majority party since 1983.

Cementing control of the Rules committee was vital to party leaders because of the increasing importance of special rules to the House. Indeed, the proliferation of restrictive special rules is probably the single biggest change in the implementation of the Reed Rules. Reed used restrictive rules in unusual cases for challenging political situations. In the thirty years after Reed's Speakership, Congress averaged about thirteen open and five restrictive rules per two-year Congress.[28] As late as 1972, at least two-thirds of special rules were simple open rules allowing all amendments.[29] Since then, restrictions have been the norm. In the modern House almost all major legislation reaches the floor under a special rule, and almost all special rules are restrictive. Since the percentage of special rules that are open has reached zero for an entire Congress under both Democratic (2009–2010) and Republican (2017–2018) leadership,[30] it is better to characterize the prevalence of open rules as low rather than on a downward trend. Restrictive, however, does not mean that bills are closed to any unsanctioned amendments. Rather, special rules are often crafted with near "surgical precision" as a complex mix of less and more restrictive provisions depending on the bill section.[31] Thus, modern House leaders have strengthened a tool introduced by Reed to overcome legislative challenges.

Special rules have become routine because they work. Functioning as "an arm of the majority party leadership,"[32] the Rules committee can use restrictive rules to make preferred outcomes more likely. A potential outcome that might be undesirable to the Rules committee, such as the approval of an amendment offered by the minority that might attract enough support from majority party members to form a majority, can be precluded by the special rule. This outcome of preventing cross-party compromise appears to have been the purpose of the first special rule offered by Reed. Although there are many goals for special rules, including protecting committees, preventing cross-party compromise remains an important goal.[33] Regardless of motivation, the use of restrictive special rules is designed to prevent losing, however it is defined. Bach and Smith explain, "The appeal of special rules with restrictive provisions is greatest to majority floor leaders and bill managers when the outcome of votes on critical amendments is most uncertain and when the policy and political consequences of losing are greatest."[34]

Although it is important to acknowledge variations in party government strength under the Reed Rules, what is ultimately more important is that the Reed Rules provide the institutional foundation for majority rule in the House. Under the Reed Rules, a House majority can stop filibustering and has substantial discretion in which proposals will receive floor votes. The longstanding function of the Reed Rules is summarized by Steven Smith: "In origin and application, the Reed rules created opportunities for a House majority to act that it may not have had otherwise."[35] In short, the Reed Rules provide congressional leaders with the tools to legislate. The success of modern leaders depends on how well they are using tools that were pioneered by Reed. Leaders who fail to use available tools can be held responsible for their lack of achievement. This was an outcome predicted by Reed at the end of the Fifty-First Congress: "Henceforth the reply of a party that it was hindered by a minority and could not act will never again be taken as answer or excuse."[36]

Party responsibility applies not only to the failure to act but also to which actions are taken. During the 1890 campaign, Reed proclaimed that "party responsibility had begun,"[37] and he invited the judgment of the electorate. By any measure, the Fifty-First Congress passed a disproportionate amount of landmark legislation. In the 1890 election, however, Republicans went from a House majority to 26 percent of seats in the following Congress. This remains arguably the largest electoral rebuke in congressional history since no House majority party ever came back with a smaller percentage in the following Congress.[38] Modern historian Richard White summarizes the outcome: "In fashioning Congress into a comparatively well-honed and efficient piece of legislative machinery, the Republicans had no idea that they were creating a political suicide machine."[39] Since a major reason why House members give procedural tools to their party leaders is to protect their electoral interests,[40] it is a testament to Reed's leadership ability that he kept his position as Republican leader after his exercise of procedural tools preceded an electoral catastrophe.

Reed's role in establishing majority rule in the House is unquestionably a tremendous achievement. The perception of Reed's leadership ability has resisted change. No timid leader in his own right, Theodore Roosevelt characterized Reed as having "extraordinary ability and iron courage with which he championed a radical revolution in our methods of applying the principles of parliamentary procedure."[41] The modern political scientist Ron Peters argues that Reed spearheaded "a metamorphosis in American democracy" through his "courage" and "political acumen."[42] The Peters formulation echoes that of Speaker Rayburn, who once said that a successful Speaker needed two things: brains and backbone.[43]

Reed also deserves credit for leadership based on principle. After his appointment to the Rules committee in 1882, Reed pursued the goal of establishing procedures that allowed a House majority to act. In summarizing the literature on congressional party leadership, Strahan observes that scholars disagree about whether congressional leaders have one overriding goal of remaining leader or pursue multiple goals.[44] Reed's dedication to principle offers evidence of multiple goals because Reed wanted both to keep his job and to strengthen majority rule in a way that could jeopardize his leadership position. It helps to explain why Reed confounds other political-science frameworks, such as the repeated instances in which a Reed-led minority party pressed for stronger majority-party rights in opposition to its underlying policy preferences. Eric Schickler explains, "Political scientists have been reluctant to deal explicitly with Reed's role because it appears too idiosyncratic for systematic analysis. . . . The Reed rules also demonstrate that important institutional changes can hinge on an entrepreneurial leader's ability to manipulate the strategic situation to align multiple interests."[45] In the language of contemporary management scholarship, Reed serves as an example of "firmly held core beliefs" sustaining values-based leadership, which is emerging in global research across organization types as a near-universal contributor to successful leadership.[46]

While Reed justifiably receives praise for his leadership in establishing majority rule in the House, he is also open to criticism for the form that it takes. In theory, Reed's conception of conditional minority rights could lead to a range of minority-party functions: "What are called the rights of minorities in deliberative assemblies are like the right of any individual in a highway, subject at all times to the control of the whole community."[47] In practice, Reed's implementation of majority rule leaves little role for the minority party. As minority leader, Reed resisted caucus pressure and refused to offer a substitute tariff bill because it would make Republicans complicit in governing. As Speaker, Reed often gave Democrats little opportunity for meaningful input in the legislative process. In Reed's partisan view of politics, the input of opposition Democrats would push policy in one direction: "I do not mean to say the difference between their average of intelligence and ours is so very great, but I say that the difference is just enough to make us take right positions on an average and for them to take wrong ones on an average."[48] Reed is credited with a pithy summary of the role of the minority party: "The right of the minority is to draw its pay, and its function is to make a quorum."[49] Excluding the minority party from meaningful participation not only eliminates potential contributions but also elevates partisan rancor.

The House's bitter partisanship, which is exacerbated by the system of parliamentary procedure, makes it difficult to reconcile the differences inherent in modern life. The pursuit of compromise, never easy under the best circumstances, is complicated by the potential for special rules to preclude a compromise amendment from being considered on the floor. The incentive to pursue compromise is reduced by knowing there is a good chance that it will not be allowed to receive a vote. Advocates for compromise cannot count on a playing field governed by standing rules for how a general class of legislation will be treated but will often encounter rules tailored to the individual bill. The perception of unfairness from amendment restriction can be further increased when special rules provide bills with individualized waiver protection from violating budget or other standing rules.[50] Since special rules are part of the calculation from the start, they can affect the entire legislative process and exacerbate a "prickly relationship between the parties."[51] This is predictable given the evidence, including experimental findings, that shows the proposer of the rule gets a greater share of the benefits under restrictive rules than under open rules.[52] Longtime House minority leader Bob Michel argued that the use of restrictive rules "effectively disenfranchis[es] millions of Americans."[53]

Party animosity is also increased by the limited opportunity to voice displeasure with legislation. Special rules routinely curtail debate to a few hours for even major legislation. It is no accident that some of the most bitterly partisan debate in the modern House occurs before a predictable party-line vote to adopt a special rule. Once the special rule is adopted, there is little that the minority can do to even briefly slow legislation from being approved by the majority. Rules shape rhetoric and the deliberative process.[54] As described by congressional scholar Matthew Green, the way that parties treat each other may lessen the chance of compromise.[55] Curtailing minority participation may eliminate an opportunity to reconcile differences.

The way that the rules amplify partisan differences should not be a surprise. As political science demonstrates, Reed built the institutional foundation of the modern Congress. He not only introduced the essential tools for congressional leaders, but he also abused them from the start. When Reed introduced the first special rule in 1883, it was widely perceived to offend the sense of fair play. *The Springfield Daily Republican* editorialized that it was "heads I win, tails you lose."[56] Reed as much as admitted it himself on the House floor when he said that he objected to the technique but was offering the special rule because of the "great emergency" for tariff legislation.[57] In the first Congress that began under the Reed Rules, Reed and House Republicans rammed through the session's two major pieces of legislation with no amendments and minimal debate one week after committees were named. Specifically, committees were named on December 21, the Democratic leader was called to the House on Christmas Day to see the final legislation, and both the tariff and bond bills were passed by December 28. This is not an ideal way to legislate.

There was nothing inevitable about majority rule taking the form of restrictive special rules and little meaningful opportunity for minority input. Although some state legislatures in the United States have established rules committees tailoring rules for individual bills, most have not.[58] Once adopted, the Reed Rules have proved resistant to change in large part because they allow the majority party to win more frequently. It is no accident that intense partisanship characterizes a House whose institutional foundation dates from one of the most partisan eras in congressional history and from one of its most partisan members.

House procedures reflect not only Reed's partisanship but also two of his leadership shortcomings—the difficulty of considering the possibility that one might not be right and being a sore loser. Using a special rule to change the rules near the end of the game to turn a defeat into a victory is a great fit for a sore loser. Minimizing the input of others is a great fit for someone who is certain about being right. When Reed famously said that William Springer did not have to worry about ever being right, there is little doubt about who Reed thought did not have to worry about ever being wrong. Reed's views of other Democrats were not much better than his views of Springer, which prompted one Reed confidante to observe that Reed regarded the Democratic Party as "synonymous" with "arrested mental development."[59] Of course, many political leaders believe that their superior mental ability allows them to be consistently right. Reed, however, took this notion to extremes. No better example exists than Reed's absurd attempt to maintain that his 1880 speech defending the disappearing quorum was not wrong and was also consistent with his later abolition of the technique because he had prefaced his remarks with the verb "seems." The refusal to admit errors and inconsistencies can undermine credibility and prevent improvement. The interdisciplinary literature on personality and leadership is increasingly emphasizing humility, including evidence suggesting a positive relationship between leader humility and organizational performance.[60]

Reed's propensity to be a sore loser approaches being a tragic flaw. This is not to take a position on the sports cliché, "show me a good loser and I will show you a loser." It is understandable to hate losing. The issue is whether a leader's response to losing will produce better outcomes in the future. Reed sometimes had a positive response to losing, especially after the voter repudiation of the Fifty-First Congress when he went back to work and against the odds got Democrats to validate his rule changes. Too many times, however, Reed responded to losses with self-defeating behavior, including harboring grudges. The pursuit of self-defeating behaviors is what scholars have in mind when they identify being a sore loser as a leadership flaw.[61] Reed took being a sore loser to extremes. His refusal to utter the name of several of his own party's presidential candidates because of grudges was so transparent that it was a running joke in Democratic newspapers. He paid a heavy price for this shortcoming. Even at the time he was seen as overly sensitive. Republican Party leader and Reed acquaintance Thomas Platt described Reed: "He lost many a friend by considering as a personal affront, to be punished by the quickest and even brutal method, any act offensive to him."[62] The level of personal isolation made it harder to work with people in a leadership role. It also likely prevented him from service as vice president that could have led to instituting procedural reform as the Senate's presiding officer or even ascending to the presidency upon the death of William McKinley.

Reed Rules in the Senate

Although Reed never served in the Senate, his system of rules has been gaining traction there. Without comparable leadership to Reed in the late nineteenth century, the Senate continued on a path of deference to minority rights, including allowing a member to prevent a vote by a filibuster that literally talks a bill to death. Over time, however, Reed's twin pillars of preventing delay and individualized bill treatment have been finding their way to the Senate. When a small number of senators were filibustering measures to mobilize for World War I, the Senate changed its rules to stop a filibuster with a two-thirds majority, which decreased to three-fifths in 1975. First implemented in 1980, reconciliation bills are immune from filibuster and allow a simple majority to prevail on budget matters when certain budgetary processes are followed. By the end of the twentieth century, Senate majority leaders were using a range of tools to shape the agenda, such as tailoring unanimous consent agreements for individual bills and limiting amendments by a procedure known as filling the amendment tree.[63] When Senate majority party leaders contemplated limits on the filibuster in 2003, the actions of Reed received renewed attention.[64]

In the process, after more than a century, a name emerged for what Reed did in January 1890. The lack of a catchy name for Reed's accomplishment had made it easier to understate its importance. Counting nonrespondents as part of the quorum could seem pedestrian, especially once congressional absenteeism declined. Yet, it was always more than that for both empirical and philosophical reasons. Empirically, political science shows that securing a quorum was the key to stopping filibusters of all types.[65] Philosophically, Reed's action was a dramatic refusal to recognize delaying tactics permitted under the rules and assert the inherent right of a simple majority to govern. The name that emerged in 2003 would not have occurred to Reed's contemporaries. The term "nuclear option" was used when persistent Democratic filibustering of President Bush's judicial nominees prompted Senate Majority Leader Bill Frist to signal that he was open to rejecting the right to filibuster judicial nominees. Unlike Reed, however, Frist allowed a standstill to drag on for years, which enabled a deal to be struck between seven Democrats and seven Republicans in June 2005 that averted the nuclear option.

Détente was short-lived. Taking a cue from a previous leader with a homonymic surname, Democratic Senate Majority Leader Harry Reid exercised the nuclear option on November 21, 2013. He refused to recognize the right under the existing rules for Republicans to filibuster President Obama's nominees unless sixty votes were obtained for cloture. Reid's parliamentary maneuver echoed Reed by rejecting the existing right to delay and being upheld by a simple majority vote. The ruling preserved the right to filibuster Supreme Court nominees, but it prohibited filibusters for other nominees to the judiciary or bureaucracy. Senate Democrats were back in the minority in 2017 and were exercising their right to filibuster President Trump's nominee to the Supreme Court, Neil Gorsuch. Republicans had no realistic chance of obtaining the sixty votes required for cloture. On April 6, 2017, Majority Leader Mitch McConnell exercised the nuclear option to confirm Gorsuch. He refused to recognize the permitted delaying tactics, insisted on majority governance, and was upheld by a simple majority.

The fallout from the nuclear exchange was to limit filibustering to legislation unattached to budget reconciliation. The Senate has changed significantly since Reed alleged that it made decisions based on "physical endurance" instead of "majority rule."[66] Although physical endurance is still required, majority rule now has a stronger foothold in the Senate. The ability of a minority to block a nomination has been curtailed. A determined simple majority that follows budget reconciliation procedures can overcome obstruction and get a final passage vote. It is no accident that the three laws with the greatest financial impact that passed in the first two decades of the twenty-first century technically cleared the Senate with simple majorities as filibuster-immune reconciliation bills—the Bush tax cuts (the Economic Growth and Tax Relief Reconciliation Act of 2001), Obamacare (the Health Care and Education Reconciliation Act of 2010), and Trump tax cuts (an Act to Provide for Reconciliation for Fiscal Year 2018). The Biden administration's first major legislation, the Covid-19 relief package, also passed through reconciliation. The Senate is still different from the House, but the historical trend is clear.

Reed Rules in American Politics

In addition to being a guide to parliamentary procedure, the Reed Rules are a metaphorical leadership style—power politics for partisan ends. The philosophy of the Reed Rules is captured by Reed's description of what happens in a democracy when 101 are on one side of an issue and 100 are on the other side: "The 100 go to the wall."[67] As implemented by Reed, the majority party sends the minority party to the wall. The Reed Rules are a take-no-prisoners approach, except when opposition party members must be taken prisoner to preserve a quorum. When Reed literally locked in members in 1890, it resulted in actual bloodshed, which did not even occur when the more bloodthirsty presiding officer Frank Underwood took a page out of Reed's playbook by securing a dramatic quorum in the American version of the fictional *House of Cards*.[68]

Politics may not always be a blood sport, but intense partisanship has a foothold across American politics. Scholars have documented the bitter partisanship that has increasingly characterized Congress,[69] the presidency,[70] and the courts.[71] Bitter partisanship also affects nongovernmental organizations, including the news media.[72] The growing partisanship of institutions reflects the increased partisanship of the American public. Support for compromise is precarious. The Pew Research Center recently asked Americans how important they thought it was that "Republican elected officials are willing to make compromises with Democratic officials" and that "Democratic elected officials are willing to make compromises with Republican officials." Although nearly 80 percent of party identifiers say that it is "very important" for elected officials of the opposing party to compromise with officials of their party, less than half of respondents say that it is important for elected officials of their own party to compromise with the opposing party.[73]

There are many causes of this bitter partisanship. Evidence increasingly points to the nature of the electoral system as having the greatest effect on amplifying partisan differences, but parliamentary procedure plays a role in the "fight club politics" of the House.[74] How the House conducts its work is vital to the functioning of American democracy. The people's chamber sets the broader tone for politics, and its members are well positioned to move into other prominent positions in state and federal government. In his quantitative analysis of polarization in the House and Senate, Sean Theriault finds that the modern Senate has become nearly as polarized as the House, in part because "the divisiveness of the House has been transported to the Senate by former House members upon their election to the Senate."[75] The House governing style can permeate the broader political system.

Bitter partisanship makes it difficult to find policy solutions. Reed envisioned a political system in which one party governs and the other party watches. Of course, many minority parties around the globe do a lot of watching. It is common that majority parties in legislatures do not give minority parties votes on preferred policies.[76] Lack of minority input, however, can be especially problematic in a system of separated powers. The House is only one part of the system and depends on other parts of the system for successful policy enactment. House majority parties that deny minority input may undermine the chance of ultimate policy success. There may be better places for the minority party to go than to the wall. It may be beneficial for the minority party to go to the negotiating table. Yet, negotiation has become more difficult in today's polarized Congress.[77] Official House historian Robert Remini sums up the implications for broader American politics: "The history of the House demonstrates repeatedly that when members fail or refuse to compromise they invite disaster."[78]

Of course, Thomas Brackett Reed is not responsible for the hyperpartisanship of contemporary American politics. He is not even responsible for the hyperpartisanship of the House of Representatives. Each House is a new body that adopts rules at the start of each Congress. It is fair to praise or criticize Reed for his leadership style and system of rules, but modern politicians are ultimately responsible for how they conduct politics. They are choosing to follow the Reed Rules. The institutional foundation of the House of Representatives is largely intact from Reed. The majority party controls the agenda by preventing delay and using special rules to shape bill consideration. Reed's foundation has proved resistant to change and conducive to his leadership style of power politics for partisan ends.

The longevity of the Reed Rules generates one final irony. The Reed Rules were designed to produce change. Fundamental to the Reed Rules is the notion that an institution is not bound by previous rules. When preferences for leadership styles change, the Reed Rules provide a path for change. The path is identified in Reed's eponymous parliamentary manual. Thus, the last word, which Reed would want to have, belongs to him: "The general principle of decision is the natural one that the majority shall govern."[79]

ACKNOWLEDGMENTS

My greatest debt in writing this book goes to Thomas Brackett Reed for documenting his reflections about life and leadership. After retiring from Congress, Reed contemplated writing a memoir and asked confidante George Gifford to return any letters from Reed that he had kept from their three-decade correspondence. Although Reed died before writing a memoir, what he preserved, if not the soul of candor, is sufficiently candid to offer unique insight into the strengths and weaknesses of a transcendent leader. Journalist Robert Gallagher commissioned most of the translations of Reed's French diary reflections cited in this book, but Gallagher died before finishing a Reed biography that he had spent years researching. That my two-decade project did not meet a similar fate required help from many others. Nobody provided more support or edited more rough drafts than Anna Broome, who balanced insights from being a policy analyst, *AudioFile* book reviewer, and wife. The University of Southern Maine provided research sabbaticals and rich interactions with students in my Congress courses. I encountered universal professionalism at archives throughout the country, especially at Bowdoin College, where most Reed papers are housed. Special thanks are also due to the Dirksen Congressional Center and the Maine State Library. I am grateful to the many scholars who provided feedback at various stages of this research, especially Douglas Harris and Burdett Loomis. At the University Press of Kansas, I received helpful anonymous peer reviews, wise counsel from Senior Editor David Congdon, and production expertise. Although others contributed, I will call it a quorum.

NOTES

Abbreviations

Archives (Paper Collections)

BC	Bowdoin College, George J. Mitchell Dept of Special Collections and Archives, Brunswick, ME (Thomas B. Reed)
BU	Brown University, John Hay Library, Providence, RI (Samuel Cox)
CHM	Chicago History Museum and Research Center, Chicago, IL (J. Franklin Aldrich)
DCR	Dartmouth College, Rauner Special Collections, Hanover, NH (Augustus Saint-Gaudens)
HU	Harvard University, Houghton Library, Cambridge, MA (Asher Hinds)
IHS	Indiana Historical Society, Indianapolis, IN (Holman-O'Brien)
ISL	Indiana State Library, Indianapolis, IN (Anna Wright)
LC	Library of Congress, Washington, DC (Nelson Aldrich, Whitelaw Reid, Theodore Roosevelt)
MEHS	Maine Historical Society, Portland, ME (Stanley Pullen, Nathan Webb)
MHS	Massachusetts Historical Society, Boston, MA (George Hoar, Henry Cabot Lodge)
MNHS	Minnesota Historical Society, St. Paul, MN (Cushman Davis)
NHHS	New Hampshire Historical Society, Concord, NH (William Chandler, Jacob Gallinger, Charles Marseilles)
OHS	Ohio Historical Society, Columbus, OH (George Myers)
PFL	Proctor Free Library, Proctor, VT (Redfield Proctor)
RBHC	Rutherford B. Hayes Presidential Center, Fremont, OH (Rutherford B. Hayes)
SCHS	Stark County Historical Society and McKinley Museum, Canton, OH (E. T. Heald)
SHMO	State Historical Society of Missouri, Columbia, MO (Champ Clark)
SU	Syracuse University, Special Collections Research Center, Syracuse, NY (J. Warren Keifer)
TSL	Tennessee State Library and Archives, Nashville, TN (Price-Gay Family)
UC	University of California, Bancroft Library, Berkeley, CA (Mark Twain)

UMO	University of Maine, Fogler Library Special Collections, Orono, ME (Hamlin Family)
UPA	University of Pennsylvania, Annenberg Rare Book & Manuscript Library, Philadelphia, PA (Samuel Randall)
UVA	University of Virginia, Albert and Shirley Small Special Collections Library, Charlottesville, VA (Thomas B. Reed)
WRHS	Western Reserve Historical Society, Cleveland, OH (Mather Family)

Letter Compilations

LTR	Morison, Elting E., ed. *The Letters of Theodore Roosevelt.* Cambridge, MA: Harvard University Press, 1951.
SRL	Lodge, Henry Cabot, ed. *Selections from the Correspondence of Theodore Roosevelt and Henry Cabot Lodge, 1884–1918.* New York: Charles Scribner's Sons, 1925.

Serials

BDG	*Boston Daily Globe*, MA
BWC	*Bangor Whig and Courier*, ME
CH	*Chicago Herald*, IL
CR	*Congressional Record* [Congress/Session]
DEA	*Daily Eastern Argus*, Portland, ME
DIO	*Daily Inter-Ocean*, Chicago, IL
DKJ	*Daily Kennebec Journal*, Augusta, ME
LEJ	*Lewiston Evening Journal*, ME
NYS	[New York] *Sun*, NY
NYT	*New York Times*, NY
NYTR	*New-York Tribune*, NY
PDP	*Portland Daily Press*, ME
PI	*Philadelphia Inquirer*, PA
SDR	*Springfield Daily Republican*, IL
SLR	*St. Louis Republic*, MO
WP	*Washington Post*, DC

Prologue

1. *Congressional Record* (hereinafter *CR*) 47/2, February 1, 1883, 1938.

2. Herbert Bruce Fuller, *The Speakers of the House* (Boston: Little, Brown, 1909), 243.

3. "Current News and Notes," *Lewiston Evening Journal*, Maine (hereinafter *LEJ*), February 3, 1883, 4.

4. "The House Roared and the Ass Brayed," *Daily Eastern Argus*, Portland, Maine (hereinafter *DEA*), February 6, 1883, 4.

5. Douglas B. Harris and Matthew N. Green, "Michel as Minority Leader: Minority Party Strategies and Tactics in the Postreform House," in *Robert H. Michel: Leading the*

Republican House Minority, eds. Frank H. Mackaman and Sean Q Kelly (Lawrence: University Press of Kansas, 2019), 101.

6. Essay, untitled draft on Reed, Champ Clark Papers, State Historical Society of Missouri, Columbia, MO (hereinafter SHMO), 2.

7. Roosevelt to Matthews, February 10, 1890, Elting E. Morison, ed., *The Letters of Theodore Roosevelt* (Cambridge, MA: Harvard University Press, 1951) (hereinafter *LTR*), 213–214.

8. Although Reed pioneered the special rule for a single occasion in 1883, the 1890 reforms paved the way for wider use through "formal recognition of the practice." Randall Strahan, *Leading Representatives: The Agency of Leaders in the Politics of the U.S. House* (Baltimore: Johns Hopkins University Press), 103.

9. Jeffery A. Jenkins and Charles Stewart III, *Fighting for the Speakership: The House and the Rise of Party Government* (Princeton, NJ: Princeton University Press, 2013), 242.

Chapter 1. Preparing for Congressional Battle

1. Samuel W. McCall, *The Life of Thomas B. Reed* (Boston: Houghton Mifflin, 1914), 7.

2. Champ Clark, *My Quarter Century of American Politics* (New York: Harper & Brothers, 1920), 1: 277.

3. Henry Wadsworth Longfellow, *The Courtship of Miles Standish and Other Poems* (Boston: Ticknor & Fields, 1858), 164.

4. C. Clark, *My Quarter Century*, 1: 284.

5. "Thomas Reed House Sold to NY Man," *Portland Evening Express*, February 4, 1969, 1.

6. Campbell Gibson, *Population of the 100 Largest Cities and Other Urban Places in the United States: 1790 to 1990* (Washington, DC: Bureau of the Census, 1998), T7.

7. "The Great Commoner Dead," *LEJ*, December 8, 1902, 1.

8. "When We Were Playmates Together," *LEJ*, July 27, 1901, B1.

9. Diary of W. F. Crowell, Reed Papers, Bowdoin College, George J. Mitchell Dept of Special Collections & Archives, Brunswick, ME (hereinafter BC).

10. Christian P. Potholm, *This Splendid Game: Maine Campaigns and Elections, 1940–2002* (Lanham, MD: Lexington Books, 2003), 18.

11. "The Free Soil Candidate for Speaker," *Boston Courier*, December 31, 1855, 1.

12. McCall, *Life*, 13.

13. McCall, *Life*, 12.

14. Charles C. Calhoun, *A Small College in Maine: Two Hundred Years of Bowdoin* (Brunswick, ME: Bowdoin College, 1993), 171.

15. Theodore Dreiser, "Thomas Brackett Reed: The Story of a Great Career," in *Theodore Dreiser's Uncollected Magazine Articles, 1897–1902*, ed. Yoshinobu Hakutani (Cranbury, NJ: Associated University Presses, 2003), 80.

16. "Reminiscences," *LEJ*, January 30, 1915, M4.

17. Scrapbook, "The Bowdoin Militia," Reed Papers, BC.

18. Diary of W. F. Crowell, Reed Papers, BC.

19. "Reminiscences," *LEJ*, February 6, 1915, M4.

20. McCall, *Life*, 27.

21. Reed to Fessenden, October 18, 1864, Reed Papers, BC.

22. Essay, "Ancient and Modern Eloquence," Reed Papers, BC.

23. Essay, "Editorial," Reed Papers, BC.

24. Dreiser, "Thomas Brackett Reed," 81.

25. *Obituary Record of the Graduates of Bowdoin College and the Medical School* (Brunswick, ME: Bowdoin College Library, 1911), 198.

26. Thomas B. Reed, *Centennial Oration* (Portland, ME: Owen, Strout, 1886), 23.

27. Dreiser, "Thomas Brackett Reed," 81.

28. McCall, *Life*, 27–28.

29. George H. Tinkham, *History of San Joaquin County California* (Los Angeles: Historic Record, 1923), 226.

30. Patricia M. Anderson and William D. Barry, *Deering: A Social and Architectural History* (Portland, ME: Greater Portland Landmarks, 2010), 78.

31. Slason Thompson, *Way Back When: Recollections of an Octogenarian* (Chicago: H. G. Adair, 1930), 128.

32. Essay, "California Essay," Reed Papers, BC.

33. William A. Robinson, *Thomas B. Reed: Parliamentarian* (New York: Dodd, Mead, 1930), 19.

34. Speech Transcript, "Loyal Legion Dinner, May 7, 1884," Reed Papers, BC.

35. Dreiser, "Thomas Brackett Reed," 82.

36. "Letter from Augusta," *Portland Daily Press*, Maine (hereinafter *PDP*), February 7, 1868, 2.

37. "Letter from Augusta," *DEA*, February 25, 1868, 2.

38. "The Speakership," *PDP*, January 4, 1869, 2.

39. "Our Augusta Correspondence," *LEJ*, January 7, 1869, 2.

40. "Our Augusta Correspondence," *LEJ*, January 8, 1869, 3.

41. Reed to Gifford, January 13, 1869, Reed Papers, BC.

42. Reed to Gifford, January 27, 1869, Reed Papers, BC.

43. Reed to Gifford, January 31, 1869, Reed Papers, BC.

44. Reed to Gifford, January 27, 1869, Reed Papers, BC.

45. "Mr. Reed on Capital Punishment," *PDP*, February 26, 1869, 1.

46. "From the Capital," *DEA*, February 20, 1869, 2.

47. "Portland Representatives in the Legislature," *PDP*, March 15, 1869, 2.

48. Reed to Gifford, September 30, 1869, Reed Papers, BC.

49. T Reed to S Reed, May 8, 1871, Reed Papers, BC.

50. "Maine Legislature," *Daily Kennebec Journal*, Augusta, Maine (hereinafter *DKJ*), March 17, 1870, 2.

51. "The Great Commoner Dead," *LEJ*, December 8, 1902, A1.

52. "To the Legislature of Maine," *PDP*, March 18, 1870, 2.

53. Hazel Dicken-Garcia, *Journalistic Standards in Nineteenth-Century America* (Madison: University of Wisconsin Press, 1989), 42.

54. "The Hoswell-Laflin Tragedy," *DKJ*, December 7, 1870, 2.

55. "The Hoswell-Laflin Tragedy," *DKJ*, December 8, 1870, 2.

56. "The Verdict in the Hoswell Case," *PDP*, December 8, 1870, 2.

57. T Reed to S Reed, October 18, 1872, Reed Papers, BC.

58. Reed to Gifford, September 28, 1872, Reed Papers, BC.

59. Reed to Gifford, June 14, 1896, Reed Papers, BC.

60. Reed to Roosevelt, May 29, 1896, Theodore Roosevelt Papers, Library of Congress, Washington, DC (hereinafter LC).

61. "First Suggested Mr. Reed for President," *PDP*, April 28, 1896, 4.

62. David S. Barry, *Forty Years in Washington* (Boston: Little, Brown, 1924), 136.

63. "Cumberland S.J. Court," *PDP*, April 25, 1877, 3.

64. Barry, *Forty Years*, 136.

65. *Parker vs. Portland Publishing*, 69 Me. 179 (1879).

66. "Superior Court," *PDP*, October 15, 1875, 3.

67. Thomas B. Reed, "Annual Report of the City Solicitor," in *City of Portland Auditors Seventeenth Annual Report* (Portland, ME: B. Thurston, 1876), 212.

68. Jamie L. Carson and Jason M. Roberts, "Strategic Politicians and U.S. House Elections, 1874–1914," *Journal of Politics* 67, no. 2 (May 2005): 474–496.

69. *Portland Advertiser*, June 28, 1876, 1.

70. "First District Convention," *Portland Advertiser*, June 30, 1876, 3.

71. "First District Convention," *PDP*, June 30, 1876, 3.

72. "Maine Politics," *Portland Advertiser*, August 12, 1876, 1.

73. Charles W. Calhoun, *The Presidency of Ulysses S. Grant* (Lawrence: University Press of Kansas, 2017), 548.

74. "Concerning a Man Named Ingersoll," *DEA*, September 1, 1876, 1.

75. *PDP*, September 11, 1876, 2.

76. "Disappointment," *DEA*, August 23, 1876, 2.

77. *PDP*, August 23, 1876, 2.

78. "Representative to Congress," *PDP*, September 18, 1876, 3.

79. "Jolification," *PDP*, September 12, 1876, 3.

80. James MacGregor Burns, *Leadership* (New York: Harper & Row, 1978), 63.

81. William K. Muir, Jr., *Legislature: California's School for Politics* (Chicago: University of Chicago Press, 1982).

82. James L. Payne and Oliver H. Woshinsky, "Incentives for Political Participation," *World Politics* 24, no. 4 (July 1972): 518–546.

83. Payne and Woshinsky, "Incentives," 540.

Chapter 2. The Bumptiousness of a Young Congressman

1. Thomas B. Reed, "The Life of a Congressman," in *The Ship of State by Those at the Helm* (Boston: Ginn, 1903), 47.

2. Richard R. John, "Who Were the Gilders? And Other Seldom-Asked Questions about Business, Technology, and Political Economy in the United States," *Journal of the Gilded Age and Progressive Era* 8, no. 4 (October 2009): 474–480.

3. Joel H. Silbey, *The American Political Nation, 1838–1893* (Stanford, CA: Stanford University Press, 1991), 219, 221.

4. Charles W. Calhoun, *From Bloody Shirt to Full Dinner Pail: The Transformation of Politics and Governance in the Gilded Age* (New York: Hill & Wang, 2010), 8.

5. Nelson W. Polsby, "The Institutionalization of the U.S. House of Representatives," *American Political Science Review* 62, no. 1 (March 1968): 146.

6. Gerald J. Baldasty, *Commercialization of News in the Nineteenth Century* (Madison: University of Wisconsin Press, 1992).

7. Charles W. Calhoun, *Minority Victory: Gilded Age Politics and the Front Porch Campaign of 1888* (Lawrence: University Press of Kansas, 2008), 21.

8. Charles W. Calhoun, "The Political Culture: Public Life and the Conduct of Politics" in *The Gilded Age: Essays on the Origins of Modern America*, ed. Charles W. Calhoun (Wilmington, DE: Scholarly Resources, 1996), 185–213.

9. Wyatt Wells, "Rhetoric of the Standards: The Debate over Gold and Silver in the 1890s," *Journal of the Gilded Age and Progressive Era* 14, no. 1 (January 2015): 49–68.

10. Richard Franklin Bensel, *The Political Economy of American Industrialization, 1877–1900* (New York: Cambridge University Press, 2000), 13.

11. Sean Dennis Cashman, *America in the Gilded Age: From the Death of Lincoln to the Rise of Theodore Roosevelt* (New York: New York University Press, 1984).

12. Thomas Piketty, *Capital in the Twenty-First* Century, trans. Arthur Goldhammer (Cambridge, MA: Belknap Press of Harvard University Press, 2014), 348.

13. Richard White, *The Republic for Which It Stands: The United States During Reconstruction and the Gilded Age, 1865–1896* (New York: Oxford University Press, 2017), 478.

14. Robinson, *Thomas B. Reed*, 40.

15. *CR* 45/2, January 10, 1878, 278.

16. "Personal," *PDP* [quoting *Boston Herald*], January 12, 1878, 3.

17. *CR* 45/2, April 12, 1878, 2481.

18. *CR* 45/2, April 12, 1878, 2485.

19. "Buncombe at the Capital," *New York Times*, NY (hereinafter *NYT*), April 20, 1878, 4.

20. *CR* 45/2, April 12, 1878, 2488, 2490.

21. *DEA*, April 17, 1878, 2.

22. *Bangor Whig and Courier*, Maine (hereinafter *BWC*), May 13, 1878, 2.

23. "Plotting," *Daily Inter-Ocean*, Chicago (hereinafter *DIO*), May 16, 1878, 1.

24. *DEA*, May 21, 1878, 2.

25. "The Democratic Mexican Committee," *Cincinnati Commercial Tribune*, May 21, 1878, 4.

26. Reed to Webb, February 16, 1878, Nathan Webb Papers, Maine Historical Society, Portland, ME (hereinafter MEHS).

27. Reed to Townsend, May 21, 1878, Miscellaneous Manuscripts—Reed, Rutherford B. Hayes Presidential Center, Fremont, OH (hereinafter RBHC).

28. "The Bulldozer's Latest," *New Orleans Republican*, March 9, 1877, 1.

29. Charles Richard Williams, *The Life of Rutherford Birchard Hayes* (Boston: Houghton Mifflin, 1914), 2: 158–159.

30. "Thomas Brackett Reed's Home," *Chicago Times-Herald*, April 7, 1895, in Scrapbook, Reed Papers, BC.

31. Select Committee on Alleged Frauds in the Presidential Election of 1876, *Testimony: Presidential Election Investigation*, 45th Cong., 3d Sess., HR Mis. Doc. 31 (1879), Part 3, 43, 46, 48, 49, 51.

32. "Anderson's Testimony," *BWC* [citing *Boston Journal*], June 7, 1878, 2.

33. Select Committee, *Testimony*, Part 3, 67.

34. "Getting the Facts," *DEA*, June 5, 1878, 2.

35. "Potter's Witness," *Cincinnati Daily Gazette*, June 5, 1878, 1.
36. "Reed as a Bulldozer," *DEA* [quoting *Boston Herald*], June 6, 1878, 2.
37. Reed to Webb, May 31, 1878, Nathan Webb Papers, MEHS.
38. Goddard to Hayes, August 1, 1878, Rutherford B. Hayes Papers, RBHC.
39. Hayes to Goddard, August 7, 1878, Rutherford B. Hayes Papers, RBHC.
40. "The Last Word," *PDP*, September 9, 1878, 1.
41. *DEA*, August 23, 1878, 2.
42. "A Mixed Contest in Maine," *NYT*, September 5, 1878, 1.
43. "The Oregon Plan," *PDP*, August 12, 1878, 1.
44. *DEA*, September 3, 1878, 2.
45. "The Last Word," *PDP*, September 9, 1878, 1.
46. *DEA*, September 9, 1878, 2.
47. "The Official Vote," *PDP*, September 11, 1878, 3.
48. "Rejoicing over the Result," *PDP*, September 10, 1878, 3.
49. *CR* 45/3, January 10, 1879, 415.
50. Select Committee, *Testimony*, Part 4, 176, 177.
51. Select Committee, *Testimony*, Part 4, 198.
52. "Tilden's Nephew's Story," *NYT*, February 7, 1879, 1.
53. "Tilden's Nephew's Story," *NYT*, February 7, 1879, 1.
54. Select Committee, *Testimony*, Part 4, 266.
55. "Mr. Marble's Testimony," *Springfield Daily Republican*, Illinois (hereinafter *SDR*), February 8, 1879, 5.
56. Select Committee, *Testimony*, Part 4, 267.
57. Select Committee, *Testimony*, Part 4, 288, 289.
58. "Piling It On," *DEA* [quoting *Chicago Times*], February 19, 1879, 2.
59. "Poor Tommy," *DEA* [quoting *New York World*], February 15, 1879, 1.
60. "Poor Tommy," *DEA*, February 15, 1879, 1.
61. *BWC*, February 10, 1879, 2.
62. *BWC* [quoting *New York Graphic*], February 14, 1879, 2.
63. Select Committee on Alleged Frauds in the Presidential Election of 1876, *Report*, 45th Cong., 3d Sess., HR Report 140 (1879), 70.
64. Karen Guenther, "Potter Committee Investigation of the Disputed Election of 1876," *Florida Historical Quarterly* 61, no. 3 (January 1983): 294.
65. "Thomas Brackett Reed's Home," *Chicago Times Herald*, April 7, 1895, in Scrapbook.
66. *CR* 46/1, April 25, 1879, 928.
67. Reed to Gifford, August 18, 1900, Reed Papers, BC.
68. "The Maine Canvass," *New Hampshire Patriot*, December 18, 1879, 2.
69. "Maine's Shame," *Boston Evening Journal*, December 24, 1879, 4.
70. "Our Washington Letter," *Troy Weekly Times*, February 12, 1880, 3.
71. M. P. Follett, *The Speaker of the House of Representatives* (New York: Longmans, Green, 1909), 184.
72. *CR* 46/2, January 28, 1880, 575.
73. *CR* 46/2, January 28, 1880, 578–579.
74. *CR* 46/2, April 20, 1880, 2568.
75. *CR* 46/2, April 21, 1880, 2609.

76. *Washington Post*, DC (hereinafter *WP*), April 22, 1880, 2.
77. *CR* 46/2, April 22, 1880, 2661.
78. *CR* 46/2, April 23, 1880, 2691.
79. *CR* 46/2, April 23, 1880, 2692.
80. "Mr. Reed's Speech," *PDP*, April 28, 1880, 1.
81. *PDP* [quoting *Philadelphia Press*], April 26, 1880, 1.
82. "The First District," *PDP*, August 11, 1880, 2.
83. "Hurrah for Hallowell," *DKJ*, August 21, 1880, 3.
84. "Victory," *DEA*, September 14, 1880, 2.
85. "Congressional Vote of First District," *DEA*, September 16, 1880, 3.
86. Reed to Gifford, March 3, 1882, Reed Papers, BC.
87. "The Campaign," *DEA*, September 16, 1880, 3.
88. "The Vote in the First District," *PDP*, September 16, 1880, 3.
89. "The Senatorship," *PDP*, November 23, 1880, 1.
90. *CR* 46/3, December 13, 1880, 117–118.
91. "Our Washington Letter," *SDR*, December 16, 1880, 4.
92. "Reed Badgering the Bourbons," *BWC*, December 15, 1880, 2.
93. *DEA*, December 16, 1880, 2.
94. *CR* 46/2, April 14, 1880, 2417.
95. *CR* 48/1, July 1, 1884, 5858.
96. *CR* 46/3, December 15, 1880, 167–168.
97. *CR* 46/3, January 13, 1881, 611–612.

Chapter 3. Elephant Avoiding Mousetraps

1. Jenkins and Stewart, *Fighting for the Speakership*, 297.
2. "Who Is to Be Speaker," *NYT*, January 29, 1881, 1.
3. Reed to Keifer, May 16, 1881, J. Warren Keifer Papers, Syracuse University, Special Collections Research Center, Syracuse, NY (hereinafter SU).
4. Reed to Hamlin, July 4, 1881, Hamlin Family Papers, University of Maine, Fogler Library Special Collections, Orono, ME (hereinafter UMO).
5. "Republican Convention," *Worcester Daily Spy*, September 22, 1881, 2.
6. "Gathering Republicans," *Boston Daily Globe*, Maine (hereinafter *BDG*), September 21, 1881, 2.
7. "The Speakership Battle," *NYT*, November 27, 1881, 1.
8. Reed to Gifford, November 7, 1881, Reed Papers, BC.
9. Reed to Roosevelt, May 29, 1896, Theodore Roosevelt Papers, LC.
10. Jenkins and Stewart, *Fighting for the Speakership*, 271.
11. Burns, *Leadership*, 105.
12. Reed to Hawes, January 31, 1880, Reed Papers, BC.
13. *CR* 47/1, May 12, 1882, 3890–3891.
14. "Our Washington Letter," *LEJ*, May 27, 1882, 7.
15. "The Geneva Award Bill," *PDP* [quoting *Rockland Courier*], June 5, 1882, 2.
16. Sarah A. Binder, *Minority Rights, Majority Rule: Partisanship and the Development of Congress* (New York: Cambridge University Press, 1997), 122.
17. Jeffery A. Jenkins, "Partisanship and Contested Election Cases in the House of

Representatives, 1789–2002," *Studies in American Political Development* 18, no. 2 (Fall 2004): 112–135.

18. "The Republican Caucus," *WP*, May 27, 1882, 1.

19. *CR* 47/1, May 29, 1882, 4307.

20. "A Parliamentary Revolution," *WP*, May 30, 1882, 2.

21. "The Contest in the House," *PDP*, June 2, 1882, 2.

22. "The Republican Revolution in the House," *WP* [quoting *Philadelphia Times*], June 1, 1882, 2.

23. DeAlva Stanwood Alexander, *History and Procedure of the House of Representatives* (Boston: Houghton Mifflin, 1916), 202.

24. Alexander, *History and Procedure*, 200.

25. *Springer v. United States*, 102 US 586 (1881).

26. *CR* 47/1, July 5, 1882, 5663.

27. *CR* 47/1, July 20, 1882, 6265–6266.

28. Paul Chambers, *Jumbo: This Being the True Story of the Greatest Elephant in the World* (Hanover, NH: Steerforth Press, 2008).

29. *CR* 47/1, July 13, 1882, 6016.

30. *Omaha Daily Herald*, July 25, 1882, 2.

31. Reed to Gifford, March 31, 1882, Reed Papers, BC.

32. "A Grand Rally," *LEJ*, August 28, 1882, 1.

33. David Mayhew, *Congress: The Electoral Connection* (New Haven, CT: Yale University Press, 1974).

34. *PDP*, September 11, 1882, 1.

35. *CR* 47/2, December 18, 1882, 405–406.

36. Samuel S. Cox, *Why We Laugh* (New York: Harper & Brothers, 1876), 123, 303, 348, 349.

37. Dean Yarwood, *When Congress Makes a Joke: Congressional Humor Then and Now* (Lanham, MD: Rowman & Littlefield, 2004), 26–27, 108.

38. Reed to Gifford, December 30, 1882, Reed Papers, BC.

39. *CR* 47/2, February 3, 1883, 2055.

40. *CR* 47/2, February 8, 1883, 2313.

41. Scott A. Hendrickson and Jason M. Roberts, "Short-Term Goals and Long-Term Effects: The Mongrel Tariff and the Creation of the Special Rule in the U.S. House," *Journal of Policy History* 28, no. 2 (April 2016): 322.

42. Essay, "The Last Weeks," Reed Papers, BC, 14.

43. Essay, "The Last Weeks," Reed Papers, BC, 14.

44. Essay, "The Last Weeks," Reed Papers, BC, 13, 15.

45. Donald R. Wolfensberger, "Suspended Partisanship in the House: How Most Laws Are Really Made" (paper presented at the annual meeting of the American Political Science Association, Boston, MA, August 29, 2002), 7.

46. "Tariff Bill Prospects," *NYT*, February 25, 1883, 1.

47. Essay, "The Last Weeks," Reed Papers, BC, 13.

48. "Tariff Bill Prospects," *NYT*, February 25, 1883, 1.

49. Hendrickson and Roberts, "Short-Term Goals," 322.

50. Hendrickson and Roberts, "Short-Term Goals," 324.

51. *CR* 47/2, February 26, 1883, 3308, 3317.

52. "Washington," *New York Herald*, February 25, 1883, 11.

53. *CR* 47/2, February 26, 1883, 3316.

54. Gary W. Cox and Mathew D. McCubbins, *Setting the Agenda: Responsible Party Government in the U.S. House of Representatives* (New York: Cambridge University Press, 2005), 20.

55. Jason M. Roberts, "The Development of Special Orders and Special Rules in the U.S. House, 1881–1937," *Legislative Studies Quarterly* 35, no. 3 (August 2010): 321, 330.

56. Essay, "The Last Weeks," Reed Papers, BC, 17.

57. Barbara Sinclair, *Majority Leadership in the U.S. House* (Baltimore: Johns Hopkins University Press, 1983), 132.

58. Robert A. Caro, *The Years of Lyndon Johnson: Master of the Senate* (New York: Vintage Books, 2003).

59. Frances E. Lee, *Beyond Ideology: Politics, Principles, and Partisanship in the U.S. Senate* (Chicago: University of Chicago Press, 2009), 140.

60. Barbara Sinclair, "Do Parties Matter?" in *Party, Process, and Political Change in Congress: New Perspectives on the History of Congress*, ed. David W. Brady and Mathew D. McCubbins (Stanford, CA: Stanford University Press, 2002).

61. Hendrickson and Roberts, "Short-Term Goals," 323, 332.

62. *CR* 47/2, February 26, 1883, 3317.

63. Burdett A. Loomis, *Time, Politics, and Policies: A Legislative Year* (Lawrence: University Press of Kansas, 1994), 23.

64. *CR* 48/1, February 4, 1884, 869.

65. Reed to Gifford, February 17, 1884, Reed Papers, BC.

66. Francis E. Leupp, "Personal Recollection of Thomas B. Reed," *Outlook*, September 3, 1910, 36.

67. "The Speakership," *St. Paul Daily Globe* [quoting *Troy Telegram*], August 17, 1889, 4.

68. "Bumptious Tom," *DEA*, May 29, 1884, 3.

69. "The Speakership," *St. Paul Daily Globe* [quoting *Troy Telegram*], August 17, 1889, 4.

70. *CR* 48/1, April 17, 1884, 3063–3064.

71. Reed to Gifford, April 23, 1884, Reed Papers, BC.

72. Thomas B. Reed, "Woman Suffrage: Views of the Minority of the Committee on the Judiciary House of Representatives Forty-Eighth Congress First Session as Submitted by Hon. Thomas B. Reed," 63d Cong., 2d Sess., Senate Doc. 497 (1914).

73. Ida Husted Harper, *The Life and Work of Susan B. Anthony* (Indianapolis: Hollenbeck, 1898), 2: 591.

74. Ruth A. Gallaher, *Legal and Political Status of Women in Iowa* (Iowa City: State Historical Society of Iowa, 1918), 168.

75. Susan B. Anthony and Ida Husted Harper, eds., *The History of Woman Suffrage* (Indianapolis: Hollenbeck, 1902), 4:52.

76. Reed to Gifford, April 23, 1884, Reed Papers, BC.

77. Reed to Hoar, April 7, 1885, Asher Hinds Papers, Harvard University, Houghton Library, Cambridge, MA (hereinafter HU).

78. Farwell to Reed, October 23, 1886, Asher Hinds Papers, HU.

79. Reed to Hoar, April 7, 1885, Asher Hinds Papers, HU.

80. "Ward Seven," *PDP*, August 20, 1884, 4.

81. "Hurrah for Robie," *PDP*, September 9, 1884, 2.

Chapter 4. Minority Leader Scolds Democrats

1. Diary, October 4, 1885, trans. Balentine, Reed Papers, BC. *Related Supplemental Source Note*: Reed's French diary is stored in the Thomas Brackett Reed Collection in the George J. Mitchell Department of Special Collections and Archives at Bowdoin College. In quoting Reed's diary entries, the English translation generally will be given. There are three sources for the translations. First, "trans. Balentine" denotes diary entries translated by Reed's own daughter Katherine Reed Balentine, who appears to have translated the first months in the French diary (1885 entries) and then stopped. Second, "trans. Gallagher" denotes diary entries whose translation was commissioned (to Jane Sutton and Ted Cottrell) by Robert Gallagher, a journalist who researched Reed in the 1970s but did not publish anything on him. Third, "trans. Klotz" denotes diary entries for March 26, 1886—January 27, 1887, that were translated by the author since Gallagher appears to have omitted this part of the diary from his commissioned translation. Where the text cites the French directly or refers only to the idea, the translation reference is omitted.

2. Diary, March 21, 1886, trans. Gallagher, Reed Papers, BC.

3. Diary, June 3, 1888, trans. Gallagher, Reed Papers, BC.

4. Diary, February 4, 1886, Reed Papers, BC.

5. Diary, January 2, 1887, Reed Papers, BC.

6. Diary, January 8, 1887, Reed Papers, BC.

7. Diary, September 30, 1885, trans. Balentine, Reed Papers, BC.

8. "The Meeting of Congress," *Boston Morning Journal*, December 3, 1885, 1.

9. Reed to Gifford, December 14, 1885, Reed Papers, BC.

10. "The Senate's President," *NYT*, December 6, 1885, 1.

11. The position at the time generally was not referred to by the formal title "minority leader" but rather by various expressions of unofficial status including "leader of the Republican minority," which was used by the *Philadelphia Inquirer*, Pennsylvania (hereinafter *PI*), November 18, 1885, 4.

12. Reed to Gifford, December 14, 1885, trans. Klotz, Reed Papers, BC. *Related Supplemental Source Note*: Reed wrote some letters to his friend George Gifford in English and other letters to Gifford in French. The choice of which language to use appears to be unrelated to substance and entirely dependent on whether Reed felt like practicing French. In citing Reed's French letters to Gifford, the English translation is by the author and "trans. Klotz" is included in the citation. Bowdoin College Special Collections makes no distinction between the French and English letters to Gifford and stores the original letters in chronological order with all other Reed correspondence in the correspondence box of the Reed Collection.

13. Matthew N. Green, *Underdog Politics: The Minority Party in the U.S. House of Representatives* (New Haven, CT: Yale University Press, 2015).

14. Frank H. Mackaman, "Bob Michel Calls It Quits," in *Robert H. Michel: Leading the Republican House Minority*, ed. Frank H. Mackaman and Sean Q Kelly (Lawrence: University Press of Kansas, 2019), 337.

15. Burnes to Cox, December 16, 1885, Samuel Cox Papers, Brown University, John Hay Library, Providence, RI (hereinafter BU).

16. *CR* 49/1, February 25, 1886, 1805.

17. Diary, February 26, 1886, trans. Gallagher, Reed Papers, BC.

18. *CR* 49/1, February 26, 1886, 1830.

19. Diary, February 26, 1886, trans. Gallagher, Reed Papers, BC.

20. *CR* 49/1, March 19, 1886, 2549.

21. Diary, March 19, 1886, trans. Gallagher, Reed Papers, BC.

22. Diary, April 5, 1886, Reed Papers, BC.

23. Diary, December 10, 1892, trans. Gallagher, Reed Papers, BC.

24. Barbara W. Tuchman, *The Proud Tower: A Portrait of the World before the War 1890–1914* (New York: Macmillan, 1966), 123.

25. Morris P. Fiorina, *Congress: Keystone of the Washington Establishment* (New Haven, CT: Yale University Press, 1977), 42.

26. Diary, April 27, 1886, trans. Klotz, Reed Papers, BC.

27. *CR* 49/1, June 12, 1886, 5614.

28. *CR* 49/1, June 12, 1886, 5614.

29. *CR* 49/1, July 21, 1886, 7274.

30. "Republican District Convention," *PDP*, June 4, 1886, 4.

31. "The Closing Rally," *PDP*, September 13, 1886, 1.

32. Diary, August 26, 1886, Reed Papers, BC.

33. Diary, March 16, 1887, trans. Gallagher, Reed Papers, BC.

34. *CR* 49/2, February 26, 1887, 2343.

35. *CR* 49/2, February 28, 1887, 2451.

36. Thomas B. Reed, "Our Outlying Province," *North American Review* 146, no. 374 (January 1888): 87, 90, 93.

37. Diary, October 8, 1887, trans. Gallagher, Reed Papers, BC.

38. Diary, October 14, 1887, trans. Gallagher, Reed Papers, BC.

39. Reed, *Centennial Oration*, 13.

40. "In Congress Thursday," *DIO*, June 25, 1886, 9.

41. *WP*, September 15, 1886, 2.

42. *CR* 50/1, December 16, 1887, 80.

43. *CR* 50/1, January 11, 1888, 388, 391.

44. Diary, February 29, 1888, trans. Gallagher, Reed Papers, BC.

45. *CR* 50/1, February 29, 1888, 1601–1603.

46. Reed to Hawes, April 8, 1888, Reed Papers, BC.

47. Fuller, *Speakers of the House*, 278.

48. "A Compromise Reached," *WP*, April 12, 1888, 1.

49. "Carlisle," *BDG*, May 20, 1888, 1.

50. *CR* 50/1, May 19, 1888, 4443, 4445.

51. *CR* 50/1, May 19, 1888, 4442.

52. "The Tariff Debate Closed," *NYT*, May 20, 1888, 4.

53. "Mr. Reed and the Tariff," *DEA*, May 21, 1888, 2.

54. "Mr. Reed's Speech," *PDP*, May 21, 1888, 2.

55. Diary, May 22, 1888, trans. Gallagher, Reed Papers, BC.

56. Diary, June 4, 1888, trans. Gallagher, Reed Papers, BC.

57. Thomas B. Reed, "Democracy at St. Louis," *North American Review* 147, no. 380 (July 1888): 39–40.

58. *CR* 50/1, June 27, 1888, 5631.

59. Diary, July 22, 1888, Reed Papers, BC.

60. Thomas B. Reed, "The Tariff Question," *Independent and the Weekly Review*, August 9, 1888, 1.

61. "The Logic of Congressman Reed," *Daily Picayune* (New Orleans), August 15, 1888, 4.

62. "Is Blaine to Be a Senator," *Columbus Enquirer-Sun*, August 5, 1888, 7.

63. "News of the Week," *Weekly Courier-Journal* (New Orleans), August 20, 1888, 8.

64. Reed to Reid, August 5, 1888, Whitelaw Reid Papers, LC.

65. "Emery at Alfred," *DEA*, August 21, 1888, 2.

66. "Washington News," *DEA*, August 17, 1888, 1.

67. "It Rained," *PDP*, September 10, 1888, 1.

68. "Glorious Victory," *PDP*, September 11, 1888, 4.

69. "Hon. T. B. Reed: A Witty and Convincing Argument on Live Issues," *Los Angeles Times*, November 3, 1888, 2.

70. *CR* 50/2, January 4, 1889, 539–540.

71. Preston S. Malone, "The Political Career of Charles Frederick Crisp," PhD diss., University of Georgia, 1962, 1, 4.

72. *CR* 50/2, January 4, 1889, 540.

73. Diary, January 7, 1889, trans. Gallagher, Reed Papers, BC.

74. "Fighters in Congress," *Weekly Courier-Journal* (New Orleans), January 21, 1889, 3.

75. "First Blood," *BDG*, January 9, 1889, 1.

76. *CR* 50/2, January 9, 1889, 630.

77. Diary, January 9, 1889, trans. Gallagher, Reed Papers, BC.

78. Fuller, *Speakers of the House*, 278.

79. Diary, January 14, 1889, trans. Gallagher, Reed Papers, BC.

80. *CR* 50/2, January 14, 1889, 746.

81. Roll-call analysis by author of vote at *CR* 50/2, January 14, 1889, 751.

82. "First Blood," *BDG*, January 9, 1889, 1.

83. Diary, January 14, 1889, trans. Gallagher, Reed Papers, BC.

84. "Split into Factions," *NYT*, January 15, 1889, 1.

85. Diary, February 23, 1889, trans. Gallagher, Reed Papers, BC.

86. Diary, January 16, 1889, trans. Gallagher, Reed Papers, BC.

87. Thomas B. Reed, "Rules of the House of Representatives," *Century Illustrated Monthly Magazine* 37, no. 5 (March 1889): 795.

Chapter 5. New Speaker Establishes Majority Rule

1. "The Speakership Contest," *WP*, January 14, 1889, 2.

2. "Out in Quest of Votes," *WP*, November 22, 1889, 1.

3. Reed to Roosevelt, November 27, 1888, Theodore Roosevelt Papers, LC.

4. Diary, January 26, 1889, trans. Gallagher, Reed Papers, BC.

5. Diary, December 18, 1888, trans. Gallagher, Reed Papers, BC.

6. "Many after One Place," *NYT*, November 20, 1889, 1.

7. Matthew N. Green and Douglas B. Harris, *Choosing the Leader: Leadership Elections in the U.S. House of Representatives* (New Haven, CT: Yale University Press, 2019), 14.

8. "Out for Gavel Stakes," *BDG*, November 17, 1889, 23.

9. HC Lodge to Anna Lodge, January 8, 1888, Lodge Papers, Massachusetts Historical Society, Boston, MA (hereinafter MHS).

10. Robinson, *Thomas B. Reed*, 197.

11. Edmund Morris, *The Rise of Theodore Roosevelt* (New York: Coward, McCann & Geoghegan, 1979), 842.

12. Roosevelt to Lodge, March 29, 1889, *Selections from the Correspondence of Theodore Roosevelt and Henry Cabot Lodge, 1884–1918*, ed. Henry Cabot Lodge (New York: Charles Scribner's Sons, 1925) (hereinafter SRL), 76.

13. Roosevelt speech, December 13, 1888, *LTR*, 151.

14. Roosevelt to Reed, September 15, 1889, Reed Papers, BC.

15. "Must End in Knock-Out," *BDG*, November 20, 1889, 1.

16. "Out for Gavel Stakes," *BDG*, November 17, 1889, 23.

17. Fred I. Greenstein, *Personality and Politics: Problems of Evidence, Inference, and Conceptualization* (Chicago: Markham, 1969).

18. Roosevelt to Lodge, August 1, 1889, *LTR*, 182.

19. Diary, January 26, 1889, trans. Gallagher, Reed Papers, BC.

20. "The Nation's Capital," *DKJ* [quoting *Boston Journal*], November 16, 1889, 1.

21. "Reed's Chances Better," *NYT*, November 27, 1889, 1.

22. "Willing to Be Speaker," *NYT*, August 20, 1889, 1.

23. "New Yorkers Will Vote for Reed," *PDP*, November 29, 1889, 1.

24. "Reed's Hot Campaign," *Morning Oregonian*, November 30, 1889, 1.

25. "Reed to Be Speaker," *WP*, December 1, 1889, 1.

26. Arthur Wallace Dunn, *From Harrison to Harding* (New York: G. P. Putnam's Sons, 1922), 22.

27. Kevin Phillips, *William McKinley* (New York: Times Books, 2003), 27.

28. "A Breezy Washington Letter," *BWC*, December 7, 1889, 2.

29. "Drenched at Woodstock," *New-York Tribune*, NY (hereinafter *NYTR*), July 5, 1889, 1.

30. Thomas B. Reed, "Obstruction in the National House," *North American Review* 149, no. 395 (October 1889): 425–428.

31. Roger Q. Mills, "Republican Tactics in the House," *North American Review* 149, no. 397 (December 1889): 669, 671.

32. Jenkins, "Partisanship."

33. Reed to Randall, January 15, 1890, Samuel Randall Papers, University of Pennsylvania, Annenberg Rare Book & Manuscript Library, Philadelphia, PA (hereafter UPA).

34. "Juggling with Rules," *WP*, January 8, 1890, 2.

35. *CR* 51/1, January 21, 1890, 747.

36. "Capitol Gossip," *WP*, January 18, 1890, 4.

37. "Notes and Opinions," *DEA* [quoting Louisville *Courier-Journal*], January 27, 1890, 2.

38. "New Code Is in Sight," *WP*, January 28, 1890, 2.

39. *NYTR*, January 29, 1890, 6.

40. L. White Busbey, *Uncle Joe Cannon: The Story of a Pioneer American* (New York: Henry Holt, 1927), 175.

41. *CR* 51/1, January 29, 1890, 949–955.

42. "Reed Rules!" *Atlanta Constitution*, January 30, 1890, 1.

43. *LEJ*, January 30, 1890, 2.

44. "Reed Rules!" *Atlanta Constitution*, January 30, 1890, 1.

45. "The New Dictator," *BDG*, January 30, 1890, 4.

46. *CR* 51/1, January 30, 1890, 983.

47. *CR* 51/1, January 31, 1890, 998–1000.
48. *CR* 51/1, January 31, 1890, 1003.
49. *CR* 51/1, February 1, 1890, 1017.
50. *CR* 51/1, February 1, 1890, 1007–1008.
51. "Mr. Reed Talks," *PDP*, February 3, 1890, 1.
52. Thomas B. Reed, "The Limitations of the Speakership," *North American Review* 150, no. 400 (March 1890): 384, 388.
53. "One-Man Power," *BDG*, February 3, 1890, 2.
54. "Majority Rule," *DEA*, February 10, 1890, 2.
55. *DEA*, February 5, 1890, 2.
56. "A Quorum Present," *NYTR*, January 31, 1890, 6.
57. "Speaker Reed's Tyranny," *BDG*, January 31, 1890, 4.
58. "Our Liberties in Peril," *PDP*, February 19, 1890, 2.
59. "Washington Letter," *DEA*, February 13, 1890, 1.
60. "Tom Reed's Revolution," *Chicago Herald*, IL (hereinafter *CH*), February 2, 1890, 4.
61. "Current Comment," *PDP*, February 13, 1890, 2.
62. Scrapbook, *Observer* clipping (n.d.), Reed Papers, BC.
63. "Speaker Reed's Nerve," *BDG*, February 6, 1890, 5.
64. "Speaker Reed's Nerve," *BDG*, February 6, 1890, 5.
65. "Mr. Reed and the Presidency," *WP*, February 9, 1890, 4.
66. "On the Volcano's Brink," *NYT*, January 30, 1890, 1.
67. "One-Man Power," *BDG*, February 3, 1890, 2.
68. "On the Volcano's Brink," *NYT*, January 30, 1890, 1.
69. "An Armed Armistice," *St. Louis Republic*, Missouri (hereinafter *SLR*), February 8, 1890, 1.
70. "Drenched at Woodstock," *NYTR*, July 5, 1889, 1.
71. *CR* 51/1, January 30, 1890, 985.
72. Barbara Sinclair, *Legislators, Leaders, and Lawmaking: The U.S. House of Representatives in the Postreform Era* (Baltimore: Johns Hopkins University Press, 1995).
73. Matthew N. Green, *The Speaker of the House: A Study of Leadership* (New Haven, CT: Yale University Press, 2010); Strahan, *Leading Representatives.*
74. Randall Strahan, "Leadership and Institutional Change in the Nineteenth-Century House," in *Party, Process, and Political Change in Congress: New Perspectives on the History of Congress*, ed. David W. Brady and Mathew D. McCubbins (Stanford, CA: Stanford University Press, 2002), 261–262.
75. Busbey, *Uncle Joe Cannon*, 175.
76. Eric Schickler, *Disjointed Pluralism: Institutional Innovation and the Development of the U.S. Congress* (Princeton, NJ: Princeton University Press, 2001), 39.
77. *CR* 51/1, February 3, 1890, 1038–1040.
78. *CR* 51/1, February 3, 1890, 1043.
79. "Pins in Mr. Reed's Chair," *NYT*, February 5, 1890, 5.
80. "Pins in Mr. Reed's Chair," *NYT*, February 5, 1890, 5.
81. Binder, *Minority Rights*, 128.
82. Cox and McCubbins, *Setting the Agenda.*
83. "The Speaker's Victory," *WP*, February 6, 1890, 1.
84. *CR* 51/1, February 13, 1890, 1293.

85. *CR* 51/1, February 14, 1890, 1341–1342.

86. *CR* 51/1, February 15, 1890, 1349.

87. Roger H. Davidson, Walter J. Oleszek, Frances E. Lee, and Eric Schickler, *Congress and Its Members*, 16th ed. (Washington, DC: CQ Press, 2018), 33.

88. Binder, *Minority Rights*, 125, 206.

89. Randall Strahan, "Thomas Brackett Reed and the Rise of Party Government," in *Masters of the House: Congressional Leadership over Two Centuries*, ed. Roger H. Davidson, Susan Webb Hammond, and Raymond W. Smock (Boulder, CO: Westview Press, 1998), 33–62.

90. Jenkins and Stewart, *Fighting for the Speakership*.

91. Andrew Taylor, *The Floor in Congressional Life* (Ann Arbor: University of Michigan Press, 2012), 42.

92. Christopher F. Den Hartog, "Limited Party Government and the Majority Party Revolution in the Nineteenth-Century House," PhD diss., University of California, San Diego, 2004, 134.

93. Sarah A. Binder, "The Partisan Basis of Procedural Choice: Allocating Parliamentary Rights in the House, 1789–1990," *American Political Science Review* 90, no. 1 (March 1996): 15.

94. John H. Aldrich, David W. Rohde, and Michael W. Tofias, "One D Is Not Enough: Measuring Conditional Party Government, 1887–2002," in *Party, Process, and Political Change in Congress, Vol. 2: Further New Perspectives on the History of Congress*, ed. David W. Brady and Mathew D. McCubbins (Stanford, CA: Stanford University Press, 2007), 111.

95. Strahan, *Leading Representatives*, 110.

96. Den Hartog, "Limited Party Government," 84, 85, 135.

97. Randall Strahan, "Reed and Rostenkowski: Congressional Leadership in Institutional Time," in *The Atomistic Congress: An Interpretation of Congressional Change*, ed. Allen D. Hertzke and Ronald M. Peters, Jr. (Armonk, NY: M. E. Sharpe, 1992), 216.

98. Douglas Dion, *Turning the Legislative Thumbscrew: Minority Rights and Procedural Change in Legislative Politics* (Ann Arbor: University of Michigan Press, 1997), 137.

99. John H. Aldrich and Kenneth A. Shepsle, "Explaining Institutional Change: Soaking, Poking, and Modeling in the U.S. Congress," in *Congress on Display, Congress at Work*, ed. William T. Bianco (Ann Arbor: University of Michigan Press, 2000), 41.

100. Strahan, *Leading Representatives*, 109.

101. Randall B. Ripley, *Party Leaders in the House of Representatives* (Washington, DC: Brookings Institution, 1967), 16.

102. "The House Rules at Last," *NYT*, February 15, 1890, 4.

Chapter 6. The Majority Party Legislates

1. Bigelow to Lodge, June 26, 1890, Lodge Papers, MHS.

2. Reed to Caruth, March 1, 1890, Reed Papers, BC.

3. Douglas B. Harris, "The Rise of the Public Speakership," *Political Science Quarterly* 113, no. 2 (Summer 1998): 193–212.

4. "When Crisp Sat Down," *WP*, April 1, 1894, 2.

5. *DEA* [quoting *New York Star*], June 23, 1890, 2.

6. Thomas B. Reed, "A Deliberative Body," *North American Review* 148, no. 156 (February 1891): 149–150.

7. "Can't Keep Him Down," *Pittsburg Dispatch*, June 6, 1890, 1.

8. *CR* 51/1, June 19, 1890, 6262.

9. *CR* 51/1, June 19, 1890, 6268.

10. "Speaker Reed Censured," *NYT*, June 20, 1890, 1.

11. *CR* 51/1, June 21, 1890, 6354.

12. "The Speaker Happy Again," *NYT*, June 22, 1890, 2.

13. Jenkins and Stewart, *Fighting for the Speakership*, 29.

14. CR 46/2, April 22, 1880, 2661.

15. *CR* 51/1, June 21, 1890, 6357.

16. Thomas B. Reed, "The Federal Control of Elections," *North American Review* 150, no. 403 (June 1890): 672, 678, 680.

17. *CR* 51/1, July 2, 1890, 6928.

18. *CR* 51/1, June 28, 1890, 6703.

19. Richard M. Valelly, "The Reed Rules and Republican Party Building: A New Look," *Studies in American Political Development* 23, no. 2 (October 2009): 115–142.

20. "A Victory for Reed," *WP*, July 3, 1890, 1.

21. "Statesmen," *WP*, July 20, 1890, 10.

22. [New York] *Sun*, NY (hereinafter *NYS*), August 6, 1890, 4.

23. *Saint Paul Daily Globe*, August 1, 1890, 4.

24. Robert Graves, "Running Up the Flags," *DEA*, October 4, 1890, 5.

25. "Big Fizzle," *DEA*, September 5, 1890, 4.

26. "Welcomed," *PDP*, September 5, 1890, 1.

27. "The Speaker Speaks," *DEA*, September 5, 1890, 3.

28. "On the Old Campground," *PDP*, September 6, 1890, 1.

29. "The Last Gun," *PDP*, September 8, 1890, 1.

30. "Republicans Celebrate," *PDP*, September 9, 1890, 4.

31. "Smiles," *SLR*, September 22, 1890, 4.

32. "The Nose and the Quorum," *NYS*, September 20, 1890, 6.

33. "Kilgore's Forced Exit," *WP*, September 19, 1890, 7.

34. *Daily Gazette* (Fort Worth), September 21, 1890, 4.

35. "Kilgore's Kick," *Pittsburg Dispatch* [quoting *Baltimore Herald*], September 20, 1890, 4.

36. "Washington," *LEJ*, September 23, 1890, 1.

37. Schuyler Colfax, "Hon. Schuyler Colfax," in *Reminiscences of Abraham Lincoln*, ed. Allen Thorndike Rice (New York: North American Publishing, 1886), 337.

38. Stephen Skowronek, *Building a New American State: The Expansion of National Administrative Capacities, 1877–1920* (New York: Cambridge University Press, 1982), 80.

39. "Reed Downed," *Boston Daily Globe*, September 30, 1890, 1.

40. "The Portland Collectorship," *PDP* [quoting *BWC*], October 1, 1890, 2.

41. Thomas Collier Platt, *The Autobiography of Thomas Collier Platt*, ed. Louis J. Lang (New York: B. W. Dodge, 1910), 213.

42. "Statesmanship: A Republican Variety," *DEA*, October 8, 1890, 2.

43. Reed to Michener, September 18, 1890, Anna Wright Papers, Indiana State Library, Indianapolis, IN (hereinafter ISL).

44. "Talked to Thousands," *DIO*, October 22, 1890, 1.

45. "Speaker Reed," *Knoxville Journal*, October 25, 1890, 8.

46. "Reed and Raum to Hoosiers," *Indianapolis Journal*, October 21, 1890, 1.

47. "Reed's Rousing Work," *Sunday Inter Ocean* (Chicago), October 26, 1890, 1.

48. "Ambitious Reed," *Daily Critic* (DC), October 3, 1890, 1.

49. "Mr. Speaker's Speech," *Sunday Herald* (Chicago), October 26, 1890, 28.

50. "Tired of Henderson," *CH*, October 31, 1890, 3.

51. "Reed as a Reformer," *CH*, October 23, 1890, 1.

52. "The Experience of Speaker Reed," *SDR*, November 7, 1890, 4.

53. *Morning World-Herald* (Omaha), November 9, 1890, 4.

54. Reed to Lodge, November 5, 1890, Lodge Papers, MHS.

55. Reed to Lodge, November 4, 1891, Lodge Papers, MHS.

56. "A Poor Excuse," *Plain Dealer* (Cleveland), November 23, 1890, 4.

57. Thomas B. Reed, "Historic Political Upheavals," *North American Review* 160, no. 458 (January 1895): 114.

58. Reed to Lodge, November 5, 1890, Lodge Papers, MHS.

59. *CR* 51/2, January 19, 1891, 1541.

60. *CR* 51/1, February 20, 1891, 2998.

61. *CR* 51/2, February 21, 1891, 3080.

62. "After Reed's Scalp," *Pittsburg Dispatch*, February 24, 1891, 1.

63. Robert McElroy, *Levis Parsons Morton: Banker, Diplomat and Statesman* (New York: G. P. Putnam's Sons, 1930), 186.

64. Gregory J. Wawro and Eric Schickler, *Filibuster: Obstruction and Lawmaking in the U.S. Senate* (Princeton, NJ: Princeton University Press, 2006), 63.

65. Thomas Adams Upchurch, *Legislating Racism: The Billion Dollar Congress and the Birth of Jim Crow* (Lexington: University Press of Kentucky, 2004), 165.

66. Unpublished Biography, "William McKinley," E. T. Heald Papers, Stark County Historical Society and McKinley Museum, Canton, OH (hereinafter SCHS), 18–43.

67. *CR* 51/2, March 2, 1891, 3820.

68. "Reed Turned Down," *Saint Paul Daily Globe*, March 5, 1891, 1.

69. "The Gavel Has Fallen," *WP*, March 5, 1891, 1.

70. *CR* 51/2, March 2, 1891, 3825.

71. "Reed's Record," *DEA*, March 9, 1891, 2.

72. "The Fifty-First Congress," *NYTR*, March 5, 1891, 6.

73. "What the Republican Fifty-First Congress Accomplished," *PI*, March 5, 1891, 4.

74. "Jubilant Republicans," *NYTR*, March 7, 1891, 1.

75. "Mr. Reed as an Advertiser," *NYS*, March 9, 1891, 4.

76. "Jubilant Republicans," *NYTR*, March 7, 1891, 1.

77. Holman to O'Brien, March 6, 1891, Holman-O'Brien Papers, Indiana Historical Society, Indianapolis, IN (hereinafter IHS).

78. McMillin to Price, May 22, 1891, Price-Gay Family Papers, Tennessee State Library and Archives, Nashville, TN (hereinafter TSL).

79. "The Billion Congress," *NYS*, March 9, 1891, 4.

80. "Jubilant Republicans," *NYTR*, March 7, 1891, 1.

81. Thomas B. Reed, "Spending Public Money," *North American Review* 154, no. 424 (March 1892): 319.

82. Gary Libecap, "The Rise of the Chicago Packers and the Origins of Meat Inspection and Antitrust," *Economic Inquiry* 30, no. 2 (April 1992): 242–262.

83. Gifford Pinchot, *Breaking New Ground* (Seattle: University of Washington Press, 1947), 85.

84. Calhoun, *Bloody Shirt*, 129.

85. "Jubilant Republicans," *NYTR*, March 7, 1891, 1.

86. Roberts, "Development of Special Orders," 312.

87. George B. Galloway, *History of the United States House of Representatives* (Washington, DC: US Government Printing Office, 1965), 50.

88. Busbey, *Uncle Joe Cannon*, 166–167.

89. "The Last Gun," *PDP*, September 8, 1890, 1.

90. Dion, *Legislative Thumbscrew*, 137.

91. William H. Riker, *The Art of Political Manipulation* (New Haven, CT: Yale University Press, 1986), 131.

92. Strahan, *Leading Representatives*, 109.

93. Author analysis of US House of Representatives, "Party Divisions of the House of Representatives, 1789 to Present," January 2021, https://history.house.gov/Institution/Party-Divisions/Party-Divisions/.

94. "The People All Right," *Ohio Democrat*, March 28, 1891, 4.

95. "A Field for the Have Beens," *DEA* [quoting *NYT*], March 17, 1891, 2.

96. Reed to Gifford, June 13, 1891, Reed Papers, BC.

97. *Le Figaro* (Paris), June 14, 1891, "Un Hote Américain," 2.

98. *Le Figaro* (Paris), June 15, 1891, "Nos Hotes," 1.

99. Reed to Gifford, June 13, 1891, Reed Papers, BC.

100. Fairchild to Lodge, July 24, 1891, Lodge Papers, MHS.

101. Sargent to Saint-Gaudens, August 21, 1891, Augustus Saint-Gaudens Papers, Dartmouth College, Rauner Special Collections, Hanover, NH (hereinafter DCR).

102. "Art Notes," *NYT*, October 26, 1891, 4.

103. *Macon Weekly Telegraph*, December 17, 1891, 4.

104. "Capitol Chat," *WP*, January 27, 1895, 4.

105. Edward P. Mitchell, *Memoirs of an Editor: Fifty Years of American Journalism* (New York: Charles Scribner's Sons, 1924), 429.

106. *Hazel Green Herald* [quoting *Brooklyn Citizen*], January 22, 1892, 2.

107. Charles Merrill Mount, *John Singer Sargent: A Biography* (New York: W. W. Norton, 1955), 191.

108. Shawn Zeller, *CQ Weekly*, "The Ash Aesthetic," June 26, 2006, 1755.

109. M. G. Van Rensselaer, "Another Portrait by Sargent," *Harper's*, December 19, 1891, 1012.

110. "Various Exhibitions," *Art Amateur*, November 1891, 131.

111. Mount, *John Singer Sargent*, 191.

112. Sargent to Saint-Gaudens, August 21, 1891, Augustus Saint-Gaudens Papers, DCR.

113. Herbert Croly, *Marcus Alonzo Hanna: His Life and Work* (New York: Macmillan, 1923), 162.

114. Hanna to Reed, November 14, 1891, Reed Papers, BC.

115. "Reed's Visit to Ohio," *DIO*, October 28, 1891, 8.

116. Croly, *Marcus Alonzo Hanna*, 161.

Chapter 7. Gladly Takes Own Medicine

1. *CR* 52/1, January 29, 1892, 680.

2. "The Reed That Was," *Morning World* (Omaha) [quoting *New York World*], December 15, 1891, 4.

3. *DIO*, December 7, 1891, 4.

4. Thomas B. Reed, "Two Congresses Contrasted," *North American Review* 155, no. 429 (August 1892), 227.

5. *CR* 46/2, January 28, 1880, 578.

6. *CR* 52/1, January 26, 1892, 557.

7. *CR* 52/1, January 28, 1892, 647.

8. Thomas B. Reed, "Mr. Speaker," *North American Review* 154, no. 422 (January 1892): 15.

9. *CR* 52/1, March 9, 1892, 1884.

10. *CR* 52/1, January 28, 1892, 649.

11. *CR* 52/1, January 29, 1892, 680.

12. *CR* 52/1, January 28, 1892, 650.

13. *CR* 52/1, February 2, 1892, 770.

14. *CR* 52/1, February 2, 1892, 769, 771.

15. *CR* 52/1, January 28, 1892, 647.

16. *CR* 52/1, February 4, 1892, 850.

17. *CR* 52/1, February 4, 1892, 856.

18. *CR* 52/1, January 26, 1892, 555.

19. *CR* 52/1, January 29, 1892, 677.

20. *CR* 52/1, January 26, 1892, 556.

21. *U.S. v. Ballin*, 144 US 1 (1892).

22. "Reed Smiles," *BDG*, March 1, 1892, 2.

23. "A Prophet with Honor," *WP*, March 9, 1892, 2.

24. *CR* 52/1, March 10, 1892, 1945.

25. *CR* 52/1, March 10, 1892, 1947.

26. "Reed's Guard," *BDG*, March 18, 1892, 8.

27. Current Comment," *PDP*, February 20, 1892, 4.

28. Reed to Lodge, April 3, 1892, Lodge Papers, MHS.

29. Reed to Hinds, May 31, 1892, Reed Papers, BC.

30. "Reed's Personal Plans," *BDG*, May 2, 1892, 8.

31. "McKinley Permanent Chairman," *BDG*, June 8, 1892, 1.

32. "Cheers for Reed," *PDP*, June 8, 1892, 1.

33. *DEA*, June 11, 1892, 4.

34. Roosevelt to Reed, June 19, 1892, Reed Papers, BC.

35. *CR* 52/1, March 7, 1892, 1830.

36. "What Funny Things We See," *DEA*, August 1, 1892, 4.

37. Reed, "Two Congresses Contrasted," 229, 235.

38. Roosevelt to Reed, July 28, 1892, Reed Papers, BC.

39. Richard F. Fenno, Jr., *Home Style: House Members in Their Districts* (Boston: Little, Brown, 1978).

40. "Mr. Reed at the Cape," *PDP*, September 6, 1892, 2.

41. "It's All Right," *PDP*, August 18, 1892, 1.
42. "Reed at Westbrook," *DEA*, August 25, 1892, 5.
43. "Enthusiasm," *DEA*, August 20, 1892, 5.
44. "Australian Ballot System," *DEA*, August 31, 1892, 5.
45. "A Perfect Knock-Down Argument," *PDP*, September 2, 1892, 5.
46. "How We Celebrated," *PDP*, September 16, 1892, 5.
47. "Tom Reedisms," *Boston Daily Journal*, October 20, 1892, 2.
48. "Reed at Lynn," *Boston Morning Journal*, October 19, 1892, 2.
49. *SLR*, October 28, 1892, 6.
50. Reed to Lodge, November 9, 1892, Lodge Papers, MHS.
51. Reed to Aldrich, November 11, 1892, Nelson Aldrich Papers, LC.
52. *CR* 52/2, February 6, 1893, 1253.
53. Diary, February 7, 1893, trans. Gallagher, Reed Papers, BC.
54. "End of the House," *DIO*, March 5, 1893, 5.
55. Richard Stanley Offenberg, "The Political Career of Thomas Brackett Reed," PhD diss., New York University, 1963, 126.
56. "Jerry Socks It to Speaker Reed for His Inaction," *Los Angeles Times*, April 8, 1897, 1.
57. "Jerry Wanted Information," *Daily Charlotte Observer*, August 20, 1893, 2.
58. *CR* 53/1, August 29, 1893, 1033–1036.
59. *CR* 53/1, September 6, 1893, 1261–1262.
60. *Kansas Weekly Capital and Farm Journal*, April 5, 1894, 4.
61. *CR* 53/1, September 20, 1893, 1630.
62. *Albuquerque Morning Democrat*, April 3, 1894, 2.
63. Diary, February 24, 1888, trans. Gallagher, Reed Papers, BC.
64. "Line Shots," *Boston Morning Journal*, October 14, 1893, 7.
65. Thomas B. Reed, "Tariff and Business," *North American Review* 158, no. 446 (January 1894): 118.
66. *CR* 53/2, January 31, 1894, 1731.
67. *CR* 53/2, January 30, 1894, A602.
68. *CR* 53/2, February 1, 1894, 1785.
69. *CR* 53/2, February 1, 1894, 1788.
70. *CR* 53/2, February 22, 1894, 2365.
71. *CR* 53/2, March 29, 1894, 3333, 3335–3336.
72. *CR* 53/2, March 30, 1894, 3350.
73. *CR* 53/2, March 30, 1894, 3354; "Reed Made to Sit Down," *WP*, March 31, 1894, 1.
74. Champ Clark, *My Quarter Century*, 2: 345.
75. Clark, 2: 345.
76. *CR* 53/2, April 12, 1894, 3707–3708.
77. "To Adopt New Rules," *CH*, April 14, 1894, 3.
78. *Worcester Daily Spy*, April 20, 1894, 4.
79. *CR* 53/2, April 17, 1894, 3791.
80. "How to Obtain Reed's Rules," *Boston Morning Journal*, March 7, 1894, 5.
81. *CR* 53/2, August 13, 1894, 8475.
82. *CR* 53/2, August 13, 1894, 8481.
83. *CR* 53/2, August 13, 1894, 8487.
84. "The Senate Bill," *Boston Daily Journal*, August 13, 1894, 2.

85. *CR* 53/2, August 13, 1894, 8469–8471.

86. Joseph Cooper and David W. Brady, "Institutional Context and Leadership Style: The House from Cannon to Rayburn," *American Political Science Review* 75, no. 2 (June 1981): 411–425.

87. Dion, *Legislative Thumbscrew*, 32.

88. David W. Brady and Phillip Althoff, "Party Voting in the U.S. House of Representatives, 1890–1910: Elements of a Responsible Party System," *Journal of Politics* 36, no. 3 (August 1974): 764.

89. Richard G. Forgette, "Reed's Rules and the Partisan Theory of Legislative Organization, *Polity* 29, no. 3 (Spring 1997): 375–396.

90. John H. Aldrich and David W. Rohde, "The Logic of Conditional Party Government: Revisiting the Electoral Connection," in *Congress Reconsidered*, ed. Lawrence C. Dodd and Bruce I. Oppenheimer (Washington, DC: CQ Press, 2001), 269–292.

91. Gary W. Cox and Mathew D. McCubbins, *Legislative Leviathan: Party Government in the House* (Berkeley: University of California Press, 1993).

92. Eric Schickler and Andrew Rich, "Party Government in the House Reconsidered: A Response to Cox and McCubbins," *American Journal of Political Science* 41, no. 4 (October 1997): 1387–1394.

93. Strahan, "Reed and Rostenkowski," 225.

94. Thomas J. Sergiovanni, "Leadership as Cultural Expression," in *Leadership and Organizational Culture: New Perspectives on Administrative Theory and Practice*, ed. Thomas J. Sergiovanni and John E. Corbally (Urbana: University of Illinois Press, 1984).

95. "A Rousing Rally," *DEA*, September 1, 1894, 2.

96. "Rousing Rally," *BWC*, September 4, 1894, 3.

97. "Reed at Brunswick," *PDP*, September 7, 1894, 1.

98. "The Situation in This District," *DEA*, September 8, 1894, 4.

99. "In City Hall," *PDP*, September 11, 1894, 5.

100. *DEA*, September 11, 1894, 4.

Chapter 8. Conspicuously Beaten for President

1. "Must Help the East," *Sunday World-Herald* (Omaha), October 21, 1894, 1.

2. "Reed's Big Greeting," *Duluth News Tribune*, October 25, 1894, 1.

3. "Home Market Club's Banquet," *Boston Journal*, November 23, 1894, 1.

4. Thomas B. Reed, "A Last Tribute," *North American Review* 160, no. 461 (April 1895): 385.

5. Reed to Lodge, June 29, 1895, Lodge Papers, MHS.

6. "Czar Reed as an Acrobat," *Wheeling Register* [quoting *Chicago Record*], February 26, 1895, 3.

7. McCall, *Life of Reed*, 215.

8. "Reed's Financial Plan," *NYS*, February 6, 1895, 5.

9. Reed to Pullen, February 9, 1895, Stanley Pullen Papers, MEHS.

10. Pullen to Reed, April 17, 1895, Stanley Pullen Papers, MEHS.

11. Reed to Pullen, April 20, 1895, Stanley Pullen Papers, MEHS.

12. Reed to Fairchild, April 4, 1895, Thomas B. Reed Papers, University of Virginia, Albert and Shirley Small Special Collections Library, Charlottesville, VA (hereinafter UVA).

13. Diary, December 29, 1886, trans. Klotz, Reed Papers, BC.

14. Reed to Pullen, September 12, 1893, Stanley Pullen Papers, MEHS.
15. "Oh, What a Fall!" *Wichita Daily Eagle*, February 15, 1895, 1.
16. Reed to Lodge, February 14, 1895, Lodge Papers, MHS.
17. "Some Capitol Chit Chat," *Plain Dealer* (Cleveland), March 10, 1895, 8.
18. "Reed and Crisp," *PI* [quoting *Zainesville Courier*], March 11, 1895, 7.
19. Reed, "A Last Tribute," 385.
20. *DIO*, March 11, 1895, 4.
21. "Tom Reed on a Wheel," *NYS*, July 14, 1895, 3.
22. Margaret Leech, *In the Days of McKinley* (New York: Harper & Brothers, 1959), 61.
23. Reed to Lodge, September 29, 1894, Lodge Papers, MHS
24. Reed to Lodge, April 19, 1895, Lodge Papers, MHS.
25. Reed to Chandler, September 2, 1895, William Chandler Papers, New Hampshire Historical Society, Concord, NH (hereinafter NHHS).
26. H. Wayne Morgan, *William McKinley and His America*, 2nd ed. (Kent, OH: Kent State University Press, 2003), 97.
27. Reed to Pullen, February 9, 1895, Stanley Pullen Papers, MEHS.
28. Thomas Bentley Mott, *Myron T. Herrick: Friend of France* (Garden City, NY: Doubleday, Doran, 1929), 48–50.
29. Hay to Mather, February 24, 1893, Mather Family Papers, Western Reserve Historical Society, Cleveland, OH (hereinafter WRHS).
30. Roosevelt to Reed, June 11, 1895, Reed Papers, BC.
31. Reed to Lodge, March 7, 1895, Lodge Papers, MHS.
32. "The Outlook for '96," *WP*, October 16, 1895, 6.
33. "House Officers," *DEA*, December 2, 1895, 1.
34. "President Expected Soon," *SDR*, December 12, 1895, 3.
35. "A Rare Curiosity," *PDP*, November 29, 1895, 1.
36. "Reed May Not Run for the Speakership," *PI*, January 24, 1897, 19.
37. *PI* [quoting *Chicago Times Herald*], December 25, 1895, 6.
38. *CR* 54/1, December 26, 1895, 305, 307.
39. *CR* 54/1, December 27, 1895, 358.
40. "A Republican House Passes the Much Needed Revenue Bill," *PI*, December 27, 1895, 1.
41. "Speaker Reed as a Humorist," *Sun* (Baltimore), December 31, 1895, 4.
42. *Wheeling Register*, December 28, 1895, 4.
43. "More Power to Mr. Reed," *NYT*, January 12, 1896, 16.
44. Strahan, *Leading Representatives*, 102.
45. *Kansas City Star*, March 24, 1896, 4.
46. Reed to Lodge, May 16, 1895, Lodge Papers, MHS.
47. Roosevelt to Cowles, January 26, 1896, *LTR*, 510.
48. Vance to Myers, February 27, 1896, George Myers Papers, Ohio Historical Society, Columbus, OH (hereinafter OHS).
49. "J. Frank Aldrich Interviewed," *DIO*, March 18, 1896, 7.
50. Kellogg and Severance to Davis, February 24, 1896, Cushman Davis Papers, Minnesota Historical Society, St. Paul, MN (hereinafter MNHS).
51. "Fate of Some Favorite Sons," *SLR*, March 30, 1896, 4.
52. Lodge to Roosevelt, October 30, 1895, SRL, 197.

53. Roosevelt to Reed, April 20, 1895, Reed Papers, BC.

54. Proctor to Mansur, May 19, 1896, Redfield Proctor Papers, Proctor Free Library, Proctor, VT (hereinafter PFL).

55. Reed to Lodge, August 21, 1896, Lodge Papers, MHS.

56. Morgan, *William McKinley*, 157.

57. R. Hal Williams, *Realigning America: McKinley, Bryan, and the Remarkable Election of 1896* (Lawrence: University Press of Kansas, 2010), 59.

58. K Reed to Marseilles, May 31, 1896, Charles Marseilles Papers, NHHS.

59. S Reed to Lodge, June 11, 1896, Lodge Papers, MHS.

60. Reed to Lodge, June 11, 1896, Lodge Papers, MHS.

61. McCall, *Life of Reed*, 224.

62. Reed to Lodge, June 12, 1896, Lodge Papers, MHS.

63. Reed to Gifford, June 14, 1896, Reed Papers, BC.

64. "Reed Nominated by Lodge," *DIO*, June 19, 1896, 3.

65. "Rushed to a Finish," *Saint Paul Globe*, June 19, 1896, 1.

66. Robert W. Merry, *President McKinley: Architect of the American Century* (New York: Simon & Schuster, 2017), 129.

67. *DIO*, June 7, 1896, 32.

68. Reed to Gifford, June 14, 1896, Reed Papers, BC.

69. K Reed to Marseilles, July 2, 1896, Charles Marseilles Papers, NHHS.

70. Gallinger to Marseilles, May 30, 1896, Jacob Gallinger Papers, NHHS.

71. *New-York Herald*, January 15, 1896, 15.

72. "M'Kinley is New Jersey's Choice," *New-York Herald*, March 30, 1896, 13.

73. "Talks About Presidential Candidates," *DEA*, April 25, 1896, 4.

74. Reed to Gifford, June 14, 1896, Reed Papers, BC.

75. Essay, "Thomas B. Reed," J. Franklin Aldrich Papers, Chicago History Museum and Research Center, Chicago, IL (hereinafter CHM), 50

76. Essay, "Thomas B. Reed," J. Franklin Aldrich Papers, CHM, 53.

77. Robinson, *Thomas B. Reed*, 332.

78. Evan Thomas, *The War Lovers: Roosevelt, Lodge, Hearst and the Rush to Empire* (New York: Little, Brown, 2010), 139.

79. Charles L. Stephens, "Presidential Possibilities," *Peterson Magazine* 5, no. 6 (June 1895): 609.

80. Johnson to Marseilles, March 12, 1896, Charles Marseilles Papers, NHHS.

81. Roosevelt to Reed, June 11, 1895, Reed Papers, BC.

82. "The Same Tom Reed," *PDP*, March 7, 1896, 9.

83. "Tactics of Tom Reed," *Jackson Citizen*, March 6, 1896, 8.

84. "Unhappy Tom Reed," *Evening Press* (Grand Rapids), February 1, 1896, 1.

85. Lyman to Lodge, April 30, 1896, Lodge Papers, MHS.

86. Morgan, *William McKinley*, 145.

87. Reed to Gifford, June 14, 1896, Reed Papers, BC.

88. "He Has Literary Ambition," *Idaho Daily Statesman*, June 9, 1896, 4.

89. McCall, *Life of Reed*, 226.

90. "Restore Confidence," *PDP*, August 27, 1896, 1.

91. "Things Can't Be Worse," *PDP*, August 29, 1896, 1.

92. "In Old York," *PDP*, July 30, 1896, 1.

93. "The Speaker's Remedy," *PDP*, September 7, 1896, 2.
94. "Enthusiastic Democrats," *DEA*, September 3, 1896, 2.
95. "Mr. Reed at Rumford," *PDP*, September 2, 1896, 1.
96. "Reed at Old Orchard," August 25, 1896, Pamphlet 2304, UMO.
97. "Mr. Reed at City Hall," *DEA*, September 11, 1896, 5.
98. "Republicans Rejoice," *PDP*, September 15, 1896, 8.
99. "Like Penance to Reed," *WP*, September 27, 1896, 20.
100. *DIO* [quoting *St. Louis Post-Dispatch*], July 28, 1896, 6.
101. "Reed's Estimate of Long," *Wichita Daily Eagle*, October 7, 1896, 4.
102. "Grander Never Held," *PDP*, October 8, 1896, 1.
103. "Injustice to Mr. Reed," *WP*, October 27, 1896, 6.
104. "Reed on Sound Money," *Kansas City Star*, October 25, 1896, 1.
105. Harper, *Susan B. Anthony*, 2: 885.
106. Essay, "Thomas B. Reed," J. Franklin Aldrich Papers, CHS, 2.
107. League of Women Voters, *Forty Years of a Great Idea* (Washington, DC: League of Women Voters, 1960), 8.
108. "Advisers to M'Kinley," *WP*, November 5, 1896, 3.
109. Roosevelt to Lodge, November 28, 1896, *SRL*, 240.
110. *CR* 54/2, March 4, 1894, 2987.

Chapter 9. War Speaker

1. David W. Brady, *Congressional Voting in a Partisan Era: A Study of the McKinley Houses and a Comparison to the Modern House of Representatives* (Lawrence: University Press of Kansas, 1973).
2. Sam Hanna Acheson, *Joe Bailey: The Last Democrat* (Freeport, NY: Books for Libraries Press, 1970), 19.
3. *CR* 55/1, March 31, 1897, 551.
4. "Opposition to Reed," *WP*, April 20, 1897.
5. *CR* 55/1, April 7, 1897, 650–651.
6. *CR* 55/1, May 3, 1897, 871.
7. "Jerry Asks Reed Where Am I At," *Kansas Semi-Weekly Capital*, May 14, 1897, 1.
8. *SDR*, May 5, 1897, 6.
9. *CR* 55/1, April 10, 1897, 672.
10. *CR* 55/1, July 1, 1897, 2190.
11. "Relief for Starving Cubans," *NYTR*, January 8, 1898, 1.
12. *CR* 55/1, May 20, 1897, 1190.
13. *CR* 55/1, May 20, 1897, 1192.
14. "Tom Reed's Muzzle," *Fort Worth Register*, May 27, 1897, 1.
15. "Too Thin," *Biloxi Herald*, June 19, 1897, 1.
16. *DEA*, June 1, 1897, 4.
17. *CR*, 55/1, July 1, 1897, 2191, 2192.
18. Lyman to Lodge, March 23, 1897, Lodge Papers, MHS.
19. "Mr. Roosevelt on the Navy," *Sun* (Baltimore), July 24, 1897, 2.
20. Roosevelt to Lodge, August 3, 1897, *SRL*, 268.
21. Roosevelt to Long, August 1, 1897, *LTR*, 651.

22. "Forest City's Guest," *PDP*, August 20, 1897, 1.

23. Lodge to Reed, August 20, 1897, Lodge Papers, MHS.

24. Reed to Lodge, August 22, 1897, Lodge Papers, MHS.

25. Lodge to Reed, August 25, 1897, Lodge Papers, MHS.

26. Reed to Lodge, August 27, 1897, Lodge Papers, MHS.

27. Reed to Lodge, September 13, 1897, Lodge Papers, MHS.

28. Lodge to Reed, September 15, 1897, Lodge Papers, MHS.

29. Reed to Lodge, September 17, 1897, Lodge Papers, MHS.

30. Roosevelt to Dana, August 16, 1897, *LTR*, 652.

31. Roosevelt to Lodge, September 24, 1897, *LTR*, 689.

32. Thomas B. Reed, "Empire Can Wait," *Illustrated American* 22, no. 408 (December 4, 1897): 713–714.

33. Reed to Crane, December 25, 1897, Reed Papers, BC.

34. *DEA*, February 22, 1898, 4.

35. Roosevelt to Long, February 19, 1898, *LTR*, 780.

36. *Times* (DC), March 7, 1898, 4.

37. "Why Speaker Reed Opposes War," *Times* (DC) [quoting Omaha *World-Herald*], March 10, 1898, 4.

38. *Independent Democrat* (Las Cruces), April 16, 1898, 2.

39. "Reed and Peace," *Times* (DC), April 5, 1898, 4.

40. Busbey, *Uncle Joe Cannon*, 191, 192.

41. Diary, March 9, 1898, Asher Hinds Papers, LC.

42. Roosevelt to Robinson, March 30, 1898, *LTR*, 805–806.

43. "In Full Revolt," *BDG*, March 30, 1898, 1.

44. "Grumbling at Washington," *NYT*, April 7, 1898, 1.

45. "House Yields a Point," *NYTR*, April 19, 1898, 1.

46. "In Leash," *St. Albans Daily Messenger*, April 22, 1898, 4.

47. Beatrice Webb, *Beatrice Webb's American Diary*, ed. David A. Shannon (Madison: University of Wisconsin Press, 1963), 32.

48. McCall, *Life of Reed*, 234.

49. Robinson, *Thomas B. Reed*, 364.

50. *Sunday News Tribune* (Duluth), May 29, 1898, 3.

51. "Reed Hostile," *BDG*, May 25, 1898, 7.

52. "The Assault upon Speaker Reed," *SDR*, June 2, 1898, 6.

53. Lewis L. Gould, *The Spanish-American War and President McKinley* (Lawrence: University Press of Kansas, 1980), 64.

54. *SLR*, May 18, 1898, 8.

55. *Tacoma Daily News*, June 3, 1898, 2.

56. *Evening Post* (Grand Rapids), June 9, 1898, 2.

57. "Fear They May Be Tricked," *WP*, June 7, 1898, 4.

58. Diary, May 29, 1898, Asher Hinds Papers, LC.

59. *CR* 55/2, May 31, 1898, 5350–5351.

60. "Want Hawaii Annexed," *WP*, June 11, 1898, 4.

61. Diary, June 19, 1898, Asher Hinds Papers, LC.

62. *SDR*, June 11, 1898, 6.

63. "Great Expectations," *DEA*, June 24, 1898, 1.

64. "At Portland Club," *PDP*, September 10, 1898, 5.
65. Reed to Crane, August 26, 1898, Reed Papers, BC.
66. Reed to Crane, August 6, 1898, Reed Papers, BC.
67. "Capitol Chat," *WP*, December 18, 1898, 6.
68. "Condensed Wisdom," *Christian Advocate*, December 15, 1898, 35.
69. "Neat Scheme," *Los Angeles Times*, February 9, 1899, 1.
70. "Speaker Reed," *Omaha Daily Bee* [quoting *Minneapolis Times*], March 13, 1899, 4.
71. Thomas B. Reed, "The Nicaragua Canal," *North American Review* 168, no. 510 (May 1899): 558.
72. Lodge to Roosevelt, December 20, 1898, *SRL*, 370.
73. "Running Mates in Congress," *WP*, February 26, 1899, 6.
74. *CR* 55/3, March 4, 1899, 2935.
75. "Mr. Reed's Disgruntlement," *WP* [quoting *St. Louis Globe-Democrat*], March 10, 1899, 6.
76. Storey to Hoar, March 9, 1899, George Hoar Papers, MHS.
77. *Tacoma Daily News*, June 3, 1898, 2.
78. "Reed's Retirement," *Seattle Post-Intelligencer*, April 22, 1899, 4.
79. "Reed Also in Georgia," *WP*, March 18, 1899, 1.
80. "Mark Hanna and Tom Reed Walk Arm in Arm," *Atlanta Constitution*, March 22, 1899, 1.
81. "All Now Harmony," *BDG*, March 22, 1899, 7.
82. William Allen White, *Masks in a Pageant* (New York: Macmillan, 1928), 218.
83. Reed to Gifford, October 18, 1899, Reed Papers, BC.
84. Brent Monahan, *The Jekyl Island Club* (New York: St. Martin's Minotaur, 2000), 193.
85. *DEA*, August 24, 1899, 4.
86. Reed to Gifford, October 18, 1899, Reed Papers, BC.
87. "Speaker Reed's Retirement," *San Diego Union*, April 23, 1899, 4.
88. *Peninsula Enterprise* (Accomac), April 22, 1899, 2.
89. "Reed's Retirement," *Seattle Post-Intelligencer*, April 22, 1899, 4.
90. Reed to Gifford, October 18, 1899, Reed Papers, BC.
91. Randall B. Ripley, "The Party Whip Organizations in the United States House of Representatives," *American Political Science Review* 58, no. 3 (September 1964): 562.
92. Reed to Crane, September 1, 1898, Reed Papers, BC.

Chapter 10. Cashing In

1. Reed to Gifford, October 18, 1899, Reed Papers, BC.
2. David J. Silbey, *A War of Frontier and Empire: The Philippine-American War* (New York: Hill & Wang, 2007), 121.
3. McCall, *Life of Reed*, 247, 248.
4. Robinson, *Thomas Brackett Reed*, 377.
5. "Ex-Speaker Reed Sums Up," *NYT*, December 17, 1899, 16.
6. Diary, January 9, 1901, Reed Papers, BC.
7. Diary, January 1, 1900, trans. Gallagher, Reed Papers, BC.
8. Thomas B. Reed, "Monopolies," *Saturday Evening Post* 172, no. 33 (February 10, 1900): 707.

9. Reed to Gifford, July 16, 1900, Reed Papers, BC.

10. Reed to Gifford, August 18, 1900, Reed Papers, BC.

11. Reed to Gifford, January 28, 1901, Reed Papers, BC.

12. Reed to Gifford, January 28, 1901, Reed Papers, BC.

13. Bartholomew H. Sparrow, *The Insular Cases and the Emergence of American Empire* (Lawrence: University Press of Kansas, 2006).

14. Reed to Gifford, May 29, 1901, Reed Papers, BC.

15. William Allen White, *The Autobiography of William Allen White* (New York: Macmillan, 1946), 336–337.

16. James Grant, *Mr. Speaker! The Life and Times of Thomas B. Reed: The Man Who Broke the Filibuster* (New York: Simon & Schuster, 2011), 369–370.

17. Grant, *Mr. Speaker*, 404; Diary, September 3, 1902, trans. Gallagher, Reed Papers, BC.

18. Diary, July 23, 1902, trans. Gallagher, Reed Papers, BC.

19. Diary, April 17, 1902, trans. Gallagher, Reed Papers, BC.

20. Reed to Gifford, January 28, 1901, Reed Papers, BC.

21. Reed to Gifford, February 19, 1902, Reed Papers, BC.

22. Diary, February 4, 1902, trans. Gallagher, Reed Papers, BC.

23. Reed to Twain, April 6, 1901, Mark Twain Papers, University of California, Bancroft Library, Berkeley, CA (hereinafter UC).

24. Diary, June 3, 1902, trans. Gallagher, Reed Papers, BC.

25. "Some of the Lamented Tom Reed's Quaint Deeds and Words and Ways," *Anaconda Standard*, December 21, 1902, 15.

26. Reed to Fairchild, February 24, 1901, Thomas B. Reed Papers, UVA.

27. Diary, June 26, 1902, trans. Gallagher, Reed Papers, BC.

28. "Thomas Brackett Reed," *LEJ*, June 25, 1902, 12.

29. "To Portlanders," *LEJ*, August 26, 1902, 4.

30. Diary, August 26, 1902, trans. Gallagher, Reed Papers, BC.

31. *SLR*, December 3, 1902, 6.

32. T. L. MacDonald, "A Brief Report of the Last Illness of the Hon. Thomas B. Reed," *Medical Century*, January 1, 1903, 1.

33. "Jokes of Illness," *Portland Evening Express*, December 5, 1902, 1.

Chapter 11. Conclusion

1. Woodrow Wilson, *Constitutional Government in the United States* (New York: Columbia University Press, 1917), 91.

2. Booth Mooney, *Mr. Speaker: Four Men Who Shaped the United States House of Representatives* (Chicago: Follett, 1964), 72, 86.

3. Walter J. Oleszek, ed., *The Cannon Centenary Conference: The Changing Nature of the Speakership* (Washington, DC: Government Printing Office, 2004), 84.

4. Charles J. Finocchiaro and David W. Rohde, "Speaker David Henderson and the Partisan Era of the U.S. House," in *Party, Process, and Political Change in Congress, Vol. 2: Further New Perspectives on the History of Congress*, ed. David W. Brady and Mathew D. McCubbins (Stanford, CA: Stanford University Press, 2007), 259–270.

5. Charles Willis Thompson, *Party Leaders of the Time* (New York: G.W. Dillingham, 1906), 154.

6. Charles O. Jones, "Joseph G. Cannon and Howard W. Smith: An Essay on the Limits of Leadership in the House of Representatives," *Journal of Politics* 30, no. 3 (August 1968): 618, 629.

7. Roberts, " Development of Special Orders," 318.

8. Cox and McCubbins, *Setting the Agenda*, 26.

9. Cox and McCubbins, 209.

10. Thomas B. Reed, *Reed's Rules: A Manual of General Parliamentary Law, with Suggestions for Special Rules* (Chicago: Rand McNally, 1898), 50.

11. Follett, *Speaker of the House*, 212.

12. Woodrow Wilson, *Congressional Government: A Study in American Government* (Cleveland: World Publishing, 1956), 70.

13. Wilson, *Constitutional Government*, 94.

14. Robert V. Remini, *The House: The History of the House of Representatives* (Washington, DC: Smithsonian Books, 2006), 250.

15. Congressional Research Service, *History of the United States House of Representatives, 1789–1994* (Washington, DC: US Government Printing Office, 1994), 180, 186.

16. Keith Poole and Howard Rosenthal, *Congress: A Political-Economic History of Roll Call Voting* (New York: Oxford University Press, 1997).

17. Cox and McCubbins, *Setting the Agenda*, 51, 69.

18. Cox and McCubbins, 71.

19. Cox and McCubbins, 112.

20. Cox and McCubbins, 25, 184.

21. Cox and McCubbins, 20, 209.

22. Barbara Sinclair, "Congressional Leadership: A Review Essay and a Research Agenda," in *Leading Congress: New Styles, New Strategies*, ed. John J. Kornacki (Washington, DC: Congressional Quarterly, 1990), 120.

23. John H. Aldrich, Mark M. Berger, and David W. Rohde, "The Historical Variability in Conditional Party Government, 1877–1994," in *Party, Process, and Political Change in Congress: New Perspectives on the History of Congress*, ed. David W. Brady and Mathew D. McCubbins (Stanford, CA: Stanford University Press, 2002), 19.

24. Cooper and Brady, "Institutional Context."

25. David W. Rohde, P*arties and Leaders in the Postreform House* (Chicago: University of Chicago Press, 1991), 38.

26. Cox and McCubbins, *Setting the Agenda*, 70.

27. Richard Bolling, *Power in the House: A History of the Leadership of the House of Representatives* (New York: E. P. Dutton, 1968), 16, 256.

28. Roberts, "Development of Special Orders," 312.

29. Stanley Bach, "Special Rules in the House of Representatives: Themes and Contemporary Variations," *Congressional Studies* 8, no. 2 (1981): 43.

30. Donald R. Wolfensberger, *House Rules Data* (Washington, DC: Bipartisan Policy Center, 2020).

31. Bach, "Special Rules," 56.

32. Douglas Dion and John D. Huber, "Procedural Choice and the House Committee on Rules," *Journal of Politics* 58, no. 1 (February 1996): 43.

33. Barbara Sinclair, "House Special Rules and the Institutional Design Controversy," *Legislative Studies Quarterly* 19, no. 4 (November 1994): 477–494.

34. Stanley Bach and Steven S. Smith, *Managing Uncertainty in the House of Representatives: Adaptation and Innovation in Special Rules* (Washington, DC: Brookings Institution, 1988), 56–57.

35. Steven S. Smith, *Party Influence in Congress* (New York: Cambridge University Press, 2007), 140.

36. Reed, "Deliberative Body," 156.

37. "Welcomed," *PDP*, September 5, 1890, 1.

38. Author analysis of US House of Representatives, "Party Divisions of the House of Representatives, 1789 to Present," January 2021, https://history.house.gov/Institution/Party-Divisions/Party-Divisions/.

39. White, *Republic*, 630.

40. Cox and McCubbins, *Legislative Leviathan.*

41. Theodore Roosevelt, "Thomas Brackett Reed and the Fifty-First Congress," *Forum*, December 1895, 417.

42. Ronald M. Peters, Jr., *The American Speakership: The Office in Historical Perspective* (Baltimore: Johns Hopkins University Press, 1990), 65, 69.

43. Oleszek, *Cannon Centenary Conference*, 92.

44. Randall W. Strahan, "Party Leadership," in *The Oxford Handbook of the American Congress*, ed. Eric Schickler and Frances E. Lee (New York: Oxford University Press, 2011), 386.

45. Schickler, *Disjointed Pluralism*, 39, 43.

46. Mansour Javidan, Peter W. Dorfman, Mary Sully de Luque, and Robert J. House, "In the Eye of the Beholder: Cross Cultural Lessons in Leadership from Project GLOBE," *Academy of Management Perspectives* 20, no. 1 (February 2006): 73.

47. Reed, "Mr. Speaker," 12.

48. *CR* 46/2, April 23, 1880, 2692.

49. Dion, *Legislative Thumbscrew*, 1.

50. William Hixon and Bryan W. Marshall, "Examining Claims about Procedural Choice: The Use of Floor Waivers in the U.S. House," *Political Research Quarterly* 55, no. 4 (December 2002): 923–938.

51. Bach and Smith, *Managing Uncertainty*, 108, 110.

52. Guillaume R. Fréchette, John H. Kagel, and Steven F. Lehrer, "Bargaining in Legislatures: An Experimental Investigation of Open Versus Closed Amendment Rules," *American Political Science Review* 97, no. 2 (May 2003): 221–232.

53. Douglas B. Harris, "Anticipating the Revolution: Michel and Republican Congressional Reform Efforts," in *Robert H. Michel: Leading the Republican House Minority*, ed. Frank H. Mackaman and Sean Q Kelly (Lawrence: University Press of Kansas, 2019), 204.

54. Kathleen Hall Jamieson and Erika Falk, "Continuity and Change in Civility in the House," in *Polarized Politics: Congress and the President in a Partisan Era*, ed. Jon R. Bond and Richard Fleisher (Washington, DC: CQ Press, 2000), 100.

55. Green, *Underdog Politics*, 187.

56. "From Washington," *SDR*, February 25, 1883, 1.

57. *CR* 47/2, February 26, 1883, 3317.

58. Jennifer Hayes Clark, *Minority Parties in U.S. Legislatures: Conditions of Influence* (Ann Arbor: University of Michigan Press, 2015), 41.

59. A. Maurice Low, "Thomas Brackett Reed," in *Twenty Years in the Press Gallery*, ed. O. O. Stealey (New York: Publishers Printing, 1906), 414.

60. Amy Y. Ou, David A. Waldman, and Suzanne J. Peterson, "Do Humble CEOs Matter? An Examination of CEO Humility and Firm Outcomes," *Journal of Management* 44, no. 3 (March 2018): 1162.

61. Rosabeth Moss Kanter, *Confidence: How Winning Streaks and Losing Streaks Begin and End* (New York: Crown Business, 2004), 97, 357.

62. Platt, *Autobiography of Platt*, 213.

63. Steven S. Smith, *The Senate Syndrome: The Evolution of Procedural Warfare in the Modern US Senate* (Norman: University of Oklahoma Press, 2014), 124, 180.

64. David D. Kirkpatrick, "Maine is Focus of Senate Battle on Filibuster," *NYT*, May 6, 2005, A25.

65. Gregory Koger, *Filibustering: A Political History of Obstruction in the House and Senate* (Chicago: University of Chicago Press, 2010), 76.

66. "Line Shots," *Boston Morning Journal*, October 14, 1893, 7.

67. *CR* 50/2, January 4, 1889, 539.

68. *House of Cards*, Netflix, season 2, episode 3.

69. Thomas E. Mann and Norman J. Ornstein, *The Broken Branch: How Congress is Failing America and How to Get It Back on Track* (New York: Oxford University Press, 2006).

70. Richard M. Skinner, "George W. Bush and the Partisan Presidency," *Political Science Quarterly* 123, no. 4 (Winter 2008–09): 605–622.

71. Lawrence Baum and Neal Devins, *The Company They Keep: How Partisan Divisions Came to the Supreme Court* (New York: Oxford University Press, 2019).

72. Matthew Levendusky, *How Partisan Media Polarize America* (Chicago: University of Chicago Press, 2013).

73. Alec Tyson, *Partisans Say Respect and Compromise Are Important in Politics—Particularly from Their Opponents* (Washington, DC: Pew Research Center, 2019).

74. Juliet Eilperin, *Fight Club Politics: How Partisanship Is Poisoning the House of Representatives* (Lanham, MD: Rowman & Littlefield, 2006).

75. Sean M. Theriault, *Party Polarization in Congress* (New York: Cambridge University Press, 2008), 197.

76. Gary W. Cox and Mathew D. McCubbins, "Managing Plenary Time: The U.S. Congress in Comparative Context," in *The Oxford Handbook of the American Congress*, ed. Eric Schickler and Frances E. Lee (New York: Oxford University Press, 2011), 451–472.

77. Sarah A. Binder and Frances E. Lee, "Making Deals in Congress," in *Solutions to Political Polarization in America*, ed. Nathaniel Persily (New York: Cambridge University Press, 2015), 240–261.

78. Remini, *House*, 503.

79. Reed, *Reed's Rules*, 28.

SELECTED BIBLIOGRAPHY

Note: This bibliography excludes newspapers and archival materials, which are summarized in the abbreviations section of the notes. Full citations for these and other bibliography exclusions, including general reference materials, are in the notes.

Acheson, Sam Hanna. *Joe Bailey: The Last Democrat.* Freeport, NY: Books for Libraries Press, 1970.

Aldrich, John H., Mark M. Berger, and David W. Rohde. "The Historical Variability in Conditional Party Government, 1877–1994." In *Party, Process, and Political Change in Congress: New Perspectives on the History of Congress,* edited by David W. Brady and Mathew D. McCubbins, 17–35. Stanford, CA: Stanford University Press, 2002.

Aldrich, John H., and David W. Rohde. "The Logic of Conditional Party Government: Revisiting the Electoral Connection." In *Congress Reconsidered,* edited by Lawrence C. Dodd and Bruce I. Oppenheimer, 269–292. Washington, DC: CQ Press, 2001.

Aldrich, John H., David W. Rohde, and Michael W. Tofias. "One D Is Not Enough: Measuring Conditional Party Government, 1887–2002." In *Party, Process, and Political Change in Congress, Vol. 2: Further New Perspectives on the History of Congress,* edited by David W. Brady and Mathew D. McCubbins, 102–112. Stanford, CA: Stanford University Press, 2007.

Aldrich, John H., and Kenneth A. Shepsle. "Explaining Institutional Change: Soaking, Poking, and Modeling in the U.S. Congress." In *Congress on Display, Congress at Work,* edited by William T. Bianco, 23–45. Ann Arbor: University of Michigan Press, 2000.

Alexander, DeAlva Stanwood. *History and Procedure of the House of Representatives.* Boston: Houghton Mifflin, 1916.

Anthony, Susan B., and Ida Husted Harper, eds. *The History of Woman Suffrage.* 4 vols. Indianapolis: Hollenbeck, 1902.

Bach, Stanley. "Special Rules in the House of Representatives: Themes and Contemporary Variations." *Congressional Studies* 8, no. 2 (1981): 37–58.

Bach, Stanley, and Steven S. Smith. *Managing Uncertainty in the House of Representatives: Adaptation and Innovation in Special Rules.* Washington, DC: Brookings Institution, 1988.

Baldasty, Gerald J. *Commercialization of News in the Nineteenth Century*. Madison: University of Wisconsin Press, 1992.

Barry, David S. *Forty Years in Washington*. Boston: Little, Brown, 1924.

Baum, Lawrence, and Neal Devins. *The Company They Keep: How Partisan Divisions Came to the Supreme Court*. New York: Oxford University Press, 2019.

Bensel, Richard Franklin. *The Political Economy of American Industrialization, 1877–1900*. New York: Cambridge University Press, 2000.

Binder, Sarah A. *Minority Rights, Majority Rule: Partisanship and the Development of Congress*. New York: Cambridge University Press, 1997.

———. "The Partisan Basis of Procedural Choice: Allocating Parliamentary Rights in the House, 1789–1990." *American Political Science Review* 90, no. 1 (March 1996): 8–20.

Binder, Sarah A., and Frances E. Lee. "Making Deals in Congress." In *Solutions to Political Polarization in America*, edited by Nathaniel Persily, 240–261. New York: Cambridge University Press, 2015.

Bolling, Richard. *Power in the House: A History of the Leadership of the House of Representatives*. New York: E. P. Dutton, 1968.

Brady, David W. *Congressional Voting in a Partisan Era: A Study of the McKinley Houses and a Comparison to the Modern House of Representatives*. Lawrence: University Press of Kansas, 1973.

Brady, David W., and Phillip Althoff. "Party Voting in the U.S. House of Representatives, 1890–1910: Elements of a Responsible Party System." *Journal of Politics* 36, no. 3 (August 1974): 753–775.

Burns, James MacGregor. *Leadership*. New York: Harper & Row, 1978.

Busbey, L. White. *Uncle Joe Cannon: The Story of a Pioneer American*. New York: Henry Holt, 1927.

Calhoun, Charles W. *From Bloody Shirt to Full Dinner Pail: The Transformation of Politics and Governance in the Gilded Age*. New York: Hill & Wang, 2010.

———. *Minority Victory: Gilded Age Politics and the Front Porch Campaign of 1888*. Lawrence: University Press of Kansas, 2008.

———. "The Political Culture: Public Life and the Conduct of Politics." In *The Gilded Age: Essays on the Origins of Modern America*, edited by Charles W. Calhoun, 185–213. Wilmington, DE: Scholarly Resources, 1996.

———. *The Presidency of Ulysses S. Grant*. Lawrence: University Press of Kansas, 2017.

Caro, Robert A. *The Years of Lyndon Johnson: Master of the Senate*. New York: Vintage Books, 2003.

Carson, Jamie L., and Jason M. Roberts. "Strategic Politicians and U.S. House Elections, 1874–1914." *Journal of Politics* 67, no. 2 (May 2005): 474–496.

Cashman, Sean Dennis. *America in the Gilded Age: From the Death of Lincoln to the Rise of Theodore Roosevelt*. New York: New York University Press, 1984.

Clark, Champ. *My Quarter Century of American Politics*. 2 vols. New York: Harper & Brothers, 1920.

Clark, Jennifer Hayes. *Minority Parties in U.S. Legislatures: Conditions of Influence*. Ann Arbor: University of Michigan Press, 2015.

Colfax, Schuyler. "Hon. Schuyler Colfax." In *Reminiscences of Abraham Lincoln*, edited by Allen Thorndike Rice, 331–349. New York: North American Publishing, 1886.

Congressional Research Service [updating George Galloway]. *History of the United States House of Representatives, 1789–1994*. Washington, DC: US Government Printing Office, 1994.

Cooper, Joseph, and David W. Brady. "Institutional Context and Leadership Style: The House from Cannon to Rayburn." *American Political Science Review* 75, no. 2 (June 1981): 411–425.

Cox, Gary W., and Mathew D. McCubbins. *Legislative Leviathan: Party Government in the House*. Berkeley: University of California Press, 1993.

———. "Managing Plenary Time: The U.S. Congress in Comparative Context." In *The Oxford Handbook of the American Congress*, edited by Eric Schickler and Frances E. Lee, 451–472. New York: Oxford University Press, 2011.

———. *Setting the Agenda: Responsible Party Government in the U.S. House of Representatives*. New York: Cambridge University Press, 2005.

Cox, Samuel S. *Why We Laugh*. New York: Harper & Brothers, 1876.

Croly, Herbert. *Marcus Alonzo Hanna: His Life and Work*. New York: Macmillan, 1923.

Davidson, Roger H., Walter J. Oleszek, Frances E. Lee, and Eric Schickler. *Congress and Its Members*. 16th ed. Washington, DC: CQ Press, 2018.

Den Hartog, Christopher F. "Limited Party Government and the Majority Party Revolution in the Nineteenth-Century House." PhD diss., University of California, San Diego, 2004.

Dicken-Garcia, Hazel. *Journalistic Standards in Nineteenth-Century America*. Madison: University of Wisconsin Press, 1989.

Dion, Douglas. *Turning the Legislative Thumbscrew: Minority Rights and Procedural Change in Legislative Politics*. Ann Arbor: University of Michigan Press, 1997.

Dion, Douglas, and John D. Huber. "Procedural Choice and the House Committee on Rules." *Journal of Politics* 58, no. 1 (February 1996): 25–53.

Dreiser, Theodore. "Thomas Brackett Reed: The Story of a Great Career." In *Theodore Dreiser's Uncollected Magazine Articles, 1897–1902*, edited by Yoshinobu Hakutani, 331–349. Cranbury, NJ: Associated University Presses, 2003.

Dunn, Arthur Wallace. *From Harrison to Harding*. New York: G. P. Putnam's Sons, 1922.

Eilperin, Juliet. *Fight Club Politics: How Partisanship Is Poisoning the House of Representatives*. Lanham, MD: Rowman & Littlefield, 2006.

Fenno, Richard F., Jr. *Home Style: House Members in Their Districts*. Boston: Little, Brown, 1978.

Finocchiaro, Charles J., and David W. Rohde. "Speaker David Henderson and the Partisan Era of the U.S. House." In *Party, Process, and Political Change in Congress, Vol. 2: Further New Perspectives on the History of Congress*, edited by David W. Brady and Mathew D. McCubbins, 259–270. Stanford, CA: Stanford University Press, 2007.

Fiorina, Morris P. *Congress: Keystone of the Washington Establishment*. New Haven, CT: Yale University Press, 1977.

Follett, M. P. *The Speaker of the House of Representatives.* New York: Longmans, Green, 1909 [first published 1896].

Forgette, Richard G. "Reed's Rules and the Partisan Theory of Legislative Organization." *Polity* 29, no. 3 (Spring 1997): 375–396.

Fréchette, Guillaume R., John H. Kagel, and Steven F. Lehrer. "Bargaining in Legislatures: An Experimental Investigation of Open Versus Closed Amendment Rules." *American Political Science Review* 97, no. 2 (May 2003): 221–232.

Fuller, Herbert Bruce. *The Speakers of the House.* Boston: Little, Brown, 1909.

Gallaher, Ruth A. *Legal and Political Status of Women in Iowa.* Iowa City: State Historical Society of Iowa, 1918.

Galloway, George B. *History of the United States House of Representatives.* Washington, DC: US Government Printing Office, 1965 [first published 1962 as House doc. 246].

Gould, Lewis L. *The Spanish-American War and President McKinley.* Lawrence: University Press of Kansas, 1980.

Grant, James. *Mr. Speaker! The Life and Times of Thomas B. Reed: The Man Who Broke the Filibuster.* New York: Simon & Schuster, 2011.

Green, Matthew N. *The Speaker of the House: A Study of Leadership.* New Haven, CT: Yale University Press, 2010.

———. *Underdog Politics: The Minority Party in the U.S. House of Representatives.* New Haven, CT: Yale University Press, 2015.

Green, Matthew N., and Douglas B. Harris. *Choosing the Leader: Leadership Elections in the U.S. House of Representatives.* New Haven, CT: Yale University Press, 2019.

Greenstein, Fred I. *Personality and Politics: Problems of Evidence, Inference, and Conceptualization.* Chicago: Markham, 1969.

Guenther, Karen. "Potter Committee Investigation of the Disputed Election of 1876." *Florida Historical Quarterly* 61, no. 3 (January 1983): 281–295.

Harper, Ida Husted. *The Life and Work of Susan B. Anthony.* 2 vols. Indianapolis: Hollenbeck, 1898.

Harris, Douglas B. "Anticipating the Revolution: Michel and Republican Congressional Reform Efforts." In *Robert H. Michel: Leading the Republican House Minority,* edited by Frank H. Mackaman and Sean Q Kelly, 186–215. Lawrence: University Press of Kansas, 2019.

———. "The Rise of the Public Speakership. *Political Science Quarterly* 113, no. 2 (Summer 1998): 193–212.

Harris, Douglas B., and Matthew N. Green. "Michel as Minority Leader: Minority Party Strategies and Tactics in the Postreform House." In *Robert H. Michel: Leading the Republican House Minority,* edited by Frank H. Mackaman and Sean Q Kelly, 94–114. Lawrence: University Press of Kansas, 2019.

Hendrickson, Scott A., and Jason M. Roberts. "Short-Term Goals and Long-Term Effects: The Mongrel Tariff and the Creation of the Special Rule in the U.S. House." *Journal of Policy History* 28, no. 2 (April 2016): 318–341.

Hixon, William, and Bryan W. Marshall. "Examining Claims about Procedural Choice: The Use of Floor Waivers in the U.S. House." *Political Research Quarterly* 55, no. 4 (December 2002): 923–938.

Jamieson, Kathleen Hall, and Erika Falk. "Continuity and Change in Civility in the House." In *Polarized Politics: Congress and the President in a Partisan Era*, edited by Jon R. Bond and Richard Fleisher, 96–108. Washington, DC: CQ Press, 2000.

Javidan, Mansour, Peter W. Dorfman, Mary Sully de Luque, and Robert J. House. "In the Eye of the Beholder: Cross Cultural Lessons in Leadership from Project GLOBE." *Academy of Management Perspectives* 20, no. 1 (February 2006): 67–90.

Jenkins, Jeffery A. "Partisanship and Contested Election Cases in the House of Representatives, 1789–2002." *Studies in American Political Development* 18, no. 2 (Fall 2004): 112–135.

Jenkins, Jeffery A., and Charles Stewart III. *Fighting for the Speakership: The House and the Rise of Party Government*. Princeton, NJ: Princeton University Press, 2013.

John, Richard R. "Who Were the Gilders? And Other Seldom-Asked Questions about Business, Technology, and Political Economy in the United States." *Journal of the Gilded Age and Progressive Era* 8, no. 4 (October 2009): 474–480.

Jones, Charles O. "Joseph G. Cannon and Howard W. Smith: An Essay on the Limits of Leadership in the House of Representatives." *Journal of Politics* 30, no. 3 (August 1968): 617–646.

Kanter, Rosabeth Moss. *Confidence: How Winning Streaks and Losing Streaks Begin and End*. New York: Crown Business, 2004.

Koger, Gregory. *Filibustering: A Political History of Obstruction in the House and Senate*. Chicago: University of Chicago Press, 2010.

Lee, Frances E. *Beyond Ideology: Politics, Principles, and Partisanship in the U.S. Senate*. Chicago: University of Chicago Press, 2009.

Leech, Margaret. *In the Days of McKinley*. New York: Harper & Brothers, 1959.

Leupp, Francis E. "Personal Recollections of Thomas B. Reed." *Outlook*, September 3, 1910, 36–40.

Levendusky, Matthew. *How Partisan Media Polarize America*. Chicago: University of Chicago Press, 2013.

Libecap, Gary. "The Rise of the Chicago Packers and the Origins of Meat Inspection and Antitrust." *Economic Inquiry* 30, no. 2 (April 1992): 242–262.

Loomis, Burdett A. *Time, Politics, and Policies: A Legislative Year*. Lawrence: University Press of Kansas, 1994.

Low, A. Maurice. "Thomas Brackett Reed." In *Twenty Years in the Press Gallery*, edited by O. O. Stealey, 409–415. New York: Publishers Printing, 1906.

Mackaman, Frank H. "Bob Michel Calls It Quits," in *Robert H. Michel: Leading the Republican House Minority*, edited by Frank H. Mackaman and Sean Q Kelly, 332–351. Lawrence: University Press of Kansas, 2019.

Malone, Preston S. "The Political Career of Charles Frederick Crisp." PhD diss., University of Georgia, 1962.

Mann, Thomas E., and Norman J. Ornstein. *The Broken Branch: How Congress Is Failing America and How to Get It Back on Track*. New York: Oxford University Press, 2006.

Mayhew, David. *Congress: The Electoral Connection*. New Haven, CT: Yale University Press, 1974.

McCall, Samuel W. *The Life of Thomas B. Reed.* Boston: Houghton Mifflin, 1914.

McElroy, Robert. *Levi Parsons Morton: Banker, Diplomat and Statesman.* New York: G. P. Putnam's Sons, 1930.

Merry, Robert W. *President McKinley: Architect of the American Century.* New York: Simon & Schuster, 2017.

Mills, Roger Q. "Republican Tactics in the House," *North American Review* 149, no. 397 (December 1889): 665–672.

Mitchell, Edward P. *Memoirs of an Editor: Fifty Years of American Journalism.* New York: Charles Scribner's Sons, 1924.

Mooney, Booth. *Mr. Speaker: Four Men Who Shaped the United States House of Representatives.* Chicago: Follett, 1964.

Morgan, H. Wayne. *William McKinley and His America.* 2nd ed. Kent, OH: Kent State University Press, 2003.

Morris, Edmund. *The Rise of Theodore Roosevelt.* New York: Coward, McCann & Geoghegan, 1979.

Mott, Thomas Bentley. *Myron T. Herrick: Friend of France.* Garden City, NY: Doubleday, Doran, 1929.

Mount, Charles Merrill. *John Singer Sargent: A Biography.* New York: W. W. Norton, 1955.

Muir, William K., Jr. *Legislature: California's School for Politics.* Chicago: University of Chicago Press, 1982.

Offenberg, Richard Stanley. "The Political Career of Thomas Brackett Reed." PhD diss., New York University, 1963.

Oleszek, Walter J., ed. *The Cannon Centenary Conference: The Changing Nature of the Speakership.* Washington, DC: Government Printing Office, 2004.

Ou, Amy Y., David A. Waldman, and Suzanne J. Peterson. "Do Humble CEOs Matter? An Examination of CEO Humility and Firm Outcomes." *Journal of Management* 44, no. 3 (March 2018): 1147–1173.

Payne, James L., and Oliver H. Woshinsky. "Incentives for Political Participation." *World Politics* 24, no. 4 (July 1972): 518–546.

Peters, Ronald M., Jr. *The American Speakership: The Office in Historical Perspective.* Baltimore: Johns Hopkins University Press, 1990.

Phillips, Kevin. *William McKinley.* New York: Times Books, 2003.

Piketty, Thomas. *Capital in the Twenty-First Century.* Translated by Arthur Goldhammer. Cambridge, MA: Belknap Press of Harvard University Press, 2014.

Pinchot, Gifford. *Breaking New Ground.* Seattle: University of Washington Press, 1947.

Platt, Thomas Collier. *The Autobiography of Thomas Collier Platt.* Edited by Louis J. Lang. New York: B. W. Dodge, 1910.

Polsby, Nelson W. "The Institutionalization of the U.S. House of Representatives." *American Political Science Review* 62, no. 1 (March 1968): 144–168.

Poole, Keith, and Howard Rosenthal. *Congress: A Political-Economic History of Roll Call Voting.* New York: Oxford University Press, 1997.

Potholm, Christian P. *This Splendid Game: Maine Campaigns and Elections, 1940–2002.* Lanham, MD: Lexington Books, 2003.

Reed, Thomas B. "Annual Report of the City Solicitor." In *City of Portland Auditors Seventeenth Annual Report*, 212. Portland, ME: B. Thurston, 1876.

———. *Centennial Oration*. Portland, ME: Owen, Strout, 1886.

———. "A Deliberative Body." *North American Review* 148, no. 156 (February 1891): 148–156.

———. "Democracy at St. Louis." *North American Review* 147, no. 380 (July 1888): 37–44.

———. "Empire Can Wait." *Illustrated American* 22, no. 408 (December 4, 1897): 713–714.

———. "The Federal Control of Elections." *North American Review* 150, no. 403 (June 1890): 671–680.

———. "Historic Political Upheavals." *North American Review* 160, no. 458 (January 1895): 109–116.

———. "A Last Tribute." *North American Review* 160, no. 461 (April 1895): 385–395.

———. "The Life of a Congressman." In *The Ship of State by Those at the Helm*, 41–63. Boston: Ginn, 1903.

———. "The Limitations of the Speakership." *North American Review* 150, no. 400 (March 1890): 382–390.

———. "Monopolies." *Saturday Evening Post* 172, no. 33 (February 10, 1900): 706–707.

———. "Mr. Speaker." *North American Review* 154, no. 422 (January 1892): 1–16.

———. "The Nicaragua Canal." *North American Review* 168, no. 510 (May 1899): 552–562.

———. "Obstruction in the National House." *North American Review* 149, no. 395 (October 1889): 421–428.

———. "Our Outlying Province." *North American Review* 146, no. 374 (January 1888): 86–95.

———. *Reed's Rules: A Manual of General Parliamentary Law, with Suggestions for Special Rules*. Chicago: Rand McNally, 1898 [first published 1894].

———. "Rules of the House of Representatives." *Century Illustrated Monthly Magazine* 37, no. 5 (March 1889): 792–795.

———. "Spending Public Money." *North American Review* 154, no. 424 (March 1892): 319–327.

———. "Tariff and Business." *North American Review* 158, no. 446 (January 1894): 110–118.

———. "The Tariff Question." *Independent and the Weekly Review*, August 9, 1888, 1–2.

———. "Two Congresses Contrasted." *North American Review* 155, no. 429 (August 1892): 227–236.

———. "Woman Suffrage: Views of the Minority of the Committee on the Judiciary House of Representatives Forty-Eighth Congress First Session as Submitted by Hon. Thomas B. Reed." 63d Cong., 2d Sess., Senate Doc. 497 (1914).

Remini, Robert V. *The House: The History of the House of Representatives*. Washington, DC: Smithsonian Books, 2006.

Riker, William H. *The Art of Political Manipulation*. New Haven, CT: Yale University Press, 1986.

Ripley, Randall B. *Party Leaders in the House of Representatives.* Washington, DC: Brookings Institution, 1967.

———. "The Party Whip Organizations in the United States House of Representatives." *American Political Science Review* 58, no. 3 (September 1964): 561–576.

Roberts, Jason M. "The Development of Special Orders and Special Rules in the U.S. House, 1881–1937." *Legislative Studies Quarterly* 35, no. 3 (August 2010): 307–336.

Robinson, William A. *Thomas B. Reed: Parliamentarian.* New York: Dodd, Mead, 1930.

Rohde, David W. *Parties and Leaders in the Postreform House.* Chicago: University of Chicago Press, 1991.

Roosevelt, Theodore. "Thomas Brackett Reed and the Fifty-First Congress." *Forum,* December 1895, 410–418.

Schickler, Eric. *Disjointed Pluralism: Institutional Innovation and the Development of the U.S. Congress.* Princeton, NJ: Princeton University Press, 2001.

Schickler, Eric, and Andrew Rich. "Party Government in the House Reconsidered: A Response to Cox and McCubbins." *American Journal of Political Science* 41, no. 4 (October 1997): 1387–1394.

Select Committee on Alleged Frauds in the Presidential Election of 1876. *Report.* 45th Cong., 3d Sess., HR Report 140 (1879).

———. *Testimony: Presidential Election Investigation.* 45th Cong., 3d Sess., HR Mis. Doc. 31 (1879).

Sergiovanni, Thomas J. "Leadership as Cultural Expression." In *Leadership and Organizational Culture: New Perspectives on Administrative Theory and Practice,* edited by Thomas J. Sergiovanni and John E. Corbally, 105–114. Urbana: University of Illinois Press, 1984.

Silbey, David J. *A War of Frontier and Empire: The Philippine-American War.* New York: Hill & Wang, 2007.

Silbey, Joel H. *The American Political Nation, 1838–1893.* Stanford, CA: Stanford University Press, 1991.

Sinclair, Barbara. "Congressional Leadership: A Review Essay and a Research Agenda." In *Leading Congress: New Styles, New Strategies,* edited by John J. Kornacki, 97–162. Washington, DC: Congressional Quarterly, 1990.

———. "Do Parties Matter?" In *Party, Process, and Political Change in Congress: New Perspectives on the History of Congress,* edited by David W. Brady and Mathew D. McCubbins, 36–63. Stanford, CA: Stanford University Press, 2002.

———. "House Special Rules and the Institutional Design Controversy." *Legislative Studies Quarterly* 19, no. 4 (November 1994): 477–494.

———. *Legislators, Leaders, and Lawmaking: The U.S. House of Representatives in the Postreform Era.* Baltimore: Johns Hopkins University Press, 1995.

———. *Majority Leadership in the U.S. House.* Baltimore: Johns Hopkins University Press, 1983.

Skinner, Richard M. "George W. Bush and the Partisan Presidency." *Political Science Quarterly* 123, no. 4 (Winter 2008–09): 605–622.

Skowronek, Stephen. *Building a New American State: The Expansion of National Administrative Capacities, 1877–1920.* New York: Cambridge University Press, 1982.

Smith, Steven S. *Party Influence in Congress.* New York: Cambridge University Press, 2007.

———. *The Senate Syndrome: The Evolution of Procedural Warfare in the Modern US Senate.* Norman: University of Oklahoma Press, 2014.

Sparrow, Bartholomew H. *The Insular Cases and the Emergence of American Empire.* Lawrence: University Press of Kansas, 2006.

Strahan, Randall W. "Leadership and Institutional Change in the Nineteenth-Century House." In *Party, Process, and Political Change in Congress: New Perspectives on the History of Congress,* edited by David W. Brady and Mathew D. McCubbins, 237–269. Stanford, CA: Stanford University Press, 2002.

———. *Leading Representatives: The Agency of Leaders in the Politics of the U.S. House.* Baltimore: Johns Hopkins University Press, 2007.

———. "Party Leadership." In *The Oxford Handbook of the American Congress,* edited by Eric Schickler and Frances E. Lee, 371–395. New York: Oxford University Press, 2011.

———. "Reed and Rostenkowski: Congressional Leadership in Institutional Time." In *The Atomistic Congress: An Interpretation of Congressional Change,* edited by Allen D. Hertzke and Ronald M. Peters, Jr., 199–229. Armonk, NY: M. E. Sharpe, 1992.

———. "Thomas Brackett Reed and the Rise of Party Government." In *Masters of the House: Congressional Leadership over Two Centuries,* edited by Roger H. Davidson, Susan Webb Hammond, and Raymond W. Smock, 33–62. Boulder, CO: Westview Press, 1998.

Taylor, Andrew. *The Floor in Congressional Life.* Ann Arbor: University of Michigan Press, 2012.

Theriault, Sean M. *Party Polarization in Congress.* New York: Cambridge University Press, 2008.

Thomas, Evan. *The War Lovers: Roosevelt, Lodge, Hearst and the Rush to Empire.* New York: Little, Brown, 2010.

Thompson, Charles Willis. *Party Leaders of the Time.* New York: G. W. Dillingham, 1906.

Thompson, Slason. *Way Back When: Recollections of an Octogenarian.* Chicago: H. G. Adair, 1930.

Tuchman, Barbara W. *The Proud Tower: A Portrait of the World before the War 1890–1914.* New York: Macmillan, 1966.

Upchurch, Thomas Adams. *Legislating Racism: The Billion Dollar Congress and the Birth of Jim Crow.* Lexington: University Press of Kentucky, 2004.

Valelly, Richard M. "The Reed Rules and Republican Party Building: A New Look." *Studies in American Political Development* 23, no. 2 (October 2009): 115–142.

Wawro, Gregory J., and Eric Schickler. *Filibuster: Obstruction and Lawmaking in the U.S. Senate.* Princeton, NJ: Princeton University Press, 2006.

Webb, Beatrice. *Beatrice Webb's American Diary.* Edited by David A. Shannon. Madison: University of Wisconsin Press, 1963.

Wells, Wyatt. "Rhetoric of the Standards: The Debate over Gold and Silver in the 1890s." *Journal of the Gilded Age and Progressive Era* 14, no. 1 (January 2015): 49–68.

White, Richard. *The Republic for Which It Stands: The United States during Reconstruction and the Gilded Age, 1865–1896*. New York: Oxford University Press, 2017.

White, William Allen. *The Autobiography of William Allen White*. New York: Macmillan, 1946.

———. *Masks in a Pageant*. New York: Macmillan, 1928.

Williams, Charles Richard. *The Life of Rutherford Birchard Hayes*. 2 vols. Boston: Houghton Mifflin, 1914.

Williams, R. Hal. *Realigning America: McKinley, Bryan, and the Remarkable Election of 1896*. Lawrence: University Press of Kansas, 2010.

Wilson, Woodrow. *Congressional Government: A Study in American Government*. Cleveland: World Publishing, 1956 [first published 1885].

———. *Constitutional Government in the United States*. New York: Columbia University Press, 1917.

Wolfensberger, Donald R. "Suspended Partisanship in the House: How Most Laws Are Really Made." Paper presented at the annual meeting of the American Political Science Association, Boston, MA, August 29, 2002.

Yarwood, Dean. *When Congress Makes a Joke: Congressional Humor Then and Now*. Lanham, MD: Rowman & Littlefield, 2004.

INDEX